CALIFORNIA SAINTS

A 150-Year
Legacy In The
Golden
State

CALIFORNIA SAINTS

A 150-Year Legacy In The Golden State

Richard O. Cowan
William E. Homer

Religious Studies Center
Brigham Young University
Provo, Utah

Library of Congress Catalog Card Number: 96-68224
ISBN 1–57008-200-6

First Printing, 1996

Distributed by BOOKCRAFT, INC.
Salt Lake City, Utah

Printed in the United States of America

CONTENTS

Preface vii
1. Where Shall We "Gather"? 1
2. Samuel Brannan and the Eastern Saints . . . 11
3. The Saga of the *Brooklyn:* 1845–46 23
4. California Beginnings: 1846 41
5. The Epic March of the
   Mormon Battalion: 1846–47 59
6. A Year of Decision: 1847 81
7. Saints and Gold: 1848 105
8. Apostles amid Gold Seekers: 1849 127
9. The Golden Sun Sets: 1850 143
10. The San Bernardino Colony: 1851–57 167
11. The Pacific Mission: 1851–57 185
12. A Spiritual Wilderness: 1857–87 207
13. New Beginnings: 1887–1900 229
14. Roots and Branches: 1900–19 247
15. A California Kaleidoscope: 1919–29 263
16. The Depression Years: 1929–39 283
17. World War II: 1939–45 301
18. Celebration and Commemoration: 1945–55 . . 317
19. Buildings and Blessings: 1950–64 337
20. Challenge and Change: 1964–85 361
21. Building Bridges: 1984–96 381
22. California Saints Today and Tomorrow . . . 401

Appendices

A: California Highlights 411
B: California Growth 419
C: California Missions 421
D: California Stakes 423
E: California Historic Sites 431

Photo Acknowledgments 437
Index 439

PREFACE

This project—a history of The Church of Jesus Christ of Latter-day Saints in California—had its beginning with William E. Homer, a realtor and writer who is a native of Utah but has been a Californian for over twenty years. As a member and director of the LDS public affairs council in the San Francisco Bay Area, he sought out historical background for Church activities in the Golden State but often lacked the sources he needed. Therefore, over a decade ago he began researching and compiling this book.

In 1992 Richard O. Cowan, chair of the Department of Church History and Doctrine at Brigham Young University, joined him as coauthor. Born in Los Angeles, Dr. Cowan received his Ph.D. in 1961 from Stanford University in the field of American church history. He soon discovered that primary sources available at BYU could enrich the compilation.

The authors gratefully acknowledge that many others have provided valuable assistance essential to move the project forward. Michael Nelson conducted extensive research in primary sources and provided important perspectives from his training in the writing of history. The staff at the Historical Department of The Church of Jesus Christ of Latter-day Saints in Salt Lake City capably provided access to important manuscript materials and photographs. Jack and Pat Marshall spent hours locating local resources. Richard and Lou Jean Grant of San Jose gave early encouragement, shared personal resources, history, and computer facilities, and in other meaningful ways helped William Homer complete his part of the project. Verna

Wolfgramm and her assistants in the office of the Department of Church History and Doctrine facilitated the finishing of this work. Kent P. Jackson and his associates in the Religious Studies Center provided insightful editing, set the type, and designed the book for printing. Finally, the authors appreciate the enthusiastic encouragement of Keith J. Atkinson, the Church's Director of Public Affairs in California.

We expect this work will provide new information and insights for those interested in Latter-day Saint history. We particularly hope it will help California Saints appreciate their rich heritage of 150 years in the Golden State.

Where Shall We "Gather"?

1

Between two and three hundred men, women, and children lined the railing of the old sailing ship as it gently rocked and groaned its way through the Golden Gate. Eyes strained against an abundant fog that revealed, then hid, the bush-covered hills. As they approached a sandy beach, a dozen or so small, primitive buildings came into view. Not a very imposing place, most perhaps thought. But they were happy to see land again after nearly six months at sea. Many may have thought about comfortable homes left behind in New York City and other civilized East Coast locations. And they may have wondered how they would acclimate themselves to such a primitive place. The date was 31 July 1846, and most of these pilgrims, leaving behind forever their friends and families, had sold all they had in order to make the voyage.

These newcomers, California's first large group of Anglo settlers, were members of The Church of Jesus Christ of Latter-day Saints, better known at the time as Mormons. They were making a religious pilgrimage to establish a new settlement in an unknown and largely unsettled location. Who were these people, and what had brought them? An understanding of their East Coast origins and their belief in "gathering" helps answer these questions.

"THIS IS MY BELOVED SON. HEAR HIM!"

*Stained-glass window depicting the First Vision; formerly
in Los Angeles's Adams Ward chapel, now on display at the Museum
of Church History and Art in Salt Lake City*

Their story began with Joseph Smith. As a boy, he was confused by conflicting religious perspectives during an unusually intense revival atmosphere near his home in western New York.[1] In the early spring of 1820, he, a fourteen-year-old who lacked knowledge but was full of youthful faith, sought guidance through prayer. He recorded that as he knelt in a grove of trees, God the Father and his Son, Jesus Christ, appeared to him in a glorious vision, assuring him that "the fulness of the gospel" would subsequently be made known to him and that through him the New Testament Church would be restored.[2]

Joseph spent the next three years doing the ordinary tasks of frontier farming. In 1823, he was visited by another heavenly messenger. An angel, surrounded by brilliant light, identified himself as *Moroni* and told Joseph about the thousand-year history of a group of ancient American Christians. Moroni, the last prophet of their extinct civilization, had been entrusted with a history that his father, Mormon, had prepared on gold plates. Joseph Smith was called to translate the record and publish it to the world as the Book of Mormon, affirming that its prime objective was to convince "Jew and Gentile that JESUS is the CHRIST" (Book of Mormon, Title Page).

With many of the first converts to his message present, Joseph Smith organized The Church of Jesus Christ of Latter-day Saints on 6 April 1830, the term *Saints* simply referring to Church members.[3] They were also called Mormons because of their belief in the Book of Mormon. Due to the extraordinary events that led to the Church's organization, Latter-day Saints accepted Joseph Smith as a prophet and as God's authorized

---

[1] See Whitney R. Cross, *The Burned Over District* (Ithaca, N.Y.: Cornell University Press, 1982); and Milton V. Backman Jr., *Joseph Smith's First Vision* (Salt Lake City: Bookcraft, 1971).

[2] *History of The Church of Jesus Christ of Latter-day Saints*, ed. B. H. Roberts, 2d ed., rev. (Salt Lake City: Deseret Book, 1957), 1:5, 4:536 (hereafter *HC*).

[3] Ibid., 1:74–80.

spokesman. His successors, as presidents of the Church, have been likewise regarded (D&C 1:38).

The Gathering

Six months after the Church's organization, Joseph Smith recorded a revelation directing the Saints to gather to a central location (D&C 29:8; 37:3). "Gathering" became an important theme throughout the history of the Latter-day Saints and was significant in bringing them to California's shore.

From 1831 until 1838, Kirtland, a town in northeastern Ohio, was the main gathering place. The Church erected its first temple there. "Stakes" were established as gathering places in Missouri as well as in Ohio. The term stake was adopted from the writings of the Old Testament prophet Isaiah, who referred to stakes figuratively as supporting the tent of God which would cover and shelter his people (Isa. 54:2; see also D&C 115:5–6).

Such gatherings undoubtedly strengthened the young Church, which was made up of converts from diverse traditions. They were able to mingle together, to be fed spiritually, and to hear the Church's doctrine accurately expounded through personal contact with their Prophet. However, gathering also brought adversity. Much of the Church's intense persecution stemmed from earlier settlers who felt threatened by a sudden influx of people with different religious and social views; therefore, they endeavored to stop the "Mormons'" gatherings.

In 1838–39, the Saints were forced to flee from both Missouri and Ohio. Missouri's governor, Lilburn W. Boggs, decreed that they either be exterminated or driven from his state.[4] Church pleas for redress from the federal government were ignored.

---

[4] Ibid., 3:175.

Joseph Smith in uniform of the Nauvoo Legion

Fleeing to Illinois, the Latter-day Saints purchased land and began constructing another city. They named it *Nauvoo*, from a Hebrew word meaning "beautiful." The area had been a swamp prior to their settlement, but soon the land was drained, and Nauvoo became one of Illinois's largest cities as the growing Church gathered and began constructing a second temple.

California Considered

Soon it became apparent that permanent peace could not be achieved in Illinois either. After about four years, earlier residents and state officials began demanding that the Mormons move again. As mob pressures mounted, Church leaders became convinced that the Saints would once again need to flee for their lives. Where could they go? The Church gave much thought to this question. As early as 1831, while still in Ohio, Church members had spoken of going to the Rocky Mountains.[5]

Now, even as they built the city of Nauvoo, Joseph Smith looked forward to yet another haven for his people. In 1842 he declared that his followers would continue to be persecuted

---

[5] Ronald W. Walker, "Seeking the 'Remnant': The Native American During the Joseph Smith Period," *Journal of Mormon History* 19, no. 1 (spring 1993): 8–10.

but that many would "build cities and see the Saints become a mighty people in the midst of the Rocky Mountains."[6]

In 1844, as Nauvoo continued to grow, opposition increased. It was in this context that California was first specifically mentioned as a possible gathering place. On 20 February, Joseph Smith "instructed the Twelve Apostles to send out a delegation and investigate the locations of California and Oregon, and hunt out a good location, where we can remove to after the temple is completed, and where we can build a city in a day, and have a government of our own, get up into the mountains, where the devil cannot dig us out, and live in a healthful climate, where we can live as old as we have a mind to."[7] At that time California was a rather ambiguous region encompassing much of what is now the western United States south of Oregon, from the Rockies to the Pacific.

Martyrdom and a New Leader

As some Illinois citizens became more resentful, a series of clashes culminated in the murder of Joseph Smith by a mob on 27 June 1844, leaving the Twelve Apostles to preside over the Church.[8] The enemies of the Saints speculated that the Prophet's death would scatter the Church and break it up. Instead, the martyrdom became a rallying cry, and under the apostles, the Church flourished.

Although Brigham Young, president of the Twelve, had almost no formal schooling, he had developed great qualities of leadership which Joseph Smith recognized the first time they met. On that occasion the Prophet declared, "The time will come when brother Brigham Young will preside over this Church." Becoming one of the original Twelve Apostles in 1835, Brigham Young demonstrated unwavering loyalty. This earned him the nickname "Lion of the Lord." He presided over

---

[6] *HC* 5:85.

[7] *HC* 6:222, 224.

[8] "History of Brigham Young," *Millennial Star* 25 (11 July 1863): 439.

Brigham Young in 1850

the Church until his death in 1877, first as president of the Quorum of the Twelve Apostles, and after 1847 as president of the Church.

Gathering Plans Solidified

After becoming the Church's leader, President Young continued to examine various gathering options. On New Year's Day in 1845, he recorded in his diary: "I met in council with my brethren of the Twelve. The subject of sending a company to California was further discussed."[9] During the spring and summer of that year, published accounts of John

[9] Preston Nibley, *Brigham Young: The Man and His Work* (Salt Lake City: Deseret Book, 1970), 63.

C. Fremont's western expeditions became available, and those positive reports were studied eagerly by leaders of the Church.

By August 1845 the idea of a central settlement in the Rocky Mountains, together with gathering places on the Pacific Coast, was fairly well established in the minds of President Young and other Church leaders. He wrote to Addison Pratt, who was serving a mission in the Pacific Islands:

> If any of the brethren of the islands wish to emigrate to the continent here, then [have them] come to the mouth of [the] Colombia River in Oregon, or the Gulf of Monterry or St. Francisco, as we shall commence forming a settlement in that region during [the] next season and make arrangements with agents in each of those places so emigrants will be enabled to get all necessary directions, and provisions for going to the settlements. The settlement, will probably be in the neighborhood of Lake Tampanagos [Utah Lake] as that is represented as a most delightful district and no settlement near there.[10]

Elder Parley P. Pratt of the Twelve (Addison's distant relative) described the plan in a letter to a Church member in New Jersey: "I expect we shall stop near the Rocky Mountains about 800 miles nearer than the coast say 1,500 from here [Nauvoo] and there to make a stand until we are able to enlarge and to extend to the coast."[11]

It was about this time that Latter-day Saints began singing lyrics penned by Elder John Taylor:

> The Upper California. O! that's the land for me,
> It lies between the Mountains and great Pacific Sea. . . .
>   A land that blooms with endless spring,
>   Our tow'rs and temples there shall rise
>   Along the great Pacific Sea.[12]

---

[10] Brigham Young to Addison Pratt, 28 August 1845, Brigham Young Papers; LDS Church Archives.

[11] Parley P. Pratt to Isaac Rogers, 6 September 1845, Parley P. Pratt Papers; LDS Church Archives.

[12] Quoted in J. Kenneth Davies, *Mormon Gold: The Story of California's Mormon Argonauts* (Salt Lake City: Olympus, 1984), 4.

Months of intense preparations culminated in the Saints' exodus from Nauvoo early in 1846, followed by the epic westward trek across the Great Plains. Yet not all Latter-day Saints were part of this main body of overland immigrants. There was a substantial number in the northeastern United States, and Church leaders devised an alternate plan for their migration.

Samuel Brannan and the Eastern Saints

2

As the Book of Mormon was being distributed throughout the eastern United States by missionaries and others, not all converts gathered to the Midwest. A substantial number remained in the New England and Central Atlantic states. Some descended from a long line of American Pilgrims, pioneers, and patriots. Others were first-generation Americans or immigrants from Europe. Perhaps few individuals then had a greater impact on the lives of Church members in the eastern United States than the gifted young man, Samuel Brannan.

The Early Years

Brannan was born on 2 March 1819 in Saco, a town near the southern coast of Maine. He spent his entire childhood there. His family's religious background is not known. He was the son of a hard-drinking, sometimes cruel father and a somewhat kinder mother.

Perhaps to remove Samuel from this less-than-desirable home or to have another able-bodied young man to help them in a new wilderness home, Samuel's older sister, Mary Ann, and her husband, Alexander Badlam, took him with them when they moved to northeastern Ohio. They settled at Painesville, only a few miles from the Latter-day Saints' center at Kirtland. Upon their arrival in 1833, fourteen-year-old Samuel became apprenticed to a printer. Just when he became a Latter-day Saint is not known. However, at age sixteen he was among some one hundred who had worked on the Kirtland Temple and were blessed by Joseph Smith on 7 March 1835.[1]

After completing a three-year apprenticeship, Brannan became involved in a prevailing spirit of land speculation and sustained a "temporary loss" when things went amiss during the nationwide depression of 1837.[2] Kirtland tax records indicate that eighteen-year-old Brannan sold fifteen acres which he and another individual owned there.[3]

As he became an adult, he wanted to see other parts of the country. During the next few years, by his own report, he "visited every State in the Union."[4] He traveled to New Orleans, where he was reunited with his brother, Thomas. They purchased a press and launched a weekly publication. Three years later, an outbreak of malaria took Thomas's life and, with it, their publishing venture.

Thomas's death changed Samuel's plans. Taking whatever printing jobs he could find, he began working his way up the Mississippi. Eventually, he returned to Painesville, where he met and married Harriet Hatch. Soon a daughter was born; however, the marriage was unhappy and quickly ended in separation.[5] He was also called as a missionary to southern

---

[1] *History of The Church of Jesus Christ of Latter-day Saints*, ed. B. H. Roberts, 2d ed., rev. (Salt Lake City: Deseret Book, 1957), 2:205–6 (hereafter *HC*).

[2] Samuel Brannan, "A Biographical Sketch Based on a Dictation," 2, MS, C-D 805; Bancroft Library, University of California at Berkeley.

[3] Milton V. Backman Jr., *A Profile of Latter-day Saints of Kirtland, Ohio and Members of Zion's Camp 1830–1839* (Provo, Utah: Department of Church History and Doctrine, Brigham Young University, 1982), 135.

[4] Brannan, "A Biographical Sketch," 3.

[5] Reva Scott, *Samuel Brannan and the Golden Fleece* (New York: Macmillan, 1944), 42. Scott indicates that she relied on family interviews and traditions for her fictionalized biography. According to Will Bagley, who is preparing a biography of Brannan, no other documentation has been found concerning this first wife.

*Samuel
Brannan*

Ohio, where he met with some success before his mission was cut short by his own bout with malaria.

Mission Among the Eastern Saints

After recuperating from malaria, Brannan went to Nauvoo, from where the leaders of the Church sent him to New York City to assist with a Latter-day Saint newspaper for the Eastern States Mission.[6] During this early period of Church history, it became customary to hold general conferences at Church headquarters twice a year, in April and October. The Church's missions held corresponding local conferences. The April 1844 conference of the Eastern States Mission in New York City approved Elder G. T. Leach's proposal to publish a weekly paper to make known the principles of the Church. Subsequently, the first issue of *The Prophet* appeared on 18 May,

---

[6] B. H. Roberts, *A Comprehensive History of The Church of Jesus Christ of Latter-day Saints* (Salt Lake City: Deseret News Press, 1930), 3:38.

published at 7 Spruce Street by "The Society for the Diffusion of Truth," with Leach as its president.[7]

Leach edited the first few issues. In the fall, mission president William Smith, brother of the recently slain Prophet, succeeded Leach, with Brannan as publisher. Then, beginning with the 23 November issue, the newspaper listed Samuel Brannan as both editor and publisher.

While in the East, Brannan met a boardinghouse proprietress, Fanny Corwin, and her daughter, Eliza Ann.[8] He fell in love with "Lizzie" and soon married her.

In addition to his editorial responsibilities, Brannan often visited branches throughout the mission and solicited funds for the paper. Unfortunately, he created some problems while doing so. Elder Wilford Woodruff of the Twelve, who spent some time in the eastern states on his way to England, assessed conditions in the mission and found mischief afoot. On 9 October 1844, he wrote that "much difficulty appeared to be brewing in New York and Philadelphia." William Smith, without Church sanction, had authorized Brannan to marry people for eternity. These two, together with George J. Adams, taught the doctrine of "spiritual wives"—that women could have sexual relations with any men they pleased. Elder Woodruff also observed that many of the eastern Saints thought the Twelve were aware of and condoned these activities. In a follow-up letter, he requested that an apostle be sent from Nauvoo to take charge of the mission.[9]

Elder Parley P. Pratt received this assignment and arrived in New York City in late December 1844. As he analyzed what was going on, he was astounded that "Elders William Smith, G. J. Adams, S. Brannan, and others, had been corrupting the Saints by introducing among them all manner of false doctrine and immoral practices." Consequently, Elder Pratt sent Smith

---

[7] *The Prophet*, 18 May 1844.

[8] This name has also been given as Ann Alexia and Elizabeth Ann.

[9] Journal History, 9 October 1844, 22 October 1844, 3 December 1844; LDS Church Archives.

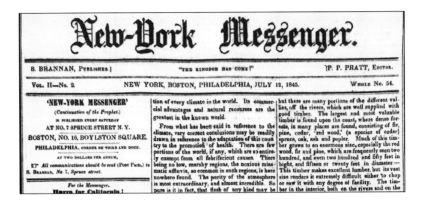

NEW-YORK MESSENGER, featuring information on California

and Adams to Nauvoo, where they were cut off from the Church. However, in Brannan's case, Elder Pratt merely warned the young man to "repent speedily of all such evil practices," which Brannan promised to do.[10] Nevertheless, based on Wilford Woodruff's earlier observations, leaders at Nauvoo disfellowshipped him.[11]

When a report of this disciplinary action reached New York, Elder Pratt urged Brannan to go to Nauvoo immediately and ask for reconsideration (an action Elder Pratt later came to regret; see chapter 11). Brannan promptly made the trip of over a thousand miles and arrived on 22 May. The next two days he met with the Twelve. After the matter was thoroughly investigated, they did not find his conduct as bad as had been reported and restored him to full fellowship.[12] He then returned to New York City.

Meanwhile, the last issue of *The Prophet* had appeared on 24 May (the very day Brannan had been restored to fellowship in Nauvoo). Under Elder Pratt's direction, Brannan launched a new weekly paper, the *New-York Messenger*, beginning on

---

[10] *Autobiography of Parley P. Pratt* (Salt Lake City: Deseret Book, 1938), 37–38.

[11] *HC* 7:395.

[12] Brigham Young to Parley P. Pratt, 26 May 1845, Brigham Young Papers; LDS Church Archives.

5 July. It was regarded as a continuation of *The Prophet*. Its first issue published a letter from Brigham Young and the Twelve reporting Brannan's restoration to fellowship and encouraging the eastern Saints "to sustain him in his office, and in his Publishing department, and bless him with their faith and prayers."[13]

Plans for Migration from New York

Soon after Brannan's return to New York, Elder Orson Pratt of the Twelve replaced his brother as president of the Eastern States Mission, and Parley returned to Nauvoo. During this time Church leaders were deciding where the Saints would settle. On 15 September 1845, Brigham Young wrote to Brannan: "I wish you together with your press, paper, and ten thousand of the brethren were now in California at the Bay of St. Francisco, and if you can clear yourself and go there, do so and we will meet you there."[14]

Such correspondence prompted increased discussion among eastern Saints concerning their own westward migration. The 1 November issue of the *Messenger* was filled with information and counsel concerning overland migration. The same theme continued into the first half of the next week's edition. At that point, perhaps while the paper was actually being printed, Church leaders in the eastern states received instructions from "our worthy Presidents, the Twelve . . . to council us to make our journey to the place of our future destiny by water, as soon as arrangements can be conveniently made."[15]

Thus, the second half of the 8 November issue announced: "We have ascertained that saints in the Eastern states can emigrate to the other side of the Rocky Mountains by water,

---

[13] *New-York Messenger*, 5 July 1845.

[14] Brigham Young to Samuel Brannan, 15 September 1845, Brigham Young Papers; LDS Church Archives.

[15] *New-York Messenger*, 15 November 1845.

with half the expense attending a journey by land, and they can take many things that could not be taken over the mountains." The paper promised to discuss this plan further in future issues, and it did.

Following the apostles' instruction, Elder Orson Pratt wrote a letter to the Saints that was published in the next edition. He admonished them to flee "as exiles from this wicked nation." Those who could afford a more costly overland migration could go to Nauvoo and join the main body of the Church in its exodus. However, the poor would have to raise means to pay their passage by sea around Cape Horn to the western coast of North America. If enough chose to go by water, a ship could be chartered and the fare would be "scarcely nothing." Elder Pratt encouraged them to leave as soon as possible in order to sail around Cape Horn during the Southern Hemisphere's summer months.

"Elder Samuel Brannan is hereby appointed to preside over, and take charge of the company that goes by sea," Elder Pratt continued, "and all who go with him will be required to give strict heed to his instruction and counsel."

"Do not be faint hearted nor slothful," he counseled, "but be courageous and diligent, prayerful and faithful, and you can accomplish almost any thing that you undertake. What great and good work cannot the saints do, if they take hold of it with energy, and ambition? Brethren awake!—be determined to get out from this evil nation next spring," he exhorted. "We do not want one saint to be left in the United States after that time. Let every branch in the East, West, North, and South, be determined to flee out of Babylon, either by land or by sea."[16]

Accordingly, the eastern Saints met at American Hall in New York City on 12 November 1845 and unanimously approved Elder Pratt's instructions. It must have been difficult for the Saints to turn their backs on a country which their ancestors had fought to secure as a land of freedom and opportunity. And yet, the promised justice for all seemed not

---

[16] Ibid.; see also *HC* 7:515–19.

to apply to Latter-day Saints, as was pointed out by Brannan in the following resolution he presented to the conference:

> *Whereas,* we as a people have sought to obey the great commandment of the dispensation of the fullness of times, by gathering ourselves together; and as often as we have done so, we have been sorely persecuted . . . our houses burned, and we disinherited of our possessions, . . . And . . . inasmuch as the people and authorities of the United States have sanctioned such proceedings without manifesting any disposition to sustain us in our constitutional rights, . . . *Resolved,* That we hail with joy the Proclamation of our brethren from the City of Joseph [Nauvoo] to make preparations for our immediate departure, . . . *Resolved,* that the church in this city [New York] move, one and all, west of the Rocky Mountains, between this and next season, either by land or water; and that we most earnestly pray all our brethren in this eastern country to join with us.[17]

The conference, comprised mostly of United States citizens, also unanimously approved this resolution to forsake their country. Brannan then invited all who wanted to go with him on the ship to come forward and sign up. Thus was his leadership established. His potential was reflected in his receiving stewardship, at the age of only twenty-six, for the lives of all who would sail with him.

Brannan's young printer apprentice, Edward Kemble, described his employer as a "hard featured man" who, despite being "debilitated by a long attack of Western fever [malaria]," was nevertheless "a power" among his flock.[18] He was described by others as energetic and fearless, with rough manners, but genial and generous, with a brilliant personality.[19] He had the ability to express himself forcefully, and he possessed impressive personal charisma that made him a natural leader. Nevertheless, because he was impulsive and quick-tempered, he was unable to successfully arbitrate disputes among members of his company.

---

[17] *HC* 7:520–21.

[18] See Edward Cleveland Kemble, "Twenty Years Ago," *Sacramento Daily Union*, 11 September 1866, and *A Kemble Reader: Stories of California, 1846–1848*, ed. Fred Blackburn Rogers (San Francisco: The California Historical Society, 1963), 14.

[19] Stewart H. Holbrook, *The Yankee Exodus* (New York: Macmillan, 1950), 149.

A Challenging Task

As the Saints returned home following the conference in November 1845, they must have considered the enormous significance of the pledge they had made. Some perhaps reflected on the voyage of their Pilgrim forebears. They, like their Latter-day Saint counterparts, were members of an unpopular religious group who became exiles sailing in a small ship to an unknown and untested destination. The 120 Plymouth Pilgrims were under the spiritual leadership of William Brewster, a seasoned, schooled, and respected man in his fifties who had served in the queen's court. In contrast, there would be twice as many Saints setting out on a voyage five times as long and led by Samuel Brannan, who was half Brewster's age and had much less experience. And they, unlike the well-organized and well-funded Pilgrims, had no backup help or support. The Saints' voyage of 18,000 miles (which actually became 24,000 miles) was perhaps the longest religious sea-pilgrimage in history.

Left largely to his own devices in New York, young Samuel Brannan faced an almost superhuman task. Time was short. A ship had to be ready to sail in only about two months and in the middle of winter. The voyage around the tip of Cape Horn was treacherous. No restrictions were imposed regarding the age or health of potential passengers. Brannan had to convince a sufficient number of Saints to place themselves at the mercy of a potentially hostile captain and crew at a time when anti-Mormon sentiment and persecution were widespread. Being on a ship at sea, there would be little margin for error. They could not be certain they would be granted landing privileges in Mexican-controlled California. The passengers would be confined to close quarters for nearly six months, possibly leading to disagreements and temptations. They would have no contact with general Church leaders for nearly two years. Finally, most of the Saints were too poor to pay their passage.

Perhaps most problematic of all, Samuel Brannan—young, brash, articulate, and arrogant—had no experience at sea or in leading any group of people. Yet the voyagers' very lives depended on his attention to the smallest detail, both at sea and in an unknown wilderness destination. Just why they were left at such a critical moment with unseasoned leadership is not clear. Perhaps Brannan, despite his weaknesses, was the best available.

Regardless of these many difficulties, many faithful eastern Saints began backing the spirit of the conference with solid actions. Possessions were sold as they assented to put their lives into Brannan's hands to lead them to a place none had ever visited or seen. In the midst of the details Brannan attended to, he confided in a letter to President Brigham Young: "I feel my weakness and inability and desire your blessing and prayers that I may be successful. My cares and labors weigh me down day and night, but I trust in God that I shall soon have a happy deliverance."[20]

The challenges faced by Brannan, Brigham Young, and the rest of the Saints were further complicated by a deteriorating international situation. Many in the United States believed it was the "Manifest Destiny" of the U.S. to occupy the continent from the Atlantic to the Pacific. In July 1845, President James K. Polk, hoping to annex much of the Southwest, including California, ordered troops into territory claimed by Mexico. War was in the air. It was possible that the only welcoming party the *Brooklyn* would encounter would be the Mexican army or a gunboat ready to rebuff them. At this same time, American relations with Great Britain were also strained, because both powers wanted to possess the Oregon Territory.

In this potentially explosive climate, some government officials were concerned that because of the Saints' mistreatment at the hands of their fellow Americans, they might go west and ally themselves with either Great Britain or Mexico. Certainly the New York Saints' unanimous acceptance of

---

[20] *HC* 7:588.

Orson Pratt's letter and Brannan's resolution, each of which assailed the United States, made such an occurrence seem possible.

Church members, in turn, feared that the government might try to stop their emigration, whether by land or by sea. "I have received positive information," Brannan wrote to Brigham Young, "that it is the intention of the government to disarm you after you have taken up your line of march in the spring."[21] Church leaders therefore hesitated to divulge exactly where they were going. Despite the clarity of earlier communications to the Saints, they began a campaign of disinformation. For example, George A. Smith later recalled, "It was thought, proper not to reveal the secret of our intention to flee to the mountains; but as a kind of put off, it was communicated in the strictest confidence to General Hardin, who promised never to tell of it, that we intended to settle Vancouver's Island. This report, however, was industriously circulated, as we anticipated it would be."[22]

Brigham Young was reluctant to disclose his full intentions for the main body of the Church even to leaders like Brannan, as illustrated by the following exchange:

Brannan:	Where are you going to settle?
Young:	"I will say we have not determined to what place we shall go, but shall make a location where we can live in peace."
Brannan:	How soon will you leave?
Young:	"When the grass is sufficient."
Brannan:	What will be your route?
Young:	"The best route we can find."
Brannan:	How many are going?

---

[21] Ibid.

[22] *Journal of Discourses* (Liverpool: F. D. Richards, Latter-day Saints' Book Depot, 1855–86), 2:23.

Young:	"Uncertain but all . . . are [of] a mind to go."
Brannan:	How long will the journey take?
Young:	"I will tell you when we get to the end."[23]

Thus, Brannan and his company did not know with any certainty what the Church's final destination would be. Later, one of the group, John Horner, recalled that "the Twelve counseled the eastern Saints to charter a ship, get on board, and go around Cape Horn to upper California, find a place to settle, farm and raise crops, so that when the Church pioneers should arrive there the following year they would find sustenance."[24]

As he pondered what to do with Brannan's press, Orson Pratt wrote to Brigham Young: "Brother Brannan thinks it will be difficult to take his printing establishment and go to California unless he goes away dishonorably without paying debts. . . . He is very anxious to go and is willing to do anything he is counseled. He says that the church perhaps would consider it wisdom to buy his establishment and still keep up the paper."[25] As things worked out, Brannan took the press with him. No one could have imagined the key role that it would play in American history.

[23] Brigham Young to Samuel Brannan, 26 December 1845, Brigham Young Papers; LDS Church Archives; quoted in Ronald K. Esplin, "'A Place Prepared': Joseph, Brigham, and the Quest for Promised Refuge in the West," *Journal of Mormon History* 9 (1982): 102–3.

[24] John M. Horner, "Voyage of the Ship 'Brooklyn,'" *Improvement Era* 9, no. 10 (August 1906): 795.

[25] *HC* 7:509.

The Saga of the
BROOKLYN: 1845–46

3

While Latter-day Saints from the northeastern states gathered in New York City during the closing weeks of 1845 and the beginning weeks of 1846, the pace of preparations quickened. Samuel Brannan scoured the harbors of New York and Boston for a vessel suitable for the Saints' long voyage to California. With war on the horizon, sea captains, hoping to secure more lucrative government contracts, were reluctant to agree to a lengthy voyage. Brannan persisted, however, and chartered the sailing ship *Brooklyn*.

Preparing for the Voyage

This three-masted, square-rigged cargo ship had two decks and measured 125 x 28 feet.[1] After being refitted, the adapted vessel had 2,500 square feet of living quarters—the size of a modern four-bedroom home. Between two and three hundred individuals were squeezed together into that space for six months. The vessel was approximately eleven years old and was described as "one of the old time build, made more

---

[1] Conway B. Sonne, *Ships, Saints, and Mariners* (Salt Lake City: University of Utah Press, 1987), 32.

for work than beauty or speed." It was chartered because it "could be had cheap."[2] It was owned by three men: two brothers, Abel W. and Edward Richardson, and Stephen C. Burdette, all of New York. Abel would be the ship's skipper during the voyage.[3]

On 15 December 1845, Brannan wrote in the *New-York Messenger:*

> We have chartered the ship *Brooklyn,* Capt. Richardson, of four hundred and fifty tons, at twelve hundred dollars per month, and we pay the port charges; the money to be paid before sailing. She is a first class ship . . . a very fast sailor. . . . The between decks will be very neatly fitted up into one large cabin, with a row of state rooms on each side, so that every family will be provided with a state room, affording them places of retirement at their pleasure. . . . The ship will sail on the 24th of January. . . . All persons that can raise fifty dollars will be able to secure a passage.[4]

Since the average wage at that time was about one dollar per day, the fifty dollars amounted to about two months' pay for the average worker. In addition to this basic fare, each person paid twenty-five dollars (another month's pay) for simple provisions. Children sailed for half this rate. A special issue of the *Messenger* decried the fact that of the three hundred individuals who initially expressed interest in participating in the voyage, only about sixty had sufficient means to carry their plans through. However, by 12 January 1846, that number was augmented to "about one hundred and seventy-five" who were able to go.[5]

When the voyagers arrived in town, they loaded their heavier baggage on board and temporarily moved, with only

---

[2] Augusta Joyce Crocheron, "The Ship Brooklyn," *Western Galaxy* 1 (1888): 79. Because Crocheron was an infant at the time of the voyage, her accounts must be based on information supplied by her parents or others. Crocheron claimed that her mother, Caroline Joyce, kept a meticulous diary, since lost, of the voyage.

[3] Sonne, 33; Lorin Hansen, "Voyage of the Brooklyn," *Dialogue* (fall 1988): n. 2.

[4] *New-York Messenger,* 15 December 1845, quoted in *Times and Seasons* 6 (1 February 1846): 1112–14.

[5] *History of The Church of Jesus Christ of Latter-day Saints,* ed. B. H. Roberts, 2d ed., rev. (Salt Lake City: Deseret Book, 1957), 7:588 (hereafter *HC*).

the bare essentials, into a boarding house which Brannan had secured for them. Brannan cautioned the Saints to keep a low profile and call one another "Mr. or Mrs.," rather than "Brother or Sister," to avert unwanted attention.[6]

Brannan and the Saints had prepared well. In addition to their personal belongings, the passengers gathered all the implements needed for survival. The cargo included the following: a large assortment of machinery, tools, and equipment (including Brannan's printing press with printing supplies for two years); two sawmills; a grist mill; farm machinery; implements and tools for eight hundred men including plows, plow-irons, shovels, hoes, scythes, and forks; blacksmith, carpenter, and millwright tools; lathes, sawmill irons, and nails; utensils of glass, brass, copper, tin, and crockery; a large assortment of seeds; a large quantity of dry goods for resale; several cases of smoothbore muskets; two milk cows, forty pigs, and several crates of fowl; educational supplies for schools and libraries, including books on grammar, mathematics, geography, history, astronomy, and Hebrew; and a 179-volume set of *Harper's Family Library*. They also took along effects belonging to Church members not traveling on the vessel who planned to make the trip overland and then reclaim their property when they reached the coast.

To help defray the cost, the voyagers agreed to stop in Hawaii and deliver five hundred barrels of merchandise, including Bibles for a Protestant mission located there.[7]

As the cargo accumulated, carpenters reconditioned and converted the ship to accommodate passengers. Sixteen thousand dollars were spent in creating thirty-two small staterooms along the outside walls between the decks. Between these rows of staterooms a long table, almost the length of the ship, was constructed. This area was used for church and other meetings, meals, school, sewing, and other projects, as well as recreation. Backless benches were nailed in place around the

---

6 *New-York Messenger*, 15 December 1845.

7 *Friend*, 1 July 1846, 103.

table. Except for berths, there was no other seating. Brannan later claimed to have had this reconditioning done "at his own expense."[8]

Some Last-Minute Dramas

As the departure date drew near, several small dramas unfolded. Isaac Robbins's wife, Ann, was in line to receive an inheritance from her father's family in New Jersey. She and Isaac visited the family and asked them for the inheritance to help them emigrate. Ann's father, already displeased over her conversion, now became enraged. He seized Ann and the children and forced Isaac out of the house at gunpoint. Isaac, praying that his father-in-law's heart would be softened before the appointed departure time, went to New York City to secure passage. Ann and the children did arrive, having traveled afoot as fugitives over New Jersey's snowy back roads.[9]

Another bit of human drama occurred as Abraham Combs headed to the wharf with his wife and a daughter from a former marriage. His former wife's brother, reluctant to have his young and favorite niece leave her friends and home to live in a strange land, planned to abduct her. He therefore contrived to have Combs badgered and arrested—on false pretenses—to separate him from the girl. The alert father, however, foiled the scheme by attracting a friendly crowd who succeeded in rescuing her and escorting her safely to the ship.[10]

One couple married just before the voyage. Twenty-five-year-old John Horner married Elizabeth Imlay at his family's home in New Jersey. The next day the newlyweds, hoping to improve their economic opportunities, joined the Saints who

---

[8] Samuel Brannan, "A Biographical Sketch Based on a Dictation," 2, MS, C-D 805; Bancroft Library, University of California at Berkeley.

[9] Kate B. Carter, *The Ship Brooklyn Saints* (Salt Lake City: Daughters of Utah Pioneers, 1960), 569–71.

[10] *New York Herald*, 5 February 1846.

were gathering in New York. Horner later described the voyage as "a rather uncommon wedding tour."[11]

The biggest drama, however, unfolded behind the scenes. Because of concerns that the persecuted Saints might ally themselves with either Great Britain or Mexico, some speculated that the government would stop the ship from sailing and confiscate all arms. The day of departure was postponed several times while Brannan negotiated with two influential men, Amos Kendall, who had served as Postmaster General from 1835 to 1840, and his partner, A. G. Benson, a New York businessman. These two, greedy for personal holdings in California, formed a partnership called "A. G. Benson and Company."

They offered to use their influence to ensure President Polk's support. In exchange, Kendall and Benson demanded half the land settled by the Saints. They warned the Saints that if they failed to cooperate, the president would claim that the Mormons planned to side with other nations against the United States and would therefore order them to be disarmed and dispersed. Eventually, Brannan signed their agreement. On 27 January 1846, he forwarded it to Brigham Young for ratification.

We do not know if a young, naive Brannan was baffled by Kendall and Benson or if a clever, cunning Brannan outsmarted them, manipulating the pair to finance the voyage—including the sixteen thousand dollars to outfit the ship. Brannan may have suspected that Brigham Young would never agree to the terms and that the ship would head for a foreign destination where it would be difficult to enforce an American contract. In any case, President Young balked at the agreement and refused to sign.[12]

Meanwhile, Captain Richardson and the Saints were anxious to leave. They did not want to chance a Cape Horn winter, nor did they like paying good money for the barren

---

[11] Quoted in Hansen, 49.

[12] *HC* 7:587–91.

boardinghouse and its atrocious food while simultaneously paying for their rented ship to stand at anchor. The crew also grew restless. Realizing that there was not enough time to wait for Brigham Young's response, Brannan and Captain Richardson decided to leave New York on Wednesday, 4 February 1846. Interestingly, that was the same day the first group of Pioneers abandoned Nauvoo for the West.

Setting Sail

Although the weather had been stormy earlier in the day, the sun shone brightly at 2 P.M. when the *Brooklyn* departed from the wharf opposite Franklin Market. Despite the Saints' desire for a low profile, there was a crowd on hand to see them off. As the last of the heavy ropes was hauled in, the crowd on the dock erupted with "three hearty cheers, which were returned as heartily by the emigrants . . . on deck." A reporter from the *New York Herald* wrote that these "bold pioneers . . . deserve our sympathies and most heartfelt wishes of success."[13]

The rarity of such a sight was captured by young Edward Kemble, one of the few *Brooklyn* passengers who was not a Latter-day Saint. "Ship loads of emigrants arriving from foreign countries were scenes of daily occurrence but a vessel crowded with emigrating Americans departing for a distant and almost unknown shore was a sight of rarer if not unprecedented novelty."[14]

After being towed out into the main shipping channel by the steamboat *Sampson*, the *Brooklyn*'s crew unfurled her sails. In keeping with the general tenor of disinformation about where the Saints were going, the *Brooklyn*, upon entering the Narrows and passing Fort Lafayette, flew from her main mast

---

[13] *New York Herald*, 5 February 1846.

[14] Edward Cleveland Kemble, *A Kemble Reader: Stories of California, 1846–1848*, ed. Fred Blackburn Rogers (San Francisco: California Historical Society, 1963), 17.

a banner proclaiming *Oregon* in large letters.[15] The Saints' prayers were answered as they left the port without incident.

The actual number that sailed is not known. It has long been said there were 234 passengers, including 70 men, 63 women, and 101 children.[16] Yet, if every name listed on every known roster were counted, the total would be closer to 300, including a four-person crew: Captain Richardson, Frank Ward, a cook, and a stewardess.

To help supervise the Saints' religious and other activities, Elder Brannan, following the pattern of Latter-day Saint Church governance, appointed two counselors. Those chosen to assist him were E. Ward Pell and Isaac Robbins, both married men with children.[17] Each would celebrate his forty-first birthday during the voyage.

Shipboard routine followed a set of rules which Brannan had published before departure. "Reveille" sounded every morning at 6 A.M., at which time all but the sick were to arise and dress before leaving quarters. "Immediately after the beating of reveille," the corporal was to visit every stateroom and "receive the names of all the sick and of those . . . not able to do duty and report the same to the officer of the day"; two other passengers were chosen to care for those who were ill. Every stateroom was swept and cleaned, and beds were made by seven o'clock. A "health officer" was appointed each day to inspect every stateroom for cleanliness and neatness. Children were the first to eat at 8:30 A.M. and adults forty-five minutes later; everyone then returned to the staterooms or went on deck so the tables and halls could be cleared by 10 A.M. During the day all stateroom doors were left open to admit fresh air. From 10 A.M. to 2 P.M. various chores and labors were performed. Dinner was served to the children at 3 P.M. and to the adults an hour later. By five o'clock the tables were cleared so the next three hours could be "occupied in reading, singing, or other

---

[15] Kemble, 18; compare *HC* 7:588.

[16] Hansen, 52 n. 4.

[17] Ibid., 54; Carter, 566, 570.

innocent amusements." On behalf of those who preferred eating late, there was a cold luncheon at 8 P.M. By 9 P.M. the table was cleared and everybody retired. One cook and three "cook police" were appointed each week from among the passengers.

On the Sabbath, "divine service" began at 11 A.M., "when all that are able must attend, shaved, and washed clean, so as to appear in a manner becoming the solemn, and holy occasion."[18] One passenger recalled that in the Sunday preaching the company was "admonished to live together in harmony and love."[19]

The group gathered morning and evening in the large central room for prayers. Soon a choir was organized and the Saints enjoyed singing the "songs of Zion." The *Brooklyn's* passengers settled into their daily routine as the ship headed out into the Atlantic.

Southward in the Atlantic

Less than a week after leaving New York, a powerful storm beset the ship. All the sails were lowered except a small one that "rested against the shrouds of the main mast."[20] For safety, everyone was confined below. Ventilation was poor. Food was prepared with great difficulty. The daily routines which had been so carefully planned were largely abandoned.[21] At night, women and children had to be lashed to their bunks to keep them from falling out as the ship pitched. Furniture also tumbled back and forth, "endangering limb and life."[22] Most of the passengers were afflicted with seasickness from "being rolled

[18] *Times and Seasons* 6 (15 February 1846): 1127–28.

[19] Samuel Stark, *Life and Travels of Daniel Stark* (Salt Lake City: Samuel Stark, 1955), 26.

[20] John M. Horner, "Voyage of the Ship 'Brooklyn,'" *Improvement Era* 9, no. 10 (August 1906): 797.

[21] Kemble, 20.

[22] Crocheron, 81.

from one side of the ship to the other."[23] Nonetheless, a passenger noted:

> Some that were more resolute than others struggled to the deck to behold the sublime grandeur of the scene,— to hear the dismal howl of the winds, and to see the ship with helm lashed pitching, rolling, dipping in the troughs of the sea and then tossed on the highest billow. These . . . sights once beheld are never to be forgotten. It was only by realizing the Lord has said He holds the waters in His hand, that we could have faith to be delivered from our perilous condition.[24]

Captain Richardson came below and bluntly told his passengers, "I have done all I can to save the ship. If any of you have not made your peace with God, you would better do it now, as the ship may go down any minute."[25] Although some passengers were frightened, the majority had a calm "trust in God that all would be well." Some expressed their confidence by singing the song "We Are Going to California." The captain was amazed "that any could sing while in such peril."[26] However, the Saints never lost faith, despite the captain's bleak outlook. One of the women remarked, "We left for California and we shall get there," and another said she had no more fear than if she were on dry ground.[27] When the storm subsided, Captain Richardson declared it to be the worst that he had ever experienced in his years at sea.

Their faith was vindicated. In fact, the winds had carried them nearly to the Cape Verde Islands off the northwest coast of Africa. Ships often went that far east to be in position to take advantage of easterly trade winds without being blown into the coast of Brazil.[28]

---

[23] *New-York Daily Tribune*, 27 August 1846.

[24] William Glover, *The Mormons in California* (Los Angeles: Glen Dawson, 1954), 14.

[25] Horner, 797.

[26] Glover, 14.

[27] Crocheron, 81.

[28] Horner, 797; see also Hansen, 54–55.

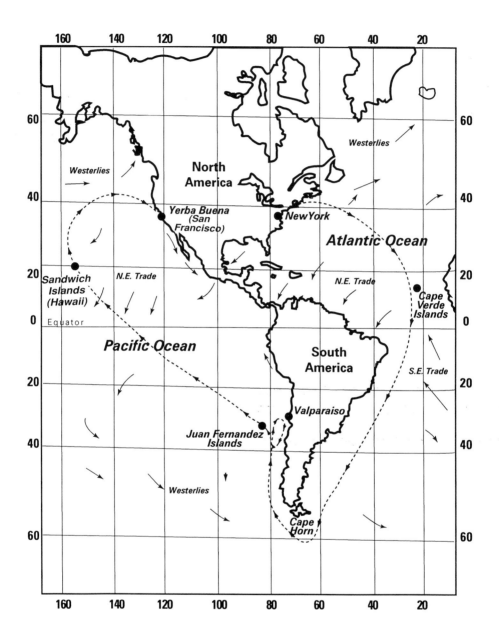

Route of the BROOKLYN

Though death claimed a total of ten passengers on the voyage,[29] there were occasions when there was new life. After the terrible Atlantic storm, a baby boy was born to the Burrs, who lost an older son about three weeks later. They named their infant John Atlantic Burr. Dr. John Robbins and his wife also buried two sons in the Atlantic. Later, en route to Hawaii, a girl, Georgiana Pacific Robbins, was born to them.

On about 3 March, as the ship crossed the equator, a good-natured crew played customary pranks on the passengers.[30] In the summerlike weather, children spent their days on deck "attending their schools, jumping rope, and engaged in all the other amusements resorted to pass off the time."[31] In the tropics, the passengers were "amused by the many flying fishes and the porpoises racing along the ship, first in the water then leaping high into the air."[32]

Into the Pacific

On 10 April the ship uneventfully rounded the tip of South America, a notorious graveyard for vessels. "It was fine weather when we doubled Cape Horn," John Horner recalled. "The women were making bread, pies, cakes, frying doughnuts, etc., and the children were playing and romping about the deck."[33] The captain then continued farther south, as far as sixty degrees latitude, to find winds that would enable him to get far enough west.[34]

Many supplies, especially water, were becoming scarce as they traveled northward along the Chilean coast. The water, described as being green and ropy with algae, was rationed at a pint per day per person. Firewood for the galley was

---

[29] *Friend*, 1 July 1846, 101.

[30] Stark, 26.

[31] *New-York Daily Tribune*, 27 August 1846.

[32] Stark, 26.

[33] Horner, 797.

[34] *New-York Daily Tribune*, 27 August 1846.

exhausted, which meant no hot meals nor warmth below deck. Captain Richardson decided to stop at Valparaiso to replenish supplies. Following nearly three months at sea, the passengers eagerly anticipated this opportunity to go ashore. However, as they were about to enter the harbor, another storm battered the ship, holding it out at sea for three days and blowing it southward, back toward the Cape. During the storm, Sister Laura Goodwin, mother of seven children, fell off a galley ladder and lay dying on her bunk.

Finally, instead of continuing the attempt to land at Valparaiso, the captain headed for Juan Fernandez Island. They arrived there on 4 May 1846 and dropped anchor. Paying tribute to the captain's navigational skills, John Horner asserted that "he hit every thing he aimed at, and nothing which he did not want to hit."[35]

Soon after arriving, the Saints buried Laura Goodwin. Of the pilgrims who died en route, she was the only one to have a final resting place on solid ground. Two or three Chilean families on the island, together with the captain and crew, joined the Saints in the funeral service.

The voyagers then replenished the ship. Its casks were filled with eighteen thousand gallons of pure drinking water.[36] Firewood for the galley was gathered, baled, and stowed on board. Goats, wild boars, and fish were salted and stored. Fruits from abandoned orchards as well as wild fruits were a delicious change from sea biscuits and brined pork. The huge crawfish in the island's streams rivaled the voyagers' eastern lobster. In all, it was a welcome respite from the sea and a most providential renewal of diet, supplies, and spirits. "If we had gone to Valpiraso," passenger William Glover reflected, "it would have cost us hundreds of dollars; thus showing to us the hand of the Lord and His overruling Providence and care for His people."[37]

---

[35] Horner, 795–96.

[36] *New-York Daily Tribune*, 27 August 1846.

[37] Glover, 16.

Their ship next headed for the Hawaiian Islands to drop off its commercial cargo. During this leg of the voyage, typically pleasant South Pacific weather was with them. Edward Kemble recalled "riding gayly along with all sails set before a six or seven knot breeze, over a sea just sufficiently agitated to give grateful variety to a motion without retarding progress."[38] When they hit the equatorial "doldrums" the "ship ran into a calm sea, not a breeze blowing." After several days and much anxious prayer on the part of the Saints, "they felt a breeze, and the ship began to move toward their longed for land."[39]

The ship BROOKLYN

During this part of the voyage, trouble erupted. Samuel Brannan excommunicated four persons for promoting what he regarded as false and dangerous doctrines and "for their wicked and licentious conduct."[40] His brash action became a

---

[38] Kemble, 22.

[39] Stark, 27.

[40] *Millennial Star* 9, no. 20 (15 October 1847): 307.

sore point and subject of much argument. Some accused him of misuse of authority or at least of overreacting.

Edward Kemble praised the young Latter-day Saint women he observed, who "were modest and discreet, and probably no emigrant ship ever crossed the ocean—certainly none ever sailed to California—whose female passengers at the end of a long voyage preserved their reputations as unspotted as did those of the Brooklyn." He noted that even though the quarters were extremely cramped, "there was rarely an infraction of discipline or decorum among the members of the company, even in the most trying times, such as were occasioned by heat or stress of weather."[41]

Captain Richardson likewise praised the Saints' conduct: "They have lived in peace together, and uniformly appeared to be quiet and orderly" and "during most of the voyage they have maintained orderly and well conducted religious exercises."[42]

Arrival at Honolulu

On 20 June, 136 days since they had left New York and six weeks after leaving Juan Fernandez Island, the ship reached land again at Oahu, Hawaii, and anchored at Honolulu. There the group found themselves next to an American warship, the *Congress*. The United States had declared war on Mexico the previous month, and this naval vessel was there to take on provisions for sailing to the same California coast to which the Saints were headed. Some undoubtedly rejoiced at the news that California might soon be part of the United States. To others, it was a "severe shock" that they might be returning to the very nation which had persecuted them, and which they had hoped to leave behind.[43] Many of the Saints began voicing

---

[41] Kemble, 17.

[42] *Friend*, 1 July 1846, 101.

[43] Stark, 28; Kemble, 23–24.

apprehensions about going on to California now that war was breaking out. Some suggested that they go on to Oregon, others to Victoria Island, and still others believed that they should turn around and head back to New York.

Nevertheless, Brannan insisted that they had set out for California, and that was where they would go. The *Congress*'s commander, Commodore Robert F. Stockton, confided that he would begin attacking and seizing the California shoreline at Monterey. He candidly suggested to Brannan that the Saints might want to go to San Francisco rather than their advertised Oregon destination. Of course, that was their real intention. The plan, though possibly dangerous since no one knew what the strength of the Mexican forces might be, offered the possibility that these Saints might be the first Americans to claim San Francisco Bay for the United States.

Despite all the confusion and disinformation, Brannan prematurely told a reporter from Honolulu's newspaper, the *Friend*, that California was to be the "grand central rendezvous" for the Saints who were then crossing the Great Plains and that the "beautiful region around San Francisco Bay is the chosen spot" where the Latter-day Saints would settle.[44]

On to California

After spending ten days in Honolulu and taking on needed supplies, the *Brooklyn* sailed on 30 June. Despite the concerns of some about returning to the United States, the *Brooklyn* Saints conducted "a spirited celebration" on the Fourth of July, hoisting flags, firing guns, and singing patriotic songs.[45]

There were still worries that they might not be allowed to land in California. Brannan encouraged his company to "be prepared for any emergency." The women on board began

---

[44] *Friend*, 1 July 1846, 101.

[45] Horner, 798.

sewing uniforms from blue denim purchased in Hawaii. With Captain Richardson's approval, the muskets were uncased, and the men began military drills on deck. Samuel Ladd, who had spent years in army service, was placed in charge. He succeeded in making the men "tolerably proficient in military duty and prepared for any exigencies that might arise."[46]

During the voyage "the people were called together and organized, and an agreement drawn up and signed by all of the men . . . that they would work together as a company to clear the debt of the ship and make all the preparations they could for the coming of the Church."[47] Specifically, they agreed to "give the proceeds of their labors for the next three years into a common fund from which all were to draw their living."[48] This pact proved to be more troublesome than useful, however, and led to disagreement and strife.

The voyage's last leg from Hawaii took just one month. Finally, on Friday morning, 31 July 1846, the scrubby hills of Yerba Buena were sighted. As their new home came into view, Carolyn Joyce noticed how "barren and dreary" the country seemed.[49] As the ship entered the bay and approached the fort—present-day Presidio—Captain Richardson, unsure of how his ship would be received, ordered the passengers below deck as a precautionary measure. Once past the fort, the captain allowed all hands back topside.[50]

The *Brooklyn* passengers strained through the mist to see what they could of their new home. They could discern American flags, one flying from the mast of a warship anchored in the harbor and another above a low, red-tiled building on the hamlet's center square. The Saints knew then that the United States had claimed and secured the area. The U.S. flag had been

[46] Kemble, 24–25; Stark, 28.

[47] Glover, 15.

[48] Crocheron, 83.

[49] Carolyn Joyce Jackson, quoted in Edward W. Tullidge, *The Women of Mormondom* (New York: Tullidge and Crandall, 1877), 446.

[50] Kemble, 7–11.

raised three weeks earlier. Brannan is reported to have exclaimed in surprise, and perhaps disappointment, "There is that damned flag again!"[51] Nevertheless, he gratefully realized that the Saints would not have to pay an anticipated twenty thousand dollars in import duties which might have been collected had Mexico still been in control.[52]

Cannons on shore boomed a salute to the new arrivals. These shots were answered from the *Brooklyn's* muskets. A rowboat from the U.S. sloop *Portsmouth* brought a group of sailors on board. An officer said, "Ladies and gentlemen, I have the honor to inform you that you are in the United States."[53] The Saints responded with three hearty cheers.

The *Brooklyn* and its passengers were finally at rest. "Of all the memories of my life," Carolyn Joyce reflected, "not one is so bitter as that dreary six months' voyage, in an emigrant ship around the Horn."[54]

As far as we have ascertained, the *Brooklyn* Saints were the first colony of home-seekers with women and children to sail around Cape Horn, the first group of Anglo settlers to come to California by water, and the first group of colonists to arrive after United States forces took California.

The *Brooklyn* arrived in Yerba Buena one year before Brigham Young and the overland Pioneers reached the Salt Lake Valley. Thus, this forlorn little California outpost, later renamed San Francisco, was the first city in the American West colonized by Latter-day Saints.

---

[51] Hubert H. Bancroft, *History of California* (San Francisco: The History Co., 1886), 5:550.

[52] *Millennial Star* 9, no. 20 (15 October 1847): 307.

[53] Tullidge, 446.

[54] Ibid.

California
Beginnings: 1846

4

The year 1846 was the beginning for both modern-day California and Latter-day Saint settlement in the West. For the first time, California attracted more settlers than Oregon. After the year began, thoughts of Latter-day Saint immigration brought concerns to California residents who feared they might be forced to capitulate to a unique group of new arrivals.

Thomas O. Larkin, the United States consul at Monterey, received word from a correspondent at the *New York Sun* that the Saints intended "to have a body of 100,000 persons" in California by spring.[1] Apparently, someone had added an extra zero to Brigham Young's letter to Brannan that requested ten thousand Church members in "St. Francisco." Latter-day Saint membership in the Golden State did not reach this level for over a century.

Another correspondent gave a more realistic figure when he wrote that there were "about 10,000 Mormons ready to start for California & that they will reach out 25 miles with their waggons etc. Look out for an avalanch." He also warned Larkin to "settle all your affairs promptly next spring. You will have

---

[1] A. E. Beach to Thomas O. Larkin, 24 December 1845 in *The Larkin Papers*, ed. George P. Hammond (Berkeley and Los Angeles: University of California Press, 1953), 4:129.

all the Mormonry among you, who will act towards you as the Israelites did to the nations among whom they came, kill you all off & take possession of your worldly gear."[2]

Such reports, though unfounded, upset even the native Mexican "Californios." The French consul at Monterey reported that the Mexicans had "a terrible fear" of the Saints, and were ready "to give themselves up" to anyone who would "deliver them from this plague."[3] Even Mexican governor Pio Pico was concerned about the approaching "Mormonitas," who claimed California as their "promised land."[4] On 6 March 1846, Consul Larkin reported that news of the approaching Saints had "caused some excitement and fear among the natives."[5]

Eastern Pilgrims

Though California's population was sparse, the *Brooklyn* Saints did not exactly arrive in a vacuum. In fact, it is possible that a few Latter-day Saints may have reached California even before Brannan and the *Brooklyn* colony. A group of immigrants arriving in 1845 was led by William Brown Ide, who had participated in the "Bear Flag Revolt" a month before the *Brooklyn* arrived. A year before, Ide had been a delegate to a convention in Illinois which had named Joseph Smith as a candidate for United States president. Hence he is presumed to have been LDS, though he later denied it. His group of some fifty men and families perhaps included other Latter-day Saints, but there is no conclusive evidence.

---

[2] John H. Everett to Thomas O. Larkin, 12 December 1845, in *Larkin Papers*, 4:119, 121.

[3] A. P. Nasatir, "The French Consulate in California, 1843–56," *California Historical Society Quarterly* 11 (December 1932): 355.

[4] Hubert H. Bancroft, *Archives of California*; Department of State Papers, IX–XVI; Misc., 9:16–17, as quoted in Lorin Hansen, "Voyage of the Brooklyn," *Dialogue* (fall 1988): 65 n. 13.

[5] Larkin to the Secretary of State, 6 March 1846 in *Larkin Papers*, 4:232.

In any case, the Latter-day Saints proved to be more benign than anticipated. There are few if any accounts of troubles between the *Brooklyn* Saints and their neighbors. They also established an early American tone of faith and sobriety that, although short-lived, can still be looked upon with a certain satisfaction.

Just as the eastern coast of the United States was settled by religious Pilgrims, so it was with the western coast. Both coasts were initially claimed by people who came in the name of religion: New England by Protestant Pilgrims, and California by Roman Catholic Franciscans, who rather than conquering or banishing the natives established instead a chain of missions to educate them and teach them Christianity. Now Latter-day Saints, religious heirs of New England Pilgrim and Puritan stock, began to transplant their religious ideals from the Atlantic seaboard to the Pacific coast. New England values and institutions began replacing Native American, Mexican, and Roman Catholic counterparts.

On 14 June 1846, just six weeks before the arrival of the *Brooklyn*, a small group of Yankee settlers raised their "bear flag" in revolt against Mexican rule. On 7 July, Commodore John D. Sloat, commander of the U.S. Pacific Fleet, raised the U.S. flag over the customs house at Monterey. And on 9 July, Capt. John B. Montgomery of the U.S. sloop *Portsmouth* raised the American flag at the plaza in Yerba Buena. Yet, it was the *Brooklyn* which, on 31 July, brought an adequate number to implant firmly and permanently, without armed conflict, the Yankee way of life. In fact, by the end of 1846, a majority of the American settlers in California were eastern-bred Latter-day Saints. It has been said that of all the cities in the West, San Francisco is most like those of the East. Those early pioneers made it so from its earliest American beginnings.

"Thus," California's eminent historian Hubert H. Bancroft writes, "San Francisco became for a time very largely a Mormon town. All bear witness to the orderly and moral conduct of the saints, both on land and sea. They were honest and industrious citizens, even if clannish and peculiar."[6]

California's first newspaper, the *Californian*, in its initial edition published in Monterey on 15 August 1846, described the recently arrived Latter-day Saints as a "plain industrious people."[7]

Although the *Brooklyn* group was young—the median age was around twenty with only eleven over fifty—many among them had varied skills; there were doctors, teachers, editors, mechanics, carpenters, farmers, and millers. The degree to which their industry and talents helped develop the new town and maintain cordial relations confirms that they were a boon to California. When they arrived, Yerba Buena consisted of only about thirty buildings, including nine adobe dwellings scattered over the clear space that stretched back from the beach. There were several Mexican families, a half-dozen

1846 view of Yerba Buena

---

[6] Bancroft, 5:551.

[7] *The Californian: Facsimile Reproductions* (San Francisco: John Howell, 1971), 3.

Americans, and about one hundred Indians, as well as the officers and men of the *Portsmouth*.

Getting Established in Yerba Buena

Immediately after the *Brooklyn* was boarded by sailors from Captain Montgomery's ship, Brannan and his two counselors were taken to the captain to explain their presence. Montgomery gave his permission for the Saints to land and disembark. Several men then went ashore on one of the *Brooklyn*'s shore boats, at what eventually became the foot of Clay Street, a high-tide landing spot.

The next day, Saturday, other passengers began disembarking. The tide was high enough until midmorning for continued landings, and soon the beach was strewn with baggage of every description— crates of chickens, what was left of the forty pigs, and the two milk cows. As the tide went out, the boats changed their landing place to the foot of a rocky bluff— later named Clark's Point—below the peak of Loma Alta, which eventually became San Francisco's famous Telegraph Hill.

"The ship *Brooklyn* left us on the rocks at the foot of what is now Broadway," wrote Carolyn Joyce Jackson. "From this point we directed our steps to the old adobe [the postmaster's "Casa Grande"] on . . . Dupont [now Grant] Street. It was the first to shelter us from the chilling winds. A little further on (toward Jackson Street), stood the adobe of old 'English Jack,' who kept a sort of depot for the milk woman, who came in daily, with a dozen bottles of milk hung to an old horse."[8]

The following day was Sunday, normally a day of rest and worship for the sailors in port. Captain Montgomery invited the Saints to attend religious services on board his ship. One of the *Portsmouth*'s sailors recalled, "Anxiety to see and examine the female portion of this strange sect, was apparent

---

[8] Edward W. Tullidge, *The Women of Mormondom* (New York: Tullidge and Crandall, 1877), 447.

BROOKLYN Saints preparing to disembark

on the faces of all." The sailors set up chairs under an awning on the quarter deck and eagerly awaited their guests' arrival. The crew's curiosity was heightened by rumors that Mormons were a strange class of people who grew horns. As the visitors came on board "curiosity appeared to fade away" and one sailor muttered, "D—nation, why they are just like other women." There was no chaplain, but it was Montgomery's custom to read a printed Episcopalian sermon to his men. After the service the Saints lunched with the captain, were escorted on a tour of the vessel, and then left for their own ship, "having created a most favorable impression among the hardy Tars of the good ship *Portsmouth*."[9]

On Monday morning, Montgomery directed his men to help unload the *Brooklyn*. One of his men left a written account: "The cargo of the *Brooklyn* consisted of the most heterogeneous mass of material ever crowded together; in fact, it seemed as if, like the ark of Noah, it contained a representative for every mortal thing the mind of man had ever conceived. Agricultural,

---

[9] Joseph T. Downey, *Filings From an Old Saw*, ed. Fred Blackburn Rogers (San Francisco: John Howell, 1956), 45–46.

mechanical and manufacturing tools were in profuse abundance; dry goods, groceries, and hardware, were dug out from the lower depths of the hold, and speedily transferred on shore, our men working with a will which showed the good feeling they bore for the parties to whom they belonged. A Printing Press and all its appurtenances, next came along."[10] All the careful preparations made before sailing contributed from that day to the ceaseless flourishing of Yerba Buena. *Brooklyn* passenger William Glover noted, "There was a continual improvement in the city, almost from the day of our landing."[11]

Getting the cumbersome five-ton press set up was one of Samuel Brannan's first challenges. He chose a spot for it on the second floor of an old gristmill. Some wondered about getting it up the rickety outside stairs and onto the second floor. But with many hands helping, it was quickly put in place.

The influx of such a large group taxed the village's sleeping quarters, so most pitched tents. This made the little town look like an army encampment. The American owner of the Casa Grande, the town's largest structure, graciously allowed nine families, including Brannan's, to spread blanket-beds on the floor. Sixteen other families crowded into the customs house, which Montgomery had converted into military barracks, their living spaces being divided by quilts or other flimsy partitions. Cooking was done outdoors.[12]

On Sunday, 16 August, the bedrolls and personal belongings crammed into the Casa Grande were sufficiently cleared to convert it from a dormitory into a chapel for Latter-day Saint services—the first non-Catholic religious meeting in Yerba Buena. The Mexican Roman Catholic priest had fled when Montgomery arrived, so Brannan was the only recognized religious figure in town. Thus, some non-Mormons attended, too, and the crowd spilled out the front door, across the porch,

---

[10] Ibid., 47.

[11] William Glover, *The Mormons in California* (Los Angeles: Glen Dawson, 1954), 19.

[12] Augusta Joyce Crocheron, "The Ship Brooklyn," *Western Galaxy* 1 (1888): 83.

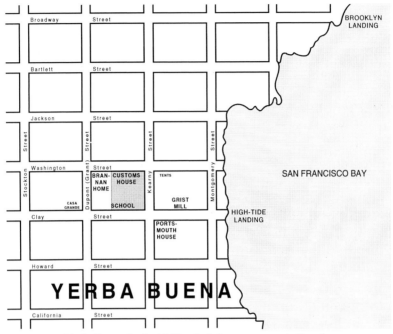

*Yerba Buena in the 1840s; shaded area represents the plaza,
now Portsmouth Square*

and into the street. John H. Brown, an English sailor who had settled in Yerba Buena the year before, indicated that Brannan's sermon was the first given at Yerba Buena in the English language and was "as good a sermon as anyone would wish to hear."[13] Thereafter, Brannan often preached on Sundays. An early historian of San Francisco described Brannan's preaching style as "fluent, terse, and vigorous."[14] Later, the people met in various private homes, "being called together by a small hand

[13] John H. Brown, *Early Days of San Francisco* (San Francisco: Presses Grabhorn #13, 1933), 34.

[14] Zoeth Skinner Eldredge, *The Beginnings of San Francisco from the Expedition of Anza, 1774 to the City Charter of April 15, 1850* (New York: John C. Rankin, 1912), 2:710.

bell which was rung on Portsmouth Square, usually by Samuel Brannan himself."[15]

An immediate problem for the new arrivals was food. The *Brooklyn* had only a one-month supply left. There was little to buy in such a tiny, unsettled place and even less money with which to buy it. However, there were abundant cattle and a little Mexican wheat. The settlers bartered for beef jerky, wheat, and whatever foodstuffs the frequent whaling ships brought with them.

William Glover cheerlessly recalled that some families had "nothing to eat, but boiled wheat and molasses, until their wives began to take in washing from the sailors and supported themselves and their husbands."[16] However, Carolyn Joyce gratefully acknowledged, "When I soaked the mouldy ship-bread, purchased from the whale-ships lying in the harbor, and fried it in the tallow, taken from the raw hides lying on the beach, God made it sweet to me, and to my child."[17]

Several other Latter-day Saint women went to work for John H. Brown in his newly opened Portsmouth House hotel: Mrs. Mercy Narrimore as housekeeper, Lucy Nutting as waitress, and Sarah Kittleman as cook.

Not all of the LDS families settled in the village of Yerba Buena. A small group found homes in the old cloistered buildings of the Franciscan Dolores Mission, about four miles to the southwest. Here, nineteen-year-old Angeline Lovett "taught the first school in California where the English language was used."[18]

The men also sought employment. Though initially hesitating at the suggestion, Captain Richardson, realizing that the Saints were destitute, agreed to accept a shipload of valuable redwood timber to pay off the remaining expense of the

[15] Florence M. Dunlap, "Samuel Brannan" (master's thesis, University of California at Berkeley, 1928), 45.

[16] Glover, 21–22.

[17] Tullidge, 446.

[18] Annaleone D. Patton, *California Mormons by Sail and Trail* (Salt Lake City: Deseret Book, 1961), 16.

voyage. Brannan called for volunteers to go north across the Bay to present-day Marin County where they could obtain the redwood. "Part of the company went to South Seleter [Sausalito]," Glover wrote, "hired a sawmill, hauled the logs, sawed and delivered the lumber and paid the debt."[19]

Several men got jobs "to make adobies, dig wells, build houses and haul wood to make money to keep up the expenses of the company."[20] John Horner and James Light went east to Marsh's Landing (present-day Antioch), where Dr. John Marsh employed them in planting wheat.[21] Some went to work in lumber camps on the Marin Peninsula, in the East Bay hills, and in the Santa Cruz mountains south of the Bay. Others went to work around Sutter's Fort. Sutter's Fort had been built only a few years earlier by John A. Sutter, an immigrant from Germany who sought to establish a colony in Central California. The walled compound, located at what is now Sacramento, included storehouses, granaries and other facilities. It was typically the first outpost travelers would reach after crossing the Sierra Nevada. Men from the *Brooklyn* worked at the Fort and also at the gristmill and the sawmill that Sutter was building in the foothills.

There was also the matter of security. Though the village had been claimed by the United States, it was by no means secure. Mexican soldiers were still around, and they opposed the idea of the Yankees taking over. Skirmishes continued throughout the territory. Montgomery immediately pressed into service the seventy partly prepared soldiers of the *Brooklyn* to aid him in defending against what he thought could be an imminent Mexican attack. The Saints mostly served as night watchmen, though they drilled daily in the town square in preparation for an attack that never came.

---

[19] Glover, 18.

[20] Ibid.

[21] John M. Horner, "Adventures of a Pioneer," *Improvement Era* 7, no. 8 (June 1904): 571.

Only an occasional false alarm disturbed the peace. For example, the officer in charge of the marines who guarded the town secretly visited John Brown at the Portsmouth House late each night to have his flask filled with whiskey. He would go to John Brown's window, rap twice on the shutter, and then say in a barely audible voice, "The Spaniards are in the brush"—a signal that he needed whiskey. One night, Brown was sleeping soundly and did not hear the knocking at his window. In frustration, the officer, who had already been drinking, "fired off one of his pistols, and sang out at the top of his voice, 'The Spaniards are in the brush.'" Immediately an alarm was sounded in the barracks, and quickly the Saints "were all up and on hand with arms and ammunition, ready to furnish what service they could." They remained on guard for three hours. "There were several shots fired by those on duty, thinking they were shooting at Californians; but they found the next day, to their great surprise, that instead of dead bodies, some scrub oaks had received the shots."[22]

Capt. John C. Fremont came to Yerba Buena to recruit men for his "California Volunteers." At first, many Saints were interested in signing up, but when William Glover pointed out that Fremont's company included many "Missouri mobbers," all but two declined to join.[23] On 15 November, these two participated in the Battle of La Navidad, near Salinas, where the Mexicans defeated Fremont and his soldiers.

New Hope Colony

During the late summer or early autumn of 1846, Samuel Brannan took communal funds to the San Joaquin Valley, about seventy miles east of Yerba Buena, to acquire land and begin a farm. At Marsh's Landing, Dr. Marsh convinced him to buy a discarded whaleboat, convert it into a sailing launch,

---

[22] Brown, 39–40.

[23] Glover, 19.

*1948 COMET monument with transcontinental
railroad bridge in background*

and use it to carry supplies up the San Joaquin River. Brannan took farm implements, sawmill irons, seed wheat, and a small flour mill to establish the farm. He also called a crew of twenty men, headed by Thomas Stout, to work the farm. Ezekiel Merritt, an old trapper who knew the area well, drew a map for Brannan of the land he regarded as the "purtiest of all."[24]

> Along the headwaters of the majestic San Joaquin River, at the juncture of the Stanislaus, slept a land of breathtaking natural beauty, boundless level acres, and a climate which rivaled Italy. Its soil, the old trapper assured him, was deep, it had wild game in plenteous abundance, and more important, it possessed a natural waterway to a seaport site on the bay. A more perfect setting could scarcely be imagined. Samuel believed he had marked the site of another Kirtland, Nauvoo, or perhaps even the New Jerusalem of the latter days.
>
> Round about, elk and antelope went in droves by thousands; deer were plentiful; the ground covered with geese; and rivers with ducks, while the willow swamps along the river banks were filled with grizzly bear. The tracks were as well worn in the swamps as cattle paths today. Three hours of good hunting could provide meat enough for a week, for the whole colony. Bear's oil served as lard, and the only provisions which

---

[24] *San Jose Pioneer*, 23 June 1877.

1948 New Hope monument

Samuel Brannan had to send from Yerba Buena were unground wheat, sugar and coffee.[25]

Captain Fremont called the area "scenic as Switzerland, balmy as Italy, and fertile as the Nile Delta."[26]

Quartus Sparks, one of the twenty called to work at the farm, was dispatched on mule-back to Livermore via Santa Clara and San Jose, to buy a yoke of oxen and farming equipment. In the meantime, the others converted the whaler, renamed it the *Comet*, and made a couple of trips up the river to transport small equipment and seed.

Sparks, with oxen and mules, met Brannan and the others at Marsh's Landing. From there they drove over the relatively trailless country into the valley, where they set up camp. A few hours later, the launch arrived carrying heavy equipment. The *Comet* was the first sailing vessel to ascend the San Joaquin River, and Brannan had the distinction of starting the first farm in the now-famous San Joaquin Valley.

From where the *Comet* stopped, the men carried the seed wheat, implements, and machinery to the site of "New Hope"—a distance of about twenty miles—on the north bank of the Stanislaus River about a mile and a half from its junction with the San Joaquin. They set to work building three log houses and a gristmill. They fenced and planted eighty acres of wheat, along with vegetables and redtop (a forage crop), hoping to get their seeds into the ground before winter rains

---

[25] Ibid.

[26] Patton, 21.

set in. However, storms that winter were early and heavy, and most of the crops were lost to flooding.

Growth Continues in Yerba Buena

Two of Brannan's concerns were economics and industry. The communal pact signed aboard the *Brooklyn* was converted into a firm known as "Samuel Brannan and Company," which owned all means of production: the printing press, the saw-mills, the flour mill, and various other tools and implements. The company also purchased city lots and farms and built homes and other buildings. During the fall of 1846, Brannan moved into a one-and-one-half-story frame home which he had either leased or built (the reports vary). It was located on a prominent corner lot directly behind the old Customs House.[27]

Samuel Brannan's home in San Francisco

But the *Brooklyn* Saints seemed to be no more ready to live under the constraints of a cooperative organization than were those in Kirtland. The grumbling that began on the ship continued and intensified, some feeling that "communal" ownership meant "Brannan" ownership.

---

[27] Frank Soulé, John H. Gihon, and James Nisbet, *The Annals of San Francisco* (New York: D. Appleton, 1855), 347.

Furthermore, Brannan excommunicated three men for drunkenness or other infractions. These, along with the excommunications during the voyage, caused a permanent rift within the *Brooklyn* colony. Some importuned Captain Montgomery for redress. Brannan complained that "a few of the passengers on our arrival endeavored to make mischief and trouble, by complaints of the bad treatment they had received during the passage, which induced Capt. M. to institute a court of enquiry, before which the larger portion of the company were cited to appear, for private examination. But the truth was mighty and prevailed!"[28]

Another suit was brought against Brannan by William Harris, a non-Mormon who had boarded the *Brooklyn* in Hawaii. He demanded that he be released from the communal pact and be given his share of the stock. The mayor, Washington A. Bartlett, acted as judge, and a jury of peers was impaneled. Attorneys were found to represent both parties, with Brannan doing most of his own talking. Each of those who had been disfellowshipped testified against him, accusing him of betraying their trust by mismanaging their common funds. Others gave compelling testimony in his behalf. Brannan pointed out that Harris had paid only his fifty-dollar fare but had been supported out of the common stock of provisions; therefore, he "had received more than his services were worth." Furthermore, if the association were to pay its debts, there would be nothing left to divide. The court decided in Brannan's favor, "that the contract, which had been signed for three years, could not be broken." Thus ended California's first jury trial.[29]

Despite the clamor, by the fall Brannan was earning a steady income publishing documents and bulletins for government officials and the general public. On 24 October, he published an "extra" in advance of his newspaper, which

---

[28] *California Star-Extra*, 1 January 1847, quoted in *Millennial Star* 9 (15 October 1847): 307.

[29] Soulé, Gihon, and Nisbet, 750–51; see also Dunlap, 46–48.

began regular publication two and one-half months later. He had planned this paper while still in the East and had prepared a masthead bearing the title the *California Star*.

Overland Arrivals

On 29 October 1846, a Latter-day Saint pioneer family arrived with the Lilburn Boggs wagon train from Missouri. Thomas Rhoads, a Kentuckian, joined the Church in Illinois in 1835 and was ordained an elder in Missouri in 1837. Though he was apparently a faithful Church member, he remained in Missouri, owning land and slaves after the general exodus of the Saints in 1839.

Upon learning of the expulsion of the Saints from Nauvoo, and possibly with direction from Brigham Young, Rhoads gathered most of his family and some friends together and headed west for California, planning to join the Saints there. Why Rhoads was traveling with the notorious Latter-day Saint enemy, Boggs, or how many others in the party were Church members, is not known.

After passing through Emigrant Gap, or Donner Pass (just a few weeks before the ill-fated Donner Party became stranded there), the Rhoads family settled east of Sutter's Fort in the vicinity of Dry Creek and the Consumnes River. The older daughters soon married prominent non-LDS pioneers in the area. The Rhoads family participated in two of California's most famous pioneer experiences. Sons John and Dan figured prominently in the rescue of the Donner Party that winter, and Thomas may have been the true discoverer of California gold, mining it successfully for some time before Marshall's more famous discovery in 1848.

Another group coming overland in 1846 included a Latter-day Saint widow, Lavinia Murphy, and her family. She had been hired by the Donner Party as a cook and laundress to pay her family's way. Although she and two sons died, four other children survived. One of these was Mary, for whom the city of Marysville was named.[30] There is no record that the Murphy children had any subsequent affiliation with the Church.

Besides the Rhoadses and the Murphys, other individuals and small, independent parties of Saints came to California in 1846. Among them was the Wimmer family, some of whom were present at the discovery of gold. This family is sometimes confused with the Winner family of the *Brooklyn*.

Thus Latter-day Saints were in California while it was still a Mexican province. They came as pilgrims and as farmers. Though they hailed from both the North and the South, they were primarily from New England and played a vital role in setting the American tone of what would later become the most populous state in the United States.

Some of the authenticated "firsts" attributed to these pioneers in California are as follows: the first Anglo birth (a baby born to the William Glovers); the first marriage (Lizzie Wimmer and a serviceman, Basil Hall, performed by Brannan); the first divorce (hotel owner J. H. Brown and Hettie Pell); the first court case (several *Brooklyn* passengers v. Brannan); the first English language school (Angelina Lovett's); and the first wheat grown in the San Joaquin Valley.

As the *Brooklyn* and other Latter-day Saint immigrants helped set the early tone in Northern California, another larger group was coming to the South—the "Mormon Battalion," which was undertaking an epic march. This battalion would soon play its own role in planting Latter-day Saint and American ideals in early California soil.

---

[30] Erwin Gudde, *California Place Names* (Berkeley and Los Angeles: University of California Press, 1974), 194.

The Epic March of the Mormon Battalion: 1846–47

5

The story of the Mormon Battalion began with the desperate need the Saints had, both individually and collectively, for cash. Having been driven from Nauvoo in the cold winter, many were sick and destitute. During the spring and summer of 1846, they scattered throughout Iowa, many working as day laborers to scrape enough money together to outfit themselves for the trek west.

To assist the Pioneers with their monetary needs, Church leaders in Nauvoo publicly announced in a circular their desire to obtain a government contract to build a chain of stockade forts along the Oregon Trail.[1] But given the prevailing anti-Mormon attitude and the tense situation with Mexico, government leaders would not sanction any plan that would give the Saints so much military influence in the West.

Behind-the-Scenes Negotiations

On 26 February, Brigham Young wrote to Jesse C. Little, a thirty-year-old New Englander, appointing him to preside

---

[1] *History of The Church of Jesus Christ of Latter-day Saints*, ed. B. H. Roberts, 2d ed., rev. (Salt Lake City: Deseret Book, 1957), 7:570.

over the Eastern States Mission. President Young continued to encourage California settlement, instructing Little: "If our government shall offer any facilities for emigrating to the western coast, embrace those facilities if possible."[2]

In Philadelphia, Little was introduced to Col. Thomas L. Kane, who understood the Saints' dilemma, and the two became fast friends. Kane wrote a letter to the vice president of the United States urging the government to aid the Saints, who, he testified, "still retain American hearts, and would not willingly sell themselves to the foreigner."[3]

Little arrived in Washington, D.C., on 21 May 1846, one week after the United States declared war on Mexico. Two days later, with the assistance of A. G. Benson, Little was able to secure an appointment with Amos Kendall, the former postmaster general who had sought to extort Brannan and who still wielded considerable influence in the U.S. capital. Kendall "thought arrangements could be made to assist our emigration by enlisting one thousand of our men, arming, equipping, and establishing them in California to defend the country."[4]

On 27 May, Kendall informed Little that he had broached the subject with President James K. Polk, who by this time "had determined to take possession of California," and was considering, with his cabinet, the possibility of using Latter-day Saint volunteers to "push through and fortify the country."[5] The president and his cabinet had already dispatched Col. Stephen W. Kearny, then stationed at Fort Leavenworth, to travel via Santa Fe to California.

By 1 June, Little had not received any definite word on the proposed use of Latter-day Saint troops, so he wrote a lengthy letter to the president in which he requested "some pecuniary assistance" for the westward migration of his persecuted people. "We would disdain to receive assistance from a foreign

---

[2] Quoted in Journal History, 6 July 1846 (hereafter JH); LDS Church Archives.

[3] Ibid.

[4] Ibid.

[5] Ibid.

power," Little wrote, "unless our government should turn us off in this grant" and thus "compel us to be foreigners."[6]

President Polk's diary entry for the following day records that Colonel Kearny was specifically "authorized to receive into service as volunteers a few hundred of the Mormons who are now on their way to California. . . . The main object of taking them into service would be to conciliate them, and prevent them from assuming a hostile attitude towards the U.S. after their arrival in California."[7] On 3 June, Jesse Little had a three-hour interview with the president, who stated that he had received Little's letter and wished to help him but had not worked out all the details.

That same day, however, President Polk and the secretary of war finalized the orders to Colonel Kearny: "It is known that a large body of Mormon emigrants are en route to California, for the purpose of settling in that country. You are desired to use all proper means to have a good understanding with them, to the end that the United States may have their co-operation in taking possession of and holding, that country. . . . You are hereby authorized to muster into service such as can be induced to volunteer; not, however, to a number exceeding one-third of your entire force." He indicated that the Saints would be paid like other volunteers and be able to nominate some of their own men to serve as officers.[8] On 5 June, President Polk, in another interview, informed Little of this decision.[9]

Recruiting the Battalion

On 19 June, just a week before he left Fort Leavenworth for Santa Fe with his first contingent of troops, Kearny complied

---

[6] Ibid.

[7] *The Diary of James K. Polk*, ed. Milo Milton Quaife (Chicago: A.C. McClurg, 1910), 1:444, 446.

[8] U.S. Congress, Senate, 30th Cong., 1st sess., 1847–48, Senate Executive Document no. 60, as quoted in John F. Yurtinus, "A Ram in the Thicket: The Mormon Battalion in the Mexican War" (Ph.D. diss., Brigham Young University, 1976), 34–35.

[9] JH, 6 July 1846.

and dispatched Capt. James Allen to the Latter-day Saint camps in Iowa to raise five hundred volunteers. Accompanied by three dragoons (armed cavalry), Captain Allen arrived at Mount Pisgah just one week later. There was some grumbling among the Saints about being asked to serve a country that had allowed them to be expelled; some even believed that this was a plot to destroy them. Nevertheless, Brigham Young immediately endorsed the proposal and went with Allen throughout the scattered camps, chastening the naysayers and soliciting volunteers. On 7 July, President Young "addressed the brethren on the subject of raising a Battalion to march to California." Jesse C. Little, who had just arrived the day before from the East, spoke to the same gathering. As a result, sixty-six men volunteered.[10] Captain Allen explained that forming a Mormon battalion "gives an opportunity of sending a portion of their young and intelligent men to the ultimate destination of their whole people, and entirely at the expense of the United States, and this advanced party can thus pave the way and look out the land for their brethren to come after them."[11]

Furthermore, as Brigham Young concluded, "the Mormon Battalion was organized from our camp to allay the prejudices of the people, prove our loyalty to the government of the United States, and for the present and temporal salvation of Israel." Battalion members would be able to send money to their families in Iowa, which would help finance their westward migration.[12]

In less than a month, the quota was filled. The volunteers enlisted into service on 16 July 1846 for a period of twelve months. Brigham Young instructed them that after being disbanded they could work on the coast if they wished, but holding to his original plan for the Saints' settlement, he emphatically reminded them that the next temple would not be built there, but in the Rocky Mountains, "where the brethren

---

[10] Ibid.

[11] "Circular to the Mormons," quoted in JH, 26 June 1846.

[12] JH, 14 August 1846.

will have to come to get their endowments." He further explained that the Saints were going to the Great Basin, where they would be safe from mobs and that the Battalion would "probably be dismissed about 800 miles from us."[13]

No one could have known just how difficult the twelve months of Battalion service would be. Throughout the march, conditions were generally bad. Nevertheless, President Young promised the recruits that none would be killed in battle "if they will perform their duties faithfully without murmuring and go in the name of the Lord, be humble and pray every morning and evening."[14]

The approximately five hundred volunteers were joined by thirty-five women—some of them serving as army laundresses—and many children. The Latter-day Saint soldiers buttressed Kearny's "Army of the West."

The Battalion marched from Council Bluffs on 21 July and recorded its first fatality the following day, when Samuel Boley became ill and died. They endured unbearably hot weather, torrential rain, and even a tornado. Many became sick from exposure and lack of provisions before they marched the two hundred miles to Fort Leavenworth for supplies.

On 29 July they marched through St. Joseph, Missouri, and found the townspeople astounded that the Latter-day Saints had volunteered to serve a United States government that had turned a deaf ear to their cries for redress. On 1 August, the day after the *Brooklyn* dropped anchor in San Francisco Bay, the Battalion reached Fort Leavenworth and was amply outfitted—a mixed blessing since each soldier would have to carry a heavy pack. A Missourian, George B. Sanderson, became Battalion doctor; the Saints viewed this as a most unfortunate appointment. Each man received his allotted forty-two dollars clothing allowance for the year, but instead of purchasing new

---

[13] Willard Richards Diary, 14 July 1846 and 18 July 1846, as cited in Yurtinus, 53–54, 59.

[14] Elden J. Watson, *Manuscript History of Brigham Young* (Salt Lake City: E. J. Watson, 1971), 264.

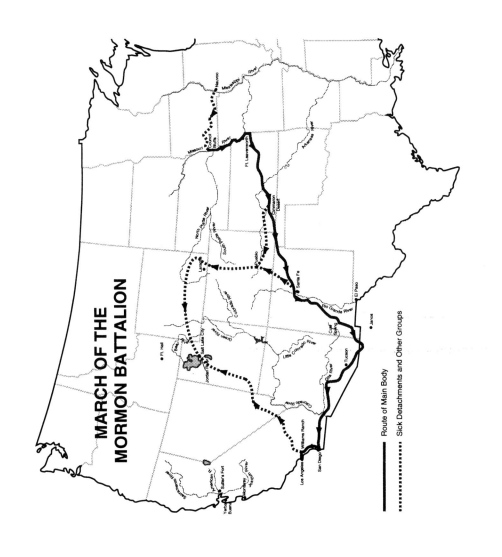

MARCH OF THE
MORMON BATTALION

Route of Main Body

Sick Detachments and Other Groups

uniforms, many sent the money back to aid their families and the general emigration effort. The paymaster noticed that the Battalion men, unlike many illiterate soldiers, could sign their names. In fact, the several detailed diaries kept made it one of history's best-documented military marches. They also conducted religious services throughout their march—an unusual practice for soldiers.

Along the Santa Fe Trail

The Battalion followed the old Santa Fe Trail through what is now Kansas, Colorado, Oklahoma, and eastern New Mexico into Santa Fe. The trail "was no mere line of ruts connecting two towns, two cultures. It was a perilous cruise across a boundless sea of grass, over forbidding mountains, among wild beasts and wilder men, ending in an exotic city offering quick riches, friendly foreign women and a moral holiday." Travelers "knew only darkness, fatigue, cold and sunburn, the insistent wind, the drenching downpour, the lone danger of guard duty while the wolves howled from the hills and the skulking Comanche fitted an arrow to his bowstring."[15]

Upon leaving Fort Leavenworth on 13 August, the Battalion's original leader, James Allen, who was popular with the men, became ill, remained behind, and died ten days later. The agreement with the Battalion was that if for any reason they lost their commander, they were to choose one of their own to take his place. They chose Capt. Jefferson Hunt.

Less than a week after they left Fort Leavenworth, a powerful storm hit them. "About sun down," wrote Henry Standage, "the wind commenced blowing very hard accompanied with large drops of rain and continued to blow till our tents were all blown down and our cooking utensils scattered all over the Prairie."[16] Robert Bliss, a fellow soldier, described

---

[15] Stanley Vestal, *The Old Santa Fe Trail* (Boston: Houghton Mifflin, 1939), preface, viii.

[16] Frank A. Golder, *The March of the Mormon Battalion: From Council Bluffs to California* (New York: The Century Co., 1928), 148.

the storm this way: "We had hardly time to pitch our tents before the storm came down upon us, it tore our tents from their fastenings, overturned our light wagons and prostrated men to the ground. The vivid lightning and the roar of the thunder and hail caused horses and mules to break from their fastenings and flee in every direction on the wide prairie. . . . Lieutenant Ludington's carriage was overturned with his wife and Mother in it and our Orderly's Carriage was sent before the storm 15 or 20 rods and he in pursuit of his wife in it."[17]

On 29 August, two weeks after the Battalion departed Fort Leavenworth, Lt. Andrew Jackson Smith of the regular army intercepted the Battalion and took command from Captain Hunt, a move which violated the agreement between the U.S. Army and the Church. Lieutenant Smith, a West Point graduate, disliked Mormons, and the Saints viewed his appointment as another unfortunate choice. The volunteers concluded that there was an unholy alliance between Smith and his accomplice, George B. Sanderson, the Battalion doctor. Smith, who looked on the LDS volunteers and their accompanying women and children as unfit for army service, confronted them with long, forced marches, making them sick. Then Dr. Sanderson concocted medicines of calomel and arsenic which, the men believed, either cured or killed. Brigham Young counseled the recruits by letter to turn to faith and priesthood ordinances for healing, and "let surgeon's medicine alone."[18]

Marching just a few days ahead of them was a large group of Missouri volunteers, some of whom were members of mobs that drove the Saints from Missouri eight years before. The two groups were sufficiently separated that, with the exception of brief confrontations at the crossing of the Arkansas River and at Santa Fe, they had no trouble with each other. The Indians, who fought against the incursions of the Whites both the year

---

[17] Robert S. Bliss Diary, 19 August 1846; typescript, LDS Church Archives.

[18] Daniel Tyler, *A Concise History of the Mormon Battalion in the Mexican War* (Glorieta, N. Mex.: Rio Grande Press, 1881), 146; see also Susan E. Black, "The Mormon Battalion: Conflict Between Religious and Military Authority," *Southern California Quarterly* 74, no. 4 (winter 1992): 313–28.

before and the year after, were strangely quiet that year. They ambushed, killed, and took the scalps of a few Missourians, but the Battalion was never bothered.

Through this part of the trek, the biggest problems were forced marches and dust. Pvt. Azariah Smith, who had just celebrated his eighteenth birthday during the march, recorded the following in his diary: "Tuesday Sept 1st. 1846. . . . I and Thomas went ahead this morning as my eyes were so sore that I could not travail in the dust of the Battalion. We travailed 15 miles and camped by a Spring on the prairy, called the Lost Spring. We arived at the Spring about 2 oclock, dry and dusty. . . . Monday Sept 14th. . . . The time goes very well with me except my eyes being very Sore."[19]

On 10 September, the Battalion met a group of messengers en route to Fort Leavenworth with the report that on 18 August Kearny, who had been promoted to general, had taken Santa Fe without firing a shot. He wanted the volunteers to go directly to Santa Fe rather than taking the longer route via Bent's Fort in Colorado. Lieutenant Smith followed orders and took the more direct but more difficult route through the Cimarron Desert.

On 16 September, Smith ordered a group of fifteen sick families, who he believed could not make the difficult march, to leave the main body and proceed instead to Pueblo, Colorado. There they joined fourteen families of Saints from Mississippi who had set up a semi-permanent camp while awaiting the main body coming overland with Brigham Young.

In the desert there were long stretches without water, except for occasional pools polluted with the urine and dung of animals. An increasing number of men and animals became sick. During the next three weeks there were only two days during which they had fresh water.

---

[19] Azariah Smith, *The Gold Discovery Journal of Azariah Smith*, ed. David L. Bigler (Salt Lake City: University of Utah Press, 1990), 23, 26.

On 2 October the Battalion received word that General Kearny would discharge them unless they reached Santa Fe by 10 October. Consequently, the officers decided to split the command into two detachments: the able and the feeble. The able-bodied were force-marched to Santa Fe, arriving on 9 October. The feeble entered the town three days later. When the first group arrived they learned that Kearny had already pushed on toward California and had left Alexander W. Doniphan in charge at Santa Fe. General Doniphan had come to the defense of the Latter-day Saints at a crucial time during the Missouri persecutions eight years before. Now, as the Battalion marched into Santa Fe's central plaza, he ordered his men to give them a one-hundred-gun salute from the rooftops of surrounding adobe buildings.

A New Wagon Road to the Coast

When General Kearny learned of Colonel Allen's death, he appointed Lt. Col. Philip St. George Cooke, another West Point graduate, to take command of the Mormon Battalion at Santa Fe. Having anticipated the glories to be earned on the battlefield, Cooke was likely disappointed with this assignment to shepherd a group of inexperienced volunteers. His initial impression of the Battalion was quite discouraging: "It was enlisted too much by families; some were too old,—some feeble, and some too young; it was embarrassed by many women; it was undisciplined; it was much worn by travelling on foot, and marching from Nauvoo, Illinois; their clothing was very scant;—there was no money to pay them,—or clothing to issue; their mules were utterly broken down; the Quartermaster department was without funds, and its credit bad; and mules were scarce."[20] These were hardly the criteria for an

---

[20] Philip St. George Cook, *The Conquest of New Mexico and California in 1846–1848* (Chicago: Rio Grande, 1964), 91.

Lt. Col. Philip St. George Cooke

efficient battle-force. Nevertheless, as a recent historian has pointed out, the Battalion had "hidden yet great potential."[21]

The preferred route from Santa Fe to the Pacific Coast was the Old Spanish Trail—through what is now central Utah to Southern California. There were trails on the more direct route from New Mexico through the Gila Valley of Arizona, but wagons had not been taken over them. Kearny, who left Santa Fe on 25 September intending to take wagons with him over the Gila route, soon abandoned them to make better time. He appointed Colonel Cooke and the Battalion to open the wagon road.

After the harsh conditions caused a second "sick detachment" to be dispatched to Pueblo, the Battalion left Santa Fe on 19 October with 397 men and twenty-five wagons, each wagon pulled by eight mules. Though their march would last another ninety days, the quartermaster was able to give the men only enough flour, sugar, coffee, and salt for sixty days, along with rations of salt pork for thirty days and soap for twenty.

The original plan was for the Battalion to follow Kearny's route as closely as possible. Two weeks later, however, Cooke received word from Kearny advising him that wagons could not cross the mountains on the most direct route to the Gila and

---

[21] Dwight L. Clarke, *Stephen Watts Kearny: Soldier of the West* (Norman, Okla.: University of Oklahoma Press, 1961), 166.

consequently directed him to go farther south along the Rio Grande before turning west. This more southerly route was completely unexplored, and it was here that the Battalion made a significant and far-reaching contribution.

The rations were never increased but were often decreased. Though the Battalion passed through numerous Mexican villages, the curious natives were generally too suspicious or poor to part with food, except for a few apples and grapes. The terrain consisted of such deep sand, in so many places, that the animals could not pull wagons through without assistance. Battalion members, already burdened with heavy packs, had to use ropes to assist the animals in pulling the wagons much of the way. "Today the Captain had us divided off ten to a wagon, to push them up hills and over bad places," Azariah Smith recorded. "We have only half rations now of flour and live cheafly on beaf which is very poor and tough."[22]

On 10 November, about 250 miles from Santa Fe, fifty-five men became too weak to travel further and were sent back to Pueblo to join the other invalids. Now numbering about 360, including women and children, the Battalion continued down into the Rio Grande Valley. Along the way they saw intricate irrigation systems, some several miles long. Their observations were fortuitous, as the knowledge of irrigation later became a necessary survival skill both in California and in Utah.

On 13 November the volunteers left the banks of the Rio Grande and headed southwest to get around the end of the mountains. A strong north wind brought very frigid temperatures. "It was exceedingly cold last night," Colonel Cooke recorded in his diary, "water froze in my hair this morning whilst washing."[23]

---

[22] Smith, 47.

[23] Philip St. George Cooke, William Henry Chase Whiting, François Xavier Aubry, *Exploring Southwestern Trails 1846–1854*, ed. Ralph P. Bieber (Glendale, Calif.: Arthur H. Clark, 1938), 105.

About a week after leaving the Rio Grande, the Battalion's scouts reported that they could not find adequate sources of water or a suitable pass ahead. A few of the men, therefore, hoping to attract someone who could recommend a better route, scaled a nearby hill and built a signal fire. A group of helpful Mexicans told them that just over a hundred miles farther south was an established westward trail passing through some settlements in what is currently northern Mexico. Cooke decided to take this detour. This decision again antagonized the Battalion; they felt it was not consistent with their mission to go straight to the coast. Daniel Tyler recalled that "a gloom was cast over the entire command." That evening, fifty-five-year-old David Pettigrew encouraged the men to pray that the Lord might change the colonel's mind, that he "might not lead up into battle or directly through the enemies strong holds where in all probability they would give up battle."[24]

Nevertheless, the next morning Cooke led the Battalion directly south toward the Mexican settlements. After going only two miles, however, the trail turned southeast, and Cooke became alarmed that he would get too far to the east and run into unforeseen problems. That would rob him of his chance to carve a trail to the West Coast. Cooke "arose in his saddle and ordered a halt. He then said with firmness: 'This is not my course.'"[25] He swore that he would be "damned if he was going all around the world to get to California."[26] He then directed the bugler to "blow the right," thus turning the troops due west. Witnessing this, David Pettigrew blissfully exclaimed, "God bless the Colonel!" Tyler recalled that the colonel "glanced around to discern whence the voice came, and then

---

[24] Henry W. Bigler Diary, Book A, 48; typescript in possession of Larry C. Porter, Brigham Young University.

[25] Tyler, 207.

[26] Henry W. Bigler, *Bigler's Chronicle of the West*, ed. Erwin G. Gudde (Berkeley and Los Angeles: University of California Press, 1962), 28.

his grave, stern face for once softened and showed signs of satisfaction."[27]

During this part of the journey, the men curried favor with their commander through an ingenious solution to the problem of dragging the wagons through deep sand. A double file of foot soldiers went ahead of the wagons, stomping down the sand in ruts so the wagon wheels had firmer ground to roll over. The double column was rotated every hour. This unconventional plan worked rather well and was therefore followed from this point on.

After passing over the Continental Divide, the Battalion, on 30 November, lowered their wagons over a two-hundred-foot precipice in Guadalupe Canyon and emerged into what is now southeastern Arizona.

While marching along the San Pedro River on 11 December, the Battalion engaged in its only fight—a battle with wild bulls. Herds gathered along the line of march. Some of the bolder animals attacked the soldiers and gored several mules to death. The men had been ordered to march with their weapons unloaded, but they now loaded them to defend themselves, and "the rattle of musketry was for once heard all along the line."[28]

Colonel Cooke wrote in his diary: "The animals attacked in some instances without provocation, and tall grass in some places made the danger greater." Tyler was standing next to Cpl. Lafayette Frost when they saw an "immense coal-black bull" about one hundred yards away charging toward them. Frost aimed his musket deliberately but did not fire until the beast was only six paces away. Colonel Cooke feared that "one man's 'ignorance with some stubbornness' was about to receive a terrible retribution." But when he saw the huge bull

---

[27] Tyler, 207.

[28] B. H. Roberts, *The Mormon Battalion: Its History and Achievements* (Salt Lake City: The Deseret News, 1919), 38.

lifeless at their feet, "how changed must have been his feelings."[29]

The bulls became even more ferocious when wounded. Dr. William Spencer shot one animal five times: twice through the lungs, twice through the heart, and once through the head, yet the culprit "would alternately rise and fall and rush upon the doctor" until it was shot a sixth time directly between the eyes. Reports of the number of wild bulls killed ran from twenty to sixty, and one writer put the figure at eighty-one.[30]

At this point in the journey, a decision had to be made. The Battalion could march through Tucson for needed rest and supplies and shorten their route by one hundred miles. But Tucson was a village of five hundred, garrisoned by two hundred Mexican troops with cannons. After a cursory consideration, Cooke decided to take the shortcut and capture Tucson.

1969 statue of Mormon Battalion soldier, sculpted by Edward Fraughton

Upon the Battalion's arrival, the two armies engaged in conversing, posturing, gesturing, threatening, arresting of emissaries, and so forth. But there was no gunfire. Finally, on 16 December the Battalion marched into town and found that the Mexican soldiers had abandoned it. The natives were friendly and shared their food. The soldiers in turn were respectful, though Cooke confiscated two thousand bushels of grain left behind by the Mexican Army.

The next leg of the trek was especially trying. Water

[29] Tyler, 220.

[30] Roberts, 38–39; Tyler, 219–20.

became extremely scarce. For several days the men and their animals trudged along with no water except for occasional small, muddy ponds. On 19 December the main body of soldiers did not camp until after dark, but to cope with their exhaustion, some "stopped without leave being worn out. The Brethren were passing by at all hours through the night," Henry Standage recorded in his journal, "still hoping that the Command had found water, travelling two or three miles at a time and resting."[31]

When someone complained about the bawling, thirst-crazed mules, Colonel Cooke curtly rejoined, "I don't care a damn about the mules, the men are what I am thinking of."[32] When some pools of freshly fallen rainwater were finally found, Battalion men not only quenched their own thirst but also helped their fellow soldiers. For example, Lieutenant Rosencrans went back along the line "on a mule loaded with Canteens of water relieving those of Co C. who had lain out."[33] Out of these difficult circumstances emerged an increasing mutual respect between Colonel Cooke and his men.

The Battalion reached the Gila River near the Pima Indian villages on 21 December, completing their assignment to open a wagon road from the Rio Grande. The significance of this accomplishment cannot be overestimated: they pioneered a new route through previously unexplored deserts between the mountainous Apache strongholds on the north and the Mexican frontier settlements on the south. This route would become a key link in a proposal for a southern transcontinental railroad. This in turn would make the 1853 Gadsden Purchase necessary, bringing what is now southern Arizona and New Mexico into the United States.

Colonel Cooke thought it might be easier to float supplies down the Gila River than to carry them to the river's confluence with the Colorado. A raft was built of two wagon boxes and

---

[31] Golder, 197.

[32] William Coray Diary, 19 December 1846, quoted in Yurtinus, 415.

[33] Golder, 197.

loaded with foodstuffs. However, the river's sandbars soon overcame the raft and the precious food, both of which were lost. At this same time, on New Year's Day 1847, Battalion members received from a group of eastward-bound travelers their first word that the colony of Saints from New York had successfully landed and was preparing a base of operations at San Francisco Bay.

After crossing the Colorado into California on 10 January, things got worse. Although General Kearny had dug some wells for the trailing Battalion, many had become dry, so new ones had to be dug. Colonel Cooke described the days between 12 and 16 January as the hardest of all. Tyler concurred:

> We here found the heaviest sand, hottest days and coldest nights, with no water and but little food. . . . At this time the men were nearly barefooted; some used, instead of shoes, rawhide wrapped around their feet, while others improvised a novel style of boots by stripping the skin from the leg of an ox. . . . Others wrapped cast-off clothing around their feet.[34]

As the Battalion left the desert and entered the Coast Range, they came to Box Canyon, which was too narrow for their wagons. Even though most of their tools had been lost with the makeshift raft on the Gila River, the men now had to chisel a passage through "a chasm of living rock." Colonel Cooke set the example by wielding one of the axes.[35]

On 21 January, the Battalion reached Warner Ranch (now in the Cleveland National Forest, northeast of Escondido),

Original Warner Ranch building

---

[34] Tyler, 244–45.

[35] Roberts, 47–48.

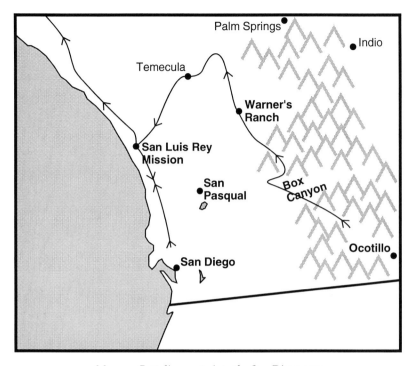

Mormon Battalion route into the San Diego area

where one Anglo man and three hundred Indians lived. Warner, upon hearing of their approach, hid all his foodstuffs, leaving the soldiers to dine on unsalted beef and a few pancakes made by the Indians. However, there were hot and cold springs—healing balm for aching feet, limbs, and joints.

Upon leaving the ranch, the soldiers passed without incident by San Pasqual, a small village where just over a month before, General Kearny's soldiers had encountered a group of Mexican "Californio" defenders who had killed Capt. Benjamin D. Moore and seventeen of his men. The Mormon Battalion first headed toward Los Angeles then received orders to detour into San Diego instead. By this time, California's landscape had taken on the luscious, emerald-green coat of January. As they marched through picturesque wooded hills and verdant winter valleys, they marveled at the fauna and flora, including vast seas of yellow-flowered mustard greens, which became new elements in their diet.

Sighting the Pacific

On 27 January 1847 the Mormon Battalion sighted the Pacific Ocean. Every soldier who kept a diary attempted to put his feelings into words. Typical is the entry of Daniel Tyler:

> The joy, the cheer that filled our souls, none but worn-out pilgrims nearing a haven of rest can imagine. Prior to leaving Nauvoo, we had talked about and sung about "the great Pacific Sea," and we were now upon its very borders, and its beauty far exceeded our most sanguine expectations. . . . The next thought was, where, oh where were our fathers, mothers, brothers, sisters, wives and children.[36]

On 29 January, almost exactly six months after the *Brooklyn* landed at San Francisco, the march ended. The Latter-day Saint soldiers were quartered near the Catholic mission some five miles outside San Diego. Both the Battalion's grueling land march and the *Brooklyn*'s arduous sea voyage had taken six months. Both groups had known danger, storms, sickness,

San Diego Mission

---

[36] Tyler, 252.

shortness of provisions, and an equal number of deaths. And both were happy to be at their Pacific destination.

Despite Col. Philip St. George Cooke's initial misgivings about taking over a ragtag group of worn-out volunteers, he became attached to the Battalion and inspired by their admirable courage and long-suffering over the epic 1,100-mile trek from Santa Fe to San Diego. The day after arriving, Cooke wrote the following commendation, which was subsequently read to the Battalion:

> The Lieutenant-Colonel commanding congratulates the battalion on their safe arrival on the shore of the Pacific Ocean, and the conclusion of their march over two thousand miles.
>
> History may be searched in vain for an equal march of infantry. Half of it has been through a wilderness where nothing but savages and wild beasts are found, or deserts where, for want of water, there is no living creature. There, with almost hopeless labor we have dug deep wells, which the future traveler will enjoy. Without a guide who had traversed them, we have ventured into trackless table-lands where water was not found for several marches. With crowbar and pick and axe in hand, we have worked our way over mountains, which seemed to defy aught but the wild goat, and hewed a passage through a chasm of living rock more narrow than our wagons. To bring these first wagons to the Pacific, we have preserved the strength of our mules by herding them over large tracts, which you have laboriously guarded without loss. The garrison of four presidios of Sonora concentrated within the walls of Tucson, gave us no pause. We drove them out, with their artillery, but our intercourse with the citizens was unmarked by a single act of injustice. Thus, marching half naked and half fed, and living upon wild animals, we have discovered and made a road of great value to our country.
>
> Arrived at the first settlement of California, after a single day's rest you cheerfully turned off from the route to this point of promised repose, to enter upon a campaign, and meet, as we supposed, the approach of an enemy; and this, too, without even salt to season your sole subsistence of fresh meat. . . . Thus, volunteers, you have exhibited some high and essential qualities of veterans.[37]

As one might expect, Cooke's words were "cheered heartily by the Battalion."[38]

---

[37] Cooke, *Conquest*, 197.

[38] Tyler, 255.

Impressive monuments in California and Utah, as well as a staffed visitors center in San Diego, would in later years celebrate the Mormon Battalion's accomplishments. But their service did not end with their epic march. They had much more to contribute to early California. Their community work and their key roles in one of the state's most historic events—the discovery of gold—are also stories worth telling.

A Year of Decision: 1847

The year 1846 has been called "the year of decision" because of its key place in American history.[1] The following year, 1847, played a similarly pivotal role in Latter-day Saint history.

During 1847, three major groups of Latter-day Saints were involved in building the American West: (1) The main body of the Church was at Winter Quarters on the Missouri River. In the spring, Brigham Young led the first party from this group toward the Rocky Mountains; (2) The Mormon Battalion completed its march to California and made significant contributions to several communities there; and (3) The *Brooklyn* colony was developing its settlement on the San Francisco Bay.

In Yerba Buena, Samuel Brannan began the year on 1 January by issuing another extra in advance of his regular publication of the *California Star*. He announced: "We shall commence publishing a paper next week, which will be the government organ by the sanction of Colonel Freemont, who is now our Governor."[2]

Brannan sent a copy of the extra, together with a circular, to the Church newspaper in Great Britain, the *Millennial Star*.

---

[1] Bernard de Voto, *The Year of Decision, 1846* (Boston: Houghton Mifflin, 1943).

[2] Quoted in *Millennial Star* 9 (15 October 1847): 307.

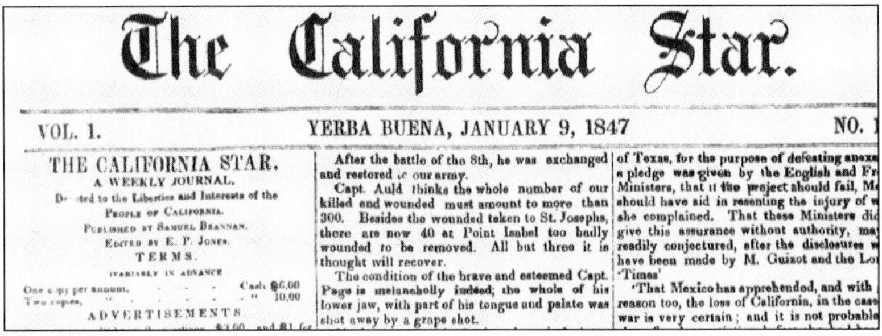

The California Star.

VOL. 1. YERBA BUENA, JANUARY 9, 1847 NO. 1

THE CALIFORNIA STAR.
A WEEKLY JOURNAL,
Devoted to the Liberties and Interests of the People of California.
Published by Samuel Brannan.
Edited by E. P. Jones.
TERMS.
INVARIABLY IN ADVANCE
One copy per annum, - - - - Cash $6,00
Two copies, " - - - - - " 10,00
ADVERTISEMENTS

After the battle of the 8th, he was exchanged and restored to our army.
Capt. Auld thinks the whole number of our killed and wounded must amount to more than 300. Besides the wounded taken to St. Josephs, there are now 40 at Point Isabel too badly wounded to be removed. All but three it is thought will recover.
The condition of the brave and esteemed Capt. Page is melancholly indeed; the whole of his lower jaw, with part of his tongue and palate was shot away by a grape shot.

of Texas, for the purpose of defeating anexa a pledge was given by the English and Fr Ministers, that if the project should fail, Me should have aid in resenting the injury of w she complained. That these Ministers did give this assurance without authority, may readily conjectured, after the disclosures w have been made by M. Guizot and the Lo 'Times'
'That Mexico has apprehended, and with reason too, the loss of California, in the case war is very certain; and it is not probable

THE CALIFORNIA STAR

He reported: "In relation to the country and climate we have not been disappointed . . . but, like all other new countries, we found the accounts of it very much exaggerated."[3]

On 9 January 1847, Brannan began weekly publication of the *California Star*. The newspaper was California's second and began publication just five months after Monterey's *Californian*, which in May was moved to San Francisco where it competed directly with the *Star*. In contrast to the *Prophet* and the *Messenger*, which Brannan had published in New York, this paper "was not issued as an organ of Mormonism," but rather as a general newspaper.[4] Although Samuel Brannan was the paper's proprietor, by April Edward Kemble, the non-Latter-day Saint who had acted as Brannan's assistant in New York and who had come with the group on the *Brooklyn*, assumed the editorship.

The Donner Tragedy

The 1846–47 winter was early and violent. It trapped the Donner wagon train of sixty immigrants in the Sierra Nevada mountains without adequate provisions. By mid-January a few of the party had snowshoed out of the mountains to Johnson's Ranch, near present-day Marysville. Winter rains had flooded

---

[3] Ibid., 306.

[4] Hubert H. Bancroft, *History of California* (San Francisco: The History Co., 1886), 5:552.

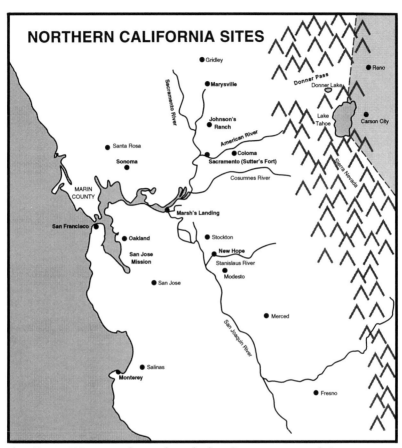

the Bear River and rendered the Sacramento plains a vast quagmire. Nevertheless, there was no time to waste. John Rhoads, a Latter-day Saint whose family had arrived overland just three weeks earlier, volunteered to go to Sutter's Fort for help. Lashing two pine logs together with rawhide and forming them into a raft, he crossed the Bear River. Taking his shoes in his hands and rolling his pants up above his knees, he waded through water that was frequently three feet deep. Sometime during the night he reached the fort although the journey generally took about two days.[5] Volunteers were

[5] Annaleone D. Patton, *California Mormons by Sail and Trail* (Salt Lake City: Deseret Book, 1961), 67.

scarce because the war with Mexico had brought about a shortage of men. With some difficulty, a group of twenty was recruited and dispatched from Sutter's Fort. After several attempts hindered by defections, only seven rescuers remained, including John Rhoads and his brother Daniel. To reach the summit, they had to break a trail through soft, waist-deep snow.

They finally reached the Donner Party camp on 18 February. "They saw only snow, and a sudden fear fell upon them that they had struggled so hard only to arrive too late. Spontaneously, they hallooed together. At the sound they saw a woman emerge, like some kind of animal, from a hole in the snow. They floundered toward her, and she, tottering weakly, came toward them. She spoke, crying out in a hollow voice, unnerved and agitated: 'Are you men from California, or do you come from heaven?'"[6]

The rescue party was not large enough to take all the survivors out. They had to make the painful choice of who would go and who would stay. John Rhoads remembered his promise to Harriet Pike, one of those who had walked out to Johnson's Ranch and a daughter of the Latter-day Saint laundress, Lavinia Murphy. He had promised that he would bring her babies out if he had to tie them on his back. Upon searching the camp, Rhoads found that Mrs. Murphy and her seventeen-year-old son had just died. John quickly rolled the one surviving Pike child, Naomi, in a blanket and hastened up the snow ramp to overtake the rescue party with its twenty-two immigrants. He carried her in the blanket, even after horses were obtained, as the child was too emaciated and frail to ride alone. Surprisingly, she lived to be ninety-three years old. She was one of the last Donner survivors when she died.

Meanwhile, word of the Donners' plight reached Yerba Buena. Samuel Brannan published the story in his paper and expressed hope that the community would do something to

---

[6] George R. Stewart, *Ordeal By Hunger: The Story of the Donner Party* (Boston: Houghton Mifflin, 1988), 191.

help the immigrants.[7] Under the leadership of Washington A. Bartlett, supplies were gathered and a new rescue party of twenty men, including *Brooklyn* passenger Howard Oakley, was dispatched four days later.

By early March, lingering snow had caused most of the rescue party to give up. Oakley was one of only seven who continued through the deep snow over the pass. The group found eleven survivors huddled around a fire which had melted a big hole in the snow. Oakley received the assignment to bring out seven-year-old Mary Donner.[8]

Samuel Brannan's Challenges

The Latter-day Saints in California had their own problems. In his New Year's Day circular, Samuel Brannan lamented that "about twenty males of our feeble number have gone astray after strange gods, serving their bellies and their own lusts," rather than cooperating in efforts to help the Saints provide for one another.[9] Such chronic dissension widened the already existing rifts.

Brannan faced another difficult and perplexing challenge as the New Hope Colony declined into an abyss of suspicion and greed. Feeling it was commensurate with his status as presiding elder, William Stout claimed for himself all the acreage that had been improved and tilled, as well as the first house built there.

Brannan knew he had to contact Brigham Young, not only to tell him of the paradise he had found in California, but also to obtain advice and support in dealing with his increasingly contentious and dwindling flock. Leaving William Glover in

---

[7] *California Star*, 16 January 1847.

[8] Stewart, 243–46.

[9] *Millennial Star* 9 (15 October 1847): 306.

charge of the settlement, Brannan set out on 4 April 1847 to meet President Young on the Plains.[10]

The first stop was the New Hope Colony, where, after trying to reason with Stout, Brannan settled the issue by expelling him. Despite difficulties, the Saints did plant several acres of crops, but, as John Horner admitted, since it was "late in the

---

[10] Andrew Jenson, comp., "The California Mission" (hereafter CM); LDS Church Archives.

season, and the grasshoppers numerous, we got only experience from this venture."[11]

The next stop was Sutter's Fort, where Brannan found an experienced trail guide, Charles Smith (said to have been a Latter-day Saint in Nauvoo), to accompany him together with another unnamed young man. The thousand-mile journey through Indian country and harsh natural conditions was hazardous for such a small party, attesting to Brannan's courage and the urgency he felt.

Brannan wrote:

> We crossed the Snowy Mountains of California, a distance of 40 miles, . . . in one day and two hours, a thing that has never been done before in less than three days. We traveled on foot and drove our animals before us, the snow from twenty to one hundred feet deep. When we arrived through, not one of us could scarcely stand on our feet. The people of California told us we could not cross them under two months, there being more snow on the mountains than had ever been known before, but God knows best, and was kind enough to prepare the way before us.[12]

The Mormon Battalion in California

While Brannan traveled east, members of the Mormon Battalion were helping to build Southern California. Hostilities related to the Mexican War had barely ceased when the Battalion arrived. In December 1846, the forward contingent of Gen. Stephen W. Kearny's Army of the West, which had preceded the Battalion by about one and one-half months, secured the peace. By 10 January 1847 the American flag was hoisted over Los Angeles, and three days later, just two weeks before the Battalion soldiers first sighted the Pacific, John C. Fremont accepted the final surrender of Mexican forces. Hence the Battalion's service in California was not primarily military in nature. Furthermore, its assignments were influenced more by

---

[11] John Horner, "Voyage of the Ship 'Brooklyn,'" *Improvement Era* 9, no. 10 (August 1906): 795.

[12] *Millennial Star* 9 (15 October 1847): 305.

*San Luis Rey
Mission*

the power struggle between Colonel Fremont and General Kearny than by the conflict between the United States and Mexico.

After only two days in San Diego, the Battalion was ordered to go to San Luis Rey, about forty miles north. Arriving there on 3 February, the soldiers found a decrepit and abandoned Franciscan mission situated in another beautiful and fertile winter valley. This was also a strategic location from which they could be ordered into action, if needed, to defend San Diego against a Mexican invasion or to check Fremont should he attempt to take over Los Angeles. While stationed at San Luis Rey, the soldiers improved their skills in military drills and skillfully cleaned and repaired the mission buildings. Perhaps more important, they demonstrated their good behavior and loyalty to Colonel Cook and General Kearny.

As the Latter-day Saint soldiers conducted religious activities at San Luis Rey, the long-festering conflict between their own military and spiritual leaders worsened.[13] Jefferson Hunt, whom Brigham Young had appointed captain of Company A,

---

[13] Larry D. Christiansen, "The Struggle for Power in the Mormon Battalion," *Dialogue* 26, no. 4 (winter 1993): 51–69.

claimed authority to call and direct religious services. Levi Hancock, however, criticized Hunt and the other captains, saying they had been deficient in living the gospel, and refused to defer to their military rank. As one of the original Seven Presidents of the Seventy called to serve directly under the Twelve, Hancock believed he should take the lead in spiritual matters and thus made his own plans for worship services. Together with David Pettigrew, he also initiated ceremonial washings and anointings in hopes of sparking a spiritual revival.[14]

In March, Company B, with only two hours' notice, was sent back to San Diego to assume garrison duty.[15] The industriousness and good behavior of these Latter-day Saint soldiers in San Diego helped overcome deceitful rumors and prejudice and earned them a favorable reputation. Army doctor John S. Griffin reported that "the prejudice against the Mormons here seems to be wearing off—it is yet among the Californians a great term of reproach to be called a Mormon—yet as they are a quiet, industrious, sober, inoffensive people—they seem to be gradually working their way up—they are extremely industrious—they have been engaged while here in digging wells, plastering houses, and seem anxious and ready to work."[16]

In San Diego, Company B organized among themselves debating teams, a chorus, and other educational and cultural activities—something which the citizens found unusual for soldiers. They also constructed a kiln and fired forty thousand bricks, with which they paved sidewalks and lined several of the fifteen or twenty wells they had dug. They built a brick courthouse, which also served as a school.[17]

---

[14] John F. Yurtinus, "A Ram in the Thicket: The Mormon Battalion in the Mexican War" (Ph.D. diss., Brigham Young University, 1975), 539–42.

[15] Ibid., 543–45.

[16] Ibid., 557.

[17] Daniel Tyler, *A Concise History of the Mormon Battalion in the Mexican War* (Glorieta, N. Mex.: 1881), 290; Henry W. Bigler, *Bigler's Chronicle of the West*, ed. Erwin G. Gudde (Berkeley and Los Angeles: University of California Press, 1962), 61.

Before the Battalion came, residents of San Diego had been able to procure water only at some distance from town. The soldiers' proposition to dig a well in the village was met with scorn by the townsfolk. Nevertheless, a thirty-foot well was dug and abundant water of a superior quality became available. An American sailor described how the locals would "hardly take time to finish their breakfast in the morning, but out they go and SIT AROUND THE WELL, smoke their cigaritos, while one of the party is everlastingly drawing up a bucket for the edification of the company."[18]

"I think I whitewashed all San Diego," Battalion member Henry G. Boyle recalled. "We did their blacksmithing, put up a bakery, made and repaired carts, and, in fine, did all we could to benefit ourselves as well as the citizens."[19] Appreciative local residents petitioned the military to keep the Battalion there. When told that it was impossible, they asked that another contingent of Mormons take their places. "When we came to leave the place," one of the soldiers recalled, "they seemed to cling to us, as though they had been parting with their own children."[20]

Meanwhile, when Col. Philip St. George Cooke left San Luis Rey for Los Angeles on 19 March, he took the four remaining companies of the Battalion with him. When they arrived in Los Angeles four days later, the soldiers were impressed with the beautiful ranches, orchards, and vineyards surrounding the small town. The day after their arrival, Fremont's "California Volunteers" would not recognize the authority of Kearny and Cooke and refused to turn over their artillery. Cooke declined to press the issue because he feared that by so doing he might fan into "civil war" the long-standing antagonism

---

[18] Capt. S. F. DuPont, *Extracts from Private Journal-Letters*, quoted in Yurtinus, 561.

[19] Quoted in Leo J. Muir, *A Century of Mormon Activities in California* (Salt Lake City: Deseret News Press, 1952), 65.

[20] William Hyde Diary, June 1847, quoted in Yurtinus, 561.

between his Mormon troops and the Missourians among Fremont's Volunteers.[21]

One of the Saints recorded that Fremont's men had "been using all possible means to prejudice the Spaniards and Indians against us by telling them we would take their wives &c. thereby rousing an excitement through the country."[22] Occasionally, the Latter-day Saints and "bullies" among the former Missourians clashed in town. Regular soldiers of the First Dragoons sometimes came to the defense of the Battalion men, telling them, "Stand back; you are religious men, and we are not; we will take all of your fights into our hands" and with an oath promising, "You shall not be imposed upon by them."[23]

Colonel Cooke ordered the men to enlarge the breastwork which had been constructed the previous January on the hill overlooking Los Angeles. At first, twenty-eight men from each company put in ten-hour days building the fort, members of the crew being rotated every four days. However, as the threat of conflict subsided the pace of construction slackened.[24]

On 8 May, Colonel Cooke sent a detachment of twenty Battalion men to protect Isaac Williams's Rancho Santa Ana de Chino, near present-day Pomona. This was the beginning of a long-lasting relationship between Williams and the Saints. While on patrol, some of the Battalion surprised a small group of marauding Indians. Amid the ensuing conflict, five Indians were killed and two Battalion men slightly wounded. This was "their first and only battle with other humans in which blood was spilled."[25]

A Fourth of July celebration featured the raising of the U.S. flag on the new 150-foot flagpole—the first such celebration in the little village of Los Angeles. The New York Volunteers

---

[21] Yurtinus, 500.

[22] Frank A. Golder, *The March of the Mormon Battalion: From Council Bluffs to California* (New York: The Century Co., 1928), 219.

[23] Tyler, 280.

[24] *Encyclopedia of Historic Forts* (New York: Macmillan, 1988), 80; Yurtinus, 572.

[25] Yurtinus, 574.

band, which had come from Santa Barbara, played the "Star-Spangled Banner," and the First Dragoons fired a thirteen-gun salute. An officer read the Declaration of Independence while the soldiers stood in formation. Levi Hancock then sang a patriotic song which he had earlier composed. On this occasion, Fort Moore was officially dedicated—named for Capt. Benjamin D. Moore, a member of Kearny's First Dragoon who was killed the previous December in the Battle of San Pasqual.[26] Over a century later, a large memorial, adjacent to the Los Angeles civic center, would commemorate Fort Moore.

While these events were unfolding in Southern California, Gen. Steven W. Kearny and Col. John C. Fremont headed east to Washington—Kearny to make his report to the president and Congress, and Fremont, following slightly behind, to stand trial for insubordination and usurpation of authority in declaring himself governor of California. General Kearny chose fifteen Mormon Battalion soldiers to go with him as his personal escort. This honor denoted a marked contrast to his denouncement of Fremont's California Volunteers for their poor treatment of local residents. The general assured the Battalion that his report of them would be favorable.

Leaving Monterey on the last day of May, this group followed the California Trail, the same route Samuel Brannan had taken a few weeks earlier. Upon reaching Fort Leavenworth on 22 August, members of the Mormon escort were discharged, each receiving a payment of $8.60 for his extra five weeks of service. Within a week, these soldiers traveled up the Missouri River to Winter Quarters, where they gave the Saints their first eyewitness report of the Battalion's activities.[27]

Meanwhile, Battalion members in California became increasingly anxious to hear about their families and the main body of the Church. Their anxiety was heightened by the few fragmentary and confused reports they were able to receive. For example, a passenger on a sailing vessel told the men in

---

[26] Ibid., 579–80.

[27] Ibid., 504–26.

San Diego that "a party of Mormons had been caught in the snows while crossing the Sierra Nevadas. The few that survived existed on human flesh."[28] The Battalion men had no way of knowing that this report referred to the comparatively small Donner Party rather than to the great Latter-day Saint exodus. Another report indicated that Samuel Brannan had gone east across the mountains to meet the main Pioneer company under Brigham Young and to lead them to California, and that "the brethren at San Francisco were doing all in their power to prepare a home for their friends."[29]

As 16 July, the end of the Battalion's year-long enlistment, drew near, the men had to decide whether to reenlist. Jefferson Hunt and other Battalion officers, believing that the Saints would ultimately "settle in the vicinity of the Bay of San Francisco," favored another year of service. However, the rank and file, influenced by Levi Hancock and other religious leaders, favored an early discharge because the war with Mexico had already ended.[30] Henry W. Bigler reported that "all hands were now busy making preparations to leave for their homes wherever that was; whether on Bear River, California, or Vancouver Island up in the British possession. For the truth is we do not know where President Young and the Church is!"[31]

California's military governor, Richard Mason, wrote to the adjutant general in Washington concerning the Mormon Battalion:

> Of services of this battalion, of their patience, subordination, and general good conduct, you have already heard; and I take great pleasure in adding that as a body of men they have religiously respected the rights and feelings of these conquered people, and not a syllable of complaint has reached my ears of a single insult offered or an outrage done by a Mormon Volunteer. So high an opinion did

---

[28] Ibid., 555.

[29] Quoted in ibid., 556.

[30] Golder, 227–30; Yurtinus, 585–89, 591–92; see also Susan E. Black, "The Mormon Battalion: Conflict Between Religious and Military Authority," *Southern California Quarterly* 74, no. 4 (winter 1992): 324–25.

[31] Bigler, 57 n. 19.

> I entertain for the battalion, and of their special fitness for the duties now performed by the garrisons in this country, that I made strenuous efforts to engage their services for another year.[32]

Many promises were made to induce the Battalion members to reenlist, including one that the government would pay to have their families transported to California to join them.

On the appointed date, the Battalion's companies were gathered at the nearly completed Fort Moore to either reenlist or be mustered out. They had put in a long year and were anxious to be reunited with their families. Nevertheless, eighty-one chose to reenlist.[33] Henry G. Boyle, one of those who reenlisted, explained his decision:

> I did not like to reenlist, but as I had no relatives in the Church to return to, I desired to remain California til the Church became located, for it is impossible for us to leave here with provisions to last us any considerable length of time. And if I Stay here or any number of us, it is better for us to remain together, than to Scatter all over Creation.[34]

The eighty-one men who reenlisted were organized into the "Mormon Volunteers" and assigned duty in San Diego. Learning this, the residents there "anxiously awaited" the soldiers' return. "Some even went out to greet the returning soldiers a day before they came."[35]

The majority of those who were discharged chose to go to Northern California to find work in San Francisco or at Sutter's Fort before rejoining their families. Three miles outside Los Angeles, these soldiers met at an appointed spot in a river-grove to make preparations for their journey. Within a few days two large groups headed north, one captained by Jefferson Hunt along the coast and one by Levi Hancock inland. Thus the rift between the Battalion's military and religious leaders

---

[32] Quoted in Bancroft, 5:492 n. 20.

[33] Yurtinus, 607.

[34] Henry G. Boyle Diary, 20 July 1847; typescript, Brigham Young University Archives.

[35] Yurtinus, 612–13.

was now reflected in an actual split into two groups. The largest group, 164 men led by Levi Hancock and David Pettigrew, organized themselves in ancient Israelite fashion, with captains of tens, fifties, and hundreds. Taking the central route into the San Joaquin Valley, they reached Sutter's Fort on 26 August.

When Jefferson Hunt discussed the possibility of recruiting an entirely new Mormon Battalion to serve under his leadership, army authorities in Southern California suggested he detour, via the coastal route to Monterey, and present this idea to Governor Mason.[36] Hunt's group of about one hundred reached Monterey on 10 August, where Mason endorsed Hunt's proposal. While most of the group continued on to the San Francisco Bay Area to find work, three stayed in Monterey to work as carpenters and roofers on several buildings, including the town hall.

Members of the Hunt and Hancock groups reunited at Sutter's Fort. Since "many of them were poorly clad, and otherwise short of means to fit themselves out for Salt Lake," they took employment with Captain Sutter. Hiring about fifty-six of the "Mormon boys" enabled him to move forward with his plans to build a gristmill on the American River about four miles from his fort and also a sawmill at Coloma nearly forty miles further upstream. At the same time he "had at Coloma nearly three hundred thousand bushels of wheat to harvest and thresh."[37] The remainder of the soldiers then turned east to cross the Sierra Nevada en route to rejoin their families and the main body of the Saints.

Brannan Meets the Pioneers

After passing through Fort Hall (in present-day Idaho), Samuel Brannan arrived on 30 June at Brigham Young's camp on the Green River in present-day Wyoming. Pioneer William

[36] Pauline Udall Smith, *Captain Jefferson Hunt of the Mormon Battalion* (Salt Lake City: The Nicholas G. Morgan, Sr., Foundation, 1958), 122.

[37] *The Journals of Addison Pratt*, ed. S. George Ellsworth (Salt Lake City: University of Utah Press, 1990), 335.

Clayton recorded: "After dinner . . . Elder Samuel Brannan arrived, having come from the Pacific to meet us, obtain counsel, etc."[38]

President Young listened patiently as Brannan, using his best salesmanship, enthusiastically laid before him all the obvious reasons for settling in California. However, the wise Church leader was not impressed. He had consistently maintained that the main body of the Church would locate eight hundred miles inland from the coast in the Rocky Mountains. Furthermore, he had seen the final destination in a vision, and Brannan's descriptions did not sound like the right place. Most importantly, the better Brannan made California sound, the more President Young knew it could never provide permanent peace, since it would also appeal to the Saints' enemies. He later remarked: "When the pioneer company reached Green River we met Samuel Brannan and a few others from California, and they wanted us to go there. I remarked: 'Let us go to California, and we cannot stay there over five years; but let us stay in the mountains, and we can raise our own potatoes and eat them; and I calculate to stay here.'"[39]

As Brannan tarried with Brigham Young at the Green River, an advance party from Pueblo, Colorado, representing the group of Battalion sick and some southern Saints, approached the camp. One of these scouts was Elder Amasa M. Lyman, who had been a missionary among the southern Saints. He had been dispatched from Brigham Young's main camp to provide leadership in Pueblo. Because some of the soldiers were considering returning east to their families rather than continuing west to California, as they had been enlisted to do, the Battalion's reputation was at stake. Desertion by a few could mean loss of pay for many. Brannan was just the man needed to convince them to continue on to California. He was appointed to meet the Saints from Pueblo, who were under the

---

[38] *William Clayton's Journal* (Salt Lake City: Deseret News Press, 1921), 281.

[39] Preston Nibley, *Brigham Young: The Man and His Work* (Salt Lake City: Deseret Book, 1970), 97.

charge of Capt. James Brown, a Mormon Battalion officer who was a Latter-day Saint, and to escort them to the main body of the Pioneers.

Brigham Young's camp pressed on toward the Great Basin, arriving in the Salt Lake Valley on 24 July 1847. Just five days later, Brannan arrived with the Pueblo contingent. He was disappointed to learn that President Young was already planning a city in the valley large enough to accommodate those still remaining on the trail. President Young had also designated a temple site. Brannan's hope that he could guide the main body of the Church to California was dashed. His trip was seemingly wasted.

While in the Salt Lake Valley waiting for Captain Brown and his party to make final preparations for the trip with him to California, Brannan accepted the invitation of his old friend, Elder Orson Pratt, to show the Pioneers how to make California adobe bricks. The adobe dwellings constructed that summer provided shelter for the Saints, including President Young's family, to survive the following harsh winter.

Instead of sending all the Battalion soldiers on with Brannan, Brigham Young changed his mind and advised most of them to remain in the Salt Lake Valley and help out there, since their enlistment time had elapsed. He had their military leader, Captain Brown, discharge them and sent him to collect their final pay.

On 7 August, two days before Brannan and Brown left for California, Brigham Young, on behalf of the Quorum of the Twelve Apostles, wrote two letters of greeting to the Saints there. In the first letter, addressed specifically to members of the Mormon Battalion, he declared:

> When you receive this and learn of this location, it will be wisdom for you all, if you have got your discharge as we suppose, to come directly to this place, where you will learn particularly who is here, who not. If there are any men who have not families among your number, who desire to stop in California for a season, we do not feel to object; yet we do feel that it will be better for them to come directly to this place, for here will be our headquarters for the present, and

our dwelling place . . . and we want to see you, even all of you, and talk with you, and throw our arms around you.[40]

In the second letter, addressed to the California Saints as a whole, President Young praised the excellence of the Salt Lake Valley's soil, water, and climate. He then added:

> You are [also] in a goodly land; and if you choose to tarry where you are, you are at liberty so to do; and if you choose to come to this place, you are at liberty to come, and we shall be happy to receive you, and give you an inheritance in our midst . . . not that we wish to depopulate California of all the saints, but that we wish to make this a stronghold, a rallying point, a more immediate gathering place than any other; and from hence let the work go out, and in process of time the shores of the Pacific may be overlooked from the temple of the Lord.[41]

After getting outfitted at Fort Hall, the Brown-Brannan party followed the California Trail west. Along the way, Brannan and Brown parted company. One of the Battalion soldiers, Abner Blackburn, detailed their conflicts: "Brannan and Cap Brown could not agree on anny subject. Brannan thought he knew it all and Brown thought he knew his share of it. They felt snuffy at each other and kept apart." On 5 September in Truckee Canyon, their frictions came to a head: "Cap Brown wanted [to] travel on several miles before breakfast. Brannan said he would eat breakfast first. Brown sayes the horses would goe anny how for they belonged to the government and were in his care. They both went for the horses and a fight commenced. They pounded each other with fists and clubs until they were sepperated. They both ran for their guns. We parted them again." The group parted and Brannan rode on ahead.[42]

The next day, near Donner Lake, Brannan intercepted the approximately 140 Battalion soldiers heading east. He shared Brigham Young's counsel that those who did not have sufficient provisions to winter in the Salt Lake Valley should remain

---

[40] Journal History, 7 August 1847 (hereafter JH); LDS Church Archives.

[41] Ibid.

[42] Abner Blackburn, *Frontiersman: Abner Blackburn's Narrative*, ed. Will Bagley (Salt Lake City: University of Utah Press, 1992), 65, 102.

in California until spring.[43] Daniel Tyler recorded that Brannan's description of the Salt Lake Valley "was anything but encouraging. . . . It froze there every month. . . . [T]he ground was too dry. . . . [If] irrigated with the cold mountain streams, the seeds planted would be chilled and prevented from growing, . . . [and] all except those whose families were known to be at Salt Lake had better turn back and labor until spring, when in all probability the Church would come to them."[44]

The following day, Captain Brown's party came into camp. After he shared with them the letter he was carrying from the apostles, about half of the soldiers decided to continue east under Levi Hancock's leadership. Apparently, Hancock and Jefferson Hunt forged at least a partial reconciliation, because Hunt also went with the group. They reached the Salt Lake Valley in October. Some, whose families were not yet there, immediately went on to Winter Quarters, arriving in December. Of those who returned to the settlements in California, about half found work with Sutter.[45] This left over five hundred Saints in California: eighty reenlistees in San Diego and four to five hundred scattered about the state, mostly in the North.

Among the Battalion men who parted were a father and son who had served together for over a year. Albert Smith went on to the Great Basin while his son Azariah, who had just celebrated his nineteenth birthday, returned to Sutter's Fort.[46]

Brannan also traveled on to Sutter's Fort. There he and his trail partner, Charles Smith, rented a one-room adobe, acquired a small boat to bring merchandise from San Francisco, and set up a general store.[47] Smith remained at Sutter's Fort to manage

---

[43] CM, 18 September 1847; Horner, 30–31.

[44] Tyler, 315.

[45] Yurtinus, 630–32.

[46] Azariah Smith, *The Gold Discovery Journal of Azariah Smith*, ed. David L. Bigler (Salt Lake City: University of Utah Press, 1990), 102–3.

[47] Although Sutter later recalled the partner's name as *George Smith* or *Gordon Smith*, he was probably the same Charles Smith who served as Brannan's guide.

the store. This little enterprise became a foundation that eventually brought Brannan unimagined wealth.

Meanwhile, Captain Brown, accompanied by his son, Jesse, went on to San Francisco then headed south to Monterey. There he met Governor Mason, who ordered the paymaster to give Brown ten thousand dollars in Spanish doubloons (nearly a million dollars in today's currency) as payment in full for his service and the service rendered by the Battalion members who had not been able to complete the march to the Pacific because of illness. Brown immediately transported the gold to the Salt Lake Valley, arriving on 15 December. After paying the soldiers, Brown, with Church leaders' sanction, used the remaining three thousand dollars to purchase a ranch with a few dilapidated buildings at the mouth of Weber Canyon. There, "Brownville" was settled by James Brown and others who were deeded plots of land on the ranch. This settlement grew into the city of Ogden, Utah. The ranch also contained the Great Basin's only established cattle herd. It supplied milk, meat, and cheese, which allowed the Pioneers to survive their first harsh winter. It is said that the ten thousand dollars in gold doubloons was virtually the only money circulated in Utah until miners brought gold from California the following year.[48]

Brannan's Return to San Francisco

While Brannan was away, growth continued in San Francisco (as Yerba Buena was now called because of an order ascribed to Mayor Bartlett).[49] Two auctions were held for San Francisco city lots, which were purchased in just a few hours, many by Latter-day Saints. The *Star* disclosed that as of 30 June the town's population had reached 459 and that half of its 157 buildings had been constructed since 1 April.[50] Thus in less

---

[48] Archie Leon Brown and Charlene L. Hathaway, *141 Years of Mormon Heritage* (Oakland: Archie Leon Brown, 1973), 103–6.

[49] *California Star*, 30 January 1847.

[50] *California Star*, 28 August 1847 and 4 September 1847.

Addison Pratt

than one year, Church members had likely erected more than one hundred dwellings for themselves, their families, and their community.

At about this time, Addison Pratt arrived in San Francisco from his mission in the Society (Tahitian) Islands. He discerned discord existing among the San Francisco Saints:

There was much dissatisfaction among the *Brooklyn* brethren as to Brannan's proceedings while on board of the *Brooklyn*, and several of them proposed to me to take charge of the spiritual affairs among them. But I told them it was not my place to meddle with their affairs in any wise as Brannan was the man that was appointed by the church to look after them, and my mission was to another part of the world altogether.[51]

Upon Brannan's return to San Francisco on 17 September 1847, he wrote to Jesse Little:

"I found everything on my return far better than my most sanguine expectation. . . . When I landed here with my little company there was but three families in the place and now the improvements are beyond all conception. Houses in every direction, business very brisk and money plenty. Here will be the great Emporium of the Pacific and eventually of the world." Brannan was a man of vision: if California were accounted as a separate country today, it would rank seventh in the world economically.

Although apprehensive comments were heard before the Saints' arrival, attitudes had already changed dramatically. Brannan gratefully acknowledged in his letter to Jesse Little that "the Mormons are A No. 1 in this country."[52] William Glover had just been elected to San Francisco's original six-

[51] *Journals of Addison Pratt*, 330.

[52] Samuel Brannan to Jesse C. Little, in CM, 18 September 1847.

member town council and a few days later was appointed to the school board.[53]

President Young's August letter to the California Saints had counseled: "We do not desire much public preaching or noise or confusion concerning us or our religion in California at the present time." It also expressed support for Brannan's leadership:

> We are satisfied with the proceedings of Elder Brannan. We believe that he is a good man and that it is his design to do right. No doubt that he has been placed in very trying circumstances in connection and common with you, since your journey to California was first contemplated; and if he or you have erred . . . we feel to exhort you at all times to cultivate the spirit of meekness, kindness, gentleness, compassion, love, forgiveness, forbearance, long-suffering, patience, and charity one towards another; and look upon others faults and follies as you want others to look upon yours; and forgive as you want to be forgiven.

President Young also urged the *Brooklyn* Saints to honor the balance of the three-year compact to labor "unitedly for the good of the whole."[54]

The Church's decision to settle in the Great Basin rather than going to the Coast changed the plans of many of the California Saints. "You can imagine our disappointment," William Glover recalled. The company was broken up as many Saints began making preparations for going to the mountains. Glover also disapproved of what happened at New Hope: "The land, the oxen, the crop, the houses, tools, and launch, all went into Brannan's hands, and the Company that did the work never got anything for their labor."[55] In October, contrary to Brigham Young's counsel, Brannan took steps to liquidate the common fund. In the *Star*, he advertised that all the holdings of "the firm of S. Brannan & Co." were for sale.[56]

---

[53] *California Star*, 18 September 1847.

[54] JH, 7 August 1847.

[55] William Glover, *The Mormons in California* (Los Angeles: Dawson, 1954), 21.

[56] *California Star*, 9 October 1847.

Monument to San Francisco's first schoolhouse, at Portsmouth Square

A few days later, Samuel Brannan wrote to Brigham Young and the Twelve:

> I hope, brethren, that you will not suffer your minds to be prejudiced or doubt my loyalty from any rumors. . . . I want your confidence, faith and prayers, feeling that I will discharge my duties under all circumstances, and then I will be happy. . . . To you I stand ready at any moment to render an account of my stewardship.[57]

Over two years would pass before Brannan would have any face-to-face contact with higher Church leaders.

With the group planning to leave and the Church discouraging overtly religious activity, Brannan increasingly channeled his energy into civic and business enterprises. He continued drumming up support in the *Star* for a public school. As early as the paper's second issue, he had offered to donate a plot of land and fifty dollars to erect one. By December, San Francisco's first schoolhouse was completed on Clay Street next to the plaza.[58] A memorial, erected by San Francisco's Centennial Commission and local Masonic lodge, stands today in Portsmouth Square in recognition of that school.

On 2 December, Brannan called a meeting to organize the San Francisco Branch with Addison Pratt as president. Disconcerted, Pratt recorded:

> To my presiding, I objected perhaps too strongly, but not withstanding, they voted me in, and I then felt it my duty to act. Strong

---

[57] JH, 17 October 1847.

[58] *California Star*, 16 January 1847 and 4 December 1847.

accusations were presented against Brannan by the "Brooklyn" company to the effect that he had devised ways and means whereby he had swindled them out of their property with the pretense that he was collecting for the church. . . . But there were two parties, one for Brannan, and the other against him, and the Battalion boys gradually allowed themselves to be drawn in some on the one side and some on the other, and party feelings were thus fast growing in spite of my best efforts to keep it down. . . . I also learned that Br. Brannan expected me to rule the branch, and that I in turn was expected to be ruled by him. But when he found that I had some notions of my own that should be consulted, I became very obnoxious to him.[59]

Soon Brannan, Pratt, and the entire Latter-day Saint colony were overcome by a tide of unforeseeable events that swept away the branch and the town's recently planted spiritual roots.

---

[59] CM, 24 January 1848.

Saints and Gold: 1848

7

Latter-day Saints were intimately involved in the discovery of gold in 1848. Under the direction of foreman James Marshall, several Saints were employed digging a race for Capt. John A. Sutter's sawmill on the American River. "Some of the Mormon boys had been raised among the gold mines in the Southern States," Addison Pratt pointed out, "and among the hills about the upper mill they saw strong indications of the precious metal . . . but as their work press'd them hard, they had no time to spare for prospecting, altho it was often talked of."[1]

The crew's cook, Elizabeth Jane (Jenny) Wimmer, a Latter-day Saint who had lived among the gold mines of Georgia, was dismayed. The men detested the water she put on the table because it characteristically had a heavy sediment in it. They teased her when she suggested, from her experience with the gold mines in the South, that the sediment could be gold dust. No one bothered to check into it.

---

[1] Andrew Jenson, comp., "The California Mission," 24 January 1848 (hereafter CM); LDS Church Archives.

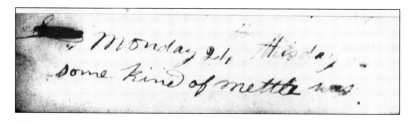

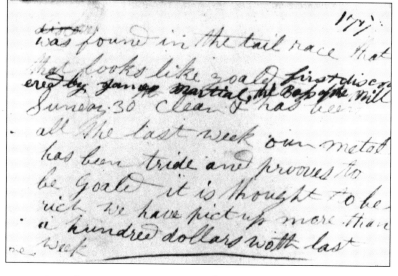

Pages from Henry Bigler's journal, showing date of gold discovery

The Discovery of Gold

For many years, the precise date of the gold discovery was a topic of debate. However, the diary of Henry W. Bigler, a Mormon Battalion soldier, ended the controversy. Bigler's entry for 24 January 1848 reads: "Monday 24th this day some kind of mettle was was found in the tail race that that looks like goald."[2] A former Mormon Battalion private, James S. Brown, nephew of Capt. James Brown, later described what happened:

[2] Henry W. Bigler, *Bigler's Chronicle of the West*, ed. Erwin G. Gudde (Berkeley and Los Angeles: University of California Press, 1962), 88.

It had been customary to hoist the gates of the forebay when we quit work in the evening, letting the water through the race to wash away the loosened sand and gravel, then close them down in the morning. . . . On January 23 . . . Mr. Marshall came along to look over the work in general, and went to where the tail race entered the river. There he discovered a bed of rock that had been exposed by the water the night before. . . . Mr. Marshall called me to him as he examined the bed of the race, and said: "This is a curious rock." Then he probed a little further, and added: "I believe it contains minerals of some kind, and I believe there is gold in these hills."

Mr. Marshall was determined to investigate further, but it was no use that night. He rose and said: "We will hoist the gates and turn in all the water that we can tonight, and tomorrow morning we will shut it off and come down here, and I believe we will find gold or some other mineral here."

Each of us went our way for the night, and did not meet again till next morning. I thought little of what Marshall had said of finding gold, as he was looked on as rather a "notional" kind of man; I do not think I even mentioned his conversation to my associates. At an unusually early hour in the morning, however, those of us who occupied the cabin heard a hammering at the mill. "Who is that pounding so early?" was asked, and one of our party looked out and said it was Marshall shutting the gates of the forebay down. This

Reconstructed sawmill at gold discovery site

recalled to my mind what Mr. Marshall had said to me the evening before, and I remarked, "Oh, he is going to find a gold mine this morning."

A smile of derision stole over the faces of the parties present. We ate our breakfast and went to work.

This was the 24th day of January, 1848. When we had got partly to work, Mr. Marshall came, with his old wool hat in his hand. He stopped within six or eight yards of the sawpit, and exclaimed, "Boys, I have got her now!" Being the nearest to him, and having more curiosity than the rest of the men, I jumped from the pit and stepped to him. On looking into his hat I discovered ten or twelve pieces or small scales of what proved to be gold. I picked up the largest piece . . . held it aloft and exclaimed, "Gold, boys, gold!"

At this juncture all was excitement. We repaired to the lower end of the tail race, where we found from three to six inches of water flowing over the bed of rock.

As soon as we learned how to look for it, since it glittered under the water in the rays of the sun, we were all rewarded with a few scales.[3]

Present on that day were several Latter-day Saints. Positively identified are Henry W. Bigler, James S. Brown, William James Johnston, Alexander Stephen, and Azariah Smith. William W. Barger and the Peter Wimmer family were other Latter-day Saints employed at the site.

Peter Wimmer later described how Mr. Marshall gave him a nugget and told him to have Jenny "boil it in saleratus [baking soda] water; but she being engaged in making soap, pitched the piece into the soap kettle, where it was boiled all day and night. The following morning the strange piece of stuff was fished out of the soap, all the brighter for the boiling it received." Marshall gave her the gold nugget, and she is said to have worn it on a necklace for many years.[4]

Over the next month, the men panned as much as twenty-five dollars per night while being paid one and one-half dollars per day by Sutter to finish the mill, which was completed on 11 March. Most of Sutter's workmen deserted him, leaving

[3] James S. Brown, *Life of a Pioneer* (Salt Lake City: Geo. Q. Cannon & Sons, 1900), 96–101.

[4] Quoted in Rodman W. Paul, *The California Gold Discovery* (Georgetown, Calif.: Talisman Press, 1966), 135, 176–77.

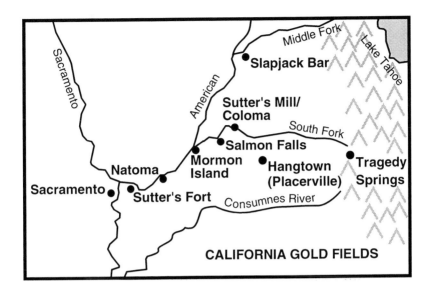

CALIFORNIA GOLD FIELDS

projects unfinished and crops rotting in the fields. "One after another of my people disappeared in the direction of the gold fields," Sutter later recalled. "Only the Mormons behaved decently at first. They were sorry for the difficulties in which I found myself, and some of them remained on to finish their jobs. But, in the long run, they too could not resist the temptation."[5]

Meanwhile, Latter-day Saints were involved in other gold discoveries. On 2 March, Sidney Willis and Wilford Hudson, both former Battalion soldiers, made one of the richest finds further down the river at what came to be known as "Mormon Island."[6] When Sidney Willis and his brother Ira went to San Francisco on business and informed Samuel Brannan of their discovery, Brannan advised all Battalion men to go to work in the mine and pay their tithing to him as head of the Church.[7] Brannan also received a report of the discovery from his

[5] Erwin G. Gudde, *Sutter's Own Story* (New York: G.P. Putnam's Sons, 1936), 208–9.

[6] Hubert H. Bancroft, *History of California* (San Francisco: The History Co., 1888), 6:48.

[7] Bigler, 108.

partner, Charles Smith, in the store at Sutter's Fort. When a Swiss teamster came in to buy some brandy, Smith requested payment in cash. The teamster instead offered him gold dust. Skeptical, Smith went to Sutter, who confirmed that the substance was gold. "The secret was out," Sutter lamented.[8]

Publicizing the Gold Strike

James Marshall, who was a partner with John Sutter, feared that "it would break him up in business" if news of the gold strike got out before the mill was completed. He was also (unsuccessfully) petitioning Governor Mason for a clear title to the land, which was being leased from the Indians. "He there fore asked the brethren to keep everything quiet," Addison Pratt reported, and "the Mormon boys were true to him and continued their labors with him . . . until the mill was running."[9] The two weekly newspapers in San Francisco, the *Californian* and the *California Star*, first mentioned the discovery rather casually in mid-March.

However, Brannan's 1 April edition of the *Star* broke the news to the world. He was organizing an express mail service from San Francisco to Independence, Missouri, using Mormon Battalion riders to carry his newspaper east. With this promotional issue of the *Star*, he hoped to test his new mail service and at the same time convince those coming west on the Oregon Trail to turn south to California. The gold discovery was treated in the last paragraph of a larger piece on the virtues of the Sacramento Valley, where his store was located:

> It has a mine of gold and a probable estimate of its magnitude cannot be derived from any information we have received. It was discovered in December last [actually 24 January], on the south branch of the American Fork, in a range of low hills forming the base of Sierra Nevada distant 30 miles from New Helvetia [Sutter's Fort]. It is found at a depth of three feet below the surface, and in a strata of soft sand

---

[8] Gudde, 201.

[9] CM, 24 January 1848.

rock. Explorations made southward, the distance twelve miles, and to the north five miles, report the continuance of this strata, and the mineral equally abundant. The vein is from twelve to eighteen feet in thickness. Most advantageously to this new mine, a stream of water flows in the immediate neighborhood, and the washing will be attended with comparative ease.[10]

Samuel Brannan thus became the first in a series of promoters to capitalize on California's allure. His promotion, like so much that followed, was biased by his involvement in land speculation. He wanted an ever-increasing stream of immigrants who would be willing to pay high prices.

On 3 April, Brannan loaded two thousand copies of his booster edition onto a launch and headed out with them. At the embarcadero, two miles below Sutter's Fort, a packtrain of mules waited to take the papers east—a journey that had significant consequences. Six of the ten men accompanying the train were Latter-day Saints, five of them known by name: William Hawk and his son Nathan, Silas Harris, Richard Slater, and Sanford Jacobs.

With the newspapers heading east, Brannan proceeded to the gold country to see for himself the riches that could be had there. He liked what he saw and took immediate steps to get his share. Foreman James Marshall had given the Battalion men permission to hunt gold at Sutter's mill, claiming 50 percent of all that was found.[11] Samuel Brannan, also in a position of power, now followed his example.

There is no evidence that either Marshall or Brannan ever had any authority to grant mining privileges or take a cut of the findings. Nevertheless, Brannan entered into an agreement with the Willis brothers to collect 30 percent "tithing" from those working at Mormon Island. Brannan also made certain that his store was well-stocked and that he was secure in his partnership with the Willises. He then returned to San Francisco on his launch.

---

[10] *California Star*, 1 April 1848.

[11] Azariah Smith, *The Gold Discovery Journal of Azariah Smith*, ed. David L. Bigler (Salt Lake City: University of Utah Press, 1990), 110 n. 43.

Gold Fever Hits the California Saints

Problems in the Church's San Francisco Branch had not gone away. In a letter to Brigham Young dated 29 March 1848, Brannan asserted that there were "many calumniators" leveling charges against him because of "jealousy and misrepresentation." He claimed that branch president Addison Pratt lacked "natural stableness of purpose and firmness in decision and character" and was therefore unable to resolve this dissension. Brannan was convinced that because he had not received his own temple endowment blessings, those who had received them were "disputing [his] priesthood, and joining their influence with the slanderer, in order to strengthen their own influence and exalt themselves."

Perhaps to increase his influence, he organized with two others "The United Order of Charitable Brothers." He reported confidentially to President Young that a "subordinate lodge" called "Samaritan Lodge No. 1" included "the majority of the most respectable citizens of this place."[12] At a Sunday service one month later, Brannan sought to dispel criticism against him by delivering "a lecture on the disaffection that existed in the branch and called for those that found fault with him to bring forth their charges."[13]

On Wednesday evening, 10 May, Brannan called another meeting. He told the Saints about the gold mine the Willis brothers had found and "gave his advice for all to go & work in it."[14] Shortly thereafter he decided the time was right to make this news even more public. With a bottle of gold dust in one hand, and waving his hat with the other, Sam went through the streets of San Francisco shouting, "Gold! Gold! Gold from the American River!"[15] Within a week the city was deserted, and

---

[12] Journal History, 29 March 1848 (hereafter JH); LDS Church Archives.

[13] John Borrowman Diary, 30 April 1848; typescript in possession of Larry C. Porter, Brigham Young University.

[14] Borrowman Diary, 10 May 1848.

[15] Bancroft, 6:56.

Brannan and others no longer had any hired help. The *Star* then sought to diffuse the mounting gold fever, labeling it "a sham as supurb [a] takein as was ever got up to guzzle the gullible."[16]

Nonetheless, prospects of great and sudden wealth upset old standards of faith and judgment. Even the little school, which had begun classes just six weeks earlier with ten students and had rapidly expanded to thirty-seven, was deserted. The schoolmaster bought a gold pan and left, as did most of his students. Henry Bigler described the residents of the area as "panic-struck and so excited and in such a hurry to be off, that some of the mechanics left their work, not taking time even to take off their aprons."[17]

The first rush was to Mormon Island. One hundred to 150 Saints flocked there, to be followed later by people from every part of the United States. Gold seekers worked in groups of five, each working five square yards of land. They generally worked Monday through Saturday, each making from ten to fifty dollars a day. So numerous were the Latter-day Saint miners by this time that the name "Mormon" was given to many sites: Mormon Island, Mormon Bar, Mormon Gulch, and so forth.

Branch president Addison Pratt had already been thinking about leaving California to rejoin his family in Utah. Because he saw "no prospects of the condition of the branch changing for the better," he resigned.[18] He boarded one of the first boats to Mormon Island, leaving behind the house he and fellow South Seas missionary Seth Lincoln had built. Brannan appointed Lincoln as branch president in Pratt's stead, but there was not much of a branch. John Horner summed up the situation: "The gold mines being discovered . . . threw the ship *Brooklyn* company into confusion. It was disorganized, the

---

[16] *California Star*, 20 May 1848.

[17] Bigler, 111.

[18] CM, 24 January 1848.

settlement was abandoned, and every member thereafter followed the counsel of his own will."[19]

Sutter observed that during March and April only "small parties of curious people from San Francisco" had passed the Fort on their way to the gold fields. "The big rush did not set in until the middle of May; then the whole country seemed to have gone mad. Merchants, physicians, lawyers, sea captains left their wives and families in San Francisco in order to become gold diggers. . . . Everything was in confusion and most people did not know what to do."[20]

There was good reason for this excitement: what they found was incredible, and it was there for the taking. With no more equipment than a pick and shovel or pan, almost everyone who tried found his share. The gold had been deposited in stream beds and rock crevices, little by little, over vast periods of time. Now it lay exposed and inviting, diversified into dust, flakes, and even "fist-sized nuggets." "The gold existed in such abundance that it was not so much mined as harvested."[21] It is estimated that as much as ten million 1848 dollars was gleaned by the end of the year.

Initially, the most common method of extraction was to scoop up a panful of gravel from a stream and swirl it around in water, flushing the lighter gravel and dirt over the side and leaving the gold dust, flakes, and nuggets in the bottom. Soon it was apparent that the only limitation to how much gold one found was the amount of gravel that could be scooped and washed.

An ingenious device called a "rocker" was invented at Mormon Island. Made from wood, it was about the size and shape of a baby cradle. It was tilted at an angle and fitted with a screen at the top end which filtered out the coarser particles. It had a slanted, riffled bottom that settled the gold in the

---

[19] John M. Horner, "Voyage of the Ship 'Brooklyn,'" *Improvement Era* 9, no. 10 (August 1906): 795.

[20] Gudde, 212.

[21] T. H. Watkins, *California, An Illustrated History* (New York: American Legacy, 1973), 84.

Street named for Samuel Brannan in modern San Francisco

grooves as the water and lighter gravel washed through. Rocking the gadget with one hand and scooping up water and gravel with the other allowed an individual to multiply the amount of stream gravel processed. When two men cooperated, even more could be handled.

Sutter observed, "The clever fellows did not stay in the gold fields, but returned immediately to San Francisco to buy up everything that they could lay hands on."[22] As Latter-day Saints deserted their little town, it was filled by enterprising Chinese immigrants—mostly merchants, traders, and men of means, few of whom went into the mining district.[23] Within a year, the Chinese in San Francisco numbered several hundred. They set up shops on Sacramento Street between Kearny and DuPont [Grant] Streets, sometimes "squatting" on properties the Latter-day Saints had abandoned.[24] Today, excepting the monument on Portsmouth Square commemorating the little schoolhouse, almost all evidence of the dynamic Latter-day Saint settlement has been effaced. Only a few scattered streets with the original pioneer names of *Brooklyn, Joice, Glover, Corwin, Pratt*, etc., remain in and around Chinatown. In another part of town, a major street bears Brannan's name.

---

[22] Gudde, 212.

[23] James O'Meara, "The Chinese in the Early Days," *Overland Monthly* 3 (May 1884): 477–78.

[24] Thomas W. Chinn, ed., *A History of the Chinese in California* (San Francisco: The Chinese Historical Society of America, 1969), 9–10.

Undoubtedly, one of the "clever fellows" Sutter referred to was Brannan, whose 30 percent "tithing" could have amounted to quite a sum. There were conflicting understandings as to where this money would go. According to Brannan's original agreement with the Willises, 10 percent would be earmarked as regular tithing—10 percent his share for securing a title and 10 percent for a temple he maintained would be built in California. "The most I made in a day was sixty five dollars after the toll was taken out," Azariah Smith stated, "which was thirty dollars out of a hundred, which goes to Hudson and Willis, that discovered the mine, and Brannon who is securing it for them."[25]

On the other hand, a skeptical Addison Pratt was told that the entire amount would go to the Church to buy cattle for the Saints in the Salt Lake Valley. "I had seen enough of Brannan's tricks," he reported, "to convince me that the church would never see any cattle brought to them through that channel. There was much dissatisfaction on the part of the brethren that went up from Francisco about it." Pratt suspected that if he set the example of not paying this "unjust" tax, others would follow. Brannan could then turn over to the Church what he had already collected and claim that he could have sent much more if Pratt had not "come out against it." Therefore, Addison reluctantly paid what Brannan demanded.[26]

Though fortunes were made easily and quickly by many Latter-day Saint miners in 1848, their gold was slippery. Battalion soldier and miner Andrew Workman tells of being discharged with his brother, then going north, panning a fortune of five thousand dollars, having it stolen, going back again, "doing well," purchasing a string of forty mules, having them stolen, then mining off and on afterward without much success. Another *Brooklyn* passenger, Ashbell Haskell, was among those working for Sutter. He panned gold after work—

---

[25] Azariah Smith, 115.

[26] *The Journals of Addison Pratt*, ed. S. George Ellsworth (Salt Lake City: University of Utah Press, 1990), 337.

amassing enough to be comfortable the rest of his life—bought some mules, loaded them with his gold, headed for Salt Lake City, but was never heard from again.[27]

The worth of California and whether such a faraway place could be adequately governed were divisive issues in the United States Congress. Some had been urging the nullification of the treaty of Guadalupe-Hidalgo which had ceded Upper California to the United States. Governor Mason and his aide, William Tecumseh Sherman (later a Civil War general), came to the mines on 4 July to celebrate and to get samples of gold to persuade Congress that California was worth keeping.

After an impressive Fourth of July celebration at Sutter's Fort, the governor's party dispersed in mid-afternoon to observe the gold-seeking. Specimens of gold were sought at both Coloma and Mormon Island, where miners lined the stream beds in knee-deep water, hundreds of rockers in motion. "Tradition says Governor Mason held samples in his hand and asked Elder William Glover to select the most convincing nuggets." These were then soldered to an old tea caddy and dispatched via military escort to Washington, D.C.[28]

When one of the miners asked Governor Mason what right Samuel Brannan had to collect his 30-percent gold tithing, he quipped: "Every right if . . . you Mormons are fools enough to pay it."[29]

Leaving for Zion

In 1848 some of the five hundred Latter-day Saints in California were planning to go to the Great Basin as quickly as

---

[27] J. Kenneth Davies, *Mormon Gold: The Story of California's Mormon Argonauts* (Salt Lake City: Olympus, 1984), 48, 67–69.

[28] Annaleone D. Patton, *California Mormons by Sail and Trail* (Salt Lake City: Deseret Book, 1961), 46.

[29] Memoirs of General William T. Sherman, 4th ed. (New York: D. Appleton, 1875), 1:53.

weather and means permitted. At least three distinct groups left that year. The two from Southern California probably knew nothing of the gold strike. The third, from the north, left after deciding they had panned enough.

The first group to leave California in 1848 was a party returning to the Great Basin with needed supplies. In October 1847, when Jefferson Hunt had reached the Salt Lake Valley with the earliest returning Mormon Battalion members, he found a critical need for food. He proposed sending an expedition to Southern California where he knew there were ample supplies of grain and cattle.

Because Brigham Young had returned to Winter Quarters to lead groups of Saints to the Great Basin the following season, the High Council—the presiding body remaining in Salt Lake—considered and approved Hunt's proposal on 13 November. A selected small group was sent to "explore the southern route to California," to buy seed, grain, and cattle, and to inform military leaders there that the Saints were not interested in raising another Battalion. A party of eighteen men, including Jefferson Hunt and Orrin Porter Rockwell, departed three days later. Following the Old Spanish Trail, the group passed through Cajon Pass into Southern California and reached the Williams Ranch on Christmas Eve.

Bearing the nickname "Son of Thunder," Porter Rockwell was one of the most interesting Latter-day Saints to come to California. He spent much of his life as a U.S. deputy marshal successfully pursuing Western outlaws. He claimed that Joseph Smith had promised him that if he never cut his hair, he could not be killed. Hence, he came to be known as the "latter-day Samson."[30]

The group from Salt Lake City purchased wheat at the old Franciscan San Gabriel mission near Los Angeles and secured other needed supplies in Southern California. Traveling with

---

[30] See Richard L. Dewey, *Porter Rockwell: A Biography* (New York: Paramount Books, 1986) and Harold Schindler, *Orrin Porter Rockwell: Man of God, Son of Thunder* (Salt Lake City: University of Utah Press, 1983).

pack mules, they left for home on 14 February 1848 and arrived there in May. Rockwell, however, did not return with them. On the trip, they suffered many difficulties, including the loss of half of the two hundred cattle purchased.[31] They did, however, bring much seed wheat, which was greatly needed in Salt Lake.

Some "Mormon Volunteers" who had reenlisted and served in San Diego formed the second group going to the Rockies. They had an understanding with army officials that they would be discharged in the spring of 1848 so they could meet their families and plant crops in Utah.

When Jefferson Hunt arrived in Southern California, he brought with him an "epistle" from Church headquarters which validated the soldiers' intentions to obtain as early a discharge as possible. With Porter Rockwell available to guide them (having just traversed the route), the soldiers decided to leave. They had learned that a recent act of Congress offered any soldier serving in the army for one full year a bonus of either 160 acres of land or one hundred dollars in "treasury scrip." Much to the surprise of their army leaders, the Latter-day Saint men forfeited this bonus in order to rejoin their families. They were officially discharged on 14 March 1848, four months short of a full year's enlistment. While a majority chose to stay in California, a company of thirty-five men, 135 horses and mules, and one wagon went with Rockwell via the Williams Ranch and Cajon Pass to the Salt Lake Valley. This party was the first to take a wagon along this route.[32]

The "gold country" Saints were the third group to leave. "Home keeps running in my mind," Azariah Smith wrote in his diary on 19 December 1847, "and I feel somewhat lonesum especially Sundays, but my heart leaps with the expectation of getting home [to a place he had never seen] in the spring, and again it sometimes shrinks for fear that I will fail for want of

---

[31] Dewey, 146; Pauline Udall Smith, *Captain Jefferson Hunt of the Mormon Battalion* (Salt Lake City: The Nicholas G. Morgan, Sr., Foundation, 1958), 132–35.

[32] John F. Yurtinus, "A Ram in the Thicket: The Mormon Battalion in the Mexican War" (Ph.D. diss., Brigham Young University, 1975), 620–24.

means, but I keep up as good courage as I can."[33] He noted how "men, women and children, from the Bay and other places in California, were flocking to the gold mine, by the dozens, and by wagon loads." But he insisted that his only objective was to eke out enough to supply himself for the journey home.[34]

A group gathered, planning to depart on 15 April. Yet deep snows prevented them from going that early. Another, larger group was set to leave on 1 June. This departure was also postponed because of a heavy Sierra snowpack (and perhaps to mine a little more before leaving).

The men working for Captain Sutter agreed to notify him of their intended departure early enough for him to hire replacements, which would be difficult, since few men were willing to work for wages. Sutter noted that "so long as these people have been employed by me they have behaved very well, and were industrious and faithful laborers and when settling their accounts there was not one of them who was not contented and satisfied."[35]

In early June, the postponed groups began gathering just southeast of Hangtown (now Placerville) at a large green meadow they called Pleasant Valley. While waiting for the snow to melt, they discovered gold there as well and thus spent their idle time prospecting. Believing a more southerly route could be forged by using Carson Pass, through which John Fremont had entered California four years earlier, three men were sent to scout this trail.

The scouts were ambushed, murdered, and thrown into a shallow grave near a spring. When they did not return, the main group, consisting of forty-five men, set out in twenty-two wagons on 3 July, under the leadership of Jonathan H. Holmes. Women and children were discouraged from going with them because of the untested road. William Coray's wife, Melissa, who had traveled the entire Battalion route, went anyway.

---

[33] Azariah Smith, 107.

[34] Ibid., 115.

[35] Brown, 130–31.

Tragedy Spring tree

Smaller groups later joined them, bringing the total party to sixty-five men and two women. The second woman was *Brooklyn* passenger Rachel Reed, recently married to Battalion veteran Franklin Weaver. Also in the group was a San Francisco convert, Francis Hammond, who later settled in Huntsville, Utah, and became the boyhood bishop of future Church president David O. McKay.[36]

The following day, as they climbed the Sierras, they shot echoing salutes with two cannons they had purchased from Sutter to help defend Zion. The salute was their contribution to Governor Mason's Fourth of July celebration below. On 19 July the emigrants discovered the buried bodies of the three scouts—evidence of the danger confronting small groups. Naming the place Tragedy Spring, the travelers held a brief service and reburied the scouts beneath a tree on which they carved an inscription: "To the Memory of Daniel Browett, Ezra Allen and Henderson Cox Who were supposed to have been murdered and buried by Indians on the night of the 27th of June, 1848." Allen's pouch, filled with gold dust, was found in the brush. This was eventually given to his widow, who made a wedding ring from part of the gold and used the remainder to finance her journey across the Plains from Iowa to Utah.[37]

The site was memorialized in 1921 by the Native Sons of the Golden West. After the tree fell, the part bearing the

---

[36] Norma B. Ricketts, *Tragedy Spring and the Pouch of Gold* (Sacramento: Ricketts, 1983), 38.

[37] Ibid., 17, 30–31.

inscription was preserved and eventually placed in the visitors center at the Marshall Gold Discovery State Park in Coloma.

By early August this group had developed a wagon road through the Sierra Nevada. They eventually reached the Salt Lake Valley on 28 September.[38]

Sutter's Problems and Brannan's Fortunes

In the summer of 1848, Capt. John Sutter's son came to California. The elder Sutter had established his city-fort alone, leaving his family behind in Europe. Now this eminent pioneer had serious problems. Gold seekers squatted on his property, and their numbers were too great for him to stop them. Wages for hired help rose tenfold. In addition, he had seen the great wealth that men like Brannan were amassing through the sale of merchandise to miners. Sutter had tried, unsuccessfully, to set up a group of rival stores. By fall, unable to cope with the rapid change, he became dissipated by alcohol and financial difficulties. The Russian-American Company threatened to foreclose on his holdings. He was also deeply in debt to Brannan. In October he deeded all his property to his son and gave him power of attorney.

Meanwhile, the demand for goods at Brannan's stores was so great that he emptied his San Francisco stock entirely, as well as every ship anywhere in the vicinity and some as far away as the eastern U.S. and the Orient, trading goods for gold. When he could not find warehouse space, he converted ships deserted by their gold-seeking crews into storage facilities.

Brannan sold his newspaper, which was less profitable than the stores, to his assistant, Edward Kemble, for eight hundred dollars. Kemble also bought the rival *Californian* and merged the two, first calling the new paper the *California Star*

[38] Yurtinus, 634–37; see also Kenneth N. Owens, "The Mormon-Carson Emigrant Trail in Western History," *Montana: The Magazine of Western History*, 42 (winter 1992): 14–27.

and Californian, then the *Alta California*, which became one of the nation's most respected newspapers.

During the fall Brannan also paid fifty thousand dollars for Charles Smith's interest in the Sacramento store, which was thereafter called "S. Brannan & Co."[39] He then purchased a store at Mormon Island, giving the management to his former New Hope colony chief, William Stout, and opened a third store at Coloma. This gave him the major share of the mercantile trade in gold country. He became California's wealthiest man, its first millionaire, and an embodiment of the "California way of life."

He then formed an alliance with the younger Sutter and convinced him to divert Sutter's property to their partnership. This twosome, together with other partners, developed a city on the property and named it "Sacramento" after the river it fronted. "It was easy for Sam Brannan to win my son over to his favorite project of a city near the Fort," the elder Sutter reflected.[40]

Brigham Young on Seeking Gold

While all this was going on in California, Brigham Young was on the Plains leading Saints westward. Just when he learned about the gold discovery is not known. Perhaps it was when Brannan's newspapers traveled through, or in mid-July when he received a letter from Church authorities in Salt Lake City indicating that some of the Saints there were becoming affected with "what we call the California fever."[41]

President Young penned a reply dated 17 July urging the Saints to "get cured of the California fevers, as quick as they possibly can, and let neither them, nor any other fevers trouble

---

[39] Samuel Brannan, "A Biographical Sketch Based on a Dictation," 6, MS, C-D 805; Bancroft Library, University of California at Berkeley.

[40] Gudde, 220.

[41] JH, 9 June and 20 July 1848.

them any more, for I am well assured that if you do, the Lord will bless you and prosper you."[42]

At the end of September, the wagon train loaded with gold from Northern California arrived in the Salt Lake Valley. When Brigham Young reached the Valley at about that same time, a substantial number of the Saints already had their bags packed for California. On 1 October he reminded them that the Spaniards had looked for gold; consequently, they had been divested of their greatness and almost lost their God. In contrast, the English colonists, who had paid attention to agriculture and industry, had waxed strong. He elaborated: "If we were to go to San Francisco and dig up chunks of gold, or find it here in the valley, it would ruin us. Many wanted to unite Babylon and Zion; it's the love of money that hurts them. If we find gold and silver, we are in bondage directly. To talk of going away from this valley we are in, for anything, is like vinegar to my eyes. They that love the world have not their affections placed upon the Lord."[43] This was the first of many such pronouncements by President Young against those wanting to go to California.

But in the Salt Lake Valley, gold, or other liquid capital, was needed to finance various public works. Although Samuel Brannan was collecting 30 percent "tithing" from the gold miners, he was sending none of these funds to the Church in Salt Lake. Therefore, as an alternate means of securing capital, Brigham Young decided to send some men to California as "missionaries" to mine gold for individuals and for the Church. Most of these assignments were kept confidential because he did not want to cause a mass exodus.[44]

Although there was no public mention of it at the October 1848 general conference, as many as three groups of gold missionaries were sent to California or went with President Young's blessing. The last of these was formed on 26 Novem-

---

[42] Ibid., 17 July 1848.

[43] Ibid., 1 October 1848.

[44] Davies, 69–73.

ber, when Elder Amasa Lyman, Porter Rockwell, and about eighteen others were called "to go to California bay, on a mission."[45] However, it was so late in the year that Rockwell and Elder Lyman did not go until the next spring.

Brigham Young also began a minting operation in November 1848. Those coming to the Salt Lake Valley with raw gold dust and nuggets were encouraged to deposit the gold in exchange for coin from the mint. During the next three years, well over one hundred thousand dollars in California gold was minted. Thus, as one historian has concluded, for Latter-day Saints "the most important crop of 1849–1851 was harvested, not in the Salt Lake Valley, but at Sutter's Mill, near Coloma, California."[46]

The News Spreads East

Copies of the *California Star* found their way to St. Joseph, Missouri, where the news was republished on 28 July 1848. On 19 August, the *New York Herald* published the discovery. Even though the *Herald* article was credited to a "California correspondent," the wording was exactly the same as that of the 1 April article in Brannan's *Star*, which had just reached the East. Though the *Herald* gave Brannan no credit, it plagiarized his words which had been printed on the old press brought around the Horn on the *Brooklyn*. Thus Brannan helped trigger gold fever not only in San Francisco and along the West Coast, but also throughout much of the world.[47]

On 17 August, California's Governor Mason issued an official report to Washington. He predicted that there would be enough gold taken out of the country to pay for the war with Mexico more than a hundred times over. On 1 December

---

[45] JH, 26 November 1848.

[46] Leonard J. Arrington, *Great Basin Kingdom: An Economic History of the Latter-day Saints, 1830–1900* (Cambridge, Mass.: Harvard University Press, 1958), 66.

[47] Douglas S. Watson, "Herald of the Gold Rush," *California Historical Society Quarterly* 10, no. 3 (September 1931): 298–301.

his report reached Washington, D.C., along with the gold-encrusted tea caddy, which was placed on public display in the War Department. The debate over California's wealth was over. President Polk declared in his 5 December State of the Union Address that "the accounts of the abundance of gold in [California] are of such an extraordinary character as would scarcely command belief were they not corroborated by the authentic reports of officers in the public service who have visited the mineral district and derived the facts which they detail from personal observation."[48]

Given legitimacy by the presidential declaration, what had been rumor through much of the country now became substantiated fact. Ships began heading for California. From towns and villages throughout the United States, wagons began rolling to the West. The local gold rush was over. An international gold rush was on.

---

[48] James D. Richardson, ed., *A Compilation of the Messages and Papers of the Presidents* (Washington: Bureau of National Literature, 1911), 4:2486.

Apostles amid
Gold Seekers: 1849

8

The once-rare sight of a ship sailing with emigrants from New York City was now a daily occurrence. During the first two months after President Polk's address confirming the gold discovery, at least 178 vessels sailed from the eastern seaboard to California. Before the year ended, eighty-nine thousand people flocked to California seeking gold: forty-two thousand overland, forty-one thousand by sea, and six thousand from Mexico.[1]

Initially, Brigham Young continued to discourage the Saints from going to California. As the year wore on, however, he temporarily softened his stance in an attempt to broaden the Latter-day Saints' political influence in California and to enhance the flow of gold through Salt Lake City.

The 1848–49 winter in the Great Basin was again harsh. Many there learned of the California wagon train that had come to Utah the previous fall laden with gold. There were those, including the contingent of southern Saints that Brannan was originally to have escorted to California, who still wanted to leave Utah. In addition to the lure of gold, they were also

---

[1] J. S. Holliday, *The World Rushed In: The California Gold Rush Experience* (New York: Simon and Schuster, 1981), 297.

unaccustomed to harsh winters. Open questioning of President Young's leadership and wisdom was occasionally heard as some wondered aloud whether they would have been better off if they had gone with Brannan.

On 24 February 1849, Robert Crow presented a petition on behalf of himself and others that they be allowed to go to California under official Church sanction. Crow's petition was denied. On Sunday, 29 February, Brigham Young confronted this issue in a discourse to a large audience in the bowery of Salt Lake's Old Fort:

> The time has not come for the Saints to dig gold. It is our duty first to develop the agricultural resources of the country. . . . The worst fear that I have about this people is that they will get rich, . . . forget God, . . . wax fat, and kick themselves out of the Church and go to hell. This people will stand mobbing, robbing, poverty, and all manner of persecution, and be true. But my greater fear for them is that they cannot stand wealth.[2]

One biographer regarded this speech as a high point of Brigham Young's leadership career. Even though "his audience stood before him in the snow, poorly clad, shivering in the cold weather," he convinced them that they were better off working in Utah's harsh climate than they would be in wealth and comfort in California.[3]

In similar circumstances, Heber C. Kimball, one of President Young's two counselors, prophesied with startling discernment: "It will be but a little while, brethren, before you shall have food and raiment in abundance, and shall buy it cheaper than it can be bought in the cities of the United States." President Kimball himself wondered how this could be. He later admitted that "the Lord led me right, but I did not know it."[4]

---

[2] Preston Nibley, *Brigham Young: The Man and His Work* (Salt Lake City: Deseret Book, 1970), 128.

[3] Ibid., 128–29.

[4] Orson F. Whitney, *Life of Heber C. Kimball* (Salt Lake City: Bookcraft, 1975), 391.

Gold seekers, when traveling through Utah, ensured the fulfillment of this prophecy. Many wintered among the Saints in the Rockies, paying for lodging and supplies. Others, trying to quicken their pace and beat those in front of them to the gold, abandoned goods along the way to lighten their loads. Almost all of them paid Latter-day Saint ferrying companies to take them across the various rivers. Blacksmithing also became highly profitable. "Thus," as one Latter-day Saint acknowledged, "in a few years in this desolated part of the mountains we were beginning to enjoy to some degree that which might have taken years had not the Lord provided for the poor saints by His providence in opening up the gold mines in California and inspiring the Gentiles with a lust for gold."[5]

One of those "Gentiles" traveling to California was a young German emigrant. In the central Utah town of Fillmore he met an attractive young lady. "He was so attracted to her that he later panned just enough gold to pay for a wedding ring and then hastened back to marry her and later join the Church!" Their great-grandson, James E. Faust, would later become an apostle and then a counselor in the First Presidency in 1995.[6]

The Church Directs Attention to California

For the previous two or three seasons, the Church had devoted its resources to getting the large body of refugees safely across the Plains and settled in the mountains. Though the Saints in California had needed the Church's help for some time, they had been too few and far away to be a priority to Church leaders. Over three years had passed since an apostle, Elder Orson Pratt, had been with the *Brooklyn* Saints in New York City. However, now that the Church was settled in the

---

[5] James Holbrook, quoted in Leonard J. Arrington, *Great Basin Kingdom: An Economic History of the Latter-day Saints, 1830–1900* (Cambridge, Mass.: Harvard University Press, 1958), 71.

[6] Neal A. Maxwell, "President James E. Faust: 'Pure Gold,'" *Ensign*, August 1995, 14.

Amasa M. Lyman

Salt Lake Valley, leaders were able to give the members in California more attention. As the April 1849 general conference drew near, they gave further thought to the assignment given to Elder Amasa M. Lyman the previous fall. They determined to send Elder Lyman and Porter Rockwell to "look after the interest of the Church and the Saints, and to return with those who might be coming to the valley in the fall."[7] On 8 April, as part of the conference, Elder Lyman was blessed and set apart for his mission.

While Elder Lyman made final preparations for his departure, another apostle, Charles C. Rich, who had been called to the Quorum of the Twelve only a few weeks earlier, received a similar assignment to California. On the same day Elder Lyman was set apart, Elder Rich was "appointed to go and establish a settlement or stake on or near the Bay of San Francisco." Church leaders instructed him to "gather the Saints, preach the gospel, and preside over the affairs of the Church on the Western Coast."[8] His departure date was postponed until the fall, however, "it not being considered safe . . . while the route west was so full of emigrants."[9]

One of the letters Elder Lyman carried to California was written by Brigham Young to Samuel Brannan on 5 April. It was a response to Brannan's report of complaints among the Saints. President Young responded that the man "who is always doing right has no occasion to fear any complaints." He further said that he expected a hundred thousand dollars in

---

[7] Journal History, 26 and 31 March 1849 (hereafter JH); LDS Church Archives.

[8] Ibid., 12 February, 31 March, 8 and 12 April 1849.

[9] Quoted in J. Kenneth Davies, *Mormon Gold: The Story of California's Mormon Argonauts* (Salt Lake City: Olympus, 1984), 159.

tithing if Brannan had, according to reports, accumulated a million dollars to tithe. President Young cautioned:

> If you want to continue to prosper, do not forget the Lord's treasury, lest he forget you. . . . And when you have settled with the treasury, I want you to remember that Brother Brigham has long been destitute. . . . He wants you to send him a present of twenty thousand dollars in gold dust . . . but a trifle when gold is so plentiful. . . . My council will not be equal with me unless you send $20,000 more to be divided between Brothers Kimball and Richards, who like myself are straitened. A hint to the wise is sufficient. So when this is accomplished, you will have our united blessing. . . . But should you withhold, when the Lord says give, your hopes and pleasing prospects will be blasted in an hour you think not of and no arm to save. . . . But I am persuaded better things of Brother Brannan. I expect all I have asked when Brother Lyman returns.[10]

It is impossible to determine the exact intent of this unusual entreaty, but it should be considered in light of the fact that Church leaders devoted their adult lives to unpaid Church service, and there was therefore no clear distinction between private and ecclesiastical property. While the Church in Utah was in poverty and Brannan was wealthy, he was being asked to devote some of his great wealth to support the leaders of the Church.[11] It may also have been a test of Brannan's loyalty to the Church and its leaders or a test of his willingness to share with those in Utah the prosperity which his position and the common labors of the Saints in California had won.

Amasa Lyman and Porter Rockwell

Amasa Lyman's party of twenty men left for California on 12 April. Even though President Young was adamant that he would "not fellowship" those going to California without authorization, Robert Crow's family and several other

---

[10] JH, 5 April 1849.

[11] Eugene E. Campbell, "A History of The Church of Jesus Christ of Latter-day Saints in California, 1846–1946," (Ph.D. diss., University of Southern California, 1952), 135–38; Davies, 113–14.

unconvinced southern Saints likely went with Elder Lyman.[12] Elder Lyman later remembered how "that singular epidemic raged to a wonderful extent, known as *gold fever*. It resulted in carrying off some eighty families, besides [Elder Lyman's] party of twenty men."[13] Despite Brigham Young's caution, many of those enticed were stalwart Church members. Half the "Captains of Ten" from the 1847 Utah Pioneers eventually ended up in California.[14]

Elder Lyman's party took the northern route via the California Trail. Traveling by horseback, they made good time across the desert but found the deep snow in the Sierra Nevada mountains an impediment. "After four toilsome and hazardous days, with nothing to feed their weary horses," they reached Sutter's Fort on 25 May, where the party split up.[15] Elder Lyman went directly to San Francisco. Many, including Porter Rockwell, scattered throughout gold country, where more friends and relatives from the southern states later joined them.

Elder Lyman found chaotic conditions in California. The main body of "forty-niners" from the East had not yet arrived; therefore, those already panning in gold country were scrambling to get all they could before the onslaught. "In their mania for sudden riches they had neither time nor inclination to listen to Amasa's message. Even members of the Church, for whose sake in particular he had been sent, were distracted with eagerness to find the yellow metal or were drunken with a sense of wealth because they had found it."[16]

Elder Lyman's most pressing assignment was to find the Latter-day Saint miners and gather up tithing gold for the mint and money system in the Salt Lake Valley. By 6 July, he had

---

[12] Davies, 110–11.

[13] *Millennial Star* 12, no. 14 (15 July 1850): 214–15.

[14] Davies, 86.

[15] Albert R. Lyman, *Amasa Mason Lyman: Trailblazer and Pioneer from the Atlantic to the Pacific* (Delta, Utah: Melvin A. Lyman, 1957), 201.

[16] Ibid.

collected $4,152 in tithing and donations. He had also induced several successful miners to begin forming a wagon train in order to emigrate with their gold.

What became known as the "Mormon Gold Train," captained by Thomas Rhoads, left Sacramento on 14 July. It was made up of those Elder Lyman had convinced to emigrate. In addition to the four thousand tithing dollars, Rhoads took about seventeen thousand in gold. William Glover, probably still nominally on the San Francisco town council, took about five thousand, which he promptly gave to the Church upon his arrival in Salt Lake City. In all, the train carried between twenty-five and thirty thousand dollars in gold for the Church's mint. The train arrived on 29 September with little fanfare. Nevertheless, the gold that the group infused into the

Great Basin economy "probably saved the Mormon money system and provided much of the liquid capital essential for continued economic growth."[17] Brigham Young called Rhoads the wealthiest miner to come from California. He became a public figure in Utah for at least a decade and served as counselor to the president of the Salt Lake City Stake.

Orrin Porter Rockwell

Meanwhile, after finding the hard work of panning gold distasteful, Porter Rockwell opened three saloons. He learned quickly that miners were not stingy when it came to alcohol: "The most accessible money was not in the [gold] claims, but in the pockets of those who worked them."[18] "When [Porter Rockwell] hauled whiskey from Sacramento by mule train he would arrive at a hilltop above town and blare his

[17] Davies, 156.

[18] Harold Schindler, *Orrin Porter Rockwell: Man of God, Son of Thunder* (Salt Lake City: University of Utah Press, 1983), 186.

bugle. His partner at the tavern would fire a shot in the air. Gold panners along the river knew it was time to celebrate."[19]

Rockwell used the alias "Brown" because there were many, particularly former Missourians, who wanted him killed. Former Missouri governor Lilburn W. Boggs and his sons were convinced that Rockwell was the assailant who had shot and wounded the governor over a decade earlier. Rockwell is said to have claimed that he could not possibly have been the assassin, because Boggs was still alive. Nonetheless, the Boggs family wanted revenge.

It must have amused Rockwell to hear tavern patrons tell "Porter Rockwell stories" without realizing that he was behind the bar. For protection, he kept loaded pistols and a trained dog at his side. When he traveled on horseback, the dog rode behind him with its paws on his shoulders and searched the trail ahead for trouble. It was trained to lick his face rather than bark—a silent alarm.[20]

Civic and Business Enterprises

Several Latter-day Saints now played important roles in the economic and cultural development of San Francisco and Sacramento. The *Brooklyn* Saints were particularly enterprising and productive. The Robbins brothers purchased a horse off a boat from Sydney, Australia, and started the first express business in San Francisco. William Evans opened the first tailor shop on the West Coast on the corner of Market Street and Van Ness Avenue in San Francisco. Carolyn Joyce, known as the "Mormon Nightingale," accompanied her songs with the first melodeon in the city.[21]

---

[19] Richard Lloyd Dewey, *Porter Rockwell: A Biography* (New York: Paramount Books, 1987), 155.

[20] Ibid.

[21] Amelia D. Everett, "The Ship *Brooklyn*," *California Historical Society Quarterly* 37 (1958): 236–37.

But Samuel Brannan, dabbling in a dozen or more enterprises, was the most famous and successful. In order to stock his gold-country stores, he began planning for a wharf in San Francisco to accommodate the largest sailing vessels. He was among the principal stockholders in the company that built the "long wharf." It stretched nearly half a mile into the Bay at the very spot where he had first landed nearly three years before.[22] This was one of Brannan's most visible enterprises. He frequently put capital at risk and encouraged others to join with him in improving the city. He was among those who guided the transition of San Francisco from a forlorn outpost to a thriving metropolis which easily became the most important city on the West Coast for half a century.

He was also actively developing the city of Sacramento and promoted a fellow Latter-day Saint, John Fowler, as mayor. Fowler had been with Brigham Young's advance party of overland Pioneers who went to Utah. He had come to California with Brannan in 1847 to reunite with his wife, Jerusha, a *Brooklyn* passenger. Brannan and Fowler, using surplus lumber from one of Sutter's mills, erected an elegant $100,000 hotel on the Sacramento waterfront. In September, they staged a gala grand-opening. The hotel was an instant success, netting them about thirty thousand dollars per year.

Brannan also built a fine home in San Francisco where he entertained eminent dignitaries. Located on the southeast corner of Washington and Stockton Streets, it looked out over the town below. It quickly became a popular meeting place for such elite figures as Commodore Stockton, Governor Mason, and the mayor of Sonoma, ex-Missouri governor Lilburn Boggs.

---

[22] Zoeth Skinner Eldredge, *The Beginnings of San Francisco from the Expedition of Anza, 1774 to the City Charter of April 15, 1850* (San Francisco: Zoeth S. Eldredge, 1912), 2:573–74; Reva Scott, *Samuel Brannan and the Golden Fleece* (New York: Macmillan, 1944), 240–41.

Brannan also became embroiled in a cause that eventually contributed to his loss of standing in the Church: the movement that became the San Francisco Vigilance Committee. The gold rush had attracted some unsavory characters, and San Francisco was now plagued by a particularly tough and lawless gang of ex-soldiers called the "Hounds" or "Regulators," whom a contemporary described as "virtually a gang of public robbers." The "town was paralyzed with terror" because of them.[23] Their *modus operandi* was to set large fires, and then, while the citizens were occupied as volunteer firemen, loot and pillage the citizens' homes. Having no regular police force, Mayor T. M. Leavenworth was powerless to stop their thievery. The gang's activities climaxed on Sunday evening, 15 July, with an attack in which several people were injured, robbed, or beaten. This attack "finally roused the community from its lethargy."[24] The next day Brannan joined other citizens in urging Leavenworth to immediately help the community organize to defend itself.

In response, Leavenworth directed all citizens to meet that afternoon in the plaza. Standing on the roof of the mayor's office, Brannan addressed the crowd "and denounced in forcible terms the depredations and many crimes of the 'hounds.'" He suggested that a collection be taken up for the relief of the victims of the previous night's riot. Two hundred thirty men were soon enlisted as "special constables." Each was given a musket and told to patrol in groups. After ten days' duty, the men formed the nucleus of a permanent militia that policed the city as it thought appropriate. The group's activities curbed the lawlessness that summer and fall; however, on Christmas Eve another mysterious fire broke out. Nearly half the city went up in smoke. Brannan's new home escaped only because the wind shifted at the last minute. This narrow escape motivated

---

[23] Frank Soulé, John H. Gihon, and James Nisbet, *The Annals of San Francisco* (New York: D. Appleton, 1855), 227.

[24] Roger W. Lotchin, *San Francisco 1846–1856: From Hamlet to City* (Lincoln, Nebr.: University of Nebraska Press, 1974), 191.

Charles C. Rich

him to fashion bolder, more extreme measures the following year.

Charles C. Rich's Journey to California

The postponement of Elder Rich's journey to California did not result in a safe, uneventful passage. Of all the groups of Saints that traveled the route between the Great Basin and California, Elder Rich's group probably suffered the most difficulty. The group was comprised mostly of non-Latter-day Saints. They interviewed Jefferson Hunt and hired him to lead their hundred-wagon train for ten dollars per wagon.[25] This was his third trip to California in three years, and although he had been over the route on horseback, he had never taken any wagons. However, in his estimation the journey could be made successfully if they followed the trail he knew. Addison Pratt, who had been called to return as a missionary to Polynesia, and his companion, gold-strike miner and former Battalion private James S. Brown, also joined this train.

This was just one of several large trains Brigham Young authorized to go to California that fall as the Salt Lake Valley experienced its own small gold rush. Along with those anxious to go, some young men, including George Q. Cannon and former Battalion member Henry W. Bigler, responded to calls as missionaries to mine gold.[26]

The Rich-Hunt train left Utah Valley via the southern route on 2 October. It included many Missourians and Illinoisans

---

[25] William Lewis Manly, *Death Valley in '49* in *March of America Facsimile Series*, no. 90 (Ann Arbor, Mich.: University Microfilms), 105.

[26] See Henry Bigler, "Journal Extracts of Henry Bigler," *Utah Historical Quarterly* 5, no. 3 (July 1932): 101; George Q. Cannon, "Twenty Years Ago: A Trip to California," *Juvenile Instructor*, January–June 1869; 16 January 1869, 13.

Jefferson Hunt

who did not trust a Latter-day Saint leader. When Hunt organized them in military fashion and demanded discipline, including rotating the lead wagon, they rebelled. As the trail grew hotter and more difficult, they became more irritable and aggressive. Some even threatened his life.

After three weeks they were overtaken by James Flake's train of about twenty gold missionaries and a mounted party headed by a man named O. K. Smith,[27] who had a map showing a shorter route. Smith, usurping Hunt's authority, offered to lead the train himself. For the next several days the large group debated the merits of Smith's cutoff through Walker's Pass. This alternate route to the gold fields was several hundred miles shorter than the route through Los Angeles. The gold missionaries, riding on horseback and hoping to get to the gold mines before the rainy season, decided to go with Smith through the cutoff.

They urged Elder Rich to leave the wagon train and join them. "He was impressed with the idea," wrote George Q. Cannon, "that if he did not do so, some of us, if not all, would perish."[28] On 29 October, a split occurred when the "packers" (on horseback) left the wagons behind and three days later reached the point where the cutoff left the Old Spanish Trail.

The wagons, traveling more slowly, reached the same point four days later. That evening the group had to decide whether to take the cutoff. Most were in favor but wanted to hear Hunt's opinion. He acknowledged that he personally did not have any factual information about the proposed route but felt that it was unsafe. Exasperated, he continued, "You all know I was hired to go by way of Los Angeles, but if you

---

[27] Possibly *Brooklyn* passenger Orin K. Smith.

[28] Cannon, 13 February 1869, 28.

all wish to go and follow Smith I will go also. But if even one wagon decides to go the original route, I shall feel bound to go with that wagon."[29] The following morning "team after team turned to the right while now and then one would keep straight ahead as was at first intended. Capt. Hunt came over to the larger party after the division was made, and wished them all a hearty farewell and a pleasant happy journey."[30]

Hunt secretly hoped that those who had threatened his life would choose Smith's cutoff. An excerpt from the journal of Addison Pratt, who stayed with Hunt and shared his concerns, recalls:

> As we began to give each other the parting hand, Br. Hunt put on a verry long face as if he was about to shed tears. I could not but smile at his sad looks. . . . I laughed at him a little about his crocodile tears. "Ah," said he, "It was a policy for me to affect something before them for many of them have treated me very kindly and would to God! that I could get them out of the trouble they are now going into. They cannot get through with their waggons that way and I hardly think Br. Rich with the horsemen can, but they stand by far the best chance, but I told Br. Rich, if he found mountains that they could not pass, to be sure and slide back onto this trail, quick as possible and come on and overtake us. This," continued he, "is one of the happiest days of my life. I cannot recollect the time when I have made so lucky escape from death as I have in getting rid of that company."[31]

As Hunt predicted, Smith's caravan, including Elder Rich and the gold missionaries, soon ran into trouble with almost impassable terrain. Several days of excessive heat without water brought excruciating thirst. Bigler recorded:

> An emigrant of Captain Smith's company came into our camp and said he would pay any price for a drink of water, there was none for sale. The day had been hot and my canteen was dry having drank and divided it with others. I said to this man that I was so dry myself that if I had a drink, I would not take fifty dollars for it. Brother Rich,

---

[29] Manly, 110.

[30] Ibid., 111.

[31] Quoted in Pauline Udall Smith, *Captain Jefferson Hunt of the Mormon Battalion* (Salt Lake City: The Nicholas G. Morgan, Sr., Foundation, 1958), 154.

who was sitting by, said to me, "have you no water"? I replied, no sir, in a few minutes afterwards he called to me, it was away from the fire in the dark. I went, he handed me his canteen and said, "Drink, drink, you are welcome." The canteen seemed to be two-thirds full. I said, no Brother Rich, but he urged me to drink, saying, he had not been very thirsty himself that day and I was welcome to a drink. I said to myself, God bless the man.[32]

The next day the struggling group descended into a canyon, where, after several hours, they discovered a small spring. "Pure, sparkling, cold water was there," Cannon recalled, "gurgling as it ran over the rocks in the channel. Oh, what music to our ears was in the sound! How ravishing the sight! It was not a large stream; but it was sufficient; and a body of water as large as Lake Superior could not have produced more joy or thankfulness."[33]

After four more days without enough water, it began to rain. Soon the water was coming down in torrents. "I rode on horseback," described Cannon, "and I turned up the rim of my hat, and made it something like a dish. By carrying my head very steady I contrived to catch some rain, to which the hat gave a smoky flavor; but it quenched thirst. . . . I have always believed that this shower of rain was sent to save our lives."[34] O. K. Smith also acknowledged that "it was plain to him that the finger of the Lord was in the rain."[35]

The Smith group found the trail increasingly difficult. Elder Rich urged them to follow Hunt's advice and return to the original trail. "We were relieved by his remarks," Cannon confessed. "They made us feel glad; for we knew that he, not Captain Smith, had the right to lead us, and that if we should be saved from our perilous circumstances, it would be through him. It seemed as though the Lord had permitted us to wander . . . to arouse every one to a sense of the peril we were in, that

---

[32] Bigler, 107–8.

[33] Cannon, 10 April 1869, 60.

[34] Ibid., 24 April 1869, 68.

[35] Bigler, 109.

he whose right it was to lead us might be justified in the eyes of all in dictating our future movements."[36]

Elder Rich and the gold missionaries did turn back and intercepted Hunt on 18 November. Smith, stubbornly holding to his original plan, swore, "If you do not hear from me, you may know that I died with my face westward." After only a day and a half's further travel, however, he, too, returned to the original trail. "By this time Smith had either forgotten his oath, or thought dying with his face westward was not so pleasant as he had imagined it would be."[37] Nearly eighty of the wagons likewise turned back and rejoined the main trail.

The twenty-seven remaining wagons, including a group of young, single men known as the "Jolly Jayhawkers," and some avowed Mormon-haters, including Reverend J. W. Brier, who had influenced many to leave Hunt, kept to the "shortcut." Only a few of these dissenters lived to tell their tale. They eventually discarded their wagons and belongings and attempted to cross, on foot, California's Death Valley, which they named.[38] The dry desert heat claimed most of their lives.

In contrast, the wagons that traveled the established trail with Captain Hunt arrived in Southern California without further incident. Once again, the gold missionaries, on horseback, went ahead of Hunt's wagon train. At the Mojave River, they met an emigrant family which had been stranded there a month and had subsisted only on beef. Although the Latter-day Saints were also running low on provisions, they gave the family sufficient flour to survive. "It was a pitiable sight to see them in their condition," Bigler wrote. "The poor little children, my heart was filled for them."[39] The family was among the first of thousands who traveled to California with too little.

---

[36] Cannon, 10 April 1869, 60.

[37] Ibid., 8 May 1869, 78–79.

[38] Quoted in Erwin Gudde, *California Place Names* (Berkeley and Los Angeles: University of California Press, 1969), 85–86.

[39] Bigler, 112.

Elder Rich and the mounted group of gold missionaries reached Isaac Williams's ranch on 10 December, with Hunt and the slower-moving wagons arriving twelve days later. Elder Rich, having survived the trip, was safely in California, where his presence would influence events for nearly a decade.

The Golden Sun Sets: 1850

Some eighty-nine thousand "forty-niners" had increased California's population tenfold since the previous year. Another eighty-five thousand in 1850 nearly doubled it again. Initially, most were stricken with "gold fever," described vividly by one forty-niner:

> A frenzy seized my soul; houses were too small for me to stay in; I was soon in the street in search of necessary outfits; piles of gold rose up before me at every step; castles of marble, dazzling the eye with their rich appliances; thousands of slaves bowing to my beck and call; myriads of fair virgins contending with each other for my love . . . were among the fancies of my favored imagination.[1]

Beginning with the late arrivals in 1849, however, newcomers found more disappointment than gold. California had been exhaustively explored. The heaviest concentrations of gold had been mined out and the choicest land claimed. Many wished they had never come and therefore beat hasty retreats. One man wrote home that "many curse the day they ever started. They are not very satisfied with small wages and are inclined to run around just as we before them have done to our

---

[1] Quoted in Irving Stone, *Men to Match My Mountains: The Opening of the Far West, 1840–1900* (New York: Berkeley Books, 1982), 137.

sorrow, and they will learn so."[2] Another spoke of talking with an industrious friend who had been doing well back home:

> "Why did you come here?" I asked. "Did not all our letters discourage further emigration?" "Yes, . . . but we thought that as so many were getting rich, they only wrote such letters to keep others away."[3]

Now enough discouraging messages filtered "back home" that the traffic to California slowed. People began to come back to reality. By the latter part of 1850, immigration had ebbed, and normalcy in governmental and Church affairs began to emerge.

Two Latter-day Saint apostles were in California to work in the interest of the Church and its members. Additionally, several other Latter-day Saints played key roles in California's transition from gold-mining frontier to statehood. One of those was John Horner.

California's "First Farmer"

John M. Horner and his wife, Elizabeth, came to farm—a trade which they had learned in their native New Jersey. Almost as soon as the *Brooklyn* landed, Horner rode around the Bay looking for the most favorable locations. After a brief try at sharecropping near present-day Antioch, John and Elizabeth struck out on their own. In March 1847, they located permanently in the shadows of Mission San Jose, in present-day Fremont, about twenty-five miles northeast of the city of San Jose. They were the first Anglo family to build a home in what is now Alameda County, and they became the parents of the first Anglo baby born there.

While teaching school in New Jersey, Horner worked after hours to raise potatoes in a few unused corners of his father's

---

[2] Quoted in J. S. Holliday, *The World Rushed In: The California Gold Rush Experience* (New York: Simon and Schuster, 1981), 397.

[3] Ibid.

John Horner

corn field. He sold his crop for five dollars just before sailing on the *Brooklyn* and used this money to buy a pistol to defend himself in the "savage" country to which he was going. After arriving in California, he carried his gun for protection wherever he went. "But," Horner later recalled, "seeing no one whom I wanted to shoot and no one who wished to shoot me, I concluded my pistol was useless and traded it to a Spaniard for a yoke of oxen, the first animals I ever owned."

With this team he launched what became a multi-million-dollar farming enterprise.[4]

Having been told there was a market for grain among Russian seamen, Horner planted grain and vegetables in the spring of 1847, only to have the entire crop destroyed by insects. His fall crops were again destroyed—this time by wandering cattle. The next spring, when the Horners learned that gold had been discovered, they went briefly to seek their share in the mines. But they found that selling food was more profitable than mining gold. Miners had to eat, and they could not eat gold.

The Horners returned to their farm and planted vegetables in the fall of 1848. When the real gold rush came in 1849, they were among the few who could supply fresh produce, which skyrocketed to such prices that they, like Brannan, became wealthy in a single season. They had such a flair for farming that at the height of their prosperity, they acquired and fenced several thousand acres and employed as many as 150 men. "I

---

[4] John M. Horner, "Looking Back," *Improvement Era* 8, no. 1 (November 1904): 32–33.

John Horner's schoolhouse/meetinghouse

fully realized that I must rely upon myself and the Great Father for success," Horner reflected. "Industry, honesty, and perseverance were my guiding stars."[5]

Building the Latter-day Saint community to the point where there was talk of organizing a stake, Horner, with his wealth, encouraged and helped many Latter-day Saint settlers in and around Mission San Jose. He allowed members to settle on his properties, gave them the use of land, teams, and machinery, and sold their produce on commission. In a central location he built a schoolhouse and employed a teacher. This building also served as a social hall and on Sundays as a meetinghouse. It therefore may be regarded as the first Latter-day Saint chapel in California.

On Sunday mornings, Horner allowed the Methodists and Presbyterians to use his meeting house. In the afternoons, he personally preached to Latter-day Saint congregations of thirty to forty worshipers.[6] The building was moved several times, remaining intact until 1965 when it was burned in a fire drill.

---

[5] Horner, "Adventures of a Pioneer," *Improvement Era* 7, no. 7 (May 1904): 513.

[6] Ibid., no. 10 (August 1904): 770; Muir, 1:38.

Horner also encouraged several of his New Jersey kindred to join him and provided financial means whereby they could do so. He and his associates introduced new agricultural methods, being the first to employ "the modern mould-board plow; the first cradle for cutting grain; the first mowing machine, and the first reaping and thrashing machines ever used in California."[7] At California's first agricultural fair, which was held in 1852, he was lauded. He was the largest contributor, received the highest awards, and was given the official title of "First Farmer of California." He was the foremost pioneer of the state's largest industry.

Horner continued farming for many years. In addition to building a school/church, he laid out many of the county roads, constructed bridges, began a ferry service to San Francisco and the West Bay, instituted stagecoach lines, and founded Union City and several other towns.

San Francisco Becomes a City

In San Francisco, the old Mexican forms of administration were replaced by an American-style government. The city also took on a cosmopolitan atmosphere, populated by some of the world's brightest young men, flexible adventurers not afraid to take risks. Many were northeasterners who built the city on the *Brooklyn* colony's foundation of New England attitudes and styles. But what had once been a Latter-day Saint majority was now less than 5 percent of the population.

In three years the city had grown from a population of less than five hundred to thirty thousand, with only about two thousand of them female, including many prostitutes. There were forty-four steamers employed in river trade, twelve oceangoing steamers, seven daily newspapers, sixty brick buildings, and eight or ten first-class hotels. There were

---

[7] Horner, "Voyage of the Ship 'Brooklyn,'" *Improvement Era* 9, no. 11 (September 1906): 890.

San Francisco in 1851

107 miles of streets (seven miles planked), and most of that distance was properly sewered. Red flannel shirts and Levis (a San Francisco invention) were being replaced by white linen shirts, top hats, and wool trousers. Brannan's "long wharf" was now a focal point of commerce, and over its wooden-planked surface vehicles thundered almost constantly.

In August 1850, a group of early settlers formed the Society of California Pioneers, a socially prominent organization in San Francisco for many years, in which those who had come to California before 1 January 1849 formed the first rank. Samuel Brannan was elected as one of the three original vice presidents.[8]

---

[8] Frank Soulé, John H. Gihon, and James Nisbet, *The Annals of San Francisco* (New York: D. Appleton, 1855), 283–84, 715.

During 1850 devastating fires continued. On 4 May a fire raged for seven hours destroying three hundred houses, the City Hall, and three important business blocks adjoining Portsmouth Square. The loss was over four million dollars— equal to half the value of all the gold mined in California the previous year. Almost immediately steps were taken to rebuild the city. Just forty days later, however, another fire burned the business district from Kearny Street to the waterfront, causing another three million dollars damage. The extent of Samuel Brannan's personal losses in these fires is not known, but they must have been considerable, since his holdings were extensive.

In addition to Brannan's enterprises in San Francisco and Sacramento, he was also involved with the development of Yuba City and perhaps Marysville, located some forty miles north of Sacramento. One observer noted that in Marysville "you will see the go-ahead-iveness of the Yankee nation. In one fortnight's time $25,000 worth of lots at $250 each were sold. In ten days . . . seventeen houses and stores were put up, and what was before a ranch—a collection of Indian huts and a corral for cattle—became a right smart little city."[9] This pattern of development was repeated many times.

Elders Lyman and Rich in the North

When Elder Charles C. Rich left the Salt Lake Valley during the fall of 1849, the First Presidency gave him a letter of introduction which also instructed him to "consult" with Elder Amasa M. Lyman relative to the interests of the Church in California, to gather tithing, to receive donations for the Perpetual Emigrating Fund (a fund from which the poor could borrow money to help them immigrate to Utah, then repay it when they were settled and employed), and "to preach the

---

[9] Franklin A. Buck, quoted in Holliday, 365.

gospel as he had opportunity."[10] The First Presidency also sent Elder Lyman instructions regarding Latter-day Saint settlement in "Western California," a term being used by Church officials to encourage the combining of California and the Great Basin (called "Eastern California") into a single state: "We wish you and Brother Rich to take into consideration the propriety of continuing to hold our influence in Western California by our people remaining in that region. Our feelings are in favor of that Policy unless, all the offscouring of Hell has been let loose upon that dejected land, in which case we would advise you to gather up all that is worth saving and come hither with all speed."[11]

After their brief rest at the Williams Ranch in Southern California, Jefferson Hunt and others left on 12 January to escort Elder Rich northward. They followed the coastal road via the California missions, the same route Hunt had traveled with the Battalion dischargees two and one-half years earlier.

As the group stopped in San Jose during a legislative session, Addison Pratt, one of those in the party, visited with New Hope foreman William Stout, who was operating a boarding house. "He boasted about the immense riches he had obtained since he had arrived in California. But when I made our circumstances known to him, he began to plead poverty, that he was in a lawsuit with his wife, that she had robbed him of some thousands."[12]

Like so many others, Stout either flagrantly exaggerated or found his California gold slippery. Pratt noted that when it came to helping missionaries, "as a general thing, those that I supposed had accumulated the least gold, were the most liberal towards us."[13]

---

[10] Quoted in John Henry Evans, *Charles Coulson Rich: Pioneer Builder of the West* (New York: Macmillan, 1936), 196.

[11] Quoted in J. Kenneth Davies, *Mormon Gold: The Story of California's Mormon Argonauts* (Olympus, 1984), 160–61.

[12] *The Journals of Addison Pratt*, ed. S. George Ellsworth (Salt Lake City: University of Utah Press, 1990), 427.

[13] Ibid., 432.

Elder Rich's party reached San Francisco on 15 February, where, according to Addison Pratt, Brannan had told the local Saints that during his 1847 visit with Brigham Young he had promised to pay at a later time the two or three thousand dollars he had collected. However, in conversations with the First Presidency, Pratt had not heard of any such promise. Furthermore, he claimed Brannan never sent President Young the "thirty percent money" he collected from the Latter-day Saint gold miners.

Addison Pratt wrote that Brannan had accused him of standing in the way when Brannan was about to "make a 'heap' of money for the church" by increasing the value of several lots Brannan owned. According to Pratt, Brannan proposed that the Church build "an adobie Temple" worth some twenty-five or thirty thousand dollars. As an incentive, he promised to give the Church a quarter of the lot. Pratt wrote:

> I had seen enought of his tricks to believe he would manage the agreement so that the least failure on the part of the church would forfeit their claim to it, and it would fall back into his hands. . . . [T]he Spirit that was in me moved me to come out against it. And I now suppose that he tries to make Br. Lyman think that had I held my peace, the church would now be in possession of one fourth of a lot that would be worth from 25 to a 100,000 dollars. But I have no such notion about the matter. For he had been verry anxious to help the church, he would have long ago handed over to Br. Lyman the money that he has already swindled off of the brethren.[14]

Meanwhile, about one week before Elder Rich's arrival in San Francisco, Amasa Lyman sailed to Los Angeles, hoping to intercept his fellow apostle. When Elder Lyman arrived at San Pedro and heard that Elder Rich had already headed north, he returned to San Francisco, arriving on 13 March. But Elder Rich had left by that time for the Mariposa mining district.

On 1 April Elder Lyman took a steamer up the Sacramento toward the gold fields, stopping at Benecia on the way. Coincidentally, Elder Rich landed there about the same time,

---

[14] Ibid., 431–32.

and the two were united. Elder Lyman, who had been antici-
pating Elder Rich's arrival for nearly a year, wrote: "To strike
hands in California with a man having faith in God is a real
treat, like a fruitful flower in a parched land."[15] Both then
continued on together to Sacramento. Two days later they left
the new Brannan-Fowler hotel to accompany the Huffaker
wagon train to Greenwood, where hundreds of Latter-day
Saints were gathering.

On 10 April they selected a site in San Francisco, "on Br.
Lincoln's land," for a chapel. A few days later they appointed
Ward Pell and George Sirrine as "agents" to raise money for
the project.[16] Pell was one of those whom Brannan had excom-
municated, but he apparently remained close to the Church.
No further record has been found of this chapel.

During those weeks, Addison Pratt and James S. Brown
prepared to leave on their missions to Polynesia. On 12 April
Elders Lyman and Rich spent the day instructing them and
setting them apart. "The brethren at San Francisco put forth the
helping hand to assist us in getting started away from there,"
Addison Pratt gratefully acknowledged. The missionaries set
sail nine days later.[17]

One of the apostles' most difficult assignments was to visit
Samuel Brannan and obtain from him the tithing he had supposedly collected in the name of the Church. Elder Lyman and
Porter Rockwell had already visited Brannan for this purpose
in January. No contemporary record of this confrontation has
survived, but Sutter later wrote that when they asked Brannan
for the Lord's tithes he retorted in disgust: "You go back and
tell Brigham Young that I'll give up the Lord's money when he

[15] Albert R. Lyman, *Amasa Mason Lyman: Trailblazer and Pioneer from the Atlantic to the Pacific* (Delta, Utah: Melvin A. Lyman, 1957), 202.

[16] Charles C. Rich Diary, 10 and 18 April 1850; LDS Church Archives.

[17] *Journals of Addison Pratt*, 432–33.

sends me a receipt signed by the Lord, and no sooner."[18] Elder Lyman saw Brannan once again, about a month later, but with no better results.

The apostles had more success on 28 June when they visited Brannan together. Amasa Lyman's diary recorded that Brannan "made me a present of $500.00 made an arrangement for the books in his possession,"[19] perhaps suggesting the end of Brannan's five-year Church leadership role at the age of thirty-one. Was the five hundred dollars a pittance, or was it generous in the aftermath of the losses Brannan sustained during the recent devastating fires? Three days later, Elder Lyman dined with Brannan, possibly to pick up the promised books.

This is the last record of Brannan giving any funds to, or having any involvement with, the Church or its leaders. However, he was generous to various charitable causes and had been known to assist individual Latter-day Saints locally. Now, Elder Rich reported that Brannan confided that as far as the Saints were concerned he "stood alone and knew no one only himself and family."[20] All the references to Brannan in Amasa Lyman's diary use the title "Mr." in contrast to the more familiar "Brother" used in reference to faithful Church members— a further reflection of Brannan's estrangement. Still, the two apostles did not choose to cancel Brannan's Church membership.[21]

---

[18] Edwin G. Gudde, *Sutter's Own Story* (New York: G. P. Putnam's Sons, 1936), 202; see also Richard Lloyd Dewey, *Porter Rockwell: A Biography* (New York: Paramount Books, 1987), 152–53; and Harold Schindler, *Orrin Porter Rockwell: Man of God, Son of Thunder* (Salt Lake City: University of Utah Press, 1983), 186–87.

[19] Quoted in Davies, 222.

[20] Ibid., 222–23.

[21] Eugene E. Campbell, "A History of The Church of Jesus Christ of Latter-day Saints in California" (Ph.D. diss., University of Southern California, 1952), 162–63.

Along the California Trail

Meanwhile, during the spring, a few more Latter-day Saint pack or wagon trains left Salt Lake City for the gold country. At this time of year travelers preferred the northern route, known as the California Trail. First to leave, on about 3 April, were men assigned to carry mail to Northern California. Accompanying this small group was sixty-two-year-old Solomon Chamberlain, who had been a faithful Church member since 1830, the year of its organization. Traveling on horseback, they quickly crossed the deserts and even the Sierra Nevada snows, arriving in Sacramento by 22 June.[22]

Later in April, Thomas Orr headed another group of thirty-five families in wagons. They were held up for three weeks by the snow which the horsemen had more easily negotiated. While camped in the Carson Valley, they did some prospecting in nearby "Gold Canyon," without finding much. One of them, Abner Blackburn, later observed, "If we had known [of] the rich mines higher up the canion, the outcome would be different. We mist the great Bonanza."[23] He was referring to the Comstock Lode, the largest gold strike in North America, which fueled the area's economy for the next fifty years. Latter-day Saints had another near-miss at the Comstock. The 1848 wagon train going to Utah had found gold in the vicinity but abandoned their search to travel on.

Orr's party finally reached Pleasant Valley near Placerville on 4 July. Thomas Orr purchased a hotel at Salmon Falls on the American River, a few miles above Mormon Island. He enlarged the hotel, opened a bakery, and soon was taking in as much as fifteen hundred dollars per day. He became a deputy sheriff, and his sons operated stagecoaches to Sacramento and Marysville. Remaining in the area until 1862, he raised his

---

[22] Davies, 239.

[23] Abner Blackburn, *Frontiersman: Abner Blackburn's Narrative*, ed. Will Bagley (Salt Lake City: University of Utah Press, 1992), 173.

children as Latter-day Saints and often hosted missionaries who traveled through.[24]

On one occasion Orr encountered a former acquaintance, Porter Rockwell. When Orr called Rockwell by name, an alarmed Porter exclaimed that "his life would be worth nothing if the Gentiles knew who he was."[25]

At April general conference in Salt Lake City, Hiram Clark was called as mission president to Polynesia. He and William D. Huntington were appointed to lead a company to California—some to assist Elders Lyman and Rich, some to serve with Clark in Polynesia, and others to mine gold. This was "the last known company of approved Mormon gold miners." The group of thirty-nine "Mormons and non-Mormons" left Salt Lake City on 7 May.[26]

Traveling by carriage with this party were two sisters, Caroline Barnes Crosby, who was accompanying her husband on his Polynesian mission, and Louisa Barnes Pratt, who was to join her husband, Addison, already serving there. They were among the first female missionaries in the Church's history, and both penned forthright accounts of their journeys to California. Louisa noted that their wagon train overtook another headed by Ephraim Hanks that had left three weeks before them, even though it "travelled on the Sabbath, [and] we have not."[27]

She also described the hordes of starving gold seekers along the route, many in the same condition as the family Elder Rich's party had assisted the previous fall: "Oh, the crowds that throng this highway, going in search of gold; crowding about our wagons to be fed. We must feed them either for pay, or

---

[24] Davies, 239–42.

[25] Ibid., 241.

[26] Ibid., 244–45.

[27] Louisa Barnes Pratt, *Mormondom's First Woman Missionary: Life Story and Travels Told in Her Own Words*, ed. Kate B. Carter (Utah: Nettie Hunt Rencher, 1950), 255.

without. They must have starved to death, had we not been here with provisions."[28]

Although many were starving, there were places along the way where provisions were available. Caroline recorded that they passed "a trading post . . . a table set under a tree with liquors, groceries and provisions of almost all kinds . . . and houses made of posts set in the earth and covered with cloth looking very comfortable for summer."[29]

Another trading post belonged to Louis C. Bidamon from Nauvoo, who lived in "quite an extensive house."[30] Bidamon, who was not a Latter-day Saint, was married to Joseph Smith's widow, Emma. He was among those who had left families behind to search for gold. Writing to Emma, he confessed that finding gold was not easy: "It is obtained by the hardest of labour, harder than my constitution is able to bear. The acquisition of gold in the mines is something like a lottery, there is sometimes large amounts . . . but these are few occurrences and far between."[31] During the evening, he came to the missionaries' camp, joined them in singing and prayer, and was "delighted with some of our hymns."[32]

Descending from the mountains, the Clark-Huntington caravan met "a Mormon trading expedition" carrying supplies east to Carson Valley. With them was Solomon Chamberlain, who, finding he could not even mine enough gold to pay for his food, had seen enough of California after only about two weeks. Chamberlain later wrote: "I knelt down and asked the Lord in faith what I should do, and the voice of the Lord came unto me as plain as tho a man spake, and said, if you will go home to your family, you shall go in peace, and nothing shall harm you." Leaving everything behind and telling no one where he was going, he set out across the mountains. He was

---

[28] Ibid.

[29] Caroline Barnes Crosby Diary, July 1850; LDS Church Archives.

[30] Ibid.

[31] Quoted in Davies, 248.

[32] Crosby Diary, July 1850.

convinced that his eventual safe return from California's fray was a blessing from God.[33]

The First Presidency Sends Instructions

The missionaries arrived in California in July and carried letters of instruction from the First Presidency. In April the First Presidency had written at least two letters concerning California. Their 12 April "General Epistle" to the Saints on the subject of California migration complained that Saints frequently left or planned to leave the Salt Lake Valley without Church sanction. While "the greater portion have gone according to the council of their own wills and covetous feelings," it was "not too late for them to do good and be saved, if they will do right in their present sphere of action." The Presidency pointed out that "gold is good in its place—it is good in the hands of a good man to do good with, but in the hands of a wicked man it often proves a curse instead of a blessing. Gold is a good servant, but a miserable, blind, and helpless god, and at last will have to be purified by fire, with all its followers."

California Saints were informed that Elders Lyman and Rich would continue to collect tithing, keeping a record "of all faithful brethren." But they were also to keep a "perfect history of all who profess to be Saints and do not follow their counsel, pay tithing, and do their duty." These were to be reported in every mail, that "their works may be entered in a book of remembrance in Zion."[34]

The First Presidency directed their second letter, dated 23 April, specifically to Elders Lyman and Rich: "Gather up the brethren, if you have not already done it, and organize them, and preach to them and pray with them, and let them preach

---

[33] Quoted in Larry C. Porter, "A Study of the Origins of the Church of Jesus Christ of Latter-day Saints in the States of New York and Pennsylvania, 1816–1831" (Ph.D. diss., Brigham Young University, 1971), 363.

[34] James R. Clark, comp., *Messages of the First Presidency* (Salt Lake City: Bookcraft, 1965), 2:46.

to each other and pray for each other, and observe the Sabbath and refrain from all evil, and they will have the spirit of God and rejoice therein."[35]

The Presidency's instructions to "preach to each other" were a shift from Brigham Young's 1847 directive to curtail public preaching. Two days before delivering these instructions, even the missionaries felt it best to abbreviate their own meeting because "Brothers Rich and Lyman we understood hold none here."[36] One historian found little evidence "of any [public] preaching by the two" prior to the arrival of the "company of proselyting missionaries on their way to the Society Islands."[37]

Now, however, the apostles wasted no time implementing the new policy and preached during the evening of the day on which they met the incoming missionaries. Louisa Pratt recorded in her diary that "to see their faces and hear their voices proclaiming the truth so far from home is comforting to the soul."[38] Two days later, at a Friday evening function, the missionaries enjoyed singing hymns with the apostles and hearing from them a report of their activities during their previous year in California.[39]

On Sunday, 21 July, the apostles preached at Rockwell's tavern. Caroline Crosby recorded: "We had a very good meeting in the afternoon. Brothers Rich and Lyman said a great many good things to us concerning our mission and also counseled those who expected to stop in California to abstain from the vices of the country, viz., gambling, drunkenness, and every other that can be named."[40]

Louisa sold her faithful old carriage, the last piece of property that she and Addison had retained from their youth,

---

[35] Journal History, 23 April 1850 (hereafter JH); LDS Church Archives.

[36] Quoted in Davies, 249.

[37] Ibid., 320.

[38] Louisa Barnes Pratt, 256.

[39] Crosby Diary, 19 July 1850.

[40] Ibid., 21 July 1850.

and which had brought her and her sister to California. The two sisters then went on to San Francisco by boat and arrived there on 25 July. Louisa, finding the city less than immaculate, wrote: "Came down to the great city, that has made such a noise in the world. A great city it is, for the age of it, but so filthy it is dangerous for people to stop there."[41] Still, the sister missionaries were warmly received. Louisa found Brannan's mother-in-law, Fanny Corwin, to be "an exceedingly kind-hearted woman full of faith and good works. She lived with her daughter in a house like a king's palace." They were also well received by Sister Morey, who "shared largely of her benevolence," and by John Lewis, who transported them in his carriage to his home at Mission Dolores where they were hosted by the Saints for two weeks. "A better class of citizens never lived in San Francisco."[42] The sister missionaries remained at Mission Dolores until 15 September when, after many difficulties and delays, they finally departed for Polynesia.

Elders Lyman and Rich Return Home

Among the tired, disillusioned miners, there was a growing sense of futility. Hiram Clark wrote to Brigham Young that most of the miners he met were "not doing much and a very poor prospect of doing better." He asserted that "many of the boys here would give their old shoes to be back."[43] "I am tired of mining and of the country," Henry W. Bigler confided in his diary, "and long to be at home among the Saints."[44] Charles C. Rich reported to Brigham Young that "the brethren in the mining regions who had come from Salt Lake Valley with the

---

[41] Louisa Barnes Pratt, 257.

[42] Ibid., 259.

[43] Quoted in Davies, 255.

[44] Henry W. Bigler, *Bigler's Chronicle of the West* (Berkeley and Los Angeles: University of California Press, 1962), 131.

Gold Mission or later generally wished themselves back in the shelter of the mountains among the Saints." He therefore anticipated "a general disposition to return home this fall which I shall encourage."[45]

For several months, Elders Lyman and Rich had traveled together throughout the gold country visiting people, blessing the sick, arranging Church business, collecting tithing, and counseling the members.[46] Now, following this exhausting service, the time came for the two apostles to return home. On 17 August they, together with forty men, eight wagons, two or three women, and about one hundred animals, departed for the Rocky Mountains, taking with them another $1,007 in tithing, which they had collected between 4 July and 15 July, mostly from Saints on the San Francisco Peninsula. In the Carson Valley, Elder Rich received a letter instructing him to remain in California a little longer to complete some Church business. Elder Lyman and his group continued east, while Elder Rich retraced his steps across the mountains.

As Elder Lyman's party crossed the desert, they witnessed a ghoulish scene not to be forgotten. Thousands of rotting animal carcasses, innocent victims of gold-lust, were strewn along the trail. "The dead animals were so numerous that the stench was almost unbearable. One of our men, while he was riding along, counted 1,400 dead by the roadside, and there were hundreds more scattered over the plain."[47]

Two of the brethren in the company died of cholera, but the rest arrived safely in the Salt Lake Valley on 29 September.

Those returning were "good advertisements for the foll· of 'chasing after gold.'" Brigham Young asked Albert Thurbe if he was "disappointed in returning home with so little." Without hesitation Thurber answered, "I never felt better

---

[45] Charles C. Rich, quoted in Leonard J. Arrington, *Charles C. Rich: Mormon General and Western Frontiersman* (Provo, Utah: Brigham Young University Press, 1974), 153–54.

[46] Ibid., 153.

[47] Lyman, 203.

[than] when I got over the mountain."[48] Elder Lyman's account was equally dour. He said that the gold fields were "swamped in blood" and that the area was "depopulated by ravages of cholera." Indeed, there was a particularly virulent outbreak of cholera that fall, undoubtedly due to streams polluted by the hordes of humanity and the dead animals. Nevertheless, Elder Lyman added, "Gold is not the god of the Saints. Rather, they 'seek to build up the Kingdom of God by industry, by building cities.'"[49]

Though the Church decried the lust for wealth, there can be no denying that California gold was a gift of divine providence that brought economic viability to the otherwise isolated outposts in the Great Basin. It also relieved suffering elsewhere. That fall alone, when members were asked to donate money to the Perpetual Emigrating Fund, some six thousand dollars were raised, "mostly from California returnees."[50]

Back in California, Elder Rich visited as many of the Latter-day Saints as he could, encouraging them in their faith. During the next month and a half he collected from them well over one thousand dollars in tithing.[51] Concerned about the faith of the young gold miners, Elder Rich described to President Young a strategy he had devised to "send some Elders to the Sandwich [Hawaiian] Islands, and as many other places as I can as I think they will be better of[f] away from hear when the rainy season commences as there can be but little done at mining in this country during the rainy season. All flock to the Towns and citys and the chief employ is gambling and drink-·ng which has already allmost if not quite destroyed many of .e brethren."[52]

---

[48] Quoted in Leonard J. Arrington, *Great Basin Kingdom: An Economic History of the Latter-day Saints 1830–1900* (Cambridge, Mass.: Harvard University Press, 1958), 76.

[49] Quoted in Davies, 264.

[50] Arrington, *Great Basin Kingdom*, 77.

[51] Davies, 265–67.

[52] Quoted in Arrington, *Rich*, 154.

On 24 September, Elder Rich met with some of the Latter-day Saint miners in their tent at Slap Jack Bar. "We were glad to see him," Henry W. Bigler wrote in his diary, "for he seems to us like a father among his sons advising and telling us what to do for the best."[53] The next day Elder Rich conducted a special meeting among the miners, in which he disclosed his plan to call them on missions. Boyd Stewart was assigned to Oregon and nine others to the Hawaiian Islands: Thomas Whittle, Thomas Morris, John Dixon, George Q. Cannon (who, in addition to his mining mission, was keeping a store for the Great Salt Lake Trading Company), William Farrer, John W. Berry, James Keeler, James Hawkins, and Henry W. Bigler. These were the first Latter-day Saint missionaries sent to Hawaii. Bigler regarded his call as inspired. Just before coming with Elder Rich to California as a gold missionary, Bigler had recorded in his diary: "Last night I dreamed I was not going for goal [gold] but was going to the islands to preach the Gospel."[54]

By 5 October, Elder Rich had completed his work and left for home. One of those who accompanied him was Porter Rockwell, who left California in a hurry under unusual circumstances. When Boyd Stewart, a former member of the Battalion, challenged Rockwell to a shooting match, hundreds of miners gathered at "Brown's" Halfway House to witness the contest. Rockwell won easily. Because "Brown" was one of the most popular men in town, his winning provided an occasion to celebrate. Bitter in his defeat, Stewart wanted to get even, so he yelled out "Brown's" true identity. Many in the drunken mob were old Mormon-haters from Missouri and Illinois who bore personal grudges against Rockwell. As they surged forward to lynch him, he mounted his horse and got out of town just in time, leaving his profitable California businesses behind

---

[53] Andrew Jenson, comp., "The California Mission," 24 January 1848 (hereafter CM); LDS Church Archives.

[54] Henry W. Bigler, Book B, quoted in Campbell, 153.

forever.[55] The Rich-Rockwell party arrived safely in the Salt Lake Valley on 11 November.

The newly called Hawaiian missionaries left the mines in mid-October, and at Mormon Island they picked up their president, Hiram Clark. On 10 November they met at the home of Brannan's former counselor, Ward Pell, who lived a short distance from San Francisco, and rebaptized him in the Bay.[56] The elders finally sailed for the Islands, despite stormy weather, on 22 November.[57]

California Becomes a State

As gold fever had waned in late 1849, residents began longing for a more stable situation. Miners' law was adequate in the gold camps, where justice was swift and certain and served to prevent total anarchy. However, in the more settled areas, people were interested in a more sophisticated arrangement, including California statehood. To this end, groups began meeting in 1849 to initiate the process. Judge Peter Burnett, Joseph Smith's legal counsel at the time he and other Latter-day Saint leaders were in Missouri's Liberty Jail, was elected president of a group meeting in Sacramento.[58] Brannan and John Fowler were among the five men selected to officially write up the resolutions passed in this meeting. An election on 1 August was held to choose delegates for a constitutional convention. None of those chosen were Latter-day Saints. If the Saints had known how important this formative convention was to their leaders in Utah, they undoubtedly would have been more active in its proceedings.

Simultaneously, the inhabitants of the Great Basin petitioned for their own statehood. However, their petition had a

---

[55] Dewey, 157; Schindler, 190.

[56] CM, 10 November 1850.

[57] Ibid., September–November 1850.

[58] Hubert H. Bancroft, *History of California* (San Francisco: The History Co., 1888), 6:644.

flaw: there was insufficient population for their proposed state of "Deseret." Newly elected U.S. president Zachary Taylor, whom the Saints had supported, now sought their cooperation. Taylor wanted California in the Union but was afraid Congress would impede the effort in a protracted debate over slavery. For several years, there had been an effort in the Senate to maintain a balance between slave states and free states, but the recent admission of Texas as a slave state upset that balance.

To assure that California would be admitted as a free state, the president wanted to counterbalance the many southern transplants in California with the anti-slavery Latter-day Saints in Utah. Therefore, he proposed combining the two areas into one state to be called California, with present-day Utah being "Eastern California" and the coastal region "Western California." Since Utah's population was too small for Utah to be granted statehood independently, joining with California would allow the Saints immediate statehood.

General John Wilson, on his way to California to serve as U.S. Indian Agent, stopped in Salt Lake City in August 1849 and shared President Taylor's plan with Church leaders. Brigham Young approved President Taylor's plan with the stipulation that there be an irrevocable provision whereby "Deseret" would automatically become a separate state in 1851 without further action of Congress.[59] On 6 September, the First Presidency wrote to Amasa Lyman in California, appointing him to work with General Wilson to implement the Saints' plan. The letter to Elder Lyman maintained that regardless of the outcome, "we expect to inhabit that country [California] as well as this [Deseret]."[60] Unfortunately, however, Sierra Nevada snows prevented General Wilson from arriving in California with the petition until it was too late to be considered.

---

[59] B. H. Roberts, *A Comprehensive History of The Church of Jesus Christ of Latter-day Saints* (Salt Lake City: Deseret News Press, 1930), 3:437–39.

[60] JH, 6 September 1849.

Meanwhile, in the fall of 1849, a constitutional convention met at San Jose to consider the matter of California statehood. During the convention, the issue of the new state's eastern boundary was "fraught with the greatest diversity of opinion, fervor, and confusion."[61] While some favored including all the former Mexican territory in the proposed state, others raised questions about the "excessive cost" and even "impossibility of governing so vast a region," and the "undesirability, for some, of embracing the 'peculiar' Mormon community."[62]

When the convention adjourned on 13 October, essentially the present-day eastern boundary, near the Sierra Nevada mountains, was adopted. On 13 November the voters ratified the constitution and elected Peter Burnett as governor, together with a provisional legislature. A certified copy of the constitution was sent to Washington with Capt. A. J. Smith, former commander of the Mormon Battalion.[63]

In January 1850, when General Wilson finally arrived in California, he and Elder Lyman presented their "memorial" to Governor Burnett, who "reviewed the several proposals one by one in a message to the legislature [at San Jose], condemning them all." The pages of his voluminous recommendations outnumbered those of the petition itself. The governor believed that the coastal settlements and the Latter-day Saints in the Great Basin "were too far apart to be united even temporarily, and that 'Texas and Maine might as well be made one state as Deseret and California.'" The assembly dismissed Elder Lyman's proposal without an opposing vote.[64] Had the Saints been more attentive to civic matters and succeeded in getting elected to the legislature, they may have obtained statehood for Deseret from the process. Consequently, Latter-day Saints in

---

[61] Neal Harlow, *California Conquered: War and Peace on the Pacific 1846–1850* (Berkeley and Los Angeles: University of California Press, 1982), 345.

[62] Ibid., 346.

[63] Ibid., 351.

[64] Roberts, 3:440.

the Rocky Mountains would have to wait almost fifty years for that to occur.

President Taylor's fears about Congress were well founded, as debate regarding California's statehood and slavery droned on through the spring and summer of 1850. Finally, the historic "Compromise of 1850" provided for the admission of California as a free state and for the creation of the territory of "Utah" (rather than "Deseret"). On 9 September, California was officially admitted to the Union—the only area to gain statehood without going through a probationary period as a territory. The news reached San Francisco when the USS *Oregon* arrived on 18 October. It had taken this steamship just over a month to travel from the East Coast to San Francisco, a voyage that just four years earlier had taken the wind-driven *Brooklyn* six months. Celebrations immediately erupted in San Francisco and surrounding areas.

As 1850 ended, the sun had set on the gold rush. Church leaders who had strengthened the faith of the California Saints had returned home. But there were plans on the table in Utah for new Latter-day Saint thrusts into what was now "The Golden State."

The San Bernardino Colony: 1851–57

10

Between 1848 and 1852, discussions among Church leaders concerning California typically centered on gold and its implications for the Saints. However, as the supply of this precious metal diminished, the focus regarding California shifted. Between 1850 and 1857, the Church's energies were directed to promoting missionary work throughout the Pacific Coast, with headquarters in San Francisco, and to establishing a colony in the southern part of the state.

Plans for a Southern California Colony

Hope had glimmered regarding a Southern California LDS gathering place for four years—ever since Captain Jefferson Hunt (in May 1847) had described to Brigham Young the beauty and fertility of Isaac Williams's Rancho Santa Ana de Chino, where a contingent of the Battalion had served: "We have a very good offer to purchase a large valley, sufficient to support 50,000 families. . . . We may have the land and stock consisting of eight thousand head of cattle, the increase of which was three thousand last year, and an immense quantity of horses, by paying 500 dollars down, and taking our time to

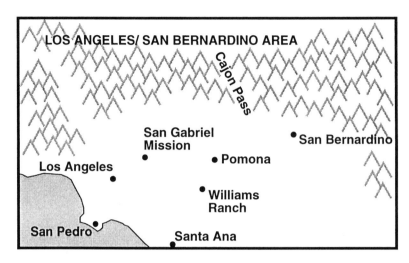

pay the remainder."[1] The owner, Isaac Williams, was an American who had married into the Spanish-California aristocracy. He had repeatedly offered his property to the Church, with attractive terms, as the various Latter-day Saint caravans stopped there for respite.

By 1849, Church leaders contemplated the advantages of having immigrant converts—even some from Europe—come to Southern California by sea and then settle there or travel overland to the Great Basin. To this end, the First Presidency, in late September, instructed Elder Amasa M. Lyman "to obtain all the knowledge he could in relation to good locations for a chain of settlements from G.S.L. City to the Pacific Coast."[2] In response, Elder Lyman took with him "Brothers Hunter, Crismond, and Clift" to ascertain "the practicability of making a settlement of our people in the lower district." He traveled to Los Angeles hoping to intercept the newly arriving Elder Charles C. Rich. Later that year, Elders Lyman and Rich determined to make a settlement in Southern California and launched efforts to purchase land.[3]

---

[1] Journal History, 14 May 1847 (hereafter JH); LDS Church Archives.

[2] Ibid., 30 September 1849.

[3] *Millennial Star*, 12, no. 14 (15 July 1850): 214–15.

In November 1849 a party of fifty, headed by Elder Parley P. Pratt, was sent to explore and recommend future colonization sites along what came to be known as the "Mormon Corridor."[4] Having explored as far as present-day southwestern Utah, the group's recommendations were heeded. The Church began sending out organized parties to colonize virtually all the suggested Utah sites. Still, Church leaders felt the need to complete the corridor by establishing settlements at strategic locations all the way to the West Coast.

Thus, when Elders Lyman and Rich returned home from their California missions, discussions about the various Southern California sites were already well under way. There seemed to be agreement with President Young that a change of focus from gold to agriculture and other pursuits would be appropriate. Since Church leaders had consistently maintained that Saints should settle in California as well as Utah, Elder Lyman began meeting with those interested in migration to the West Coast. He approached several men who had previously been in California, including *Brooklyn* Saints and Battalion veterans, to help him plan a settlement in Southern California. Among those approached were William Glover and Albert Thurber, neither of whom was interested. However, Elder Lyman found an audience among some southern Saints who had settled on a tract developed by him near Holladay, a few miles southeast of Salt Lake City, and who still felt uncomfortable in Utah's harsh climate.

Jefferson Hunt, following a year of gold mining in California, returned to Utah in early February 1851, via the southern route, carrying a letter from Isaac Williams to Charles C. Rich. Once again, Williams offered to sell the ranch:[5] "I make this

---

[4] Donna T. Smart, "Over the Rim to Red Rock Country: The Parley P. Pratt Exploring Company of 1849," *Utah Historical Quarterly* 62, no. 2 (spring 1994): 171–90.

[5] Isaac Williams to Charles C. Rich, December 1850, quoted in George William Beattie and Helen Pruitt Beattie, *Heritage of the Valley: San Bernardino's First Century* (Pasadena, Calif.: San Pasqual Press, 1939), 177.

proposition in consequence of ill health, and not being able to manage things, as the country is at present, as I could wish."

In the "President's office," on Sunday evening, 23 February 1851, Amasa M. Lyman was "set apart to take a company with Elder Charles C. Rich to Southern California, to preside over the affairs of the Church in that land and to establish a strong hold for the gathering of the Saints."[6] Brigham Young authorized Elders Lyman and Rich to recruit others to go to Southern California.

President Young directed the two apostles "to select a site for a city or station, as a nucleus for a settlement, near the Cajon pass, in the vicinity of the sea coast, for a continuation of the route already commenced from this to the Pacific [and] to gather around them the saints in California." He also wanted them to plan a mail route to the coast and to cultivate such subtropical products as olives, "grapes, sugar cane, cotton and any other desirable fruits and products . . . [and] to plant the standard of salvation in every country and kingdom, city and village, on the Pacific and the world over, as fast as God should give the ability."[7]

In March, 437 volunteers, among whom were natives of every state but two and natives of eight foreign countries, met with their 150 wagons at Peteetneet (present-day Payson, Utah, sixty miles south of Salt Lake City), anxious to go even though a sale of the Rancho had not been completed. When Brigham Young traveled south to send them off with his blessing, he "was sick at the sight of so many of the Saints running to California, chiefly after the god of this world."[8] He was so upset at the spectacle that he was unable to address them as

---

[6] JH, 23 February 1851.

[7] "History of Brigham Young," 23 March 1851, quoted in Joseph S. Wood, "The Mormon Settlement in San Bernardino: 1851–1857" (Ph.D. diss., University of Utah, 1968), 69–70.

[8] Quoted in Wood, 71; see also Leonard J. Arrington, *Charles C. Rich: Mormon General and Western Frontiersman* (Provo, Utah: Brigham Young University Press, 1974), 159.

planned. This was "one of the few recorded instances when he was without words."[9]

On 24 March the group left, accompanied by Elders Lyman, Rich, and Parley P. Pratt. Elder Pratt had been appointed mission president "of all the islands and coasts of the Pacific," with headquarters in San Francisco. In addition to his role in selecting the corridor's way station sites, Elder Pratt knew many of the *Brooklyn* Saints from their East Coast days and thus was also prepared to address the difficult matter of Sam Brannan.

The journey was grueling. The California-bound party encountered blizzards, mud, and Indian attacks in Utah, and thirst in the deserts of Nevada and California—at one point going fifty miles without water.[10] On 11 June the last wagon arrived at a previously designated sycamore grove on the edge of the San Bernardino Valley near Devore.

Securing a Place to Settle

Amasa Lyman and Charles Rich went ahead to negotiate with Williams. However, to their astonishment and dismay, he had changed his mind and now refused to sell at any price. One historian has wondered if the boom in the cattle business, due to the growing population in Northern California, had been "a recuperative influence on Williams' health."[11] The party remained camped all summer in the sycamore grove while a search went forward for another site.

The situation became increasingly grave. After extensive searching, the only available land they could buy was the Lugo

---

[9] J. Kenneth Davies, *Mormon Gold: The Story of California's Mormon Argonauts* (Salt Lake City: Olympus, 1984), 306.

[10] "A Mormon Mission to California in 1851 from the Diary of Parley Parker Pratt," ed. Reva Holdaway Stanley and Charles L. Camp, *California Historical Quarterly* 14, no. 1 (March 1935): 59–69; *Autobiography of Parley P. Pratt* (Salt Lake City: Deseret Book, 1970), 371–81.

[11] Wood, 83.

brothers' San Bernardino Rancho. Elders Lyman and Rich had hoped to purchase between eighty and one hundred thousand acres for approximately fifty thousand dollars and were therefore disheartened when the Lugos demanded $77,500 for their property—much more than the price Williams had quoted earlier. Nevertheless, on 29 June, they decided to purchase it.

Elders Lyman and Rich went to San Francisco to solicit enough money from the prosperous Northern California Saints to begin buying the Ranch and to feed their large group of stranded immigrants. For the next several days, with the help of Elder Parley P. Pratt (who was already in San Francisco), Elders Lyman and Rich, graphically depicting their need for help, visited the Saints, the gold missionaries in their camps, and even non-Latter-day Saints. Within two weeks they obtained eight thousand dollars worth of provisions and supplies and seven thousand dollars in cash, including two thousand dollars tithing from John Horner, all of which Elder Rich took back to Southern California on the brig *Fremont*. Elder Lyman remained in San Francisco to continue raising funds.

When Elder Rich reached San Pedro he was met by some forty teams, which the Latter-day Saint settlers had sent to carry the provisions back to their sycamore grove. Elder Rich, deciding to spend the night in Los Angeles, took the cash with him and checked into a hotel there. He did not spend the entire night, however, because "a mysterious something told him to rise and go on." Consequently, he and his companions "took the carriage and started out." At a certain point the road to San Bernardino forked. Rather than choosing the more popular "New Road," Elder Rich decided to take the less-traveled "Old Road." One of their mules became ill near Cucamonga, causing several hours' delay.[12] As Elder Rich's party approached the Saints' settlement after midnight, they heard a gunshot behind

---

[12] A. Harvey Collins, "At the End of the Trail," *Annual Publications Historical Society of Southern California* 9 (1919): 71–72.

them and hurried the remaining distance to the camp.[13] "We learned afterwards," Elder Rich recorded in his diary, "that we were [to be] waylaid by a band of robbers, but passed them after they had given us up and laid down; in which I acknowledge the Lord's protecting hand."[14]

Finally, on 22 September 1851, the Ranch was purchased, with a down payment of seven thousand dollars, leaving a balance of over seventy thousand yet to be paid. The deed was in the names of Elders Lyman and Rich. The Saints immediately took possession of the Ranch, which included some adobe dwellings formerly occupied by Mexican laborers. Elder Lyman's eleven-year-old son, Francis Marion, later recalled that his father's five wives and their families were crowded "into a house with tile floors in two rooms. The other floors were of earth."[15]

Developments in San Bernardino

While still camped in the sycamore grove on Sunday, 6 July 1851, the immigrants held a conference and organized the first stake in California. The apostles called David Seely to be stake president and William J. Crosby to be bishop of the fledgling community. Richard Hopkins, the new stake clerk, kept a meticulous journal which became the best single source for San Bernardino history.[16]

The colonists' unity and resourcefulness were tested almost immediately. The threat of Indian warfare gripped all of Southern California in November 1851 as Chief Antonio Garra

---

[13] John Henry Evans, *Charles Coulson Rich: Pioneer Builder of the West* (New York: Macmillan, 1936), 208.

[14] Quoted in Beattie and Beattie, 181–82.

[15] Albert R. Lyman, *Amasa Mason Lyman: Trailblazer and Pioneer from the Atlantic to the Pacific* (Delta, Utah: Melvin A. Lyman, 1957), 208.

[16] Wood, 85; Eugene E. Campbell, "A History of The Church of Jesus Christ of Latter-day Saints in California, 1846–1946" (Ph.D. diss., University of Southern California, 1952), 193.

*Amasa M.
Lyman
home*

sought to lead a multi-tribe force in driving out all white settlers. Consequently, the Saints chose to follow what was by now a well-established pattern for their colonies. After the land was dedicated by prayer, a fort or stockade was erected which served as a temporary home and community center, as well as a protection against Indians. When the Saints' night-and-day labors were done, the structure was the "most elaborate fortification ever attempted in southern California."[17]

"When our people got the fort nearly inclosed," Elder Rich's wife, Emeline, recalled, "there came a terrible sand storm. It was the worst storm I have ever witnessed. The next morning we learned that this had been the night a certain band of marauders picked to drive us out. To this storm undoubtedly we owed our lives."[18]

The fort was roughly rectangular in shape and measured 300 feet by 720 feet. "The north, south and east sides were made of cottonwoods and willow trunks with the edges fitted tightly together. The logs were sunk three feet into the ground, and they projected twelve feet above. . . . Loopholes were made, bastions built, and the gateways indented to allow crossfire." Log houses along the west side formed the fourth wall, which was finished with timbers placed "in blockhouse fashion." Additional log dwellings were constructed inside the fort.

---

[17] Ibid., 103.

[18] Charles C. Rich Family Association, *Biography of Emeline Grover Rich* (Logan, Utah: 1954).

Some people slept in their wagons. Water from Lytle Creek, which ran through the enclosure, was stored in reservoirs. "A small group preferred to take their chances outside the fort, and camped on what later became the old cemetery."[19] Although Garra was captured and executed a short time after the completion of the fort, the settlers continued to live within its walls for more than a year.[20]

Throughout this period of early development, a spirit of unity prevailed. Though the settlers were restricted to the fort "in a confined space that would test even the most neighborly," there was "no evidence recorded of anything but continuous harmony."[21] Elder Amasa Lyman reported to Brigham Young in September 1852 that "it is our feelings that the spirit of the Gospel is on the increase in this branch of the church, the best evidences of which are exhibited in the disposition of the people to observe and be governed by the council ordained for their edification. They still manifest a disposition to unite their efforts with ours to accomplish the payment for the place."[22]

Church leaders in Utah shared Elder Lyman's optimistic outlook. In a letter to Elders Lyman and Rich, the First Presidency announced: "We have written to Brother Pratt at San Francisco . . . to direct the Saints of the Society Islands to emigrate to your place, and put themselves under your care. . . . Their location . . . for their comfort and convenience will be in the same warm climate, in Southern California."[23] President Young informed Elder Pratt that "we are pushing our settlements south as fast as possible, expecting that Brothers Lyman and Rich will meet us with their settlements this fall," appar-

---

[19] Annaleone D. Patton, *California Mormons by Sail and Trail* (Salt Lake City: Deseret Book, 1961), 139–40.

[20] Beattie and Beattie, 184–87.

[21] Edward Leo Lyman, "The Rise and Decline of Mormon San Bernardino," *BYU Studies* 29, no. 4 (fall 1989): 46.

[22] Quoted in ibid., 61 n. 9.

[23] Quoted in Leo J. Muir, *A Century of Mormon Activities in California* (Salt Lake City: Deseret News Press, 1952), 1:81.

ently indicating he expected the apostles to establish other settlements on the southern end of the Mormon Corridor.[24]

In December 1851, the colonists surveyed a "big field" of two thousand acres. They immediately went to work in a cooperative effort to plow the ground and plant their crops.[25] A year from the time they had purchased the land, the settlers were able to increase the yield as much as twentyfold, harvesting good crops of wheat, barley, and corn, and entering into active competition with the supply that had been coming from Chile and Peru.

Elder Parley P. Pratt, who passed through the colony in September 1852 on his way home from a brief mission to Chile, described a harvest feast in the bowery:

> The Room was highly and tastfully ornimented, and set off with evergreens, specimens of Grains, vegitables etc. While above the Stand was written in Large Letters HOLINESS TO THE LORD. . . . The entire day and evening was spent in feasting dancing etc. Every variety almost which the earth produces, of Skill could prepare, was spread out in profusion, and partaken of by all citizens, Strangers, Spaniards or Indians, with that freedom and good order which is characterestic [of] the Saints.[26]

The Saints were also interested in furthering their intellectual pursuits. They had established a school while waiting in the sycamore grove. When a new Sunday School began meetings on 11 April 1852, Hopkins, the stake clerk, noted that it included "103 as happy-looking scholars as was ever seen, joined in praising the Heavenly Father for the blessings he continually bestows on us."[27] During that same month a bowery was erected to serve as a chapel and day school for local children.[28]

---

[24] Quoted in Albert R. Lyman, 208.

[25] *Millennial Star* 14, no. 31 (25 September 1852): 491.

[26] 4 September 1852: "A Mormon Mission to California in 1851," 180.

[27] Quoted in Campbell, 201.

[28] *Millennial Star* 14, no. 31 (25 September 1852): 491.

Mill at San Bernardino

Elders Lyman and Rich laid out the city in the grid pattern used at Salt Lake City. At its center they designated a "Temple Block," although no temple was ever built there.[29] As the city began to take shape, more families constructed homes and engaged in public works. These projects required lumber, adobe, and other building materials. There was abundant timber in the nearby mountains, so the settlers decided to construct a sawmill there.

Building a road up the steep grade to the timber posed a great challenge. Every man in the settlement was called on to put in all his time and use all his teams and equipment in building the road and moving the machinery up to the sawmill. The resulting road was some twelve miles long and required over a thousand man-days of labor to complete. This was accomplished in just two and a half weeks during May 1852. The route was extremely steep, including grades of up to 41 percent. Unlike most lumber roads, which were private and charged tolls, the Latter-day Saint road was open for public use.

Jefferson Hunt, who had come with the initial colonizing group, was elected to represent them at the first board of

---

[29] Ibid.; Campbell, 201–2.

supervisors meeting in Los Angeles County. He was also elected a member of the state legislature. Largely through his efforts, San Bernardino County was formed from Los Angeles and San Diego Counties in April 1853.[30] It was, and still is, the largest county in the contiguous forty-eight states.

The colony continued to grow and by 1856 had an estimated population of three thousand, making it the largest Latter-day Saint community outside Salt Lake City.[31] Unfortunately, the early optimism, unity, and success did not last.

Problems

As the colony prospered, various forces created challenges. The Church, in a special conference in Salt Lake City on 28 and 29 August 1852, made the first public announcement of its doctrine of plural marriage, or polygamy as it has been commonly called. Though outlawed in California, it was practiced, both overtly and covertly, by some of the Saints. This created controversy among the colonists themselves, as well as animosity among their neighbors.

Slavery was another controversial issue. Several Saints from Mississippi brought slaves with them. One of them became involved in Southern California's "most important slavery case." Robert Smith had brought two black mothers, Hannah and Biddy, and their twelve children and grandchildren with him to California, treating them in a manner somewhere "between freedom and paternalism." When Smith decided to move with them to Texas (a slave state) where, he promised, their status would remain as it was, Mrs. Lizzy Rowen, who had formerly been owned by a Latter-day Saint, reported that Smith actually held them as slaves.

---

[30] Pauline Udall Smith, *Captain Jefferson Hunt of the Mormon Battalion* (Salt Lake City: The Nicholas G. Morgan, Sr., Foundation, 1958), 172; see also Beattie and Beattie, 135.

[31] Campbell, "Brigham Young's Outer Cordon: A Reappraisal," *Utah Historical Quarterly* 41, no. 3 (summer 1973): 242–43.

A trial was held and the judge, a Missouri transplant named Benjamin Hayes, ruled that Smith was viciously hypocritical, particularly in the case of four that had been born free in California. All fourteen slaves were declared free.[32]

As the economic boom fueled by the gold rush leveled off, agricultural surpluses were harder to sell, hampering efforts to make payments on the Ranch debt.[33] To further complicate matters, in 1853 the Saints learned that the property sold to them by the Lugo family contained only about thirty-five thousand acres—less than half of what the Saints believed they had acquired. This presented two substantial problems. First, because there was now less land to be partitioned and sold to individuals, Elders Lyman and Rich realized less cash toward the payment of their debt. Second, individuals interested in settling in the plush valley could purchase surrounding government property less expensively than they could purchase Ranch property. These lost revenues meant further financial difficulty.[34]

By 1853 these and other problems fueled internal strife, especially when Church leaders in Utah expressed concerns about Saints in California and when new arrivals gave only grudging deference to local ecclesiastical authorities. Even Amasa Lyman began lamenting the fact that the "foes against whom we have to contend are not shut out by adobe walls."[35]

Early in the same year, Utah Church leaders asked about apostasy in San Bernardino. Elders Lyman and Rich reported that Henry G. Sherwood, a longstanding member and one of the original Utah Pioneers who had "held many positions of honor and trust in the Church," had "totally failed to do what he promised us when on the way here which was to

---

[32] Rudolph M. Lapp, *Blacks in Gold Rush California* (New Haven, Conn.: Yale University Press, 1977), 120–21; Beattie and Beattie, 186 n. 13.

[33] Edward Leo Lyman, 47.

[34] Ibid.

[35] Quoted in ibid., 48–49.

operate in connection with us in the accomplishment of our labors here."[36]

Simmering dissent boiled over in 1855 during the county election. Although the two official Church candidates (chosen by Elders Lyman and Rich) won easily, their bids for election were contested by several other Latter-day Saints. One local resident, Battalion veteran Henry G. Boyle, observed that "these men came out in opposition to Amasa's nominations, contrary to counsel," and that they manifested a "regular mobb spirit." He specifically noted that "this is the first opposition in elections we have had since we came into the country."[37] Such open dissension rattled the faithful and encouraged the opposition. While the election itself did not cause the strife, it was "certainly a catalyst that brought the conflict into the open."[38] The opposition candidates were quickly excommunicated for apostasy and immediately organized a "factionist" or "factionalist" or "Independent" party in San Bernardino dedicated to breaking the Mormon theocratic hold on the community.

The new party grew quickly. The "factionists" included several once-loyal Church members. Henry Sherwood joined, as did William Stout (the New Hope leader) and Addison Pratt's long-time Polynesian missionary companion, Benjamin Grouard. *Brooklyn* passenger Quartus Sparks also joined and became "the most revengeful and acrimonious" of the former Latter-day Saints in San Bernardino.[39] In the fall of 1855, Richard Hopkins lamented: "The spirit of dissention is daily becoming more evident." Amasa Lyman's early prediction that problems in San Bernardino "would be started by those in our midst" was being fulfilled dramatically.[40]

---

[36] Campbell, "A History," 208; quoted in Edward Leo Lyman, 50.

[37] Henry G. Boyle Diary, 21 April 1855; typescript, Brigham Young University Archives.

[38] Edward Leo Lyman, 52.

[39] Campbell, "A History," 209–11; Wood, 215–16.

[40] Edward Leo Lyman, 53.

The May 1856 elections touched off another round of controversy. The "Independent" party presented a full slate of candidates, and "notwithstanding the fact that only 26 anti-Mormon votes were polled at the municipal election, the spirit of disunion, [a] devastating sickness, was spreading over our once happy place," wrote Hopkins. "It is almost impossible to insure the concert of action upon any object of the public interest. When will this end? The grand object appears to be the aggrandizement of private interests. To be a Latter-day Saint is becoming quite unpopular."[41]

Property claims were a major source of friction in 1856. A government land commission had granted Elders Lyman and Rich the opportunity to select which thirty-five thousand acres they would settle. They delayed a final decision until 1856, when it became apparent that the "big field" would not provide long-term productivity. The more arable lands they chose were along the river bottoms, where many outside the Church had settled during the interim. A conflict between the apostles (rightful owners of the newly designated lands) and the "squatters" heightened confrontations and ill feelings. A particularly hazardous encounter involved a disgruntled apostate named Jerome Benson. After ignoring a court order to abandon his farm, he and several others barricaded his cabin, complete with a cannon. Despite efforts to evict him, Benson remained until after the Saints left San Bernardino. At that time, he purchased a plot of government land some distance away, and his "fort" was razed.

The rift was further widened that year when the Independents decided to have "a regular old fashioned 'back east' Fourth of July celebration." The Church party, however, went ahead with its own plans, and a somewhat humorous rivalry developed between the two groups. "The Independents procured a sixty-foot flagpole. The Mormons searched the mountains until they found one a hundred feet tall." The

---

[41] Richard Hopkins Diary, quoted in Campbell, "A History," 211.

Church group fired its salutes with a "little brass cannon," which their rivals condescendingly termed the "pop gun." The Independents, on the other hand, brought a large cannon from Los Angeles "which made the mountains echo with its deep reports."[42]

Elders Lyman and Rich took various measures to strengthen the Saints. As part of a larger Church movement, the two apostles advocated a "Reformation" beginning in late 1856. They appointed new "missionaries" to the Saints themselves. These new teachers sought to remind them of their duties and encouraged them to increase their faith and obedience. In December the apostles instituted a program of rebaptism, whereby the faithful could recommit themselves. Some five hundred individuals were rebaptized in two months.[43]

To pay off the Ranch debt and solve other financial problems, Elders Lyman and Rich formed a partnership with a wealthy Latter-day Saint, Ebenezer Hanks. A faithful member, Brother Hanks saw this partnership as not only a business venture with the possibility of profit, but also as a duty to the Church. He continued selling property and working toward payment of the debt even after the apostles left in 1857.[44]

In January of that year, Elders Lyman and Rich learned that they would leave later that spring for missions in Europe.[45] At the April conference in San Bernardino, they shared good counsel with the Saints as they bade farewell. In his remarks, Elder Lyman alluded to the possibility that the colony itself, now a hybrid of Saints and apostates, might be closed:

> Suppose you are driven from this land; does this force you to apostacy and to forget God? It does not. What did you come here for? You came to build up the Kingdom of God . . . but you came to build up the Kingdom of God by improving yourselves. . . . If toil and perplexity

---

[42] Wood, 220–21.

[43] Campbell, "A History," 212–13.

[44] Edward Leo Lyman, 57–58.

[45] Arrington, 204–5.

is a reason for us to forget God, we have had plenty of that; but we have not forgotten God nor our duty, and what is true of us should be true of you.[46]

By 18 April 1857 the apostles had settled their affairs and were ready to leave. Feelings ran so high that they needed an "escort of 28 men and the sheriff to see them safely beyond reach of their blustering enemies."[47] Neither ever returned.

The difficulties continued after their departure. On 20 June, a leader of the Independents was accused of killing a Latter-day Saint during a drunken brawl. The accused was arrested and the community became further divided as rumors circulated that the dissidents would break him out of jail. Eventually he was released when a grand jury failed to return an indictment against him.[48]

Speaking in Salt Lake City that same month, President Young was well aware of the mounting difficulties:

> We are in the happiest situation of any people in the world. We inhabit the very land in which we can live in peace; and there is no other place on this earth that the Saints can now live in without being molested. Suppose, for instance, you should go to California. Brothers Amasa Lyman and Charles C. Rich went and made a settlement in South California, and many of the brethren were anxious that the whole Church should go there. If we had gone there, this would have been about the last year in which any of the Saints could stay there. They would have been driven from their homes. It is about the last year that brother Amasa can stay there. Were he to tell you the true situation of that place, he would tell you that hell reigns there, and that it is just as much as any "Mormon" can do to live there, and that it is about time for him and every true Saint to leave that land.[49]

As precarious as the situation was in San Bernardino, it would become even worse. Both internal and external events in 1857 would result in the abandonment of the colony, as will be seen in chapter 12. Nevertheless, the San Bernardino Saints

---

[46] Hopkins, quoted in Campbell, "A History," 214.

[47] Albert R. Lyman, 222.

[48] Wood, 232–34.

[49] *Journal of Discourses* (Liverpool: Latter-day Saints' Book Depot, 1857), 4:344.

left a lasting legacy in roads and structures, in education, and in farming technology. Without doubt the agricultural wealth accrued from Latter-day Saint farmers, who pioneered irrigation and other farming technologies that made agriculture viable in an otherwise uncultivated region, is a far greater heritage than the wealth contributed by digging gold. As Brigham Young surmised, it was agriculture that in the long run proved to be the backbone of California's wealth. And though the San Bernardino colony was short-lived, it made a lasting contribution.

11

The Pacific Mission: 1851–57

During the same years that Latter-day Saints were establishing and maintaining their colony in San Bernardino, the Church's focus in Northern California changed from gold mining and "not much public preaching" to public dialogue and missionary efforts both in the Golden State and beyond.

Elder Parley P. Pratt in San Francisco

Elder Parley P. Pratt was the third apostle to come to California in 1851. On 23 February, at the same meeting in which the First Presidency appointed Elders Amasa M. Lyman and Charles C. Rich to their San Bernardino missions, Elder Pratt was set apart to preside over the "islands and coasts" of the Pacific.[1]

Specifically, he was charged "to open the door and proclaim the Gospel in the Pacific Islands, in Lower California and in South America."[2] He traveled with the large wagon train which went to San Bernardino and arrived in Southern

---

[1] *Autobiography of Parley P. Pratt* (Salt Lake City: Deseret Book, 1938), 371.

[2] Journal History, 23 February, 1851; LDS Church Archives.

Parley P. Pratt

California in early June. During the next several days at Los Angeles he sold his animals, wagon, and other gear to raise money. On Sunday, 29 June, he "preached in the Coarthouse in Los Angelos, to Some forty attentive hearers, Mostly American Gentlemen."[3]

After about a month in Southern California, Elder Pratt and his wives, Phoebe and Elizabeth, took the steamboat *Ohio* from San Pedro and arrived in San Francisco after a rough four-day passage. There he established mission headquarters and renewed old acquaintances made in New York City. The following day, Elders Lyman and Rich arrived from Southern California, hoping to raise money for San Bernardino. In numerous meetings the three apostles rekindled the San Francisco Saints' faith. In the ocean near present-day Fisherman's Wharf, Elder Pratt rebaptized most of the *Brooklyn* Saints still in the area. These immersions represented new beginnings and a recommitment to faith, righteousness, and "membership . . . in all their standing."[4]

Included in this group were George and Hannah Winner, at whose home the San Francisco Branch of the Church was reorganized, with Elder Pratt as president and Philo B. Wood as clerk.[5] In August, the branch began meeting in a large room on the second floor of Barton Mowry's home on the corner of Broadway and Powell Streets.

---

[3] "A Mormon Mission to California in 1851 from the Diary of Parley Parker Pratt," ed. Reva Holdaway Stanley and Charles L. Camp, *California Historical Society Quarterly* 14, no. 1 (March 1935): 72.

[4] Ibid., 72–73.

[5] Ibid., 73.

During this period, Elder Pratt found some time to study and write. He began his noted *Key to the Science of Theology*, authored a "Proclamation of the Gospel" to "the People of the Coasts and Islands of the Pacific," and studied Spanish to prepare for a missionary trip to South America.

After about a month in San Francisco, Elder Pratt reported to Brigham Young that "several new members are being added—some of whom are young people of the old members, and others are strangers from different countries. We are upwards of fifty members in number [about one-fifth the number on the *Brooklyn*]. We have preaching twice a day on Sundays in a large theatre in the centre of the city, and prayer meetings on Sunday and Thursday evenings. Strangers give good attention. The members feel well, and are full of faith and the good Spirit."[6]

One of the converts was Col. Alden M. Jackson, a Mexican War veteran assigned to the Customs House and for whom the California city of Jackson was named. He was a friend of *Brooklyn* passenger Carolyn Joyce, who had loaned him a copy of the Book of Mormon. The Pratts lodged in Mrs. Joyce's home, and on one occasion Elder Pratt and Colonel Jackson stayed up all night discussing the book. When daylight broke, Jackson declared he was converted. He also was baptized at the spot near Fisherman's Wharf. Mrs. Joyce and Colonel Jackson were later married in San Bernardino.[7]

Samuel Brannan Disfellowshipped

As the apostles revived the faith of the Saints, there was one striking exception: Samuel Brannan. When Elder Pratt arrived, Brannan was devoting considerable energy to San Francisco's famed vigilante movement. A 9 February 1851

---

[6] *Autobiography of Parley P. Pratt*, 386.

[7] Augusta Joyce Crocheron, *Representative Women of Deseret: A Book of Biographical Sketches to Accompany the Picture Bearing the Same Title* (Salt Lake City: J. C. Graham, 1884), 106.

beating and robbery of a leading merchant stirred hostile demands for more effective justice. Two suspects were apprehended and identified by the merchant from his hospital bed. They were jailed, and Brannan's voice was loudest in crying for an immediate hanging. However, the two were never tried. Upon interrogation, one claimed that he was a victim of mistaken identity—that he was a British citizen, not an Australian criminal. The two remained in jail.

Then, following the fire of Saturday, 3 May, San Francisco citizens mounted a "determined search for arsonists, with Samuel Brannan organizing a volunteer police department to aid in such investigations."[8] This gave rise to the Vigilance Committee, "organized under the fiery, coarse-grained, and erratic yet resolute and influential Sam Brannan, as president of the executive committee, or directing council and court."[9] Two days later, the vigilantes began dispensing their unique brand of justice. On the evening of 10 June, George Virgin left his office near the Long Wharf to check on the sailing time of a vessel. As he was returning, "he saw a man hastily rowing

Early civic leaders (left to right): Jacob P. Leese, Talbot Green, Thomas O. Larkin, Samuel Brannan, and W. D. M. Howard

[8] Bernard McGloin, *San Francisco: The Story of a City* (San Rafael, Calif.: Presidio Press, 1978), 71.

[9] Hubert H. Bancroft, *History of California* (San Francisco: The History Co., 1884), 6:742; see also Frank Soulé, John H. Gihon, and James Nisbet, *The Annals of San Francisco* (New York: D. Appleton, 1855), 752.

away from the wharf in a small dinghy. In the same dinghy he also noticed his office safe! Virgin's shouts attracted the attention of other merchants and boatmen, who took out after the thief. The man in the dinghy managed to pitch the safe overboard just before he was apprehended."

As the men prepared to take the thief—whose name was John Jenkins—to the police station, George Schenck, who only a few days earlier had joined the Vigilance Committee, "had a better idea. . . . He suggested bringing Jenkins before the vigilantes, who had their headquarters in a group of vacant offices on the corner of Bush and Sansome Streets, in the building that also housed Sam Brannan's real estate brokerage." The rest of the men agreed.

> The sight of a live Australian thief stirred up the vigilantes, who so far had not done very much except draw up a long constitution and give themselves secret numbers. George Oakes, who had been one of the organizers of the committee, was also a foreman of Empire Engine Co. No. 1. He went out and rang the firebell, the prearranged signal for the vigilantes to assemble. When about thirty men had arrived, a trial was at once called in order, with Schenck as the prosecutor and Brannan as the chief judge. No one seemed to think there was any need for a defense attorney.
>
> Around eleven at night, the vigilante court found Jenkins guilty of theft and sentenced him to death by hanging. By this time a crowd of curiosity seekers had gathered outside and was buzzing with rumors. Brannan came out and harangued them about the inadequacies of the law and told them that he and some others had decided that the time had come to take the law into their own hands. At half-past one, Jenkins was led by guntoting vigilantes to Portsmouth Square. A rope was thrown over the beam of the old adobe customs house and a noose was strung at one end of it. The noose was placed around Jenkins's neck; affecting indifference, he continued to smoke a cigar.
>
> Then there was a moment's hesitation, but it was broken by Brannan's cry, "Every lover of liberty and good order lay hold of this rope!" A group of men responded by grabbing the rope. They jerked it down, broke Jenkins's neck, and lifted him off the ground. After a while they tied the rope to a post and kept Jenkins strung up all night. At dawn they allowed the coroner to cut him down.[10]

---

[10] Robert M. Senkewicz, *Vigilantes in Gold Rush San Francisco* (Stanford, Calif.: Stanford University Press, 1985), 4–5.

The committee also hanged three others that summer. One of these, another Australian, seeing that death was imminent, confessed on 11 July that he was one of the men who had beaten the merchant the previous February. He and the man who was erroneously arrested were look-alikes, both with British accents. Had the hasty, immoderate Brannan prevailed, an innocent man would have been hanged.

Many of Brannan's contemporaries, including the historian Hubert H. Bancroft, praised Brannan and the Vigilance Committee for using restraint in rescuing a lawless city controlled by criminal gangs. However others, including more recent historians, have raised questions about the vigilantes' motives.[11] Parley P. Pratt was appalled. At a sacrament service and business meeting held in the Mowry home on Monday evening, 1 September, Brannan was once again disfellowshipped, this time by Elder Pratt "for a general course of unchristianlike conduct, neglect of duty, and for combining with lawless assemblies that commit murder and other crimes."[12] Elder Pratt later reflected that Brannan was an impediment, "a corrupt and wicked man, and had the Church and myself been less long suffering and merciful [in New York during 1845], it would have saved the Church much loss, and, perhaps, saved some souls which were corrupted in California, and led astray and plundered by him. I have always regretted having taken any measures to have him restored to fellowship after he was published in Nauvoo as cut off from the Church. However, if I erred, it was on the side of mercy."[13]

Church Progress Continues

At the same meeting in which Brannan was disfellowshipped, Elder Pratt was released as president of the San Francisco Branch. George K. Winner was sustained in his stead.

---

[11] Ibid., 203–31.

[12] "A Mormon Mission to California in 1851," 176.

[13] *Autobiography of Parley P. Pratt*, 338; see also chapter 2 herein.

Taking his pregnant wife, Phoebe, with him and leaving behind his other wife, Elizabeth (whom he had been introducing as his sister), Elder Pratt departed on a boat for Chile four days later. Elizabeth apparently stayed with friends near San Jose.

Following some rather unsuccessful months in Chile, Elder Pratt and his party returned to San Francisco on 21 May 1852. The next few weeks were occupied in writing letters to the various missions and preparing for a trip home to Utah. Elder Pratt met with the Saints in San Francisco and near Mission San Jose and found them "endeavoring to serve the Lord, and to set good examples of Life, and they met often, to worship and Edify each other and as many as came to their meetings."[14]

He sought to convince others to gather with him to Utah but was able to persuade only three to join his party. "I urged the principles of Gathering, with all the energy of the Gift of God within me," he recorded in his diary, "but all seemingly almost in vain. The World and the Gain thereof Seemed to have a Strong hold and influence over them."[15] Late in July Elder Pratt and his group took a steamer to Southern California and spent over a month with the San Bernardino Saints. They then returned to Utah, arriving home on 18 October.

On 30 June 1852, just before Parley P. Pratt left San Francisco, his relative, Addison Pratt, and Benjamin Grouard returned from their South Seas missions. Being destitute, the newly returned missionaries' families found work wherever they could. Addison harvested crops for John Horner at Mission San Jose. His wife remained in San Francisco where she took in tailoring work. The older Pratt children also found jobs to earn money.

These missionaries found their return to be a difficult adjustment. In Polynesia they had been the leaders who directed their converts' activities and who guided their faith.

---

[14] "A Mormon Mission to California in 1851," 178.

[15] Ibid.

Now they became the followers. Addison found the principle of plural marriage, announced publicly just after his arrival, to be a difficult test. Addison's wife, Louisa, "would wish her husband to demonstrate his faith by adhering to the principle."[16] In September, the Grouards went to San Bernardino, and by December, Addison had decided to take his family there as well.

The regular conferences which the Church held every six months were especially helpful in promoting unity and in increasing faith. In the absence of higher officials, John Horner presided over the April mission conferences of 1853 and 1854, which were held at his home near Mission San Jose. A vote to sustain Church leaders was a regular part of these and all conference meetings. There was also a report of Church activities throughout the mission. Because the branch "was not very lively," missionary William McBride, "who had raised up a branch of the Church in Santa Clara," implored the Saints in Mission San Jose to overcome "the spirit of apostasy" and other "evil influences which manifested themselves."[17]

In the April 1854 general conference in Salt Lake City, Parley P. Pratt was called to another term as mission president in California. Several others were called to missions in the Hawaiian Islands. Elder Pratt left Salt Lake City on 5 May, joined by twenty-three other men and one woman.

One of those men was young Joseph F. Smith, son of Joseph Smith's brother, Hyrum, who had been shot and killed when the boy was just five years old. Early in his life he had to assume the duties of a man, which included driving the family's team of oxen across the Plains. His mother having just died, young Joseph was now an orphan as he headed out for a foreign mission at age fifteen. Nearly half a century later he became the Church's sixth president.

---

[16] *The Journals of Addison Pratt*, ed. S. George Ellsworth (Salt Lake City: University of Utah Press, 1990), 502–4.

[17] Andrew Jenson, comp., "The California Mission," 10 April 1853, 23 April 1854 (hereafter CM); LDS Church Archives.

Young Joseph F. Smith was destitute when he reached San Bernardino, so along with William W. Cluff, another young missionary on his way to the Islands, he went to work making shingles for one of the Saints in the mountains. He then went to San Francisco, where he tried preaching but was bothered by the impertinent things some people implied about his father. He sailed to Hawaii on 8 September.

After spending a few days in Southern California, Parley P. Pratt continued on to San Francisco, arriving there on 1 July. About a month later, George Q. Cannon, Henry W. Bigler, and others who had been sent out by Elder Charles C. Rich four years earlier, returned from their Hawaiian missions. Elder Pratt advised most of them to remain in California until the following spring to earn funds for their trips home. Although times were hard and many people were out of work, most of these elders were able to find employment across the Bay digging potatoes for John Horner. Elder Cannon stayed forty days and helped Elder Pratt write his autobiography. He returned in October to Utah via San Bernardino.

This pattern of missionaries passing through San Francisco on their way to or from missions in the Pacific became increasingly common during the 1850s. At one point, mission authorities even bought their own ship to transport the elders as well as immigrating converts. "An old sea captain" was employed and the missionaries were the crew. When the captain ordered the missionaries to do things they considered "below their dignity and unbecoming to ministers of the Gospel," he almost had a mutiny on his hands. Soon the ship was found to be unseaworthy. Elder Pratt sold it at a loss and abandoned this plan.[18]

Late in August 1854, a colorful and amusing newspaper duel began between Elder Pratt and various Protestant ministers in the area. The 15 September *Christian Advocate* accused the Latter-day Saints of mistreating travelers who

---

[18] *Life of Joseph F. Smith*, comp. Joseph Fielding Smith (Salt Lake City: Deseret Book, 1969), 166–67; *Autobiography of Parley P. Pratt*, 409.

were passing through Utah. In a letter to the *Advocate*'s editor, Elder Pratt vigorously condemned what he considered untrue attacks against the Saints: "You know in your own hearts that you have published lies enough about the 'Mormons' to sink you and those who patronize your publications to the lowest hell with murderers."

The editor sarcastically responded:

> To have a man possessed of divine authority, and capable of raising the dead, threaten us so, is truly awful. Men have pursued us with bludgeons and revolvers before, but this thing of being sent straight to the bottom of the bad place, is a sprinkle more terrific than carnal weapons. . . . A few more such [letters] will cause us to retire to private life.[19]

Elder Pratt also confronted his antagonists in person. On 19 December he lectured on the subject of plural marriage at the Oakland Lyceum, holding forth until 11 P.M. A Presbyterian minister and others responded, but as Elder Pratt later reflected, "Truth was triumphant, and my adversaries confounded."[20]

"Polygamy meets us everywhere," Elder Pratt wrote to Church leaders in Utah, "and we are compelled to satisfy their minds on that before they can possibly be satisfied with our preaching, so we have met it in the press and pulpit and the spirit of truth has almost struck them dumb with amazement and wonder."[21]

Elder Pratt summarized these events in California for readers of the *Millennial Star*, a Church newspaper published in Great Britain: "There is much agitation here, through the public press, &c. The Bible is openly renounced, to keep rid of 'Mormonism.'" He asked the British Saints to pray for him "in this dark corner of the vineyard."[22] Despite the confrontations and Elder Pratt's gloomy rhetoric, the work of the Latter-day

---

[19] *Autobiography of Parley P. Pratt*, 411–12.

[20] Ibid., 422.

[21] CM, 18 December 1854.

[22] *Millennial Star*, 17 (31 March 1855): 198.

Saint kingdom went forward. Letters written by Elder Pratt to Brigham Young during the closing weeks of 1854 reflected this progress:

> We have baptized three new members in the city of San Francisco, one in Union City, some twelve or fourteen in Santa Clara, San Jose City, Santa Cruz, Pajaro, etc., in connection with Brother McBride. Courthouses, schoolhouses, and other buildings have been kindly opened to us, and all our meetings have been well attended. Judges, lawyers, and leading spirits, and many others, have listened with attention to the old members in this country who are alive and rejoicing in spirit and doing all they can, as well as the new ones. I think there are some fifty active members in this upper country and there are many more candidates for membership.[23]

A month later, he wrote: "We have continued to interest a few in these parts and some are being baptized every week. . . . We have some good saints here, and the spirit of the Lord is upon us. We number in all this upper country some sixty or eighty members in good standing."[24]

These membership numbers were about the same as they were three years before, despite the continual outflow to Utah and San Bernardino.

"All is well here among the elders and Saints [who are] wide awake and full of the Spirit of God as a general thing especially in San Francisco and Santa Clara. I never observed a better spirit or more faithful people according to their knowledge and the Spirit of the Lord is like a melting fire in our meetings."[25] By the end of 1854 the mission had officially grown to 120 members in five branches.[26]

It was during this second term as California mission president that Elder Pratt met Eleanor McLean. She was one of several Church members who frequently brought provisions to the Pratts in San Francisco. Her husband's hatred of

---

[23] CM, 25 October 1854.

[24] Ibid., 23 November 1854.

[25] Ibid., 18 December 1854.

[26] Ibid., 31 December 1854.

Latter-day Saints created an incessant jealousy regarding his wife's association with the Saints in general and with Elder Pratt in particular. This jealousy led him to pursue Elder Pratt and murder him in Arkansas just over two years later.[27]

Elder Pratt urged Church authorities to establish a newspaper in San Francisco. He published, in March 1855, a prospectus for the *Mormon Herald* but received "scarcely any encouragement."[28] Deciding that he should return home to his family in Utah, on 16 June 1855 he set apart J. Crosby (probably Jonathan Crosby, husband of missionary Caroline Barnes Crosby) to preside over the San Francisco Conference (or District). Elder Pratt left four days later.[29] Before leaving, however, he crossed the Bay and spent a few restful days near Mission San Jose.

George Q. Cannon's Ministry

While George Q. Cannon was a missionary in Hawaii, he became particularly fluent in Hawaiian. He was a member of a committee that decided to order a printing press to publish his Hawaiian translation of the Book of Mormon. Following the same route as Brannan's press ten years before, it was shipped from New York around Cape Horn and arrived in Hawaii after Elder Cannon left. As Elder Parley P. Pratt consulted with mission leaders in Hawaii, "it was deemed the better plan to remove the press and the printing materials from the Sandwich Islands to San Francisco, California, where Elder Pratt intended to publish a paper."[30]

He asked President Young to send George Q. Cannon back to California to help him. In response, Cannon was called in

---

[27] Steven Pratt, "Eleanor McLean and the Murder of Parley P. Pratt," *BYU Studies* 15, no. 2 (winter 1975): 225–56.

[28] George Q. Cannon, *Writings From the* WESTERN STANDARD *Published in San Francisco, California* (Liverpool: George Q. Cannon, 1864), vii.

[29] CM, 16 and 20 June 1855.

[30] Cannon, v–vi.

George Q. Cannon

1855 to publish the Book of Mormon in Hawaiian and to assist Elder Pratt in publishing his newspaper. Cannon traveled to California via San Bernardino and intercepted Elder Pratt while he was at Mission San Jose. Elder Pratt set Cannon apart as his successor, "to preside over the Pacific Mission, subject to the direction of any of the Twelve Apostles who might visit or be called to labor in that part."[31] There were at the time three apostles residing in the area. One was the president of the Quorum of the Twelve, Orson Hyde, who had recently arrived in Carson Valley to preside over a colony there. The other two were Elders Lyman and Rich at San Bernardino.

Parley P. Pratt never returned to California. George Q. Cannon, on the other hand, was a young man just beginning a long life of Church service, including significant experiences in California.

Elder Cannon's first priority was to finish his Hawaiian translation of the Book of Mormon, a task which was completed 26 January 1856. Because those who set the type did not know Hawaiian, George, with the help of his wife, Elizabeth, proofread the entire text letter by letter. Two thousand copies of the book were then printed.

Next, on 23 February 1856, Cannon began publishing the newspaper Elder Pratt had suggested, calling it the *Western Standard*. In his prospectus, Cannon announced that the paper was "to be devoted to the interests of The Church of JESUS CHRIST OF LATTER-DAY SAINTS—to be an exponent of its doctrines, and a medium through which the public can derive

---

[31] Ibid., vii.

The WESTERN STANDARD

correct information in relation to its objects and progress. Its columns will also contain items of general intelligence and the current news of the day, both foreign and domestic, which from our position, situated in the Queen City of the Pacific, we will be able to obtain at the earliest dates and in ample detail."[32] The paper's masthead carried the slogan, "To Correct Mis-Representation We Adopt Self-Representation."

The *Western Standard* helped unite the Saints by giving them regular information about Church events throughout the area and by reporting other events from a Latter-day Saint perspective. Missionaries commented that the newspaper also aided them by providing helpful doctrinal articles. A non-LDS reader was prompted to write to the paper, indicating that he knew little about the Church but what he did know came from the columns of the *Standard;* he explained that he had inadequate information to say whether the Church was true, but he could say he liked the paper's "bold and manly tone."[33]

Nonetheless, criticism of the Saints intensified during Brother Cannon's California presidency. For example, John

---

[32] *Western Standard*, 1 March 1856.

[33] Cannon, 114.

Hyde, a former Latter-day Saint, addressed gatherings in San Francisco during December 1856 and January 1857. Cannon noted in the *Western Standard* that Hyde's lectures were designated to "expose the workings of Mormonism and the great danger to be apprehended from the admission of Utah into the Union." Hyde ridiculed certain Latter-day Saint doctrines and accused the Saints in Utah of immorality. The *Pacific*, a Protestant newspaper, noted that when Hyde had been in San Francisco as an advocate of the Church a few months earlier, he had preached to large audiences; but now his anti-Mormon speeches were given before only meager groups. The paper concluded, therefore, that in San Francisco it was more popular to advocate than to attack the LDS Church.[34]

The Work Spreads

During the mid-1850s, Latter-day Saint missionary work was extended into various Northern California locations. In 1855 Elder William Shearman went to the mining districts and soon became a leading missionary, finding converts in several places. In four months he and his companions "visited upwards of forty towns including the County seats of Amador, El Dorado, and Placer Counties" where they preached in the courthouses through the courtesy of local officials. They also preached in theaters, temperance halls, churches, ballrooms, and even barrooms. Shearman noted that the people were willing to listen to their message and that after hearing it once, they often extended invitations to the elders to remain and preach again—as many as five times. In their travels, these missionaries often depended on the kindness of the people for food and shelter.[35]

Elder Shearman described the miners as being generally an "intellectual, independent, and generous hearted set of

---

[34] CM, 10 January 1857.

[35] Ibid., 29 February 1856.

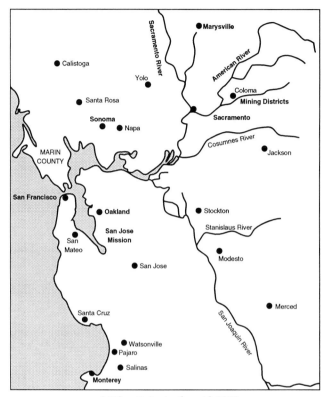

LDS activity in the mid-1850s

men." They were accustomed to think and act for themselves. Even though indisposed to embrace any religious faith, they listened "with attention and respect, with but few exceptions."[36] Elder David M. Stuart, Shearman's companion, attributed their indifference and "spiritual deadness" to their preoccupation with the world's wealth.[37]

Elders Shearman and Stuart found Latter-day Saints scattered throughout the mining districts. Many privately acknowledged Church membership but preferred that it not be known openly. An outsider observed that "while they cherish a belief in the doctrines of their Church, they seem ashamed of

---

[36] Ibid., 29 February, 1 May, and 23 June 1856.

[37] Ibid., 12 May 1856.

the faith within them, and are frequently heard to disavow having any faith or sympathy in common with Mormonism. Away from Utah they become divested of moral courage, and . . . deny what they deem essential to salvation. I speak generally, and, of course, admit that there are honorable exceptions."[38]

Occasionally, the missionaries reactivated members. At Wall's Diggings in Sacramento County, for example, the elders found "a number of stray sheep." The missionaries preached to them twice, rebaptized one, "and left a good warm feeling among the few brethren there, who promised to meet together and hold prayer meeting once a week."[39]

At the October conference of 1856, Elders Shearman and Stuart reported that the sixty identified Latter-day Saints in the mining districts were generally in good standing. At the following April conference, however, Elder Shearman lamented that there were some who were not living their religion as they should.[40]

Mission president George Q. Cannon manifested early an interest in organizing a branch in the mining districts. In February 1856, however, Elder Shearman advised him that he was incapable of sustaining a branch at that time. He pointed out that the few members who would form such a branch were so widely separated by rugged terrain that "it would be almost impossible for them to meet together."[41] To serve their needs, Elder Shearman traveled from camp to camp, keeping in touch with his scattered flock.[42]

There were also missionaries assigned to the counties north of San Francisco. At a conference held in San Bernardino in June 1855, Henry G. Boyle was set apart "to travel in the

---

[38] Ibid., 29 February 1856; quoted in Cannon, 115.

[39] CM, 1 May 1856.

[40] Ibid., 6 October 1856 and 6 April 1857.

[41] Ibid., 29 February 1856.

[42] Ibid.

counties of Sonoma, Napa, [and] Yolo."[43] Boyle fulfilled this mission until October, when he returned home. After working through the winter, he was called again to go to Northern California. He arrived in San Francisco on 22 April 1856.[44]

On 3 August, Elder Boyle reported to President Cannon from Napa City that his meetings were generally well attended and that a spirit of inquiry was manifested by many. He humorously related an incident which reflected a common attitude toward Latter-day Saints. Mr. Sheldon, a Methodist minister who did not know that Elder Boyle was a Latter-day Saint, called on him to address his congregation. Boyle gladly accepted this opportunity, and "it was only a short time until Mr. Sheldon found out that he had waked up the wrong passenger; at first he laughed, afterwards looked wild and somewhat confused, and then hastily commenced turning over the leaves of his Bible." After Elder Boyle finished, Sheldon dismissed the meeting without comment.[45]

As a result of Elder Boyle's labors, the Saints organized two branches north of the Bay. On 29 December 1856, Saints at Buckeye, Yolo County, held a baptismal service at Putah Creek. Elder Boyle baptized eight persons and confirmed them members of the Church.[46] One of them was fourteen-year-old Moses Thatcher, whose Latter-day Saint parents had neglected to have him baptized at the accustomed age of eight.[47] Two days after Moses' baptism, the Saints met again under Elder Boyle's direction and organized the Buckeye Branch. They chose Moses' father, Hezekiah, to serve as the presiding elder over the branch's eleven members.

---

[43] Henry G. Boyle Diary, 26 June 1855; typescript, Brigham Young University Archives.

[44] Ibid., 22 April 1856.

[45] CM, 3 August 1856.

[46] Ibid., 1 January 1857.

[47] Andrew Jenson, *The Historical Record* (Salt Lake City: A. Jenson, 1882–1890), 6:245.

Elder Boyle organized the second branch north of the Bay on 8 March 1857 at Dry Creek, Mendocino County, with twenty members.[48] He then ordained Moses Thatcher an elder when the latter had been a member only three months. The following month, President Cannon called Thatcher, who was "fifteen years of age—a beardless boy," to serve as a missionary and to be Elder Boyle's companion. With a look of dismay, Thatcher "plead with Elder Boyle not to call him to preach or pray in public, saying that if he could be excused from that, he would be Brother Boyle's obedient and willing servant, blacking his boots, waiting on him, caring for his horse and in every possible manner rendering himself useful to his friend." A few weeks later the young missionary attended a meeting at which the speakers ridiculed the Saints. On that occasion Thatcher overcame his timidity and spoke in defense of his faith. The boyhood courage that Elder Thatcher displayed in California not only ingratiated him to Elder Boyle but was the beginning of a life full of service to the Church. Over twenty years later he was called to the Quorum of the Twelve Apostles.[49]

The energetic young mission president, George Q. Cannon, also turned his attention to the counties south of San Francisco. In the October 1856 conference he called Charles W. Wandell to "labor in the Counties of San Mateo, Santa Clara, Santa Cruz, and Monterey." At the mission conference held six months later, Elder Wandell reported that there were no organized branches in his district, but that there were thirty members: four at Santa Cruz, nine at Pajaro, four at San Juan, two at San Jose, one at Santa Clara, two at Mountain View, and eight at West Union.[50]

However, two weeks later the Saints met at Pajaro under Elder Wandell's supervision and organized the Salinas Branch on 20 April 1857. Of the twenty-one original members, twelve had been baptized or rebaptized during the previous two

---

[48] CM, 31 December 1856, 8 March and 1 May 1857.

[49] Jenson, 6:244–48.

[50] CM, 23 April and 31 December 1854, 6 October 1856, 6 April 1857.

weeks. Harvey Whitlock was chosen to be president of the new branch.[51]

The following month, President Cannon noted on a visit to Pajaro that the public there manifested a different attitude toward the Church than found elsewhere; even though many of them were prejudiced against the Saints, they were willing to investigate.[52]

Difficult Times

After the gold rush, there were numerous economic swings, panics, and bank runs. San Francisco banker and future Civil War general, William Tecumseh Sherman, wrote: "California is a perfect paradox, a mystery. The various ups and downs are enough to frighten any prudent person."[53] Letters to Church leaders from the California missionaries inevitably reflected these ups and downs. As an example, mission president Parley P. Pratt, who in 1852 lamented the fact that with all his effort he could convince only three persons to accompany him to the Salt Lake Valley, wrote to Brigham Young just two years later that "the Spirit for Salt Lake is so prevalent here that we must be indulged in the privilege of emigrating there." About four weeks later, he noted that members were selling out and preparing to go to Utah or San Bernardino: "There is no opening as yet for a Stake of Zion here, and with the spirit that now prevails, one can hardly keep them here anyhow."[54]

Despite the ups and downs, however, many Bay Area Saints chose to remain there. One of these was John M. Horner. During the early 1850s he had prospered to the extent that he was able to bring twenty-two family members from New Jersey

---

[51] Ibid., 20 April 1857.

[52] Cannon, 427–29.

[53] T. H. Watkins, *California: An Illustrated History* (Palo Alto, Calif.: American West, 1973), 110–11.

[54] CM, 23 November and 18 December 1854.

to join him in farming near Mission San Jose. Missionaries on their way to or from the South Seas typically stopped at the Horner home, where they received welcome hospitality. In one season, for example, some forty missionaries needed to raise $6,250 for transportation to their fields of labor in such places as China, Siam, and Hindustan. When they, through their combined labor and efforts, were only able to raise $750, Horner generously provided the remaining $5,500.[55]

However, droughts and economic difficulties, climaxing in the nationwide depression of 1857, ended Horner's prosperity. Furthermore, "hoping to do good," he had unwisely endorsed notes and loaned money to many acquaintances. As times became more difficult and money became tighter, those notes were all called due; Horner lost everything, including his home. He had to sell his property for one-sixth its former value. Like Job, Horner recalled his inextricable predicament:

> As afflictions seldom come singly, so it was in my case. . . . My only daughter sickened and died, while my property was being confiscated. I was also personally afflicted. Lock-jaw came upon me with a heavy fever, which lasted a long time. My life was despaired of by my physicians, relatives, and friends. . . . My recovery was slow, and my sickness left me with but little use of my legs; for weeks I used a crutch when moving around.[56]

As Horner's health improved, his ambition returned. "The loss of my property and business placed me financially where I had commenced, eight years before, as nothing much of value was saved from the wreck, except my experience."[57] He started over, renting his former home, and once again successfully growing and selling produce and investing in San Francisco real estate.

Despite the ups and downs, however, the Church generally prospered until about 1854, when polygamy became a

---

[55] John M. Horner, "Adventures of a Pioneer," *Improvement Era* 7, no. 7 (May 1904): 511.

[56] Ibid., no. 11 (September 1904): 849.

[57] Ibid., no. 10 (August 1904): 771.

source of strife not only in San Bernardino but throughout the state, prompting the general desire among the Saints to flee again. Another crisis, in the summer and fall of 1857, compounded these feelings and would lead to the closing of the mission headquartered in Northern California as well as the abandonment of San Bernardino.

A Spiritual Wilderness: 1857–87

12

Until the mid-1850s, Latter-day Saints in California seemed to prosper. Many enjoyed a measure of wealth from mining and other activities despite wild economic swings. Church congregations, small and large, dotted the state. No one would have imagined that within a few years Church activity in California would be almost completely extinguished.

Problems in Utah

In Utah, many of the Saints were experiencing hard times. There had been droughts and crop failures. Some Saints began to waver in their faith. Church leaders suggested that the loss of land, crops, and health were punishments for ingratitude and faithlessness and called for a thorough "Reformation." As a result, some entire communities assembled to pray on their knees for forgiveness and better days.

At the same time, the Saints were being challenged by problems from without. They had chosen to settle the Utah desert primarily to avoid conflicts with their neighbors and to be left alone. Despite this, they rejoiced when their chosen land became part of the United States, even though Utah was granted territorial status rather than hoped-for statehood. But because Utah was a territory, its chief officers were federal appointees rather than Church members, and a war of words and wills resulted between them and the Saints.

For example, while Judge W. W. Drummond professed to be defending solid Puritan morals, he sometimes invited a prostitute, whom he had brought from the East, to sit with him on the judicial bench. Such behavior aroused the Saints' indignation, and under pressure, Drummond resigned. Returning to Washington via California early in 1857, he vengefully accused the Latter-day Saints of rebellion against the U.S. government. In his official letter of resignation, Drummond charged them with destroying court records and asserted that "the Mormons look up to [Brigham Young], and to him alone, for the law by which they are to be governed: therefore no law of Congress is by them considered binding in any manner."[1]

In the previous fall's election, the newly formed Republican Party had promised to eradicate the "twin relics of barbarism"—slavery and polygamy. Now, President James Buchanan and the Democrats were anxious to show the nation that they, too, opposed LDS plural marriage. In a labyrinth of lies and deception, Drummond's letter of resignation was "probably the most important factor in forming the Buchanan administration's image of the Church."[2]

Ironically, though the Church required the Saints to live with integrity, honor, and moral principles tied to sacred marriage vows, critics like Drummond used polygamy as an excuse to ridicule and persecute them but placed no such restrictions on themselves. This was particularly true in California, whose leading city was known for its numerous prostitutes, including Lola Montez, courtesan to European nobility and "special friend" to Samuel Brannan. Throughout California, the outcry

---

[1] Quoted in Andrew Love Neff, *History of Utah, 1847–1868* (Salt Lake City: Deseret News Press, 1940), 448.

[2] James B. Allen and Glen M. Leonard, *The Story of the Latter-day Saints* (Salt Lake City: Deseret Book, 1976), 297–98.

grew ever more vociferous in condemning the Saints' practice of plural marriage.

Without making any attempt to confirm the reliability of Drummond's charges, President Buchanan decided to remove Brigham Young from his office as territorial governor and to send an army of twenty-five hundred men to assure the installation of a new governor. This force was as large as General Kearny's Army of the West during the Mexican War a decade earlier. President Young vowed that no hostile army would drive the Saints from their homes again.

In this tense atmosphere, a disastrous tragedy occurred at Mountain Meadows in Southern Utah. On 11 September 1857, 120 emigrants from Arkansas, Missouri, and elsewhere were ambushed and killed by a group of angry Indians and over-zealous Mormon settlers, perhaps in retaliation for earlier persecutions in Missouri and the recent murder of Parley P. Pratt in Arkansas.[3]

The nation's presses, including some in California, began demanding Mormon blood. The *San Francisco Bulletin* announced: "Virtue, Christianity and decency require that the blood of the incestuous miscreants who have perpetrated this atrocity be broken up and dispersed. Once the general detestation and hatred pervading the whole country is given legal countenance and direction, a crusade will start against Utah which will crush out this beastly heresy forever."[4]

As the U.S. Army approached Utah, the Saints organized a guerilla force to intercept and harass it in Wyoming. The marauders appeared out of nowhere, stampeded the army's animals, blew up its ammunition, set fire to supply wagons, then disappeared again into the darkened prairie. Night after night they took their toll on the army's provisions and nerves. Hungry, freezing, and embarrassed, the army was forced to

---

[3] Allen and Leonard, 303–6; see also Juanita Brooks, *The Mountain Meadows Massacre* (Norman, Okla.: University of Oklahoma Press, 1962).

[4] *San Francisco Bulletin*, 12 October 1857.

make winter camp more than a hundred miles short of its objective.

A Call to Utah

In the fall of 1857, not knowing what the presumably hostile army would do, President Brigham Young called all missionaries who were abroad, as well as settlers in outlying colonies, to come to Utah and prepare to defend Zion. Following these instructions, various groups of Saints in California departed to join the main body of the Church in Utah. George Q. Cannon sent his family with a group of elders and remained a little longer to issue the last number of the *Western Standard* on 6 November 1857. Then, on 3 December, he and others from San Francisco joined "Orson Pratt, Ezra T. Benson, and other elders having arrived from England en route for the Valley," where they planned "to take part in the defence of [their] liberties and homes."[5]

By 2 November, Brigham Young advised the San Bernardino stake president to "forward the Saints to the valleys as soon as possible in wisdom."[6] The following February, Ebenezer Hanks sold the Rancho, paying off the mortgage with a little left over. With Elder Cannon's departure and the Rancho sold, "the official efforts on the part of the Church to maintain an organization within the state of California came to an end."[7]

Estimates of the number of California Saints who headed to Utah run as high as three thousand. Disproving the concerns of some that these Saints were "lukewarm," many loaded all their possessions into wagons and made the long, difficult

---

[5] George Q. Cannon, *Writings from the* WESTERN STANDARD *Published in San Francisco, California* (Liverpool: George Q. Cannon, 1864), ix.

[6] Eugene E. Campbell, "A History of The Church of Jesus Christ of Latter-day Saints in California, 1846–1946" (Ph.D. diss., University of Southern California, 1952), 220.

[7] Ibid., 275.

journey to Utah to fight and, if necessary, die for the kingdom. They willingly gave up everything from their years of labor and returned empty-handed. "The faithful gave up their homes, their farms, their businesses, obliged to sell out for a pittance; those who wanted to acquire the Mormon lands and buildings had only to wait a few days to take possession without any cost at all."[8]

Henry Boyle, former Battalion soldier and one of the more successful California missionaries, reported that the faithful Saints in San Bernardino were "selling out, or rather Sacrificing their property to their enemies. . . . The apostates and mobocrats are prowling around trying to raise a row." He wrote in his diary that the Saints' enemies were "trying to stir up the people to blood shed & every wicked thing." The situation became desperate: "O, is it not Hell to live in the midst of such spirits? They first thirst for & covet our property, our goods, & our chatels, then they thirst for our blood. . . . I think I shall feel like I had been released from Hell when I shall have got away from here."[9]

Joseph F. Smith, now a nineteen-year-old returning from his mission in Hawaii, joined some of the San Bernardino Saints heading for Utah. After they went a short distance and made camp, a group of drunken men approached, cursing and threatening to kill any Mormons they could find. Most of the Latter-day Saints, fearing for their lives, quickly hid in some brush along a nearby creek.

Elder Smith was just returning to the camp with an armload of firewood. "I dared not run," he later recalled, "though I trembled for fear which I dared not show. I therefore walked right up to the camp fire and arrived there just a minute or two before the drunken desperado, who came directly toward me, and, swinging his revolver in my face, with an oath cried out:

---

[8] Irving Stone, *Men to Match My Mountains* (New York: Berkeley Books, 1982), 224–25.

[9] Henry G. Boyle Diary, 16 and 17 November and 4 December 1857; typescript, Brigham Young University Archives.

Joseph F. Smith at age 19

'Are you a — — — Mormon?'" Looking him straight in the eyes, Joseph's disarming reply was, "Yes, siree; dyed in the wool; true blue, through and through." Lowering his weapon and extending his right hand, the drunken man responded, "Well, you are the — — pleasantest man I ever met! Shake. I am glad to see a fellow stand for his convictions."[10]

Many of the San Bernardino Saints settled in Southern Utah near Beaver and Parowan. Not all of the California Saints relocated to Utah, however. Of the estimated 20–50 percent who did not move, most were or became disaffected. Henry Bigler, who returned to Utah from a Pacific Islands mission in 1858, reported that the majority of his contacts in California did not wish to join the Saints in Utah for one of three reasons: some were upset over the Church's now-public practice of plural marriage; some did not wish to leave California's mild climate for a place where, as one settler commented, he would have "to wade up to my neck in snow in order to get a little fire-wood";[11] still others did not wish to be subject to Brigham Young's "high-handed authoritarianism."[12]

Jefferson Hunt, the respected pathfinder, lawmaker, and state leader, was one of the last to leave San Bernardino in early 1858. His three daughters, however, chose to remain behind.

---

[10] Joseph F. Smith, *Gospel Doctrine: Selections from the Sermons and Writings of Joseph F. Smith*, comp. Joseph Fielding Smith (Salt Lake City: Deseret Book, 1978), 532.

[11] Henry W. Bigler, Book G, quoted in Campbell, 280.

[12] Ibid., 282.

His son John returned to San Bernardino in 1859 but took his family back to Utah four years later.[13]

An aging Addison Pratt and his family were also torn apart, as expressed in a letter written by his daughter, Ellen:

> Father has an aversion to a cold climate now he is getting in years. . . . He dreads . . . making another beginning in such a hard place; that is the most disagreement he and mother have. . . . She tries every way to encourage Father about going there . . . but he thinks he cannot go: he loves the Sea air, and wants to live where he can feel it; it makes him look so vigorous and youthful: he is scarcely like the same man. Mother has better courage to live in a hard place. . . . She has great zeal for this cause. . . . Should I believe one quarter of what I hear about the doings up there [in Salt Lake City] I should never dare to come there in my life; but I am not afraid, I shall go when mother does, as sure as you live.[14]

Addison Pratt decided he would stay in California, knowing that if he chose Utah there would be problems with his health, and if he chose California, there would be problems with his marriage. This faithful missionary who had already left home and family four times for island missions and who once felt that his first mission's "exile for Christ's sake" was "penance sufficient with good behavior the rest of my days, to secure me an interest in his kingdom," resolved to stay in California even though his wife resolved to go.

He accompanied her into the Mojave Desert, where he made "every humiliating and condescending proposition, that the case demanded." But she only treated his need to stay with contempt and disdain. There on the desert they parted. "I looked at her, & thought then . . . 'that we had parted forever.'"[15]

The "Utah War" ended peacefully. Following counsel by the Saints' old friend, Col. Thomas L. Kane, in the spring of 1858 President Young allowed two federal officials and the

---

[13] Pauline Udall Smith, *Captain Jefferson Hunt of the Mormon Battalion* (Salt Lake City: The Nicholas G. Morgan, Sr., Foundation, 1958), 196, 229, 233, 238.

[14] Quoted in *The Journals of Addison Pratt*, ed. S. George Ellsworth (Salt Lake City: University of Utah Press, 1990), 510–11.

[15] Ibid., 513–16.

new territorial governor into Salt Lake City without military escort to inspect the court records, which were found to be intact.

Once the truth was discovered and a report made to Congress, the press did an about-face and insistently asked why taxpayers' money had been spent on so foolish an army expedition. A truce was finally signed, and the army entered the Salt Lake Valley peacefully. However, to make sure they understood he meant business, President Young had every dwelling piled with straw and a sentinel at each to strike a match at the least army provocation. Col. Philip St. George Cooke, who had developed respect and fondness for his Mormon Battalion volunteers, was part of the expedition and passed through the city with his head bared and his military hat over his left breast in a reverent salute.[16] The soldiers were then peaceably quartered a good distance away from Salt Lake City, where they remained until 1861.

In 1863, Louisa Pratt visited her family that had remained in California and persuaded Addison to return to Utah with her. Upon their arrival, they chanced upon a traveling party that included President Brigham Young. "Brothers Young and Kimball alighted from their carriages and came to ours, and saluted Brother Pratt in the cordial manner, congratulating me on my success in having been to California, and returning brought my husband with me. They blessed us in the name of the Lord."[17]

However, as he had suspected, Addison suffered terribly through two Utah winters before returning ill to the coast, where he made a final home for himself with his daughter in Anaheim. He died there on 14 October 1872, still full of faith

---

[16] Norman F. Furniss, *The Mormon Conflict, 1850–1859* (New Haven, Conn.: Yale University Press, 1960), 201–2.

[17] Louisa Barnes Pratt, *Mormondom's First Woman Missionary: Life Story and Travels Told in Her Own Words*, ed. Kate B. Carter (Utah: Nettie Hunt Rencher, 1950), 352.

and loyal to his Church. He was buried in the Anaheim cemetery.

The LDS Remnant in California

As the crisis in Utah passed, many of the families from San Bernardino began returning to California. By 1860, the Saints again formed a majority of the San Bernardino community.

One of those returning was David Seely, the original San Bernardino stake president. After moving to Utah, he had a disagreement with Brigham Young, who told him he might just as well go back to California.[18] Seely was dropped from the Church and remained in California looking after his timbering interests. Although more than half of the original San Bernardino colonists remained in or returned to California, none of their leaders were ever replaced, and no official Church organizations were ever reconstituted. Even without spiritual leadership, many retained their faith. Others lost their unique LDS identity, joining mainline churches or drifting away from religion altogether. Still others remained believers in the restored gospel and the mission of Joseph Smith but rejected Brigham Young and polygamy; most of those found their way into the Reorganized Church of Jesus Christ of Latter Day Saints. Where there had once been flourishing LDS congregations, RLDS groups now appeared. The San Bernardino Branch became the largest RLDS congregation in the West.[19]

Returning in 1864 from a mission to Hawaii, John R. Young discovered only a handful of still-faithful members in California. Notable among those few was John Horner, who related the story of his conversion. He said that

> when he was a boy the Prophet Joseph Smith and Oliver Cowdrey had called upon the Horner family. John M. wanted to visit with the

---

[18] Campbell, 282–83.

[19] J. Kenneth Davies, *Mormon Gold: The Story of California's Mormon Argonauts* (Salt Lake City: Olympus, 1984), 315.

young prophet, but his father insisted that he finish hoeing a piece of corn given him as a stint. Joseph, on learning of it, took off his coat and asked for a hoe and helped finish the task. As a result Horner was baptized by Oliver Cowdrey and confirmed by Joseph Smith, who predicted that the earth should yield abundantly at Bro. Horner's behest.

By the time of John Young's visit, Horner had paid some twenty thousand dollars tithing on his agricultural profits.[20]

He remained in California until 1879 when he moved to Hawaii to live out his last days. Upon journeying to San Bernardino, Young found only a few Saints and no organization. The family of Col. Alden Jackson was among the faithful, and Young spent the winter with them. During his stay he convinced the family to relocate to Utah and even drove one of their teams in order to pay his way to Salt Lake.[21]

When Porter Rockwell was recruited as a guide to escort Lt. Col. Edward Steptoe from the Great Basin to California, he visited acquaintances in the gold country. One of these was Agnes Pickett, the widow of the Prophet Joseph Smith's brother, Don Carlos. She was recovering from a bout with typhoid fever which had caused her to lose all her hair.

Rockwell, who had long been a close friend of the Smith family, knew that to both him and Agnes, hair was worth more than its intrinsic value. Like the biblical Samson, he had received prophetic promises contingent upon never cutting his hair; like Samson, he attributed his successes to it. But because he had nothing else to relieve her embarrassment, "he had his hair cut to make her a wig and from that time he said that he could not control the desire for strong drink, nor the habit of swearing."[22] However, Rockwell, despite his cut hair, lived a long life and died a peaceful death in his bed in Utah.

---

[20] "Journal History of the San Bernardino Mission," 5 December 1864, quoted in Campbell, 290–91.

[21] Ibid., 291–92.

[22] Harold Schindler, *Orrin Porter Rockwell: Man of God, Son of Thunder* (Salt Lake City: University of Utah Press, 1966), 224.

Agnes's daughter, Josephine Donna Smith (named after her uncle, Joseph, and her father, Don Carlos), was a gifted poet who was about eleven years old when her family came to California. After a tragic marriage and divorce in Los Angeles, she moved with her mother and stepfather to the San Francisco area and remained there, unmarried, for the rest of her life.

Ina Coolbrith

She took as her pen name a shortened version of her own given names (Ina), and her mother's maiden name (Coolbrith), becoming Ina Coolbrith. Just twenty years old when she moved to San Francisco, she was welcomed in local literary circles, her verse having been widely published already. Yielding to the demands of her stepfather, she did not identify herself as a Latter-day Saint. Still, her spiritual sensitivity is reflected in "this simple creed: 'Love thou thy God; thy neighbor as thyself; Forgive, as thou dost hope to be forgiven!' and lo! we have sweet Heaven about us on the earth."[23] A half-century later she was named "Poet Laureate" of California.

Coolbrith became a key factor in creating California's "Golden Age" in literature. She was closely acquainted with and influenced such illustrious writers as Bret Harte, Charles Warren Stoddard, Mark Twain, Henry George, Prentiss Mulford, Jack London, and Joaquin Miller. Jack London, remembering her as an invariably kind and gentle Oakland librarian who had befriended him and had opened the world of literature to him when he was little more than a street waif, called her his "literary mother." She never wrote an auto-

---

[23] Josephine DeWitt Rhodehamel and Raymund Francis Wood, *Ina Coolbrith: Librarian and Laureate of California* (Provo, Utah: Brigham Young University Press, 1973), 374.

biography, although friends urged her to do so. She laughingly replied: "Were I to write what I know, the book would be too sensational to print; but were I to write what I think proper it would be too dull to read."[24]

Some other notable Latter-day Saints remaining in California were members of the Garlick family. Aaron and Mary Garlick were young British converts who came west by wagon, passing through Utah and going on to California in the spring of 1857, just before the Saints were asked to abandon the Golden State. Mary was pregnant, and both she and Aaron were too exhausted and poor to go back, so they lived out of their wagon for a year, where their eldest son was born. By the time they had sufficient strength and means, the Utah crisis had passed. They bought a home at 108 2nd Street in Sacramento, where they remained for many years as the focal point of an on-again, off-again LDS branch. They became prosperous and respected Sacramento citizens.

Aaron joined the Reorganized Church, where he served diligently and even held the position of branch president. Some time in 1870, however, Garlick "discovered his mistake, and relinquished the presidency, priesthood and membership in that organization" and asked to be rebaptized a Latter-day Saint.[25]

Brooklyn Saint Thomas Eager, an Alameda County supervisor, proposed in 1856 that the communities of Clinton and San Antonio Redwoods, where he had resided since entering the lumber business in 1849, be combined into a town called "Brooklyn" in memory of the ship that had brought him to California. Eager continued his public service as a member of the California state legislature from 1861 to 1869, during which he served a term as sergeant at arms. His town bore the Brooklyn name until 1872, when it was annexed to Oakland and became that city's Seventh Ward.

---

[24] Annaleone D. Patton, *California Mormons by Sail and Trail* (Salt Lake City: Deseret Book, 1961), 152.

[25] Philip Leuba to *Deseret News*, 6 February 1896, quoted in Campbell, 294.

A former private in Mormon Battalion Company E, Daniel Brown remained in Watsonville with his mother, Mary A. Brown, and is buried there with her in the Pioneer Cemetery.

Samuel Brannan's Fortunes

Undoubtedly the best known of the Latter-day Saints—or former Latter-day Saints—who remained in California was Samuel Brannan. In 1853, two years after he had cleaned up San Francisco with his Vigilance Committee and was disfellowshipped from the Church, Brannan was elected to represent California's most important city in the state senate. He claimed he would refuse to serve but was elected over his objections as a write-in candidate. However, when he went to the East on business, he was replaced. Before he left, he agreed to reorganize the prestigious California Society of Pioneers, which he had helped found, and he served a term as its president.

According to a family tradition, on that trip he visited his first wife, Harriet, and their daughter, Almira, and brought them to California at his expense with the understanding that they would not reveal their identities. In 1855, soon after their arrival, "Hattie" went to Los Angeles and obtained a divorce.[26]

Later, when Brannan was at the height of his wealth and fame, he and his

Samuel Brannan

---

[26] Reva Scott, *Samuel Brannan and The Golden Fleece* (New York: Macmillan, 1944), 331–34, 361–62. See n. 5 in chapter 2.

Brannan's newspaper office

wife, Eliza, went to Europe, where their reputation as California millionaires preceded them. Brannan bought sheep and vines to export to California. Although he returned, Eliza insisted on staying in Europe and educating their children there.

On 21 October 1857, as George Q. Cannon prepared the last issue of the *Western Standard* and most Latter-day Saints readied to leave the state, Brannan opened his bank at the northeast corner of Montgomery and California Streets. One of his biographers asserts that he was "the acknowledged financial leader of the city and the titan to whom all other businessmen deferred."[27]

It was the practice of the time for large banks and other financial institutions to issue their own currencies, which Brannan's bank did. During the 1860s, while the United States was embroiled in a civil war, many people preferred Brannan's currency to that of the federal government.[28]

Brannan also began developing a large, mile-square resort north of San Francisco for which he coined the name "Calistoga." The resort contained a hotel, avenues lined with palms and thirty cabins, a roller-skating rink, a natural hot-springs pool, a reservoir of clear mountain drinking water (pure spring

---

[27] Ibid., 376.

[28] Paul Bailey, *Sam Brannan and the California Mormons* (Los Angeles: Westernlore, 1943), 216–17.

One of Brannan's guest cottages in Calistoga

water is still bottled and sold under the Calistoga label today), horse barns, trails, and a racetrack.[29]

For ten years after the Saints' departure from California, Brannan rode the crest of business success. In 1868, at age forty-nine, he was part of an investment group that bought nearly 180,000 acres of what is now Los Angeles. But that year his empire began to crumble.

Brannan invested $125,000 in Hawaiian land and had to sell for $45,000. He became increasingly incapacitated by alcohol when his temperate brother, who had been a steadying influence in his life, died.[30]

On top of these difficulties, a band of disgruntled workmen took possession of a sawmill they had been building for him at Calistoga. Accompanied by a force he had organized, Brannan advanced on the mill one bright, moonlit night. When the workmen ordered them to halt or be shot, the force fled, but the irate Brannan, impetuous and headstrong, continued to advance alone. A volley was discharged from inside the Mill and Brannan fell, riddled with bullets. About thirty bullets either pierced his clothing or penetrated his body. Though

---

[29] Today in the town of Calistoga, the Sharpsteen Museum preserves a diorama of the resort, together with one of Brannan's original cabins.

[30] Bailey, 224–25.

some were surgically removed, he was left a cripple, walking with a cane the rest of his life.

In 1870 Eliza returned from Europe with their grown children and sued for divorce. She demanded half their property in cash, forcing him to liquidate his assets at disastrously low prices.[31]

In 1878 Brannan went to Mexico City to press the Mexican government for repayment of the nearly $80,000 he had lent them to finance a hundred-man army in their war against France. They only sneered at him and gave him a huge tract of Sonora, but no cash. Unknown to him, the land was also claimed by a fierce tribe of Yaqui Indians, making it unusable for Brannan. He lost heavily not only in that venture, but also on every other investment he made during the depressed 1870s and outside his beloved California.

Having moved to Guaymas on the Gulf of California in 1882, at age sixty-three Brannan married an attractive thirty-one-year-old daughter of "a prominent Mexican family."[32] The following year, the *Deseret News*, the Church's newspaper in Salt Lake City, published a description of a slovenly Brannan submitted by three men who had just visited Brannan in Mexico: "He was partially paralyzed, in the depths of poverty, residing in a little shanty, friendless, and living in the most groveling forms of vice. . . . He was half naked and filthy, a pitiable spectacle to behold."[33] A reader who read the sordid description regarded these circumstances as a fulfillment of prophecy: "In 1854, while the late Parley P. Pratt was on a mission on the Pacific Coast, he was informed that Mr. Brannan, then a millionaire, was very much afraid some one would kill him for his money. Parley P. Pratt said: 'Go, tell Sam

---

[31] Ibid., 227.

[32] Samuel Brannan, "A Biographical Sketch Based on Dictation," 12, MS, C-D 805; Bancroft Library, University of California at Berkeley.

[33] *Deseret News*, 27 February 1883.

Brannan from me that he shall not die till he is in want of ten cents to buy a loaf of bread.'"[34]

When Brannan learned about these articles, he vigorously refuted them:

> With regards to the prophesy of Parley P. Pratt, as printed in the *Deseret News* sometime since, that I would die a pauper—I don't believe he ever uttered it. If so, he must have been drunk or crazy. . . . The whole yarn is a pure fabrication of their own.
>
> I can hardly consider my circumstances extremely desperate; and not withstanding they reported I was living in a "dug out." I own ten lots and two houses here, all rented at good rates. My wife also owns a large double house and lot from which she derives a nice little revenue; and we board with her daughter.[35]

However, Brannan's fortunes took another turn for the worse. Four years later, after his Mexican wife left him, he sold pencils on the streets of Nogales. He then returned to San Francisco, where he is said to have slept on a bench on a street he once owned, in front of a hotel he once owned, now unable to pay twenty-five cents for a room.[36] He visited the hall of honors at the California Society of Pioneers, stood in front of a portrait of himself as a young, handsome, powerful man, and wept.[37] He was asked by the California historian, Hubert H. Bancroft, to provide an account of his life's experiences. However, the cold weather inflamed his old wounds, and he soon left for the warmer San Diego environment where his tent house and historical manuscript were washed away in a flood.

At the bidding of Brannan's nephew, the Odd Fellows lodge, which Brannan had founded and financed, gave him a small monthly stipend. This allowed him to move into an apartment and hire a cleaning lady to help out each week.

---

[34] Ibid., 8 March 1883.

[35] *Salt Lake Tribune*, 31 May 1883.

[36] Scott, 438–39.

[37] *San Francisco Bulletin*, 20 May 1916, 1.

Samuel Brannan's grave in San Diego

Finally, in May 1889, just two months after his seventieth birthday, Brannan, isolated in his San Diego apartment, died of inflammation of the bowels.[38] There was no funeral, nor family or friends, to mourn his death or to memorialize his accomplishments. His remains lay unclaimed in a public vault for sixteen months before his nephew, Alexander Badlam Jr., arranged for a proper burial. As President Brigham Young had prophesied forty years before, there was, in the end, "no arm to save" the man once so highly esteemed by some of the nation's best and brightest.[39]

Samuel Brannan was indeed a paradox. One biographer summed up his life as follows: "'No penniless stranger seeking provisions or goods ever left his store without being supplied.' And it was true. Sam, who robbed with one hand his brothers in religion, his old friend Sutter, and others, helped with the other any needy stranger who presented himself."[40]

Brannan was buried in San Diego's Mount Hope Cemetery with only a plain wooden stake marking his grave. In 1926, someone provided a granite marker.

---

[38] Scott, 441.

[39] Journal History, 5 April 1849; LDS Church Archives.

[40] Scott, 235.

The Church Comes out of the Wilderness

During the 1870s, tentative steps were taken to reestablish the Church in California. During the fall of 1871, when Elder Philip Leuba was on his way as a missionary from Salt Lake City to his native Switzerland, he met the Garlick family during a stopover in Sacramento. On 29 October, at Aaron Garlick's request, Leuba rebaptized him a member of the Church and also ordained him to the office of elder. His wife and their two sons were also baptized. On 5 November, Leuba appointed Garlick to preside over the branch which at that time consisted of only six members. In April 1873 Garlick wrote to Brigham Young "inviting all travelling missionaries who came through Sacramento to call on the little branch."[41]

The next known attempt at reorganizing the Church in California was made in 1876. Job Taylor Smith, an Ogden businessman going to California for his health, was called to "take a mission to the Pacific States." Leaving for California by train on Christmas Day, he was startled by a man who verbally attacked the Latter-day Saints "in a very malignant manner . . . but fortunately he kept his hands off. The passengers on the car were all disposed to hear the Mormons abused, and seemed to enjoy the scene." Arriving in Sacramento on 27 December, Smith was "hospitably received and lodged at Aaron Garlick's" and found a "small branch of the church numbering about 12 persons in good standing."[42] Within four years the branch would grow to twenty members.

In January 1877 while Smith was still in Sacramento, California newspapers widely covered the execution of John D. Lee for his role in the Mountain Meadows Massacre twenty years before. The newspapers also accused Brigham Young of being primarily responsible for the tragedy. Deeply affected by these attacks, Job Smith climbed to the top of the state capitol, where

---

[41] Campbell, 292–95.

[42] Job Smith Diary.

he knelt and prayed that God would "bless the cause of Zion . . . when the Legislatures of this State, or any other body of men, shall in this State House, design, plot, discuss or enact measures for the injury, downfall or disadvantage of thy Saints. . . . May confusion enter into their counsels until they suffer defeat."[43]

On 15 January 1877, Elder Smith visited *Brooklyn* passenger William Atherton and his wife at their home in Oakland. They had joined the Reorganized Church, but Smith rebaptized them in the San Francisco Bay. On 4 March, Atherton was "appointed by unanimous consent to preside over the Saints in Oakland."[44]

Smith noted that most people in the area "revile the Mormons because of having a plurality of wives, and suppose them to be the most corrupt people upon the earth." Nevertheless, Brigham Young, who still had not given up on San Francisco, instructed Elder Smith: "We shall be glad to have you organize the branch of the church in San Francisco. We should have a place there." On 6 April, Smith helped organize a local branch of the Relief Society. Later that month he returned home to Ogden.[45]

That same year, three months before Brigham Young's death, the First Presidency wrote to Smith: "You are hereby appointed to take charge of and preside over the mission of the Church of Jesus Christ of Latter-day Saints in California, to assign the elders who may accompany you and others who may be called to labor with you in the ministry there . . . [and] to organize branches and conferences." The First Presidency also instructed him to "secure a tract of land" where the Saints could gather and live according to the principles of the cooperative "United Order." He was further instructed to investigate the profitability of raising crops and of cultivating willows for basket weaving. "Should you cultivate the grape,"

---

[43] Ibid.

[44] Ibid.

[45] Ibid.

the letter continued, "do not enter into the manufacture of wine, but cultivate the raisin grape."[46]

Smith accordingly returned to California, where he organized the Oakland Saints into a cooperative. "By putting their means together," they attempted to operate a boarding house, green grocery, and chair caning business. However, partly because the branch had only sixteen or eighteen scattered members, some of them blind and others "more or less unemployed," the branch soon fell apart. The dissolution was "amicably accomplished" in November, and Elder Smith, "having received an honorable release," returned home.[47]

The trickle of Latter-day Saints leaving Utah to make homes in California increased during the 1880s, partly because of the growing persecution in Utah of those practicing plural marriage and partly because of a "land boom" in California that rivaled the gold rush.

The passage of the Edmunds Act in 1882 intensified the anti-polygamy campaign. The first prosecutions began almost immediately with stiff prison terms handed out to convicted male violators. Dozens of federal marshals posed as census takers or peddlers, bribed children to get information about their parents, spied through windows, and in various other ways sought to apprehend polygamists. While working as a night watchman in the Church Tithing Office, Joseph W. McMurrin, who would later figure prominently in California LDS history, was shot and seriously wounded by one of those marshals.

Several husbands, often in jeopardy of being arrested, went into hiding on the "underground." Among them were the entire First Presidency—President John Taylor and his two counselors, George Q. Cannon and Joseph F. Smith. Rewards were offered for information leading to the arrest of those accused of polygamy. When a bounty of five hundred dollars

[46] Quoted in ibid.

[47] Ibid.

was placed on President Cannon's head, he was apprehended on a San Francisco-bound train, returned to Utah, and sentenced to prison.

With husbands and fathers in prison or in hiding, it was probably the women and children who suffered most from what they called "The Raid," as they were left alone without means of support. In order to avoid these problems, many individuals and families fled to outlying areas—including California—where they became the nuclei around which the Church subsequently grew.

Though Utah had already recognized the right of women to vote, in February 1887 Congress tightened their grasp on the Saints with the Edmunds-Tucker Bill, which abolished women's suffrage in Utah. The new law also required residents to swear, prior to being given the right to vote, that they were not polygamists and provided for the confiscation of the Church's assets, even including Temple Square in Salt Lake City. Later that year, President Taylor died, a polygamist in exile.

Sixty years after the Church was founded, hostile forces now seemed to prevail. The Church as an institution was left without legal charter or monetary assets. Once again, the Saints stood vulnerable to the actions of a government whose Constitution guaranteed religious liberty. Forty years earlier California gold had helped save the Saints. Now, again, they turned to their Pacific neighbor for assistance.

New Beginnings: 1887–1900

13

In its early years, California had its ups and downs. There were exciting gold discoveries and wild speculations in land, mining, and railroad stocks. But interspersed among these were periods of economic depression. By the 1880s, California had become stable and sober, providing a setting more conducive to the replanting of Latter-day Saint roots.

The Saints had likewise been through their own years of sobering and leavening. Continuous challenges—repeated persecutions, forced uprootings from their homes, an epic overland migration, a hard desert, and the onslaught of a hostile United States army—had crystallized within them a solid confidence in themselves and in their faith. This, together with improved communications and transportation, prepared them to reach out and write a new chapter in their California history.

Seeking Help in California

The new chapter began when Wilford Woodruff succeeded John Taylor as president of the Church. The changes he would institute were so dramatic that they now rank among the most important in Latter-day Saint history. His

Wilford Woodruff

life's experiences helped prepare him to provide leadership for the new opportunities which were opened to the Church during the 1890s. Interestingly, both of his counselors, George Q. Cannon and Joseph F. Smith, had spent time in California.

When President Woodruff took over, the Church's very survival was hanging in the balance. Not only had it been disenfranchised by the 1887 Edmunds-Tucker Act, but some members of the U.S. Congress were now urging even more drastic measures which would effectively deprive every Latter-day Saint of the right to vote. The situation was discouraging.

President Woodruff was convinced that he needed to take action. An aggressive pursuit of Utah statehood might be the answer. Where could he turn? Utah representatives in Washington could not help, because they had little influence there.

Some of President Woodruff's early missionary success was in Saco, Maine, where the Brannans and Badlams had lived. It was after he had served there that the Badlams took young Samuel Brannan with them to settle near Kirtland, Ohio. The Badlams' son, Alexander Jr., was now politically well connected and respected in San Francisco. So in September 1887, just a few weeks after President Taylor's death, President Woodruff made a trip to California and contacted Badlam.

President Woodruff also met with Col. Isaac Trumbo, grandson of LDS Pioneer John Reese, the man who had founded a town called Mormon Station in Carson Valley on the California-Nevada border. Trumbo had lived in Utah and still had significant business interests and connections there as well as in California. Would Badlam or Trumbo be willing to raise their voices on behalf of the Latter-day Saints?

The two men promised to enlist the help of California's powerful senator, Leland Stanford, into whose hands much of Samuel Brannan's fortune had fallen and who had visited Utah in 1869 to drive the "golden spike." It was hoped that Stanford respected the Saints enough to raise his voice on their behalf. Badlam and Trumbo promised to promote Utah statehood among national Republican leaders and even went to Washington under assumed names to lobby for this cause.[1]

In April 1889, President Woodruff took further action. He brought a prominent group of Latter-day Saints to California, where Badlam and Trumbo arranged two meetings with Senator Stanford. Though these visits were crucial events in Latter-day Saint history, little is known about their details. President Woodruff described Stanford as "a good friend of ours," who was ready "to do everything in his power for our good."[2]

Shortly after President Woodruff's return to Utah, the Church ceased authorizing new polygamous marriages and dismantled the adobe Endowment House where they had been performed. To emphasize this new position, President Woodruff issued a sworn statement dated 24 September 1890 that became known as the "Manifesto." It was subsequently canonized into Latter-day Saint scripture (Doctrine and Covenants, Official Declaration 1).

Although a few felt that their leaders had "sold out" to government demands, President Woodruff testified: "The Lord showed me by vision and revelation exactly what would take place if we did not stop this practice. . . . I went before the Lord, and I wrote what the Lord told me to write."[3] Truly,

---

[1] Thomas G. Alexander, *Things in Heaven and Earth: The Life and Times of Wilford Woodruff, A Mormon Prophet* (Salt Lake City: Signature Books, 1991), 249–50.

[2] Quoted in ibid., 252.

[3] *Deseret Weekly News*, 14 November 1891.

Wilford Woodruff's vision was a turning point, not only for the Saints in California, but for the Church as a whole.

Over the course of time, Mormonism cooled as a controversial issue. The press, which had used plural marriage to make the Church a whipping post, instead began to recognize in the LDS people some of the virtues then being advocated by the American Populist movement—industry, thrift, temperance, and self-reliance.

A little more than two years later, the government was convinced that sufficient time had passed to prove the Church's good intentions, so it issued a proclamation of amnesty to all those who had entered into polygamist relationships before 1 November 1890. Soon afterwards, the government returned the Church's confiscated property. A new climate of goodwill resulted as the Saints and their fellow Americans genuinely desired to tolerate one another. Utah was finally admitted to the Union in 1896.

The First Presidency also shifted the Church's longstanding emphasis on gathering to Utah. During the 1890s, the Church began encouraging its members to remain in their homelands, to gather others about them to help build local branches, and eventually to organize wards and stakes there. This new emphasis had been anticipated in Joseph Smith's revelations which specified that the time would come when the Saints would gather in more places than one (D&C 101:20–22; 115:17–18). In this context, and with the issue of polygamy resolved, the Church returned to California.

Sharing the Gospel in Oakland

The new beginnings in California developed around families and individuals who had fled from Utah to avoid government persecution. In fact, by the time President Woodruff issued the Manifesto, a permanent presence of Church members in California was already established.

Norman Phillips, one of the original six members in a newly formed Oakland branch, who for over twenty-three years served as clerk and then as president in the first permanent branch in the state, left an account of these beginnings. According to his record, it began in July 1890, two months before the Manifesto was issued, when Mark Lindsey, his wife, and two children arrived in Oakland as polygamous refugees from Utah. Although a few other members of the Church were in the city, Lindsey was unaware of them.

One morning, Lindsey saw a man walking in front of him whom he felt impressed to follow. This individual turned out to be Bishop Cutler from Lehi, Utah, also in hiding for plural marriage. Cutler knew of others in San Francisco and Oakland who were "on the underground," and he and Lindsey immediately began visiting them.

In Oakland they found John Pickett, through whom they learned of Alfred and Charlotte Nethercott. The Nethercotts were among those whose spiritual home during the Church's absence had been the Reorganized Church. However, they did not feel entirely comfortable there and, after repeated warnings to stop preaching the doctrines of the "Utah Mormons," they were excommunicated from the RLDS Church.

Alfred Nethercott then wrote to Salt Lake City requesting readmission into the LDS Church. As a result, Lindsey and Pickett visited the Nethercotts and on 5 December 1890 baptized them in the ocean, together with their son, Charles, and his wife, Rebecca. President Woodruff subsequently sent Lindsey and Pickett written authorization to act as missionaries. By January 1891 there were thirty-six members of the Church in the Oakland area.[4]

Norman Phillips was one of those whom Alfred Nethercott had earlier converted to the Reorganized Church. After moving to Southern California, Phillips was contacted by Lindsey, who had been sent by the Nethercotts. After about a month

---

[4] Norman B. Phillips, "History of the California Mission of the Church of Jesus Christ of Latter-day Saints," MS; Oakland California Stake Collection.

of studying with Lindsey, Phillips was baptized despite the objections of his wife, who said, "If you get baptized into that Mormon Church I will never live another day with you!" A few months later she left, and after trying for four years to convince her to return, he divorced her and remarried. He returned to Oakland, only to find that the Nethercotts had all moved to Utah, which left him "all alone without the knowledge of another Mormon in the whole state."[5] He evidently was not acquainted with any of the other Oakland members or with the Garlick family, who still held small meetings at their home in Sacramento. Pickett went to Utah and reported that there was enough interest in the Church in California that another missionary should be sent in his stead.

California Mission Reorganized

Based on Pickett's report, on 10 August 1892, thirty-five years after George Q. Cannon had closed the doors to his California mission office in San Francisco and left for Utah, President Cannon, now a member of the Church's First Presidency, participated in the decision to reopen a mission in California. Church leaders sent fifty-year-old Luther Dalton to organize and preside over local branch leaders and to supervise missionary activities. A resident of Ogden, Utah, he was born to Latter-day Saint parents in Nauvoo, Illinois, and crossed the Plains with them in 1852.

President Dalton held his first California meeting on Sunday, 28 August 1892, at the home of James Jorgensen in Fruitland (or Fruitvale), an Oakland suburb.[6] Jorgensen had recently been rebaptized. Two weeks later, Dalton rented a fraternal hall on Washington Street between Thirteenth and Fourteenth Streets, distributed hundreds of circulars advertising the meetings, and rebaptized several members.

---

[5] Ibid.

[6] Some recall these early meetings as being in a parlor at 525 Sixth Street.

On 2 October 1892 Dalton organized the Oakland Branch (which also encompassed San Francisco) as part of the Alameda Conference, which had jurisdiction over all of Northern California. The branch had six members, including the following officers: Joseph Natress, president; Dr. John Peter Phillip Van Denbergh and James Peter Jorgensen, counselors; and Norman B. Phillips, clerk. The other two branch members were the wives of Brothers Van Denbergh and Jorgensen.[7] All lived in Oakland except the Van Denberghs, who lived in San Francisco.

Two weeks later they decided to hold two meetings each Sunday, and their intentions were advertised in the *San Francisco Examiner*, the successor to the *California Star*. However, attendance was small, and the rent, fifteen dollars per month, seemed too high; therefore, they moved to the Thomas Hall at 1156½ Fourteenth Street in East Oakland. The first meeting there was held on 4 December 1892, with the great Latter-day Saint educator, Karl G. Maeser, preaching.

Meanwhile, on 27 November the sporadic little branch in Sacramento was also officially reorganized with Aaron Garlick as president. Hence, Oakland and Sacramento may claim the honor of having the longest-standing Church units in California. As this memorable year ended, four missionaries were sent to assist President Dalton: Henry B. Williams and George H. Maycock were assigned to revitalize the faith of the Saints in Southern California, and Alva Keller and James B. Cummings were assigned to do the same in Sacramento.

As anticipated, the missionaries soon found other Church members and sympathizers whose faith, without the benefit of the Church organization, had grown lax. In the north was an actor, Luke Cosgrave, who in 1890 brought a small stock company from El Paso and traveled throughout Northern California staging one-man Victorian road shows. There was

---

[7] Luther Dalton to the *Deseret Weekly News*, quoted in Eugene E. Campbell, "A History of The Church of Jesus Christ of Latter-day Saints in California, 1846–1946" (Ph.D. diss., University of Southern California, 1952), 305–6.

also *Brooklyn* Saint Sophia Patterson Clark King. In Sacramento, in addition to the Garlicks, there were Dr. Ward Pell (possibly the *Brooklyn* Saint or his son), Frederick Merriweather, and Archibald Curle.

In mid-1893, before President Dalton had been in California a year, the Oakland Branch with thirty-eight members split and created a dependent Sunday School in San Francisco. There were also twelve members in San Bernardino, twelve in Los Angeles, eight in San Diego, and thirteen others scattered about, making a total of eighty-three. By the end of that year, the number had grown to 120. President Dalton returned home in February of the following year, after eighteen months of service.

Karl G. Maeser returned to preside over the California Mission for the brief period of January to August 1894. As the Superintendent of Church Schools, he was sent primarily to arrange and direct an educational exhibit for the Church at the San Francisco Mid-Winter Fair. "The exhibit made by the Mormon schools of Utah is a very interesting and attractive one," *Campbell's Illustrated Magazine* of Chicago reported. "The work done by pupils in this display is, if anything, far superior to that shown in other exhibits, and speaks well for the system of education prevailing among the disciples of Brigham Young."[8]

Brother Maeser established mission headquarters at 29 Eleventh Street, San Francisco. He immediately began advertising and holding public meetings at this location. He also addressed small congregations and hosted several General Authorities who came to visit the fair or who were en route to assignments elsewhere. This gave these top Church leaders a firsthand look at the newly reestablished Church in California.

On 6 April 1894 the first conference of the California Mission since the renewal of activities was held. A number of fair visitors attended. When the fair ended, President Maeser

---

[8] Quoted in Alma P. Burton, *Karl G. Maeser: Mormon Educator* (Salt Lake City: Deseret Book, 1953), 62.

returned to Utah disappointed, believing that during his eight months as president progress had been imperceptible—not a single person had been baptized. The first convert baptisms did not take place until January 1895, twenty-eight months after the mission was reopened. However, President Maeser's public-relations efforts resulted in a friendlier atmosphere.

On 25 July 1894 Henry Tanner, a twenty-five-year-old future attorney, replaced Karl G. Maeser. He almost immediately became ill with what he thought was a recurrence of the malaria he had contracted as a missionary in the southern states. By the time the proper diagnosis of typhoid fever was made, the doctor said he did not have much chance of living. The Saints called a special prayer meeting for him, choosing Brother Charles Nethercott, who had returned to the Bay Area, to offer the prayer. Branch clerk Norman Phillips described this as

> one of the most eloquent prayers in behalf of the sick that I have ever heard. . . . During and after that prayer there was the greatest outpouring of the spirit of God that I ever saw. When we rose from our knees, there was not a sad face, not gloom in the building. The spirit testified to us each and all that all would be well with Brother Tanner, that he would get well and be amongst us again shortly, notwithstanding the unfavorable report given by the doctors. I will never forget that meeting. . . . The doctors were surprised at his rapid recovery; in fact they were surprised at his recovering at all.[9]

The little branch in Oakland was soon moved to San Francisco, where Dr. Van Denbergh provided for a time rent-free quarters for both the mission president and the branch. However, growth was slow until 1895, when they moved the meeting place to 909 Market Street and erected a small sign on the busy street advertising their meetings. "From that time on the branch began to grow."[10] Soon afterwards, the *San Francisco Call* carried the following:

---

[9] Phillips, 12.

[10] Ibid.

TO REDEEM THE GENTILES

Mormonism Makes its First Strong Effort
To Plant Itself Here
Many Missionaries at Work
Not Gray-Whiskered Fellows, but Nice Young
Business and Professional Men[11]

Growth in the South

In the early days, most of the Church's activity in California was concentrated in the north. However, things were happening in Southern California that would alter the face of the state and the Church.

Los Angeles was not a major focal point in early Church history, with the exception of the quartering of a Mormon Battalion Company which built Fort Moore in 1847. Nor had it been a leading California city, even though it was one of three Spanish pueblos (towns associated with missions) existing since early Spanish colonial mission times. Also, Los Angeles did not have a deep-water port and thus was not a major town until connected by rail. In 1887, the population was only eleven thousand, the same as it had been ten years earlier.

In that year, however, the Santa Fe Railroad completed a line from Kansas City to Los Angeles. A government survey in the 1850s determined that the only way for a rail line to enter Southern California was through a tunnel into the top of West Cajon Canyon, but the Southern Pacific owned the necessary approaches, hence blocking the entry of any rival. However, Fred T. Perris, an LDS convert from Australia and a San Bernardino resident (for whom the town of Perris was later named), showed how the Santa Fe could enter "through the eastern wing of Cajon Pass never before considered feasible."[12]

---

[11] *San Francisco Call*, 10 June 1895, excerpted in Leo J. Muir, *A Century of Mormon Activities in California* (Salt Lake City: Deseret News Press, 1952), 1:108.

[12] E. Leo Lyman, *Guidebook: Mormon Historical Sites in the San Bernardino Area* (Lyman, 1991), 12–13.

A memorable fare-war broke out with the Southern Pacific Railroad, which had earlier built a line down from San Francisco. As passenger fares from the Midwest plummeted from one hundred dollars to just one dollar, suddenly thousands of people who had long dreamed of going to the coast decided that now was the time.

Groups of families and friends, businesses, and farming associations made up traveling communities. The Southern Pacific alone brought 120,000 people in 1887. As these immigrants poured in, Southern California's population mushroomed. The newcomers' tents ringed the city much as they had in San Francisco when the *Brooklyn* arrived some forty years earlier. This avalanche of land boomers in Southern California matched the number that flooded into Northern California during the gold rush.

Eliza Woollacott and her home in Los Angeles

Latter-day Saints were caught up in this excitement. In July 1884 Eliza Woollacott had come to Los Angeles from Salt Lake City with her wine-merchant husband, two children, and two grandchildren. The Woollacott home, located at 220 North Grand Avenue, became the focal point of Church activity for many years. Eliza, whose gracious hospitality brought numerous Church dignitaries to her home, pleaded for missionaries to serve in her area and "wept with joy" when, in 1892, Elders

Williams and Maycock were assigned to serve in Southern California.[13]

On 20 October 1895, the first conference of Southern California members since 1857 was held in Los Angeles. A missionary, Elder Parley T. Wright of Ogden, Utah, was sustained as Southern California conference president. The Los Angeles Branch was also organized with bakery owner Hans C. Jacobson as its first president.

The Church was also growing in San Diego. In 1886, William Cooper, a Church member from Wirksworth, England, arrived to help build the famous Coronado Hotel and remained to become an important local builder and contractor. Three years later, on 2 June 1898, a branch was organized in San Diego at the home of Sister Amelia Jewell on First Street. Charles Hoag was chosen as the first branch president. This branch would have its ups and downs—sometimes flourishing, and sometimes lapsing into complete inactivity.

At the close of 1895, California's membership had increased to over two hundred—nearly doubling in two years. Los Angeles now had the largest congregation in the state, with fifty-one members. San Francisco had forty-six, Sacramento twenty-nine, San Bernardino twelve, and San Diego nine. Though mission headquarters were still in the north, from this point forward the Los Angeles area would carry the state's largest LDS population, swelling over the next century to more than a half-million members.

Noted Visitors

Even after the San Francisco Fair closed, Church leaders continued to visit California. Several notable visitors came in 1896, which happened to be the fiftieth anniversary, or "jubilee," of the Saints' first arrival in the area. On 9 February Elder Heber J. Grant of the Quorum of the Twelve spoke at a meeting

---
[13] Muir, 108–9.

of the San Francisco Branch and attracted a crowd of about two hundred people—a good number given the fact that there were only a few Latter-day Saints in the city.

Two months later, the Salt Lake Mormon Tabernacle Choir came to perform—only the second time it had left the Intermountain West. On 14 April the Choir, directed by Evan Stephens, presented a concert in Oakland's First Congregational Church. There were also five concerts in San Francisco. One of those was a Sunday service before an enthusiastic audience in Metropolitan Hall. Elder Grant spoke to the congregation in his second major San Francisco address in two months. "One could see the expression on their faces as we sang and he preached," one Choir member recalled, "and we choir members thanked God for him and that we were partakers of that memorable occasion."[14]

On 20 and 21 April the Choir performed in San Jose and in Sacramento.

The press, which until recently had maligned the Church, gave favorable reviews of the Choir's performances. The *San Francisco Call* raved: "It is impossible to describe the precision of attack, the general fidelity to key, or the noble manner in which the singers respond to the slightest movement of the leader, who plays upon them as if they were mechanical."[15] According to the *Sacramento Bee*, "the singing of the choir was indeed a revelation to lovers of choral music and an event long to be remembered."[16] The Choir's appearances undoubtedly created additional goodwill toward the Latter-day Saints.

In June 1896 President Joseph F. Smith, Second Counselor in the First Presidency, and Elder Abraham H. Cannon of the Quorum of the Twelve spent three days with the San Francisco Saints. Lorenzo Snow, President of the Quorum of the Twelve, visited them on 9 August with his wife and two daughters.

---

[14] Quoted in J. Spencer Cornwall, *A Century of Singing: The Salt Lake Mormon Tabernacle Choir* (Salt Lake City: Deseret Book, 1958), 70.

[15] Ibid.

[16] Ibid.

*Wilford Woodruff (third from left) and George Q. Cannon (left)
fishing from the Coronado pier in San Diego*

President Wilford Woodruff and his First Counselor, George Q. Cannon, spent two weeks in California later that month. The Golden State was obviously being closely observed.

In November, President Henry Tanner was released. During his administration, missionaries had been dispatched to organize branches at Stockton, Los Angeles, Fresno, Santa Cruz, San Bernardino, and the gold country town of Latrobe.

Growth continued as earlier members were identified and others moved into the state. By 1897, under a new mission president, Ephraim H. Nye, California Church membership doubled again to well over four hundred.

In 1897, the *Improvement Era* began publication; for many decades it was the official voice of the Church. To Californians living away from Church headquarters, the words of the prophets and apostles on the pages of this monthly magazine were particularly appreciated and bolstered their commitment to live the gospel though surrounded by those not of their faith.

Soon after it began, the magazine carried, over a three-year period, a series of articles written by John Horner describing the *Brooklyn*'s voyage and his role in early Latter-day Saint affairs in the San Francisco Bay Area.[17]

In 1898, Californians commemorated the discovery of gold. Four of the Mormon Battalion veterans who had been at Sutter's Mill when the discovery was made were able to attend the celebration. Henry W. Bigler, Azariah Smith, William J. Johnston, and James S. Brown were honored by the Society of California Pioneers, which sponsored the celebration. The four veterans led a parade as "the only survivors of that notable occasion, fifty years before."[18] This event generated "much favorable publicity" for the Latter-day Saints.[19]

Gold discoverers (from left to right): Henry W. Bigler, William J. Johnston, Azariah Smith, and James S. Brown at 1898 jubilee

[17] *Improvement Era* 7, no. 7 (May 1904): 510–15; 7, no. 8 (June 1904): 571–75; 7, no. 9 (July 1904): 665–72; 7, no. 10 (August 1904): 767–72; 7, no. 11 (September 1904): 849–54; 8, no. 1 (November 1904): 29–35; 8, no. 2 (December 1904): 112–17; 9, no. 10 (August 1906): 794–98; 9, no. 11 (September 1906): 890–93.

[18] James S. Brown, *Life of a Pioneer* (Salt Lake City: Geo. Q. Cannon & Sons, 1900), 515.

[19] Campbell, 333.

Notable Deaths in California

During the summer of 1898—the jubilee year of the gold discovery—ninety-one-year-old President Woodruff made another trip to California, this time to recuperate from his lingering asthma. He was accompanied by his wife Emma, President George Q. Cannon and his wife, Bishop Hiram B. Clawson and his wife, and his secretary, L. John Nuttall. Upon arriving in San Francisco on 14 August, President Woodruff and his wife became guests at Colonel Trumbo's home.

On the following Sunday, 21 August, President Woodruff addressed the Saints in the San Francisco–Oakland Branch, speaking for about twenty minutes. This was his last public address. Two days later he underwent surgery. He was well enough by the end of the week to attend a dinner in his honor at the exclusive Bohemian Club. A few days later, however, he took a turn for the worse and died peacefully on 2 September at the Trumbo home.[20] President Cannon, who had recorded significant San Francisco events in the pages of the *Western*

Isaac Trumbo home in San Francisco

Standard nearly fifty years before, meticulously recorded the following recollection of the prophet's death:

> I arose about 6 o'clock. The nurse told me he had been sleeping in the same position all the time. I took hold of his wrist, felt his pulse, and I could feel that it was very faint. While I stood there it grew fainter and fainter until it faded entirely. His head, his hands, and his feet were warm and his appearance was that of a person sleeping sweetly and quietly. There was not a quiver of a muscle nor a movement of his limbs or face; thus he passed away.[21]

---

[20] Alexander, 329–30.

[21] Quoted in Preston Nibley, *The Presidents of the Church* (Salt Lake City: Deseret Book, 1959), 133.

The Church leaders, their wives, Sister Woodruff, and Colonel Trumbo accompanied the body back to Salt Lake City. The journey was made in a special car provided by the Southern Pacific Railroad. President George Q. Cannon also died in California three years later, in April 1901, at Monterey.

These deaths near the end of the century marked the end of an era. The reopening of the Church in California was no mishap; it was a vital step in planting the kingdom of God in new areas of the United States and the world. It was now acceptable for a Latter-day Saint to live in the Golden State. This acceptance provided valuable experience in establishing the Church in predominately non-Latter-day Saint cultures outside America's Intermountain West.

Roots and Branches: 1900–19

14

The opening years of the twentieth century are known in United States history as the "Progressive Era." It was a time when the collective American mind was stretched. This expansive mood was also reflected in the Church. On New Year's Day 1901, the Church president, eighty-six-year-old Lorenzo Snow declared: "I hope and look for grand events to occur in the twentieth century. At its auspicious dawn I lift my hands and invoke the blessings of heaven upon the inhabitants of the earth. . . . Let all people know that our wish and our mission are for the blessing and salvation of the entire human race. May the twentieth century prove the happiest as it will be grandest of all the ages of time."[1]

This optimistic statement, with its broad vision, assured Latter-day Saints that gospel blessings were for all, regardless of where they lived. This, together with President Snow's emphasis on tithing, which brought the Church financial stability, gave impetus to growth in many areas, including California. Following President Snow's death later in 1901, his successor, President Joseph F. Smith, continued this same emphasis.

[1] *Deseret News*, 1 January 1901.

Joseph F. Smith

By the time Joseph F. Smith became Church president, he had served as counselor to Presidents Brigham Young, John Taylor, Wilford Woodruff, and Lorenzo Snow. A man of seemingly boundless goodwill, President Smith's cheerful optimism earlier in California while staring down the barrel of a gun was a prelude to his entire administration. Somehow he always remained open and tolerant despite blistering personal attacks from the press and others.

Following the lead of his predecessors, President Smith encouraged Church growth outside the Intermountain West, where with his nurturing the Church began to take root, branch out, and permanently flourish in a way it had not done for half a century. President Smith was already familiar with California; in addition to passing through the state to and from his boyhood mission to Hawaii, he was in California again during the 1860s and 1880s en route to the Islands. He also spent time with the Saints in San Francisco in 1896.

The California rebuilding process began in earnest when a proven leader and seasoned public servant, Joseph E. Robinson, was appointed mission president. President Robinson's eighteen-year administration, which both in time and vision mirrored that of President Smith, laid a permanent foundation for future Latter-day Saint development in California.

Born in the small Southern Utah town of Pinto to English-immigrant parents, Robinson was raised in nearby Kanab. When he left his family behind to go to California in June 1900, his assignment was that of an ordinary missionary. However, he was not the typical young elder with minimal

*Mission president
Joseph E. Robinson and
his wife Minnie*

experience, and by the end of the year he was called to be mission president. His wife and family then came to join him.

He had served as Kane County (Utah) assessor and clerk, chairman of the Republican Party, and representative in the Utah State Legislature. As a legislator, he helped write Utah's constitution and chaired the committee which purchased the site upon which the state capitol now stands in Salt Lake City. Like his prophet leader, President Robinson was a well-proportioned man of regal bearing, standing approximately six feet tall. His face was ruggedly handsome, displaying a perpetual smile. His personality reflected wisdom and compassion.

The San Francisco Earthquake

The biggest event of the early 1900s in San Francisco was an act of nature. One-third of the way into President Robinson's service, on 18 April 1906 at 5:12 A.M., a cataclysmic event occurred that changed the course of Church history in California. It was the great 1906 earthquake and subsequent fire that destroyed 490 blocks and dealt a nearly mortal blow to the city.

The night before, a missionwide conference had concluded with a Mutual Improvement Association gathering at the mission home at 609 Franklin Street. In addition to the

missionaries and local members, five elders en route to the South Seas and former apostle Matthias Cowley were also present. When one of the missionaries was called on to offer a closing prayer, he prayed that something might happen to "wake up San Francisco and make it receptive to the gospel." After the events of the following morning, the Robinsons sought to console the elder, who feared that his prayer had caused the disaster.[2]

Cowley and the five elders bound for the Pacific believed that they had received divine protection: their rooms were the only portions of their hotels which had not been damaged. When the five went to check on their luggage at the railway station, they were told that it had been transferred to a building across the street, which, by this time, had burned to the ground. Three days later, one of the missionaries was impressed to go back and check again. He was grateful to discover that all of their possessions were still in the station baggage room, and none had been destroyed or stolen.[3]

---

[2] William G. Hartley, "Saints and the San Francisco Earthquake," *BYU Studies* 23, no. 4 (fall 1983): 432.

[3] Ibid., 437, 451–52.

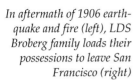

In aftermath of 1906 earth-quake and fire (left), LDS Broberg family loads their possessions to leave San Francisco (right)

Local member Harold R. Jensen described some of the quake's effects:

> My family was burned out on the first morning of the fire, and we brought what few belongings we had saved to the Hooper family home on Golden Gate Avenue, a half block from the mission house. We seemed safe there but later in the day another fire had started in the neighborhood and on our second trip to the house, we found the Hooper family with their belongings in a truck, ready to flee. Together with some of the missionaries, all of us drove away and camped that night in a barn on a ranch near Colma. The missionary house was later burned, one of the last blocks to be destroyed by fire.[4]

George C. Carpenter, special correspondent for the *Deseret News*, described the area between City Hall and mission head-quarters (609 Franklin) as "ash heaps." "All that remained of '609' was part of an iron fence, a bathtub, and a half-burned telephone pole 'to which was tacked the cards of several elders and notice to latter-day Saints to gather at Jefferson Park.'"[5] President Robinson, the missionaries, and several local Latter-day Saint families set up camp in this park three blocks away. Even though there was widespread panic among the general population, President Robinson observed a rather different reaction among the faithful Saints, whose mood was similar to

---

[4] Harold R. Jensen, interviewed by J. Edward Johnson, 15 May 1935, Oakland Stake Collection.

[5] Hartley, 454.

that of the *Brooklyn* passengers in their hour of peril sixty years before: "There was no hysteria, abandonment to grief, despair or complaint manifest. All seemed to possess that 'peace of mind that surpasseth understanding' which comes only to those whose 'hopes were secure in the promises of the Father.'"[6]

The quake had a lasting impact on Church activity in San Francisco. In the midst of such crises, people often turn from material concerns to more enduring spiritual values. Two months after the disaster, President Robinson reported that "the Saints are more attentive to their duties since the dread calamity."[7]

With the destruction of the mission home in San Francisco, President Robinson concluded that the time was right to move his headquarters to Los Angeles, where Church membership was larger and where a direct rail link with Salt Lake City had been completed the previous year. Headquarters were first established there at 516 Temple Street. Later the offices were moved to 423 West Tenth Street, where they remained for a number of years until a permanent building was constructed.

After moving his family to Southern California, President Robinson immediately returned to San Francisco, where he was involved "for some time helping the Saints readjust" and in distributing relief funds and supplies which poured in from Latter-day Saints in many areas. Relief Society women in Hawaii, for example, sent fifty dollars to help their suffering sisters.[8]

One of those devastated by the quake was Joseph F. Smith's cousin, the poet Ina Coolbrith. The quake destroyed her unpublished manuscripts and irreplaceable mementos; it also destroyed her home and left her destitute. Letters of condolence and gifts came from all over the world. Her California friends and fellow writers initiated projects to help her, one of

---

[6] Ibid., 458.

[7] Quoted in ibid., 457.

[8] Ibid., 454–55.

which was a book of short stories, poems, and articles. This and other undertakings proved successful. A substantial amount of money was accumulated, and a home was bought for the much-loved poet.

Modern-Day Pioneers

Consistent with the Church's progressive attitude, leaders continued to send clear signals that settlement in California would not only be condoned but encouraged. Consequently, during the opening decades of the twentieth century, many Latter-day Saint "pioneers" came to the Golden State. In the autumn of 1906, the California Irrigated Land Company, a farming co-op interested in utilizing water from the Feather River to bring additional acres into production, sent a representative to the Intermountain West to recruit Latter-day Saint farmers to the small Northern California town of Gridley. Those solicitations fell upon the receptive ears of some Latter-day Saints in and around Rexburg, Idaho, who agreed to settle in California despite the devastating earthquake earlier in the year.

The first party, headed by George Cole and family, arrived in California on 22 November. They boarded for a week at the Gridley Hotel at the expense of the land company. Locating approximately two miles south of town, the group increased to more than fifty by the end of the year.

On 23 February 1907, under the direction of President Robinson, the Gridley Branch was organized with the following officers: George Cole, president, and J. F. Dewsnup and Charles Larsen, counselors. Since those early meetings, Latter-day Saint activities in Gridley have been continuous.[9]

Other pioneers came individually or as families. Many were rugged, talented, and sufficiently self-assured to expose their faith to a California environment of tiny, struggling

---

[9] Gridley Reunion Committee, *History of the LDS Church in the Gridley, California Area* (Gridley, Calif.: McDowell Printing, 1980), 1–2.

branches amid a sea of disinterested, sometimes disapproving non-Latter-day Saints. The twentieth-century influx of Saints into California was in marked contrast to that of the nineteenth century. Most now came on their own rather than through Church sponsorship. "It is quite probable, however, that many would not have come to California in opposition to Church policy," one historian has concluded. "The facts seem to be that the Church leaders had ceased to oppose the movement of members away from the centers of the Church and had come to regard this movement as a possible means of strengthening the Church in the mission fields. This was especially true of the California Mission."[10]

Some Latter-day Saints participated in the early development of the motion picture industry. Waldamer Young of Salt Lake City worked for the *San Francisco Chronicle* for about a decade before moving to Hollywood in 1912; he wrote the screen scenarios for *Lives of a Bengal Lancer* and *The Plainsman*, which featured Mary Pickford, the famed silent movie star.[11] Other noted Latter-day Saint screenwriters during this period were Harvey H. Gates and Eugene B. Lewis.

The Saints engaged in business, political, social, and cultural activities. Martella Lane, an Iowa native who came to California in 1900, became known as the "Artist of the Redwoods," painting numerous landscapes of these beautiful trees. She also created murals of the Sacred Grove in at least two Southern California chapels. Daniel Lillywhite headed the Los Angeles Livestock Exchange for twenty-five years, and Nephi E. Miller pioneered large-scale honey production. James H. Cannon, an electrical contractor, presided over the Los Angeles Rotary Club; Horace T. Perry became a Bank of America executive; and W. Ed Wallace became president of the

---

[10] Eugene E. Campbell, "A History of The Church of Jesus Christ of Latter-day Saints in California, 1846–1946" (Ph.D. diss., University of Southern California, 1952), 348–49.

[11] Leo J. Muir, *A Century of Mormon Activities in California* (Salt Lake City: Deseret News Press, 1952), 1:493.

California Association of Realtors. Ettie Lee, a native of New Mexico who came to Los Angeles in 1914, became a prominent Los Angeles public school educator and philanthropist. She taught immigrant mothers and girls how to clothe themselves attractively and how to make their lives more comfortable by producing homemade quilts and rugs. She eventually founded the widely acclaimed Ettie Lee Homes for Boys. T. Earl Pardoe founded the first speech clinic at the University of Southern California, and John W. Freestone helped establish the Los Angeles College of Osteopathic Physicians and Surgeons. Businessman Jesse Knight came to develop mines in the Mojave desert, and his son, Goodwin, later became a California governor.

Hyrum G. Smith, a great-grandson of Joseph Smith's brother, Hyrum, came to Los Angeles to study dentistry at the University of Southern California. On 29 May 1910 he was appointed president of the Los Angeles Branch, the third man to serve in that capacity. Having been awarded a gold medal for proficiency in his studies, he established a local practice upon his graduation in 1911. However, he had just begun when he was called from California on 9 May 1912 to serve as Patriarch to the Church.[12] He left for Salt Lake City as the first person called as a General Authority while living in California. At that time, the Patriarch to the Church was selected among descendants of Hyrum Smith and had the responsibility of giving blessings to Church members not residing in organized stakes. The position no longer exists in the Church.

Once again the Church began calling missionaries from California to serve in various parts of the world. Perhaps the first in the twentieth century was Eliza Woollacott's grandson, Albert Henry Thomas, who left from Los Angeles on 18 June 1903 for Britain.

---

[12] Lawrence R. Flake, *Mighty Men of Zion* (Salt Lake City: Karl D. Butler, 1974), 311–12.

Early Church Buildings

In 1908 President Joseph F. Smith came to California to tour the mission, underscoring the state's growing importance. He was the first General Authority to extensively visit Church units in the state since the 1850s; he was also the first president of the Church ever to do so.

1909 Social Hall (left) and 1912 chapel (right) at Gridley

By this time, some Church branches were becoming well organized and thinking about building permanent meeting houses. The first Church building of the modern era in California was constructed in Gridley during the winter following President Smith's mission tour. The Saints called their building, which was two and one-half miles southwest of Gridley, Liberty Social Hall. Though it was not intended to be a permanent worship facility, the first religious meeting was held in this hall on Sunday, 4 July 1909.

In 1912 a more suitable chapel was built at a cost of twelve thousand dollars. This meetinghouse was the "largest house of worship belonging to the Latter-day Saints west of Salt Lake City" and the first Church-owned chapel in California.[13] The LDS group in Gridley was at that time the Church's largest branch in the Far West.

---

[13] *History of the LDS Church in the Gridley, California Area*, 3.

Anthon H. Lund (with trowel), Joseph E. Robinson (to his right), George Albert Smith (to President Lund's left), and others at 1913 cornerstone laying for Adams chapel (right)

To underscore the importance to Church leaders of a successful Latter-day Saint presence in Southern California, the first chapel in Los Angeles drew Anthon H. Lund of the First Presidency and George Albert Smith of the Quorum of the Twelve to lay the cornerstone. Upon its completion, the building was dedicated by President Joseph F. Smith on 4 May 1913. The chapel was located at 153 West Adams Boulevard, adjacent to the mission headquarters building, which was completed at that same time. This "Adams Chapel," as it came to be called, together with the Los Angeles Branch, which met there, was a focal point of Church growth and activity in Southern California for many years. It became a place where friendships for the entire Latter-day Saint community were begun and renewed.

President Smith developed such a fondness for California that he acquired a winter home in Santa Monica that same year. There he became even more intimately acquainted with President Robinson and the local California Saints.

Next, the San Diego Branch, under the leadership of its president, Stephen Barnson, purchased a chapel site at Tenth and Pennsylvania Streets. After two years of planning and raising money, a chapel was completed and dedicated on this site in the spring of 1916.

1915 World Fairs

In 1915 California celebrated the completion of the Panama Canal by sponsoring two world fairs, the Panama-Pacific International Exposition in San Francisco, and the Panama-California Exposition in San Diego. Even though the Church did not formally participate at either fair, several Latter-day Saints were involved because the state of Utah had its own building at both.

Several specialized "congresses" were organized in conjunction with the San Francisco Fair. Latter-day Saints were especially involved with the International Congress of Genealogy, with Church members being invited to organize and conduct several of the sessions. A special train called the *Utah Genealogical Special* was chartered to bring 250 persons from Utah, including the First Presidency. All three members of the First Presidency spoke at sessions of the genealogy congress.

"Utah Day" at the San Francisco Fair was observed on 24 July. In his remarks, President Joseph F. Smith recalled his memories of the Bay Area sixty years earlier, when "only a few houses were at San Francisco." The Church leaders "were cordially received and treated with great respect. Many prominent men and women called on them and sought interviews."[14]

Another significant Latter-day Saint representative was James E. Talmage of the Quorum of the Twelve, who addressed the Congress of Religious Philosophy. His outstanding lecture, "The Philosophical Basis of Mormonism," became a classic of Latter-day Saint thought and was reprinted in pamphlet form for many years.

Another fair participant was young Avard Fairbanks, a Utah artist and sculptor, who made his first visit to California to exhibit his work. Joseph Ballantyne also brought his Ogden

---

[14] Gerald Joseph Peterson, "History of Mormon Exhibits in World Expositions" (master's thesis, Brigham Young University, 1974), 38–39.

Tabernacle Choir to perform at both the San Francisco and San Diego fairs.

Ina Coolbrith, still in good health though in her seventies, undertook the task of organizing the International Congress of Authors and Journalists. She contacted nations and groups worldwide, personally writing letters by hand over a period of four years. At the conclusion of the congress on 30 June 1915, President Benjamin Ide Wheeler of the University of California crowned her with a wreath of California laurel. The state legislature passed a resolution declaring her the first poet laureate of the state of California. She was so highly regarded that on the day of her funeral in March 1928, the state legislature declared a day of mourning and named a 7,900-foot mountain in her honor. Mount Ina Coolbrith commands the north side of Beckworth Pass, through which this young niece of Joseph Smith had entered California three-fourths of a century earlier. San Francisco still honors her. A hillside park bearing her name overlooks the site of the former Latter-day Saint village and the beach at its feet.

The End of an Era

On 6 April 1917 the United States entered the First World War, which had broken out in Europe three years earlier. The Church, though it supported the position of the U.S., encouraged all members to support their own countries, even through military service.

Before the war, relatively few Latter-day Saints had moved to or made extensive visits to California. Now whole groups of LDS servicemen were trained in or passed through California, taking firsthand looks at the state. Utah's volunteer unit, the 145th Field Artillery (1st Utah), received its basic training at Camp Kearny, just north of San Diego, during the fall of 1917. Many of these servicemen later returned and made permanent homes in California.

The year 1918 marked a major milestone in the course of both world and Church events. To the world, it brought peace. To the Church, it brought the end of an era: within two weeks of the armistice, President Joseph F. Smith died. Soon after, President Robinson, who had labored diligently for nearly two decades, received his honorable release, thus ending the long and parallel Church service of the visionary prophet and the faithful California mission president. From a few hundred Church members in 1900, most of whom were migrants from Utah, membership grew to over three thousand during President Robinson's tenure. The number of branches climbed from five to nineteen. Although there were no temples or other ornate structures, the value of Church property increased from almost nothing to over one hundred thousand dollars.[15]

As a testimonial of their deep affection for President Robinson and his wife, the members of the Church in Southern California gave them a building lot on Buckingham Road in Los Angeles, together with four thousand dollars to build a home. The presentation was made on 21 April 1919, at a reception hosted by officers and members of the Los Angeles Conference. Robinson entered the real estate business and continued to be a much-loved and respected Church leader. His Sunday School class in the Wilshire Ward attracted large crowds. Following his death in August 1941, his family interred his remains in his adopted state. His former missionaries erected a fitting monument to his memory at the Inglewood Cemetery.

During the first two decades of the twentieth century, faithful California Saints proved to Church leaders and members that devotion and faithfulness could be maintained and strengthened in a modern urban setting. These Latter-day Saint immigrants stayed close to their Church—a prodigious feat given the scattered condition of Church members and the comparatively primitive communication, transportation, and

---

[15] Andrew Jenson, comp., "The California Mission," 19 April 1919; LDS Church Archives.

meeting facilities. The Church in California was now ready for its next plateau: the first stake outside of predominantly LDS communities.

A California
Kaleidoscope:
1919–29

15

The end of World War I brought a mood of celebration to the United States that lasted a decade. The "Roaring Twenties" were a time of heady optimism, nowhere felt with more fervor than in California. During this decade large numbers of Americans, including Latter-day Saints, sought to realize their dreams in the Golden State.

"The motion-picture industry . . . between the two wars did more than any other development to foster a yearning among the nation's discontented to share in what California supposedly represented."[1] As millions flocked to the neighborhood cinemas, they were infused with Hollywood's portrayal of the "California Dream." The Golden State had the traditional makings of dreams: fame, fortune, opportunity, adventure, climate, scenery, and a relaxed lifestyle. As more and more people purchased automobiles they were able to turn those fantasies into reality. A piece of the California lifestyle could be had by anyone with enough gas money to whisk him or her away to the Pacific shores.

---

[1] David Lavender, *California: A Bicentennial History* (New York: W. W. Norton, 1976), 175.

California also had oil. As the northern part of the state had become rich on gold nearly a century earlier, the south now became rich on oil, triggering a boom which made California the nation's leading oil producer for the next quarter century. A growing number of opulent mansions now overlooked the Pacific.

Taken together, these attractions were irresistible. During the 1920s, 1,900,000 out-of-state migrants entered, and of those, 1,368,000 settled in Southern California. It was the largest internal migration in the history of the United States, nearly ten times the size of the gold rush beginning in 1849 and the railroad land-boom of the 1880s.

Latter-day Saint Migration to California

As in the past, the nation's mood was reflected among members of the Church. The number of California Latter-day Saints increased more than fivefold, from 3,967 in 1920 to 20,599 in 1930. Church members came to California particularly for advanced education, a mild climate, an interesting and stimulating culture, and the comparatively favorable salaries and working conditions. These magnets quickly gave the Church an energetic and enlightened membership, and out of this comparatively small group of about twenty thousand came a disproportionately large number of future business, political, Church, and other leaders, among whom was a future Church president, Howard W. Hunter.

These high achievers transformed a few home Sunday Schools and struggling branches into a kaleidoscope of new organizations, programs, and buildings. Meeting attendance and tithing payment rose. Church auxiliary organizations proliferated, Church leadership was strengthened, and new branches blossomed everywhere.

Presiding over this period of history was Heber J. Grant, who became Church president upon the death of Joseph F. Smith in 1918. A successful businessman, President Grant showed unusual talent and imagination in commercial affairs. His personal skills and his affiliation with the Democratic Party enabled him to mingle with prominent and influential people and in the process break down opposition and remove prejudice toward the Church. His warmth opened doors that had long been closed.

Heber J. Grant and Saints at Ocean Park chapel dedication

President Grant visited California repeatedly to establish goodwill and to manage the mushrooming growth. He seemed to recognize the potential that the Golden State held for the Church, and he had a special affinity for the California Saints.

Despite the fact that the Church had encouraged growth and permanence outside the Intermountain area for thirty years, some still voiced concerns. In 1921 a group of Saints in Santa Monica, apparently responding to a rumor that the Church was again planning to call members back to Utah, wrote President Grant, asking if they were out of harmony with Church policy by living there. He answered their letter in person during one of his frequent visits to the Pacific Coast. He assured them that "at the present time the idea of a permanent Mormon settlement at Santa Monica was in full accordance

Mission president Joseph W. McMurrin and his wife Mary Ellen

with Church policies."[2] He backed this up by handpicking such successful LDS business leaders as Joseph McMurrin, George McCune, LeGrand Richards, and others, and calling them to move to California where they could lead by example.

President Grant chose sixty-year-old Joseph W. McMurrin, a member of the First Council of the Seventy, to preside over the California Mission. Elder McMurrin became the second long-term mission president, holding his appointment from 1919 until 1932. When he came, he assumed the responsibility of nearly four thousand members scattered throughout little branches or Sunday Schools in California, Arizona, Nevada, and Oregon. He therefore endured a grueling travel schedule to interview potential leaders, provide personal counseling, approve building plans, issue temple recommends, and supervise missionaries. During his first year, branches were first organized in such widely divergent places as San Jose and Bakersfield. As a General Authority, he also spoke in general conferences in Salt Lake City twice each year. He was a man of profound faith, eloquent speech, and tireless devotion.

President McMurrin was born in Tooele, Utah, in 1858 but soon went to Salt Lake City, where he lived until moving to

---

[2] Andrew Jenson, comp., "The California Mission," 29 October 1921; LDS Church Archives.

California in 1919. By trade he was a teamster and stone cutter. He had worked on the Salt Lake Temple and had helped build dams and canals in northern Arizona.

In November 1885, after he was shot twice through the abdomen by a United States deputy marshal on a polygamy raid, doctors despaired of his life. In a visit to his bedside, Elder John Henry Smith asked him if he desired to live. McMurrin affirmed his strong desire to live and enjoy the company of his wife and two children. Elder Smith then promised him he would live. His recovery was regarded as miraculous.

Temple Sites Considered

Since Brigham Young had mentioned that "in process of time the shores of the Pacific may be overlooked from the temple of the Lord,"[3] there had been talk of a California temple. While the early Church had not been strong enough to warrant the construction of one of those sacred structures in California, the many talented and faithful Latter-day Saints now coming made thoughts of a temple more plausible.

In 1921 Harry Culver, a non-LDS Los Angeles real estate developer and founder of Culver City, offered to give the Church a six-acre tract in Ocean Heights plus a contribution of fifty thousand dollars if it would build a five-hundred-thousand-dollar temple there. In December of that year, President Heber J. Grant and other General Authorities traveled to Los Angeles to inspect the property. At first Church leaders were favorably impressed, but they eventually declined the offer because of financial commitments to complete temples already in progress in Arizona and Alberta, Canada. "It might also have been said," one Church leader added, "that temples are not built to further real estate schemes or enterprises; temple locations and temple buildings stand apart from all

---

[3] Journal History, 7 August 1847; LDS Church Archives.

Harry Culver (right) offers temple site to President Heber J. Grant (next), with other leaders looking on; beginning third from left: Rudger Clawson (President of the Twelve), Charles W. Nibley (Presiding Bishop), Anthony W. Ivins (counselor in First Presidency), and Sister and President McMurrin

such considerations."[4] Despite this disappointment, Southern California Saints continued to cherish the thought that a local temple would one day grace their area.

The Saints in Northern California also began speaking of prophecies concerning a temple in their area. During the summer of 1924, Elder George Albert Smith of the Quorum of the Twelve was in San Francisco attending regional Boy Scout meetings. On that occasion he met with W. Aird Macdonald, president of the Church's small branch across the Bay in Oakland. They met at the Fairmont Hotel high atop San Francisco's Nob Hill. President Macdonald, a writer for the *San Francisco Chronicle*, later reported his memory of the occasion:

> From the Fairmont terrace we had a wonderful panorama of the great San Francisco Bay nestling at our feet. The setting sun seemed to set the whole eastern shore afire, until the Oakland hills were ablaze with golden light. As we admired the beauty and majesty of the scene,

---

[4] B. H. Roberts, *A Comprehensive History of The Church of Jesus Christ of Latter-day Saints* (Salt Lake City: Deseret News Press, 1930), 6:493.

President Smith suddenly grew silent, ceased talking, and for several minutes gazed intently toward the East Bay hills.

"Brother Macdonald, I can almost see in vision a white temple of the Lord high upon those hills," he exclaimed rapturously, "an ensign to all the world travelers as they sail through the Golden Gate into this wonderful harbor." Then he studied the vista for a few moments as if to make sure of the scene before him. "Yes, sir, a great white temple of the Lord," he confided with calm assurance, "will grace those hills, a glorious ensign to the nations, to welcome our Father's children as they visit this great city."[5]

But the Saints in both Northern and Southern California would have to wait more than thirty years for their temple dreams to become a reality.

The First California Stakes

Church growth in California occurred in a logical sequence. In areas where Latter-day Saint population was sparse, small Sunday Schools were established—often meeting in members' homes. Those were supervised and often staffed by the nearest fully organized branch. As these Sunday Schools grew, they eventually became independent branches. When branches within a given district reached a sufficient size and necessary leadership could be supplied from within the area, they were reorganized as wards and grouped into a stake. The creation of wards and stakes not only provided members with solid local support, but it also alleviated the mission president's responsibility to oversee the day-to-day operation of these individual units.

Church growth was so great and President McMurrin's schedule so heavy that it became apparent that either the mission had to be divided or self-administered stakes organized to relieve part of the load. But were the California members ready to stand on their own? In the three years after President McMurrin's appointment as mission president,

[5] Harold W. Burton and W. Aird Macdonald, "The Oakland Temple," *Improvement Era* 67, no. 5 (May 1964): 380.

membership in Los Angeles more than doubled. As opposed to just three small branches in this area when he came in 1919, eleven thriving branches were now meeting in Los Angeles, Long Beach, Ocean Park, Garvanza, Boyle Heights, Hollywood, Glendale, Alhambra, Inglewood, Huntington Park and San Pedro. Five small groups met in Lankershim, Pasadena, Redondo, Belvedere Gardens and Home Gardens.

After his appointment, President McMurrin carefully trained members to take over the leadership in Southern California. He realized early that the creation of locally administered congregations "would make the members more independent and self-reliant" and would free him to concentrate his efforts on preaching the Church's message to non-Latter-day Saints.[6]

Early in 1922, he sent his recommendation to Church headquarters that a stake be organized in Los Angeles. The recommendation was approved. In April, President Grant went to New York City where he visited with George W. McCune, who indicated his intention to make his home in California when released as president of the Eastern States Mission. President Grant asked him to accept the presidency of the proposed stake. The invitation was accepted, so McCune, his wife, three sons, and one daughter established their home in Los Angeles on 4 September 1922, four months before the stake was organized.

Born in Nephi, Utah, President McCune was an Ogden businessman and financier prior to his call to the eastern states. As he became acquainted with the people over whom he would preside, he could not help but notice the differences among the Saints since he had last visited the area three years earlier. While the members in Los Angeles had been faithful in 1919, he found them even more so in 1922. In fact he was "astonished . . . at the wonderful devotion and interest shown by our peo-

---

[6] Eugene E. Campbell, "A History of the Church of Jesus Christ of Latter-day Saints in California, 1846–1946" (Ph.D. diss., University of Southern California, 1952), 347.

ple in the gospel of our Redeemer in that portion of the vine-yard." He attended a Sunday School at Ocean Park which was so crowded that twenty-five children had to stand. "On the same day," he continued, "I attended the services at Los Angeles; and when I left that place a little over three years ago, their [Adams Boulevard] chapel was ample to accommodate them all. When I returned I found that little chapel was wholly inadequate for the Sunday night meeting, and every available space was taken for standing room."[7]

While in California, President McCune continued to nurture business interests as a real estate developer and as one of the original organizers of the Bank of America, of which he was director for many years.

In the early autumn of 1922, the announcement was made by the First Presidency that a stake was to be established in Los Angeles. When the time for the organization arrived, President Heber J. Grant personally directed the proceedings, beginning with a meeting of Church and local officers on Friday afternoon, 19 January 1923. Accompanying him were Charles W. Penrose, a counselor in the First Presidency, George Albert Smith, a member of the Quorum of the Twelve, and Charles W. Nibley, Presiding Bishop. Also assisting and counseling in the matter was President McMurrin. In the meeting, the appointment of President McCune was announced, and Leo J. Muir and George F. Harding were chosen as his counselors. The following day consideration was given to the membership of the high council and to the leaders of auxiliary organizations.

The organization of the Los Angeles Stake on 21 January 1923 was an auspicious occasion, as it marked a new precedent, not only for California but for the entire Church. Not only was California the first state outside of the Intermountain territory to have a stake, but Los Angeles was the first major urban setting for one outside of Salt Lake City. And for the first time, Church jurisdiction in California was split. Nearly four

---

[7] In *Conference Report*, October 1922, 152.

thousand stake members were now shepherded by President McCune, while members outside of stake boundaries were presided over by the mission president, Joseph W. McMurrin.

With the stake organization in place, attention was given to organizing its constituent wards. The first ward in modern California was organized on 11 March 1923, when the original Los Angeles Branch became the Adams Ward, a month and a half following the organization of the stake. Under the direction of President Grant, Hans Benjamin Nielsen was sustained as bishop of the ward with Ezra Taft Benson (a cousin of the future thirteenth Church president) and Basil T. Kerr as counselors. Other wards organized that year included Alhambra, Belvedere, Boyle Heights, Florence (later renamed Matthews in honor of a member who contributed generously to the building fund), Garvanza, Glendale, Hollywood, Huntington Park, Inglewood, Long Beach, Ocean Park, and San Pedro.[8] Signs of prejudice against the LDS people seemed to have vanished, and there was therefore little difficulty in acquiring suitable meeting places.

It was now up to the new stake to show what it could do. Attention turned to developing an efficient organization. This was a challenge, because some of the stake officers had not known each other beforehand, and many members were not familiar with stake or ward procedures. The "success formula" for this new organization embodied the cultivation of three lofty traits: a cooperative spirit, a "high standards attitude," and a habit of achieving. One member of the stake presidency later recalled that these goals stimulated both leaders and members: "Enthusiasm was wide-spread and spontaneous. Everybody seemed to rally to the challenge." The new stake quickly stepped to the forefront of the Church with high percentages in attendance of meetings and "ward teaching" visits to families in their homes.[9]

---

[8] Campbell, 351.

[9] Leo J. Muir, *A Century of Mormon Activities in California* (Salt Lake City: Deseret News Press, 1952), 1:153–54.

In just four years the stake's membership doubled. The administrative load was again too burdensome for one presidency. An assignment to divide the stake came to apostles David O. McKay and Stephen L Richards. Under their direction, details were worked out in a meeting held in the basement of the Adams Ward chapel. They also decided to divide the Adams Ward at Vermont Avenue, the western portion becoming the new Wilshire Ward. At the stake conference held on 21 and 22 May 1927, the more northerly wards became the Hollywood Stake (later renamed Los Angeles), with George W. McCune as president. The southern portion, with Leo J. Muir as president, retained the name of the Los Angeles Stake (later renamed South Los Angeles).[10]

Leo J. Muir was a Utah educator and town mayor before coming to California in 1922 to begin a new career in finance. He served a combined sixteen years as counselor and then

President Heber J. Grant, Wilshire Ward bishop David Howells, and Hollywood Stake president George McCune with their wives in front of stake center

---

[10] Ibid., 1:155.

president of the first modern stake in California. He was thus an important historical figure who later wrote a nostalgic eyewitness account of the Church's growth and development during the period.[11]

With the success of the stake in Southern California, Church leaders felt ready to create a similar unit in the north. By 1926 there were fifteen hundred members in the San Francisco area; hence local leaders wrote to mission president McMurrin urging that a stake be organized. At a conference on 10 July 1927, apostles Rudger Clawson and George Albert Smith proposed to organize a San Francisco stake. The visitors explained that the Saints "could have a stake here if they wanted it, but if they did not want it they did not need to," and that they could not proceed without knowing the feelings of the members. The congregation unanimously opted to become a stake. President McMurrin said that "the time is not far distant when there will be five new stakes in this state and the organization will continue until the entire state is organized."[12]

Oakland Branch president W. Aird Macdonald was called to preside over the new stake with J. Edward Johnson and Clyde W. Lindsay as his counselors. The new stake consisted of the Berkeley, Daly City, Dimond, Elmhurst, Martinez, Mission, Oakland, Richmond, San Francisco, and Sunset Wards, and a few branches.

President Macdonald, a native of Arizona, had resided in the Bay Area since 1911. He was an artist, writer, and photographer for local newspapers. In later years, he became an insurance agent and a member of both the California State Board of Equalization and the prestigious Commonwealth Club.

The stake was the ninety-ninth organized in the Church, with a membership of over three thousand—mostly "day

---

[11] Ibid., vols. 1 and 2.

[12] Harold R. Jensen, interviewed by J. Edward Johnson, 15 May 1935, Oakland Stake Collection.

(laborers), a few professionals, a school teacher here and there, and a lawyer or two in the Oakland Branch."[13]

Church Buildings

The Latter-day Saints in California had few permanent meeting houses. Worshiping or attending Church activities in rented halls—fraternal lodges, public auditoriums, other churches, schools, and almost every other imaginable place, including a room above a fire station at Barstow and an abandoned jail in Whittier—was an almost universal experience for pioneering members in small branches. In rented halls, it was common to sweep up cigarette butts which remained from Saturday night activities, or to detect the pungent odor of stale cigarette smoke or alcohol during sacrament services.

Typical was an experience in the Bay Area's Martinez Branch, which held services in a rented lodge hall. After Sunday School, having received word that the stake presidency would be attending their sacrament service that evening, the members carefully prepared the hall. When the Saints and stake visitors arrived a few hours later just prior to sacrament meeting, "the hall was in complete disarray. A Portuguese wedding had been held there between services and the hall was left in disorder and reeking of spilled wine and tobacco smoke."[14]

Therefore, a challenge facing stake and mission leaders was to provide adequate meeting places for the increasing number of congregations. In 1925, for example, mission president Joseph W. McMurrin reported that he had dedicated new chapels at Santa Anna, Modesto, and Sacramento and that the two branches in San Francisco had jointly built an "amusement

---

[13] Leon Baer, Oral History, 5; James Moyle Oral History Archives, LDS Church Archives.

[14] Evelyn Candland, *An Ensign to the Nations: History of the Oakland Stake* (Oakland: Oakland Stake, 1992), 28.

hall." He planned to purchase an existing building in Bakersfield and to build another "amusement hall" in San Diego.[15]

In Southern California there were only three chapels capable of accommodating wards of six hundred to one thousand people—Los Angeles, Long Beach, and Ocean Park. The fact that other wards met in rented halls generally precluded a full complement of Church activities, particularly for the youth. It was therefore with anticipation that members in the two Los Angeles stakes began planning their own buildings.

In the 1920s, local Saints raised approximately half the building costs, with general church funds providing the other half. The two stakes began raising funds for a stake center they could share. A newly formed interstake building committee conducted its first meeting in February 1927 while parked "in an automobile in front of Adams Ward Chapel." In less than two months, $110,263 "had been pledged to the fund."[16] However, the First Presidency directed that two buildings be built. Accordingly, the fund was split between the two stakes, and each began plans for its own stake center.

Stake center in Huntington Park

Ten months after the committee first met, the Los Angeles Stake, having raised sufficient funds, received final approval to begin construction—a prodigious feat given President Grant's insistence that all Church lands and buildings be procured and built without mortgages. Five months later the "Tabernacle," a large stake center completely furnished and equipped, was opened in Huntington Park.

The Hollywood Stake began building its own stake center, also known as the Wilshire Ward chapel,

---

[15] Mission Annual Reports, 1925, 64; LDS Church Archives.

[16] Muir, 1:154.

on 15 April 1928, when the cornerstone was laid by President McCune in a grand ceremony. Stake members not only donated and collected enough money to keep the $250,000 project out of debt, but they also donated countless hours in construction labor. Generally, the men did the heavy construction, while the women did the painting and interior decorating. Once, while visiting the area, President Heber J. Grant "picked up a shovel" and "did his part that day in landscaping."[17] When it was completed in April 1929, two members of the First Presidency came from Salt Lake City for its dedication.

President Heber J. Grant declared that other than the temples and the Salt Lake Tabernacle, it was the finest building in the Church. It remained California's most imposing LDS structure for the next thirty years, until the construction of the Los Angeles Temple. The building was admired by non-Latter-day Saints as well, being named the "finest cement building in

Wilshire Ward chapel

---

[17] Chad M. Orton, *More Faith Than Fear: The Los Angeles Stake Story* (Salt Lake City: Bookcraft, 1987), 86.

America" by *Architectural Concrete* in 1933.[18] Today it remains a notable example of California's art deco architecture and is a Los Angeles landmark.

Over the next several years, Church buildings multiplied, helped considerably by Swiss architect Louis Thomas, who came to Los Angeles in 1921 and began a notable career, designing over twenty LDS chapels throughout Southern California. Many others were on the drawing board or under construction in other places. As the state and nation prospered, so did the Church.

Varied Activities and "Firsts"

The scope of Latter-day Saint activity in California could be seen in the wide variety of programs instituted by the California Mission and its branches and by the newly organized stakes and their wards. The following are some of the programs which took root during that period.[19]

The Relief Society was particularly active. Following the lead of the general Church, California Relief Societies became involved in local social service agencies and maternity hospitals. When a child guidance clinic was established in Los Angeles, the stake Relief Society became a charter member. This involvement brought local LDS women leaders into active participation in many of the social welfare programs of the city, county, and state. A social welfare convention was held in the Adams Ward chapel in 1924 in which eminent social workers in Southern California participated. The stake Relief Society also contributed generously to the children's hospital and to a home for girls in Los Angeles.

Other activities or "firsts" included the following: Ada Gygi Hackel's earliest Primary for children in Los Angeles was conducted in her home at 208 East Santa Barbara Street in 1919;

---

[18] Ibid., 84–91.

[19] For a more detailed account of these activities, see Muir, vol. 1.

Los Angeles choir at San Diego's Balboa Park

the Ocean Park Branch Dramatic Club presented a three-act drama in the Women's Club at Santa Monica on 19 February 1921; a Sunday School conference met at the Adams chapel on 25 September 1921; and in 1922 the choir of the Los Angeles Conference of the California Mission presented Evan Stevens's cantata, "The Vision," to an audience of twelve thousand people in Balboa Park, San Diego.

In the autumn of 1922, Los Angeles "M Men" (young single adults) elected Jay S. Grant as their first district president. In December 1923 Wallace E. Lund of the Belvedere Ward organized the first Latter-day Saint Boy Scout troop in Southern California.

In February 1924 the first directory of stake and ward members in Southern California was published by the M Investment Company—a group of young LDS men who had gone into business together. During that same year Alma B. Summerhays launched the first Latter-day Saint news publication in Southern California—the *Los Angeles Stake Journal*—a monthly eight-page paper, eight by ten inches in size. This publication carried on for a year or two with fair success. A young men's basketball league was also organized in 1924. The Matthews Ward won the first league championship.

The first Old Folks Committee was organized on 25 March 1925. On 1 May of the same year, a genealogical conference in California convened at the Adams chapel.

Latter-day Saints were also active in commemorating their heritage. The first California chapter of the Daughters of Utah Pioneers was founded at Los Angeles in February 1927. Latter-day Saints were honored on 31 May of that year when a new San Bernardino County courthouse was dedicated on the lots where the original home of Amasa M. Lyman had stood. The following day at Sycamore Grove, a concrete, steel, and bronze monument was unveiled and dedicated to the memory of the Saints who had camped there for several weeks while negotiating the purchase of the Rancho where they founded San Bernardino.[20]

Other "firsts" during the 1920s included the commencement of missionary work among California's Spanish-speaking population and the beginnings of religious programs for college students. Both of these efforts would see significant development during the following decade.

On 8 September 1929, at the invitation of the stake presidency, the Honorable John C. Porter, mayor of Los Angeles, addressed the morning session of the Los Angeles stake conference—probably the first public official to address an LDS stake conference in California. Mayor Porter stressed the need for a religious and moral crusade in the city of Los Angeles.

Later that year, on 6 October 1929, Rachel Latham and Irmgard Kreipl Koening of the Los Angeles Stake were among the first women set apart as stake missionaries.

This period of California Church history ended abruptly with the stock market crash in the fall of 1929. Just over two years later, seventy-three-year-old Joseph W. McMurrin was honorably released as mission president because of ill health. He died in Los Angeles on 24 October 1932 and was buried in Forest Lawn Memorial Park. During his twelve-year admini-

---

[20] Muir, 1:460.

stration, he witnessed the most remarkable changes in the Church since the gold rush days.

At the beginning of his administration, he presided over all Church members in California and parts of three other states; but when he was released, fifteen thousand members in California's two largest population centers were under local stake leadership. New and beautiful buildings were in place, and the degree of Church activity had risen to new heights. The Church was now firmly and permanently rooted in California soil—a position from which it would grow, as President McMurrin had prophesied, until stakes would blanket the entire state.

The Depression Years: 1929–39

16

A s in early Church history, national events in the twentieth century affected the Church's ability to pursue its agenda. Few external forces had a greater impact on the course of modern Latter-day Saint history than did the Great Depression.

Nationally, the industrial and technological advances of the previous several decades had resulted in robust economic expansion, which in turn had engendered a spirit of unbridled optimism. This mood suddenly changed, however, with the stock market crash on "Black Tuesday," 29 October 1929. Early in 1930, business declined sharply. As a result, many factories and retail outlets were forced to close, even as surpluses piled up in warehouses. As thirteen million individuals lost their jobs, the nation's banks began to collapse under the strain. By 1932 some five thousand financial institutions were depleted of the hard-earned savings of millions of depositors and became insolvent. Many people quivered in the cold, standing in lines on city sidewalks to obtain a hot bowl of soup or piece of bread, while in agricultural areas farmers could not afford to plant new crops, and old harvests rotted in granaries or were burned as fuel.

The Great Depression hit California hard. Some half million people lost everything they had in 1930 alone. But operating on the mistaken premise that conditions had to be better in California, "thousands of hollow-eyed, wasted refugees guided their broken automobiles into the state, seeking jobs, seeking sunshine, seeking hope."[1] As the full weight of the Depression settled on the state, California was fettered with a massive surplus of labor. Thus, those who forsook their homes to pursue their dreams in California were rudely awakened as they found conditions there to be much the same as in the places they had left behind. The term "Golden State" seemed a mockery.

Migration from Utah Continues

The Depression's impact was even more severe in the Mountain West. In 1932 unemployment in Utah reached 35 percent, compared to a national peak of 24.9 percent. Average personal income in the Beehive State fell by 48.6 percent.

In this environment, many Intermountain Latter-day Saints took flight. California Church membership more than doubled again from 20,599 in 1930 to 44,784 in 1940. Church president Heber J. Grant continued to request that capable Utah businessmen relocate in order to provide leadership for the growing Church and the thousands of struggling Saints in California.

One of those businessmen was the charismatic LeGrand Richards, who at great personal sacrifice left his thriving real estate business in Salt Lake City and moved his family to Los Angeles. In the next five years he served as bishop of the Glendale Ward and then as president of the Hollywood Stake, a position he left in order to preside over the Southern States Mission.[2] He later authored his classic book, *A Marvelous Work*

---

[1] T. H. Watkins, *California: An Illustrated History* (Palo Alto, Calif.: American West, 1973), 363.

[2] Lucile C. Tate, *LeGrand Richards: Beloved Apostle* (Salt Lake City: Bookcraft, 1982), 141–65.

LeGrand Richards

and a Wonder, and served as the Church's Presiding Bishop and as a member of the Quorum of the Twelve Apostles.

Continued growth required the formation of more Church units. During the 1930s, the number of stakes in California nearly quadrupled from three to eleven. New stakes were formed out of the California Mission in Gridley, Sacramento, and San Bernardino, while division of existing stakes resulted in two stakes in San Francisco and six in Los Angeles. In areas like San Jose, Santa Barbara, Fresno, and Bakersfield, branches continued to grow. In dozens of smaller cities like Alturas, Brawley, Escondido, Eureka, Gilroy, Hanford, Hemet, Indio, Lancaster, Lompoc, Placerville, Porterville, Redding, Salinas, San Rafael, Santa Cruz, Santa Rosa, Ukiah, and Watsonville, new branches were organized. By the end of the decade, most cities and many towns had functioning wards or branches.

Church Response to Depression Problems

As economic conditions worsened, local Church leaders' shoulders strained under increasing burdens. Especially in such urban areas as Los Angeles and San Francisco, the stakes had to provide assistance to the numerous families in distress, many of which were new arrivals. Furthermore, the doubling of membership not only taxed existing Church programs and services, but it also created a need for more meetinghouses in many areas—at just the time when they could be afforded least.

In 1932 Los Angeles County had four hundred thousand cases on its relief rolls, including hundreds of Latter-day Saint families. Newcomers were not eligible for public relief. In response to these dire circumstances, the Inter-stake Employment and Relief Office was opened that year in Los Angeles under the direction of Alice H. Osborn—four years before the inauguration of a Churchwide welfare program. The Church Employment Office established contacts with superintendents and personnel directors. The Office also became a clearing house for membership records, since many people seeking assistance made dubious claims to being members of the Church. During the years in which Mrs. Osborn directed this office, some thirty-six thousand people came for information, relief, or other services. She succeeded in providing five thousand jobs, more than one for every Latter-day Saint family.[3]

The Depression also brought an enhanced and expanded role for the LDS women's Relief Society. These women were instrumental in administering relief for needy families. The ward bishop was in charge of relief funds and commodities donated by members. However, he entrusted to the Relief Society not only the investigation of family needs but also the dispensing of available funds and materials. "The product of Relief Society handicraft and the canned fruits and vegetables processed with women's help in the canning plants, represented by far the major part of the substance provided for welfare distribution."[4]

A hint that the General Authorities were considering a Churchwide effort came three years later in a 1935 Oakland Stake conference, where Elder Melvin J. Ballard of the Quorum of the Twelve declared, "Our economic problems will not be solved by a Stalin of Russia, a Hitler of Germany, a Mussolini of Italy, a Huey Long of Louisiana, nor a Sinclair of California. The Lord has a plan, and when men will follow it, our troubles will be over."[5]

---

[3] Leo J. Muir, *A Century of Mormon Activities in California* (Salt Lake City: Deseret News Press, 1952), 1:287–88.

[4] Ibid., 1:289.

[5] *Messenger*, May 1935, 1.

Upton Sinclair had run unsuccessfully for governor on the Democratic ticket the previous year. Though President Heber J. Grant was also a Democrat, he rejected Sinclair's socialist ideals, which undermined the concepts of individual dignity and responsibility. President Grant's views were widely noted in California's newspapers.

The Church's welfare plan was announced at the April 1936 general conference. The First Presidency later explained why the Church launched this effort: "Our primary purpose was to set up, in so far as it might be possible, a system under which the curse of idleness would be done away with, the evils of a dole abolished, and independence, industry, thrift and self respect be once more established amongst our people. The aim of the Church is to help the people to help themselves. Work is to be re-enthroned as the ruling principle of the lives of our Church membership."[6]

The welfare plan provided both cash and commodities to those in need. Church leaders gave renewed emphasis to the Saints' longstanding tradition of fasting two meals each month and donating the financial equivalent of those meals to the Church for the poor. These "fast offerings" were first used to help the needy within the local congregation, but any surplus was then shared with other wards and stakes. The Church purchased farms, opened canneries, and developed other kinds of projects to produce a wide variety of goods which were placed in a "bishops' storehouse" for distribution to those in need. Church members donated many hours of service working on these projects in order to help the less fortunate.

To coordinate these projects, a new level of Church administration was inaugurated. Stakes throughout the Church were grouped into thirteen "regions." In California, stakes in the south were grouped into the Los Angeles Region and those in the north into the Oakland Region. Each region, consisting of between four and sixteen stakes, was to have a storehouse

---

[6] In *Conference Report*, October 1936, 3.

where commodities produced by stakes, both local and regional, could be exchanged.[7]

Each stake was assigned a specific production responsibility. In the Los Angeles Stake, where a member, Jay Grant, owned a clothing factory, the assignment was shirts. The Gridley Stake picked peaches from local orchards and canned them at the homes of Church members. In 1937 this stake processed thirty-five thousand cans, representing thirty-five tons of peaches. The Pasadena Stake transformed the basement of the Baldwin Park Ward building into a cannery. Pear culls were purchased in truckloads and ripened and sorted on tables in a member's yard in El Monte. "Apricots, tomatoes, and other produce were harvested in the fields of the San Fernando Valley either as shares or as donations from owners who could not obtain the necessary labor to harvest them."[8]

Another part of the Church's welfare plan began in Southern California. In March 1938 the Pasadena and Hollywood Stakes joined in setting up a small workshop and salvage operation at 705 Ivy Street, Glendale, under the direction of Willard J. Anderson and Orville Shupe. The operation followed a pattern set by Goodwill Industries which had been established previously by some Protestant churches in the area. Later that year, Church leaders launched a similar Churchwide program named *Deseret Industries*.

The following year, the Glendale operation became part of the Deseret Industries system and moved to a larger, two-story facility at 116 Llewellyn Street, furnished with new equipment for processing salvage, sewing clothing, repairing furniture, etc.

Trucks collected clothing, furniture, appliances, newspapers, magazines, and other items that members wished to donate. Unemployed or disabled individuals then earned income by sorting, cleaning, and repairing these materials,

---

[7] *Deseret News*, 25 April 1936, Church section, 1, 4.

[8] Susan Kamei Leung, *How Firm A Foundation: The Story of the Pasadena Stake* (Pasadena, Calif.: Pasadena California Stake, 1994), 19.

which were then sold inexpensively in Deseret Industries retail stores. Proceeds from these sales paid the employees' wages and financed other operating expenses. Salaries were supplemented, if necessary, with commodities from bishops' storehouses. The objective was that all members, regardless of their abilities, would maintain self-respect doing worthwhile work and prove to themselves and to the world that they could earn their own way.

Deseret Industries, together with the bishops' storehouse system, provided almost every item needed to sustain life. Each Latter-day Saint family received a monthly visit from a representative of the local ward bishop and the ward Relief Society president. If a family needed help, the Relief Society president determined with the bishop and the family what those needs were. If it was cash to forestall eviction or a utility shut-off, fast offerings were used. If food, clothing, or household goods were needed, a commodities "shopping list," redeemable at a bishops' storehouse or Deseret Industries outlet, was given to the family.

In return, Church members contributed what labor they could to the Church until they were able to stand on their own. Eventually, the system was expanded to provide a full range of social services. Although it was fine-tuned over the years, the essentials of this program, outlined by the First Presidency in 1936, were kept intact. After that time, no faithful California Latter-day Saint willing to work to his or her ability went unfed, unclothed, or unhoused.

The system worked so well that the sometimes hostile press began printing more positive stories about the Church. Although the long-range trend had been toward a less distorted image of the Latter-day Saints, it was not until these years that media coverage crossed the line from a predominantly negative to a predominantly positive character. Four-fifths of all magazine articles about the Church had titles specifically referring to the Church's welfare program.

Missionary Efforts during the Depression

The Great Depression took its toll on missionary service, as fewer families were able to afford sending their sons and daughters on missions. In the California Mission, the number of missionaries plummeted from 147 in 1929 to 46 in 1932.[9] California stakes responded by calling some members to serve locally as stake missionaries. Elder J. Golden Kimball, a member of the First Council of the Seventy, "reported that hundreds had been converted to the Church" as a result of stake missionary efforts in Los Angeles and other areas.[10]

The mission president's job was as important and demanding as ever, but it was changing as larger numbers of members were organized into stakes and therefore removed from his jurisdiction. Though increasing numbers of new mission branches in smaller areas still required staffing and support, the mission president was becoming a more distant figure to members in urban stakes, most of whom no longer had close personal contact with him or his work.

Furthermore, during the 1930s, mission presidents' terms of service were shortened. In contrast to the more than ten years served by Presidents Robinson and McMurrin, two to five years became the norm, giving California three mission presidents during the decade. The high caliber of men appointed to preside over the California Mission was an indication of the importance that Church leaders attached to missionary work in the Golden State: Alonzo A. Hinckley of Millard County, Utah, became an apostle upon his release; Nicholas G. Smith of Salt Lake City, former president of the South African Mission and Acting Patriarch to the Church, later became an Assistant to the Twelve; and W. Aird Macdonald Jr. had been the first president of the San Francisco and Oakland Stakes.

---

[9] Mission Annual Reports, 1929 and 1932; LDS Church Archives.

[10] J. Golden Kimball to the Seventies, 31 January 1934, LDS Church Archives, cited in Richard O. Cowan, *The Church in the Twentieth Century* (Salt Lake City: Bookcraft, 1985), 164.

During these years, the Church continued teaching the gospel to California's Spanish-speaking population. Some of these people traced their roots back to the era when California was part of New Spain, but the majority were among the multitudes who flocked to the Golden State during the 1920s and 1930s. Most came from Mexico and settled in the barrio of East Los Angeles, which acquired a Mexican population second only to that of Mexico City itself.

Missionary efforts among Spanish-speaking Californians had been launched in 1924 when Rey L. Pratt of the Mexican Mission handpicked two elders to work in the Los Angeles area under the supervision of the California Mission. As additional missionaries became available, Spanish-speaking missionary work was expanded into such areas as San Diego and San Bernardino. Even top Church leaders became involved. On 28 August 1927, Joseph Fielding Smith of the Quorum of the Twelve spoke to over a hundred Spanish-speaking Saints at a special conference. And in February 1928 Anthony W. Ivins of the First Presidency, who had been born in Mexico, was able to speak to an even larger group in their native language.[11]

A Spanish-speaking branch was organized on 8 February 1928 in San Diego, and a similar unit was formed in Los Angeles on 16 June of the following year. Juan M. Gonzales became president of the Los Angeles Branch and continued in this office until 1944. There were fifty members when this branch was organized, but in four years it swelled to 345. Even though these Mexican Saints had been hit hard by the Depression, they somehow managed to accumulate enough funds to build their own chapel in 1938.

The rapid growth of Spanish-speaking missionary work in Southern California prompted Church leaders to move the headquarters of the Mexican Mission from El Paso to Los Angeles in 1929. The Church bought a large home at 2067 South

---

[11] Eugene E. Campbell, "A History of The Church of Jesus Christ of Latter-day Saints in California, 1846–1946" (Ph.D. diss., University of Southern California, 1952), 400–1.

Hobart Boulevard containing twenty-seven rooms, seven baths, and enough sleeping quarters for thirty missionaries. Five years later, however, Church leaders decided to return the Mexican Mission office to the more central location in El Paso. Subsequently, headquarters of the California Mission were moved from the original office at 152 West 25th Street to the larger home on Hobart.

The Mexican Mission supervised proselytizing both in Mexico and among the Spanish-speaking people of the southwestern United States. By the mid-1930s this work had grown to the point that the mission was divided along the international border. At a meeting in Los Angeles held on 28 June 1936, under the direction of Reed Smoot of the Quorum of the Twelve, a separate Spanish-American Mission was organized. The Spanish Saints in California became part of that mission, presided over by President Orlando C. Williams, whose headquarters remained at El Paso.

New Efforts in Public Affairs

With a drop in the number of missionaries during the Depression, the Church began looking for new ways to share its message. Most notably, it began to participate in mass media and public relations programs. Not since the days of Samuel Brannan had the Church involved itself so widely with the press and the community. Perhaps the recent and favorable media attention given to the Church's welfare efforts had something to do with this participation. Both by invitation and by their own initiative, California Latter-day Saints began publishing Church literature and participating more fully in local community affairs.

The effort began with local Church publications, starting with the *Los Angeles Stake Journal* in 1924, followed by Oakland's *Messenger* in 1931, then Los Angeles's *California Intermountain Weekly News* in 1935. The latter two publications

U.S. President Herbert Hoover
presenting award to Howard S.
McDonald, scoutmaster of East
Bay LDS troop and future
BYU President

continued off and on for more than thirty years with the aim of increasing the efficiency of stakes and wards.[12]

Soon these efforts were expanded into the newly invented medium of radio. In 1931 a weekly radio broadcast under the direction of the stake mission president, Isaac B. Ball, started on Oakland radio station KTAB. The following year a series of discourses were delivered over Los Angeles's KMPC by Elder James E. Talmage. The Los Angeles and Hollywood Stakes continued the KMPC programs for nearly a year.

Then, at the invitation of the Columbia Broadcasting System, the Los Angeles Stake choir was invited to perform on the weekly nationwide "Church of the Air" radio program on 18 November 1934. Following the program, an invitation was extended by the Los Angeles Council of Churches to have the choir appear with other musical groups in the Easter sunrise services at the Los Angeles Memorial Coliseum on Sunday, 21 April 1935. This began a tradition of Latter-day Saint participation in what became one of the nation's best-known and widely broadcast Easter Sunday programs. In August 1937 the Bay Area stakes took their turn appearing on the "Church of the Air," this time being invited to speak as well as sing. The Oakland Stake president, Eugene Hilton, spoke on the significance of the Restoration. In 1938 the Church was invited to be represented at the annual Easter sunrise service at Dimond

---

[12] *Messenger*, January 1931.

Park in Oakland, suggesting that the Latter-day Saints had finally gained "full acceptance into the religious community of the Bay Area."[13] Elder Melvin J. Ballard spoke at the service.

Meanwhile, at the California-Pacific International Exposition in San Diego during 1935 and 1936, the Church—for the first time—erected its own exhibit building. This was under the direction of the Church's Radio, Publicity, and Literature Committee, headed by a young, newly returned missionary (and future Church president), Gordon B. Hinckley. It was built around a shady patio, which brought a peaceful atmosphere to fair visitors. The building featured murals, stained glass, and statuary. Replicas of the Salt Lake Temple and Tabernacle outside the exhibit entrance attracted interest. Illustrated lectures on the Book of Mormon and its archaeology proved especially popular. There was also a historical parade in which the Daughters of Utah Pioneers marched in pioneer costumes.[14] Several concerts by the famed Mormon Tabernacle Choir brought additional favorable attention.

The Church was also represented in a second California fair—the Golden Gate International Exposition, held on Treasure Island in the San Francisco Bay in 1939 and 1940. Again capitalizing on the Tabernacle Choir's popularity, the Church designed its exhibit building in the form of a "miniature Tabernacle," with a fifty-seat auditorium where missionaries presented illustrated lectures on the Church's history and beliefs.

Yet another example of utilizing the media to tell the Church's story was the movie, *Brigham Young*, which depicted the trek of the Pioneers across the Plains. In October 1939 two members of the First Presidency, Heber J. Grant and his first counselor, J. Reuben Clark Jr., went to Los Angeles to confer with producers of this film.

---

[13] Evelyn Candland, *An Ensign to the Nations: History of the Oakland Stake* (Oakland: Oakland California Stake, 1992), 33.

[14] Gerald Peterson, "History of Mormon Exhibits in World Expositions" (master's thesis, Brigham Young University, 1974), 49–53; Muir 1:461.

Temple Plans Move Forward

Depression difficulties and the expense of long-distance travel kept the California Saints yearning for their own temples. Meanwhile, these Church members made hundreds, if not thousands, of trips to Mesa in Arizona and to Salt Lake City or St. George in Utah, to do temple work. But these lengthy journeys took a toll and brought tragedy on at least two occasions.

Late Friday night, 23 February 1934, thirty-six members of the Home Gardens Ward in southeastern Los Angeles left the Mesa Temple to return home. They were traveling in a bus owned by the Los Angeles Stake Genealogical Society. Slightly after one o'clock Saturday morning, the bus encountered a sharp detour where the highway was being rebuilt. Oil-burning warning lights had been set out, but they had been extinguished by winds and heavy rain. The driver was unable to make the detour safely, and the bus overturned. Passengers were thrown about the bus, and some were ejected through doors and windows. Six passengers were killed and many others were seriously injured.

Bishop Morris R. Parry ran a mile back to the town of Aguila for help. Emergency medical crews had to come from Wickenburg—over twenty-six miles away. Meanwhile the survivors in the bus, "terrified and rain-soaked, met the perilous situation as bravely as possible." The First Presidency of the Church, at the request of the Los Angeles Stake presidency, soon appropriated funds to care for the injured. "It was several weeks before the last of [the injured] were released from the hospital."[15]

A second tragedy occurred three days after Christmas in 1938. On the morning of 28 December two little girls and a teenaged boy were traveling by car to take part in ordinances

---

[15] Muir, 1:469–70.

at the St. George Temple. All three were killed on the winding road through central California's San Marcos Pass.[16]

Until this time, progress toward a California temple had been slow. But news of these tragedies intensified interest in having temples close by. Committees were formed in both the north and the south to find suitable sites.

On 23 March 1937, despite continuing economic depression, negotiations for the purchase of a 24.33-acre site in Los Angeles were finalized. The site fronted on the heavily traveled Santa Monica Boulevard and was the property of silent screen star and comedian Harold Lloyd and his motion picture company. A large stucco building with a tile roof, which previously had been the company's business offices, stood in the middle of the tract. When the Church purchased the property, however, this building was a fraternity house for students at the University of California at Los Angeles (UCLA). Though preliminary plans were drawn before 1940, World War II and resulting shortages would delay the temple's construction.

Meanwhile, the committee in the north, headed by stake president Eugene Hilton, attempted to locate the Oakland site envisioned by Elder George Albert Smith ten years before. As they searched, they were enthusiastically aided by the local chamber of commerce and city officials.

Several possible sites were considered. Though two were offered free of charge, a particular spot impressed the committee as "the one," but it was not for sale. They also faced resistance from Church headquarters after the announced purchase of the Los Angeles site, because of reluctance to build two temples in California at the same time. The committee suspended its work, but President Hilton admonished: "Let us patiently wait our time and keep silent regarding this preferred site. Let us also watch and pray that we may yet obtain it."[17]

---

[16] Ibid., 1:472.

[17] David W. Cummings, *Triumph: Commemorating the Opening of the East Bay Interstake Center on Temple Hill, Oakland, January 1958* (Oakland: Oakland Area Stakes, 1958), 10.

Other Activities during the Depression

Now that California had several functioning stakes, auxiliary programs and activities mushroomed. On a dozen different fronts, Church organizations and programs became more active. One example was an active athletic program, with an annual all-Church basketball tournament in Salt Lake City, won by the Glendale Ward in 1933.

Glendale Ward 1933 all-Church basketball champions

Depression conditions, however, posed a hurdle. In Pasadena, for example, local wards "had to wait to organize a Primary until the time when enough families could share in the transportation of the children to and from the weekly activities."[18]

A most significant California contribution to the Church during this decade came in the area of education. In 1928, several religious denominations of the Los Angeles area had united in the inauguration of the University Religious Conference adjacent to the UCLA campus. Emily Brinton Sims became the Latter-day Saint representative. The Church contributed ten thousand dollars to the erection of the Religious Conference Building and for many years supported the operation of this institution.

A few years after the establishment of the Conference, the executive secretary, Thomas St. Clair Evans, recommended that Latter-day Saint students form an organization to promote fellowship, social and religious identification, and instruction, as the Protestant, Catholic, and Jewish groups had done. Thus, the Church's first Deseret Club was organized at UCLA on

---

[18] Leung, 4.

13 January 1931. Local members instrumental in this organization were Preston D. Richards, Adele Cannon Howells, and Vern O. Knudsen (a member of the UCLA faculty). This club was eventually expanded Churchwide on campuses where there were not enough Latter-day Saint students to justify establishing a more fully organized institute of religion.

In 1935 the University of Southern California invited the Church to send a representative to instruct classes on Mormonism in its School of Religion. Elder John A. Widtsoe of the Council of the Twelve, a former university president, received this assignment. After one season, Elder Widtsoe was succeeded by G. Byron Done, who continued for some time, developing a program that reached four thousand students in Southern California. An equally active though smaller program also flourished in Northern California. This became the foundation of the Church's "institute" program in California, patterned after a similar model inaugurated at the University of Idaho in 1926.

Berkeley Institute of Religion

One of the more curious events of the decade was the election of a California governor with Latter-day Saint roots but who openly declared himself an atheist. California's twenty-ninth governor, Culbert Olson, began his career in Utah as a lawyer and Democratic politician, continuing it in California after 1920. He was a Utah-born grandson of Latterday Saint Pioneers but was also a protégé of the defeated Upton Sinclair. Olson was elected governor on the Democratic ticket in 1938—the first member of that party to hold the office since 1899. He was the only California governor to that date who refused to place his hand on the Bible when he took his oath of office. So Olson, who did not identify himself as LDS, was philosophically opposed to the more conservative position of the Church and his fellow Democrat, President Heber J. Grant.

Governors Henry H. Blood of Utah and Culbert L. Olson of California at 1939 Golden Gate Exposition

The decade dominated by the Great Depression was a period of suffering but also one of new beginnings and growth. The Church found a way to "care for its own." As the Saints were recognized for lives well lived, they were increasingly invited to participate in California affairs; consequently, the Church gained greater respect. In politics and on many other fronts, the Latter-day Saints were becoming a more vital and appreciated sector of California's citizenry. For example, the Bancroft Library at the University of California in Berkeley asked the Church to submit materials on California Latter-day Saints, past and present.

Unquestionably, the Great Depression was the dominating force of the 1930s. But powerful as this effect was, events of even greater impact were about to unfold.

World War II: 1939–45 17

World War II was perhaps the most significant, defining event of the twentieth century. It changed the way America viewed itself and the rest of the world. Prior to the war, the United States looked primarily eastward toward Europe, cradle of its culture and language and the origin of 85 percent of its immigrants. However, this war reminded the nation that its western shore faced the great cultures of Asia, which began to play an increasingly important role in U.S. affairs. For the rest of the century, most of America's major armed conflicts would be in Asia, and military operations would be funneled primarily through California. During this same time, a growing tide of Asian immigrants and products would flow toward California.

The war's repercussions in California were particularly great—altering the face of the state psychologically, economically, technologically, and sociologically. World War II profoundly changed California's demographics in ways that continued to be felt for decades. War-related activities accelerated America's internal population shift toward the Pacific Coast. The war also intensified California's ethnic diversity as hundreds of thousands of American Blacks came to work in California's war industries, permanently adding large numbers of African American faces to the Anglo, Mexican, and

Asian ones that had already been important parts of the state for a century or more. Finally, the war triggered a population bubble called the "baby boom," as many children were born just after the war ended. The war began in Europe where Adolf Hitler and his Nazi Party first rose to power in Germany then set out on a path of conquest. For a while, the United States, still smarting from the Great Depression and World War I, remained on the sidelines. However, as it became increasingly apparent that without American action Hitler could prevail, the United States reluctantly became more involved—largely ignoring the growing threat on its western flank.

But on 7 December 1941, when the Japanese launched a surprise air attack on the U.S. naval base at Pearl Harbor in Hawaii, America's attention was suddenly diverted westward. California Saints were just leaving their morning Sunday School services when reports of this event reached the mainland. Some heard the news on their car radios as they drove home.

A Future Prophet Begins His Ministry

As these scenes unfolded, a future president of the Church, Howard W. Hunter, began his service as a bishop in Los Angeles. Though he had Latter-day Saint Pioneer ancestors, his father's family had drifted away from Church activity. Young Howard was not baptized until he was twelve rather than at the accustomed age of eight. In the late 1920s, he was among those transplants whose faith deepened in California. Although he had participated in Church activities while growing up in Idaho, he later acknowledged that his "first real awakening to the gospel" resulted from attending Peter A. Clayton's Sunday School class in the Los Angeles Adams Ward. Brother Clayton had a wealth of knowledge on gospel topics and was able to motivate the young members of his class by assigning them to speak on specific gospel themes. "I think of this period of my life as the time the truths of the gospel commenced to unfold," Howard W. Hunter later recalled. "I always had a testimony of the gospel, but suddenly I commenced to understand."[1]

As a young father and *cum laude* law school graduate, he became the first bishop of Southern California's new El Sereno Ward on 1 September 1940. He said:

> Such a call had never entered my mind, and I was stunned. I had always thought of a bishop as being an older man, and I asked how I could be the father of the ward at such a young age of 32. They said I would be the youngest bishop in Southern California, but they knew I could be equal to the assignment.[2]

The new bishop's first task was to "find a place for meetings, get the ward organized and staffed, and get going." He arranged to rent the local Masonic lodge for Sunday services and for an occasional Friday night activity. The rent was fifteen dollars a month. "We didn't know where we were going to get $15," Elder Hunter later reminisced, "but we survived."[3]

The Latter-day Saints and Military Service

In May 1941, several months before the United States entered the war, the Church appointed Hugh B. Brown, who was living in Glendale, as servicemen's coordinator. A former stake president and officer in the Canadian military during World War I, and future apostle and counselor in the First Presidency, he brought stature to this new calling. He began his assignment with a visit to a group of Latter-day Saint servicemen at San Luis Obispo. He next accompanied Elders Albert E. Bowen and Harold B. Lee of the Quorum of the Twelve (the latter having been called as an apostle only a few

---

[1] Eleanor Knowles, *Howard W. Hunter* (Salt Lake City: Deseret Book, 1994), 70–71.

[2] Quoted in Susan Kamei Leung, *How Firm a Foundation: The Story of the Pasadena Stake* (Pasadena, Calif.: Pasadena California Stake, 1994), 14.

[3] Ibid.

Hugh B. Brown recalls role as servicemen's coordinator

weeks earlier) to San Diego, where several hundred Latter-day Saints were already stationed.

Wherever Hugh B. Brown went, he organized special branches for military personnel and made sure the servicemen were supplied with Church reading materials.[4] He delivered numerous inspirational sermons to military personnel—regardless of their religious affiliations—in open-air meetings, on board ships, in army huts, and in military chapels, canteens, and theaters.[5]

From these beginnings in California, a Churchwide servicemen's program developed. Because a large share of Latter-day Saints entering military service received their basic training in California, Brown and his associates played a key role. They officially appointed many of these young men to be "group leaders." Wherever they were sent, they were authorized to conduct religious services and in other ways minister to the spiritual needs of their associates.

In the April 1942 general conference, four months after the attack on Pearl Harbor, the First Presidency outlined the Church's position on war and gave counsel to Latter-day Saints

---

[4] Eugene E. Campbell and Richard D. Poll, *Hugh B. Brown: His Life and Thought* (Salt Lake City: Bookcraft, 1975), 144–46.

[5] Leo J. Muir, *A Century of Mormon Activities in California* (Salt Lake City: Deseret News Press, 1952), 1:484.

in military service: "Hate can have no place in the souls of the righteous," they declared, emphasizing the Savior's injunction to love one another. However, as citizens, the Saints should "render that loyalty to their country and to free institutions which the loftiest patriotism calls for. . . . Both sides cannot be wholly right; perhaps neither is without wrong." The First Presidency exhorted the young men and women in military service to "live clean, keep the commandments of the Lord, pray to Him constantly to preserve you in truth and righteousness, live as you pray, and then whatever betides you the Lord will be with you. . . . Then, when the conflict is over and you return to your homes, having lived the righteous life, how great will be your happiness—whether you be of the victors or the vanquished—that you have lived as the Lord commanded."[6]

Heeding the counsel of their Church leaders, Latter-day Saints responded when calls for military service came. Many servicemen were trained in California before being shipped overseas. Hence, wards and stakes in the Golden State became heavily involved in the various programs the Church implemented for servicemen. These local units frequently sponsored dances and other events to which the servicemen were invited. "Budget cards" became passports to these Church social and recreational activities.

Many Latter-day Saints in the military shared their beliefs with others. Numerous conversions resulted from the worthy examples of LDS friends, both in California and overseas. As a result, many small branches of local members sprouted in the Pacific and East Asia. Growth in these areas would impact the Church in California throughout the rest of the century, as members from these regions migrated to the state.

---

[6] In *Conference Report*, April 1942, 90–96.

Saints in the War Industries

One of the greatest challenges the war brought to California resulted from rapid population growth and escalating defense spending. California's population had already exploded. The growth of the 1920s and 1930s, the largest migration in the world's history, was now eclipsed. The number of newcomers during the 1940s was greater than the total of the previous two decades combined (see appendix B). Between 1940 and 1946 the U.S. government injected an average of seven billion dollars per year into the state's economy. Even without war, that amount would have done severe violence to the state's social and economic structure, for it was nearly twice the average annual value of the previous years' total economic output.[7]

California became one of the major manufacturing states in the nation. In Southern California the aircraft industry mushroomed from a scant twenty thousand workers in 1939 to more than 243,000 four years later.[8]

Another large industrial effort was shipbuilding. The Bay Area port of Richmond built a series of "Liberty ships" named for American heroes. One of those was the cargo ship *Joseph Smith*, built by the Kaiser shipyard and launched on 20 May 1943. The Oakland Stake president, Eugene Hilton, represented the First Presidency at the christening of this ship named for the Church's founding Prophet. Special music was provided by the Oakland Stake, and many members attended the ceremonies.[9]

These manufacturing efforts swiftly exhausted the state's available labor supply, so California industries recruited workers from all over the country. The inducements were considerable. Weekly earnings nearly doubled, and those

---

[7] T. H. Watkins, *California: An Illustrated History* (Palo Alto, Calif.: American West, 1973), 434.

[8] Ibid., 435–36.

[9] Muir, 1:475.

working in essential wartime industries were exempt from the draft. California's high wages and mild climate were powerful attractions. As a result, the total number of manufacturing workers increased from 461,000 in 1940 to 1,186,000 in 1943.[10] Thus, almost overnight, what had been a large and important state became the giant of the West, a state larger, more populous, and more prosperous than most independent countries.

Though the pace of the general migration was fast, the influx of Latter-day Saints to California continued to be even greater. LDS population grew from one in 150 in 1940 to one in 120 in 1945. The Church's percent of California's population was higher than its percent in the nation as a whole. Between 1940 and 1950, California's LDS population grew 128 percent, from 44,800 to 102,000.

The war impacted the Saints and Californians in other distinctive and significant ways. Large numbers of women left traditional roles as full-time homemakers and took places on factory assembly lines to alleviate the labor shortage. "Rosie the Riveter" not only became a wartime heroine but was the precedent for permanently altered roles for many women. Many of those whose husbands were away as soldiers went into the workplace to do their part to aid the war effort. However, rather than going back home when the war ended, many kept working, joined by ever larger numbers of women. Though Church leaders warned that removing mothers from traditional roles could have a significant impact on families, the number of working Latter-day Saint women continued to rise after the war.

The Effects of War

In January 1942, just a month after the Pearl Harbor attack, the First Presidency announced that in order to cut down on unnecessary travel, all stake leadership meetings for various

---

[10] Watkins, 439.

Church programs would be suspended for the duration of the war. Later, other Church activities and large group gatherings had to be curtailed also, because of gasoline and tire rationing and because of the difficulties in obtaining automobiles. Those restrictions especially affected California, where traveling distances were typically longer.

Elder Harold B. Lee was convinced that the timing of the Church's precautions was the result of revelation. Referring to the January 1942 restrictions on meetings and travel, he declared:

> When you remember that all this happened from eight months to nearly a year before the tire and gas rationing took place, you may well understand if you will only take thought that here again was the voice of the Lord to this people, trying to prepare them for the conservation program that within a year was forced upon them. No one at that time could surely foresee that the countries that had been producing certain essential commodities were to be overrun and we thereby be forced into a shortage.[11]

The war changed Church activities in several other interesting ways. In certain areas, owing to fears of possible air raids, the military ordered all buildings "blacked out" at night. Latter-day Saint churches took on a somber look as opaque coverings were applied to all windows. If any light was seen coming from the building during evening air-raid drills, the "block warden" ordered the lights turned off. "Motorists were even instructed not to use their headlights at night. Local Church leaders therefore canceled as many evening activities and meetings as possible to facilitate compliance with the 'black out' regulations and to minimize risk to the members." The Pasadena Stake, for example, moved its sacrament meetings from early evening to the afternoon.[12]

Building supplies were diverted for military use, so construction of meetinghouses also came to a halt, despite a rapidly growing Church population. Nevertheless, local

---

[11] In *Conference Report*, April 1943, 128.

[12] Leung, 18.

congregations tried to accumulate money in hopes of having a chapel someday. Even though the El Sereno Ward could not build its badly needed meetinghouse during the war, Bishop Howard W. Hunter led his congregation in projects to earn money which they put aside for the time when they could proceed. For example, ward members tediously trimmed onions for a nearby pickle factory, and for a sauerkraut producer they shredded cabbages which were then stamped down in large vats by men in rubber boots. "It was easy to tell in Sacrament Meeting if a person had been snipping onions," Bishop Hunter mused.[13]

He also encouraged family members to plant their own gardens and to work in the ward garden raising beans. "People in the neighborhood were amazed at the harvest we gathered," one ward member recalled.[14] These gardens were part of a nationwide "Victory Garden" campaign for families and other groups to grow as much of their own produce as possible so that commercially grown products could be fed to soldiers. Some of the gardens in the Pasadena Stake were singled out for acclaim over national radio as a stimulus to encourage other Americans to become likewise involved.

Because of the building shortage, the Church organized fewer new stakes nationwide during the war and none in California. The Church did, however, divide the California Mission. This decision coincided with the outbreak of the war. Beginning in January 1942, the new Northern California Mission, a mission headquartered once again in San Francisco, was responsible for approximately four thousand members in forty-five branches scattered throughout Northern California, western Nevada, and southern Oregon. The California Mission continued to be headquartered in Los Angeles and had nearly thirty-seven hundred members in thirty-four branches, including some in Arizona. This division was fortunate because it cut

---

[13] Knowles, 97–98; Leung, 21.

[14] *Church News*, 10 January 1981, 2, as quoted in Knowles, 101.

down the number of miles the mission president had to travel. No longer would one man have to cover the vast state of California plus portions of three other western states as well. It also doubled the availability of a mission president to give leadership and counsel to servicemen and other members. Over the course of time, both stakes and missions would continue to be divided again and again.

The Church agreed not to call young men of draft age to go on missions. Hence the number of missionaries in California plummeted as more young men entered military service during the war. While 244 missionaries were serving at the end of 1941, the total dropped three years later to only seventy-two.[15] Members living in California again assumed more responsibility to make up for the shortfall, just as they had when the number of missionaries dropped a decade earlier during the Great Depression. These Saints accepted calls as local part-time missionaries and at the same time assumed greater roles in stake, ward, district, and branch organizations.

Church members often had to function in two or more callings simultaneously. For instance, Bishop Hunter also carried the weighty load of scoutmaster.

The cutbacks in Church personnel and programs came at the very time when the Church more than ever needed to reach the growing number of members cut free from the guiding and sustaining influence of home and family. These included thousands of LDS servicemen and servicewomen, as well as LDS youth who were seeking employment in California's defense industries. Near the end of the war, more than half of the young men of high school and college age were living away from home. Church authorities encouraged local leaders to take a special interest in these youth. Despite the pressures of living away from home, however, the young Saints' faithful adherence to Church doctrines and standards was actually strengthened during the war. In several areas the contribution

---

[15] Mission Annual Reports, 1941–42, 1944; LDS Church Archives.

of tithes and fast offerings and the attendance at Church meetings increased. The California groups stood among the top wards, stakes, and missions of the Church. This was in spite of the fact that the leadership burdens in California were perhaps larger than anywhere else in the Church because of the number of members that leaders had to serve and the distances involved in reaching them.

Church members became involved in a variety of activities to help with the war effort. Even the youth found ways to assist. During the winter of 1942–43, the Church's twelve- and thirteen-year-old Beehive girls donated thousands of hours collecting scrap metal, fats, and other needed materials, making scrapbooks or baking cookies for soldiers, and tending children for mothers working in defense industries. A special "Honor Bee" award was offered for such service.

As the war dragged on, concerned Latter-day Saints in California established servicemen's "homes away from home." One was the five-room Berkeley residence of Stanley and Anna Patton, who were known as "Mom and Pop" Patton to thousands of servicemen and servicewomen. The Pattons made their basement into a free dormitory and put cots in the laundry room. The young men were given keys to these downstairs rooms, which they called "cot luck."

But the Pattons' home was more than a dormitory. They sponsored activities that ran the gamut—birthdays, engagements, weddings, births, baptisms, priesthood advancements, and farewells. On some occasions they even had to help with funeral arrangements.

After morning Sunday School, the Pattons invited two or three home for dinner. Each week there were a few more, and soon their home could not hold them all. So the sisters of the Berkeley Ward began hosting servicemen's lunches at the chapel. After Sunday School they set up long tables and brought salads or vegetables—whatever they could spare—and combined these potluck items into dinners for the servicemen. At the war's peak, as many as 150 were served

Anna Patton and her home in Berkeley

dinner each week in the ward cultural hall. Rather than going with their buddies to movies, bars, or other less-desirable places, the servicemen were invited to spend the afternoon at the church until sacrament meeting began in the evening.

The servicemen brought wives, mothers, sisters, and sweethearts to meet "Mom and Pop." For three years the LDS military personnel at nearby Treasure Island honored Sister Patton on Mothers' Day with a special program. Over the years Anna compiled more than twenty scrapbooks of correspondence from servicemen and servicewomen as they scattered throughout the world.[16]

One group of California Saints severely affected by the war were those of Japanese ancestry. Fearing that Japanese Americans might become disloyal if the coast were attacked, overly cautious government officials ordered them to leave or be concentrated under armed guard in relocation centers. Some, such as Hideo "Eddie" Kawai and his extended family chose to move to Utah, where they could remain "close to the gospel and other members of the Church during wartime." When the Kawais returned home after the war they were disappointed to find that they were still the victims of pre-

---

[16] Muir, 1:475.

judice and were therefore especially grateful for "their true friends."[17]

A Second Temple Site Secured

Despite the war, California Latter-day Saints still longed to have temples nearby. Even though no construction could be done, they, full of faith, drew plans for a temple in Los Angeles and kept their eyes on the hill in Oakland.

One of the war's few favorable impacts was the acquisition of the longed-for Oakland site. Just two weeks after Pearl Harbor was bombed, A. B. Graham, a Latter-day Saint realtor who had been on the original site-selection committee, informed Oakland Stake president Hilton that because of the war, the owner of the hill was unable to obtain building materials to go forward with his planned subdivision. He offered the entire 14.5 acres to Graham for eighteen thousand dollars. President Hilton said: "This is most important. It is an answer to our prayers. We won't wait for the mails. I will go directly to Salt Lake tonight."[18]

The First Presidency agreed to look at the proposed site. One delay after another kept President David O. McKay from coming for nearly two months, so the staunch "hill watchers passed many anxious hours" as the owner was on the verge of selling the property to others who were offering him more money. Graham's diplomacy was rewarded as the site was still available when President McKay finally arrived. He was "enraptured at what he saw" and promised to recommend its purchase. From that time on the Saints spiritedly referred to the site as "Temple Hill." The purchase of this property was consummated by August 1943.[19]

---

[17] Leung, 18–19.

[18] David W. Cummings, *Triumph: Commemorating the Opening of the East Bay Interstake Center on Temple Hill, Oakland, January 1958* (Oakland: Oakland Area Stakes, 1959), 10.

[19] Ibid.

Then followed the even more difficult task of obtaining an additional two acres, "which were absolutely necessary to provide the proper entrance to the tract itself." The owners of the two acres were not interested in selling because it was "their country home and the place where they kept their precious horses." A few years later, however, they finally agreed to sell the property—for six thousand dollars more than Church leaders in Salt Lake had authorized. Fearing that further delay might result in losing the strategic piece and lead to the entire project's undoing, "local stake authorities counseled together, and concluded to buy the two acres on their own responsibility, knowing that time would justify their actions. They proposed to raise the extra six thousand dollars among themselves, if necessary, rather than risk losing the natural 'key' to the entire project."[20]

The property was finally purchased in August 1947, after which the First Presidency informed the Oakland leaders that "we have concluded that you acted wisely and will accordingly advance the entire purchase price." Subsequent purchases brought the site's total size to 18.3 acres. Oakland leaders anticipated that this would be regarded as the "most impressive and inspiring location" of any temple site worldwide.[21]

The War Draws to a Close

During the closing years of the war, Saints in California were concerned about providing help to their fellow Saints—even those who were on the opposite side of the conflict. The Los Angeles Deseret Industries sent sixty thousand pounds of "first class salvage clothing and shoes" via the Panama Canal to Church members in Holland and Germany who had been devastated by the war. These, together with $6,100 worth of commodities sent by the Oakland Stake, were part of nearly

[20] Ibid., 19.

[21] Ibid.

four million pounds of goods supplied by the Church for relief in Europe.

In addition, in 1945 Deseret Industries trucks "collected and delivered to the U.S. government more than a hundred thousand pounds" of clothing in a national drive. The trucks visited 5,227 homes, 92 percent of which donated something.[22] Many of those supplies would be distributed in Europe immediately following the close of the war under the personal supervision of Elder Ezra Taft Benson of the Twelve.

As had been the case with Joseph F. Smith, Heber J. Grant's service as president of the Church ended as a world war came to its close. President Grant died on 14 May 1945, just one week after Germany's surrender and three months before Japan's. Throughout his twenty-seven-year administration, he had encouraged the California Saints, and there had been substantial growth in the Golden State. Much of the state was blanketed by wards and branches. In fact, as the war drew to a close, approximately 10 percent of all Latter-day Saints lived in California—a figure that would remain fairly constant from that time forward.

---

[22] Muir, 1:288–89.

Celebration and Commemoration: 1945–55

18

The years immediately following World War II were a time of celebration. Latter-day Saints rejoiced as peace superseded war, and they commemorated various pioneer centennials as worldwide Church membership surpassed the one million mark in 1947.

In California, Latter-day Saints were once again, as Samuel Brannan had expressed it over a century earlier, "A No. 1 in this country."[1] Press coverage continued to be positive. State politicians made increasingly frequent appearances at LDS events.

Presiding over the Church after the war years was President Heber J. Grant's successor, George Albert Smith, who was a lifelong devotee of Church history, especially the marking of historic sites. President Smith supervised the erection of more than a hundred substantial markers at historic sites throughout the western United States, several of which were in California. Thus, it was fitting that he presided over the Church during this time of commemoration.

[1] Andrew Jenson, comp., "The California Mission," 18 September 1847; LDS Church Archives.

President Smith stood six feet tall and was slender with a thin face and a kindly expression. He was without guile or pretense. One Californian, while investigating the Church, attended a meeting where the prophet was going to be. Expecting to see a pompous and impeccably dressed man, he was completely disarmed by President Smith's quiet, approachable, and loving manner and said he was convinced that George Albert Smith was a true and humble servant of God when he noticed that his shoes were an inexpensive department store variety with holes in the soles.

Though he never resided in California, President Smith had visited the state on numerous occasions. His 1924 vision of the future Oakland Temple imbued the Saints with a heightened desire for temples. During his administration, plans for building California temples in both the north and the south were vigorously pursued, though he died before either was completed.

Postwar Growth in California

LDS growth in California continued during the postwar years, passing the one hundred thousand mark in 1950. Many service people passed through the state on their way home from Pacific battlefields, and some never left. Others returned to the Intermountain area, then came back with families or sweethearts to settle.

New cities sprang up as the state teemed with new subdivisions of hundreds, sometimes thousands, of identical two- and three-bedroom homes. The G.I. Bill allowed returning service people to purchase one of those starter homes with no money down and low monthly payments, while earning a living as laborers, businessmen, or professionals, often using skills they had gained in the service.

California made a strong commitment to education, and many Latter-day Saints, both students and educators, benefitted. Through the G.I. Bill, the federal government also paid for veterans' college educations. In order to meet educational needs in California, a widely admired system of state and community colleges developed. At the same time, the population growth and the postwar baby boom required many new public schools.

As the school system grew, more teachers and administrators were needed. Recruiters from California were frequent visitors at Utah colleges, resulting in "a surprisingly large number of Latter-day Saint teachers and administrators in higher education" in California, as well as hundreds of teachers in California public schools, and hundreds more studying in California colleges.[2]

Of the 1,234 Latter-day Saints whose biographies were published by Leo J. Muir in 1952, 29 percent were businessmen, 17 percent educators, and 23 percent other professionals. Nearly three-fourths came from Utah or other Intermountain states. Only 10 percent, mostly young adult children of transplants, were born in California. Apparently, sixty years of active proselytizing in the Los Angeles area had not resulted in significant numbers of native converts. Only 150—12 percent of Muir's sample—were converts. Less than fifty were California-born.

Historical Societies and Centennial Celebrations

With the heavy migration into California during the Great Depression and then during World War II, an increasing number of residents in the Golden State were first-generation transplants from other areas. During the postwar years it was natural for these people to look back to their roots. Various societies sponsored activities "designed to bring former residents of individual states together in a kind of continuing

---

[2] Leo J. Muir, *A Century of Mormon Activities in California* (Salt Lake City: Deseret News Press, 1952), 1:316.

reunion."[3] This interest in places of origin was strongly manifested among the California Saints, who created several Utah-oriented organizations. The Daughters of Utah Pioneers (DUP) was perhaps the most active; from their beginning at Los Angeles in 1927, they continued organizing chapters in virtually every California stake. The first chapter of the Sons of Utah Pioneers (SUP) was organized on 28 October 1946, also in Los Angeles. Other groups included the California Utah Women and the Utah Women's Club. These LDS men and women constituted some of the most civic-minded groups in the state.

These societies became active in celebrating the Latter-day Saints' California heritage. On 30 July 1940 the San Francisco DUP chapter brought ninety-five-year-old Elizabeth Bird Howell, the only living survivor of the *Brooklyn* passengers, to be present as a bronze plaque was unveiled at the corner of Broadway and Battery Streets in San Francisco, the spot where the ship had unloaded.[4]

Although Latter-day Saint settlers arrived in California in 1846—a full year before the Pioneers entered the Great Basin—and although San Francisco was the first LDS settlement in the West, these facts went largely uncelebrated, even among local members. Instead, the arrival of the Pioneers in Utah in 1847 was the main focus.

San Bernardino's "Covered Wagon Days" featured a performance by the Salt Lake Mormon Tabernacle Choir. Participating in the celebration were President George Albert Smith and Utah governor Herbert Maw. On Sunday, 12 October, the Choir presented its 950th consecutive weekly radio broadcast, from San Bernardino's First Congregational Church. Elder Richard L. Evans, member of the First Council of the Seventy and official narrator for the Choir, conducted the proceedings. Other churches in the community were closed

---

[3] T. H. Watkins, *California: An Illustrated History* (Palo Alto, Calif.: American West, 1973), 359.

[4] Muir, 1:446.

that day as the Choir program was designated "The Union Church Service."

On 24 January 1948 Latter-day Saints participated in the "Gold Discovery Jubilee" at Coloma. From Church headquarters in Utah came Oscar A. Kirkham of the First Council of the Seventy, Gordon B. Hinckley of the Church Publicity Committee, and Henry Smith of the *Deseret News*. Grover C. Dunford, Los Angeles SUP president, presented Governor Earl Warren a memento, "a pair of handsome bookends, each a replica of the Mormon Battalion Monument on the Utah State Capitol grounds in Salt Lake City."[5] For this occasion local Church members erected a replica of a typical miner's cabin built of "random width boards and batten" to house a special exhibit. Prepared under Brother Hinckley's supervision, illuminated dioramas focused on the Mormon Battalion's achievements, including their role in the discovery of gold.[6]

The Alameda County DUP chapter raised money and in October 1949 erected two monuments in the San Joaquin Valley. Designed by Theodore Ruegg, an LDS architect from Berkeley, each consists of metal plaques mounted on cobblestone shafts (see appendix E for locations). The inscription on the monument at Ripon commemorates the New Hope Colony, where "Mormon Pioneers from the ship *Brooklyn* founded first known agricultural colony in San Joaquin valley," and planted the "first wheat."

The second marker, placed at the former site of Moss Landing on the San Joaquin River, honors Samuel Brannan's sailboat, the *Comet*, the "first known sail launch to ascend San Joaquin River from San Francisco."

The SUP celebrated the centennial of California's statehood in 1950. In March of that year, members of the Los Angeles, San Diego, and San Bernardino SUP chapters joined others who had come from Utah in several buses, traveling

---

[5] Ibid., 1:463.

[6] *Church News*, 31 January 1948, 1, 6–7.

SUP "Mormon Battalion march" at San Diego

over the final portion of the Mormon Battalion route into California. In Los Angeles, President George Albert Smith, Utah governor J. Bracken Lee, and apostles Joseph Fielding Smith and Harold B. Lee greeted them.

Governors Earl Warren and J. Bracken Lee admire gold discovery statue with sculptor Avard Fairbanks

Before a crowd of fifteen hundred on the south lawn of the city hall, they were officially received by Los Angeles mayor Fletcher Bowron and California governor Earl Warren. Avard Fairbanks, the noted Utah sculptor, presented to the governor "a miniature of the monument he had made to memorialize the discovery of gold in California."

President Smith then addressed the throng and "recounted the achievements of the Battalion." He also "related many interesting personal experiences in California" and "expressed praise and appreciation to the people of California for their goodwill" toward the Latter-day Saints. He then "outlined his formula for the cure of the evils which perplex the race of men."[7]

Members of the DUP and SUP had, over a period of several years, raised funds for a monument to the Mormon Battalion that would stand adjacent to the Los Angeles civic center. Construction of the Hollywood Freeway just after the close of World War II required the removal of part of the hill on which Fort Moore had stood. As part of a massive retaining wall (four hundred feet long), the memorial features relief sculptures of early California pioneers, including the Battalion. A sixty-eight-foot pylon flagpole bears the inscription: "Fort Moore Pioneer Memorial To the Brave men and women who, with trust in God, faced privation and death in extending the frontiers of our country to include this land of promise." The monument was finally dedicated on 3 July 1958 by former LDS Serviceman's Coordinator Hugh B. Brown, now a member of

Fort Moore memorial in Los Angeles

[7] Muir, 1:459–60.

the Quorum of the Twelve and a grandson of Battalion member and gold discoverer James S. Brown.[8]

Leo J. Muir's two-volume work, *A Century of Mormon Activities in California*, was published during this period of intense interest in Church history. The first volume briefly reviewed Church activities in the Golden State, while the second volume contained over one thousand brief biographical sketches. A major contribution of Muir's 1952 work was his collection of many interesting photographs. Another significant California LDS history was Eugene E. Campbell's doctoral dissertation at the University of Southern California, also completed in 1952.[9]

Latter-day Saints in Cultural and Professional Life

As the Latter-day Saints gained increasing respect, they became more accepted into California's cultural and professional circles. These were years of celebrity-studded fund raisers, elegant gold-and-green balls, and formal concerts. For example, on 18 November 1949, the Inglewood Stake presented a "grand musical" in Los Angeles's prestigious Shrine Auditorium as a welfare fund raiser. Many noted performers responded to invitations to volunteer their talents. The production featured well-known Latter-day Saint performers, including movie star Lorraine Day. Also in attendance were Cecil B. DeMille, Gary Cooper, Edgar Bergen, J. Spencer Cornwall, and others, who received special citations for "faithful and meritorious service to their fellow men."[10]

Individual Latter-day Saints increasingly gained prominence and thus were able to provide more support for Church activities. One example was Rose Marie Reid, who came to Los

---

[8] *Church News*, 3 May 1958, 2; 5 July 1958, 7.

[9] Eugene E. Campbell, "A History of The Church of Jesus Christ of Latter-day Saints in California, 1846–1946" (Ph.D. diss., University of Southern California, 1952).

[10] Muir, 1:361–62.

Angeles from western Canada in 1947. She became a noted designer and manufacturer of swimsuits. She frequently opened her beautiful Brentwood home for LDS social functions and became active in sharing the gospel with business associates and many others.[11]

Another noted individual who helped the Church during this period was the retired boxer Jack Dempsey. Although he had been baptized in his native Colorado, he did not participate actively in the Church after moving to California in the 1920s. Nevertheless, he was a "liberal contributor to the building of LDS chapels in California."[12]

Miss America Colleen Hutchins on Church magazine cover

On 20 January 1950, Latter-day Saint artists of the Los Angeles area presented in the Wilshire Ward building what was designated the "First Annual Art Exhibition." On display were 120 pieces from twenty-eight artists. "This was, in all likelihood the first art exhibit of the works of Mormon artists ever presented in California."[13]

A widely publicized example of Latter-day Saint recognition occurred in 1951, when the brother-sister duo of Mel and Colleen Hutchins of Southern California's Arcadia Ward achieved national fame. Colleen was crowned Miss America. Mel, playing for Brigham Young University, was named All-American and most valuable player in college basketball's National Invitational Tournament.

---

[11] Ibid., 1:396.

[12] Ibid., 1:363–64; see also Jack Dempsey, *Dempsey* (New York: Harper and Row, 1977).

[13] Ibid., 1:478.

Not only were individual members achieving recognition for their cultural attainments, but the Church as an organization was also sponsoring such activities. One example was the Mormon Choir of Southern California.

Wilshire Ward bishop Roy Utley inherited a tradition of outstanding ward choirs and went to unusual lengths to secure an accomplished director. Early in 1951, he contacted an acclaimed musician, H. Frederick Davis, a native of New Zealand

Choir conductor
H. Frederick Davis

then living in Whittier, about moving into the Wilshire Ward and directing the choir. Realtor Harold E. Phelps found a suitable home within the ward, and Davis moved to direct the choir.

When officials at radio station KMPC were planning a program entitled "Go to Church," they invited Davis and his choir to participate. The program's producer was quite impressed and therefore wanted an expanded, three-hundred-voice choir, with Davis as director, for a special program at the outdoor Hollywood Bowl. When, with the advice of Los Angeles Stake president John M. Russon, Davis agreed to serve as director, the First Presidency gave approval to organize such a choir "on a one-time basis."

A 309-voice choir was drawn from throughout the Los Angeles area. Following "a highly successful program" before an audience of eight thousand at the Bowl on 7 October, the choir was asked to perform again that same month at the San Bernardino centennial celebration. Following this concert, the choir was officially disbanded but was brought together once again to provide music for the famous Hollywood Bowl Easter sunrise service in April 1952.

The Hollywood Ministerial Association raised its voice in opposition "on the grounds that Mormons were not Christians." However, when LDS representatives explained the

Church's faith in Jesus Christ, the objection was withdrawn. The choir made such a favorable impression that it was subsequently invited to sing in the churches of some of the very ministers who had initially objected. The choir was also invited to participate in NBC's coast-to-coast radio program, "Faith in Action."[14]

Owing to the widespread acclaim and repeated requests for appearances, stake presidents in the region enthusiastically recommended that the "Mormon Choir of Southern California" become a permanent institution. The First Presidency concurred.

In following years the choir became a symbol of excellence and made over one hundred national broadcasts and many appearances. It has sung for a United States president, at the dedication of the Los Angeles Temple, and at general conference in Salt Lake City. It presented George Frederick Handel's *Messiah* at the opening of Los Angeles's new music center in December 1964.[15]

In Northern California, a group of Latter-day Saint business and professional people residing in the Oakland Stake formed the Liahona Club. Its purpose was "the advancement of the cooperative and individual well-being of its members by bringing to their collective attention the respective abilities and business talents of all its members." Just as the Liahona was a compasslike instrument used as a guide in the Book of Mormon (1 Nephi 16:10), so each club member was to be a guide or compass to his fellows.

Membership in the club was open to those who owned or operated their own businesses or were executives in private enterprise or government service. Through the years, the club undertook many projects. After the war it helped servicemen find employment. For a time, it sponsored Northern Califor-

---

[14] Chad M. Orton, *More Faith Than Fear: The Los Angeles Stake Story* (Salt Lake City: Bookcraft, 1987), 207–9.

[15] Ibid., 208–9.

nia's LDS newspaper, the *Messenger*, and also constructed and maintained camps for Latter-day Saint youth.[16]

Church members also became involved in politics. On 5 October 1953 Latter-day Saint Goodwin J. Knight, California's lieutenant governor, succeeded Governor Earl Warren, who was appointed to the United States Supreme Court. Knight thus became the second California governor with an LDS background. Born in Provo, Utah, and son of businessman Jesse Knight, he had come as an infant with his family to California in 1896. When they arrived, the Latter-day Saint population was just a few hundred. After graduating from Manual Arts High School in Los Angeles, Knight went on to Stanford University—perhaps the earliest Latter-day Saint educated from elementary school to university completely in California. His name appeared in the first recorded minutes of the Los Angeles Branch Sunday School in 1915, though in his adult years he was not commonly identified as an active Church member. In 1954 he was elected by a wide margin as governor. His political career came to an end four years later, when he ran unsuccessfully for the United States Senate.[17]

Howard W. Hunter's Ministry Continues

In 1946 Howard W. Hunter was released as bishop of the El Sereno Ward after six years of wartime service. A ward member later recalled: "As a bishop, he brought our small membership together in a united effort and taught us to accomplish goals that seemed beyond our reach. We worked together as a ward, we prayed together, played together, and worshipped together."[18]

---

[16] Muir, 1:475.

[17] *Dictionary of American Biography*, Supplement 8, s.v. "Knight, Goodwin Jess ('Goodie')."

[18] Quoted in Eleanor Knowles, *Howard W. Hunter* (Salt Lake City: Deseret Book, 1994), 101.

After his release, Brother Hunter continued to be involved in Church activities which were not as demanding on his time. With other high priests, one evening each week he visited church members at Los Angeles County General Hospital to give them blessings or help in other ways. Like most members of the period, he and his two sons spent many evenings and Saturdays working on a new ward meetinghouse. They put chicken wire on a wall of the chapel for plastering and installed acoustic tiles on the ceiling. The chicken-wired walls were later plastered by some inactive members who agreed to help. As a result, they once again became fully involved in Church activity.

Howard Hunter's respite from heavy Church responsibility ended on 26 February 1950, when he was sustained as president of the Pasadena Stake. An important assignment came just over a month later during the April 1950 general conference in Salt Lake City, when he and the other Los Angeles stake presidents were summoned to the office of President Stephen L Richards of the First Presidency. President Richards explained that the time had come to consider a new early morning seminary program in California.

In earlier decades the Church had organized seminaries to provide religious education for high school students. In the LDS communities of the Intermountain West, such instruction had been offered as a regular part of students' curriculum, but a different pattern was needed for areas where Latter-day Saints were more scattered and not dominant in the population. As early as 1941 the institute director in Los Angeles had reported that there were five high schools having more than one hundred LDS students each and that several others were approaching that number. However, wartime restrictions did not permit any new programs.

Now, at the 1950 meeting in President Richards's office, Howard W. Hunter was appointed chairman of the committee to survey the various high schools in the area to see where such a program could be feasible. Following this evaluation, the eleven Los Angeles area stake presidents unanimously urged that early morning seminaries be started at once.[19]

This was no trivial undertaking. Formidable obstacles had to be overcome. Most classes had to serve more than one high school, each having a different schedule; hence, classes had to begin at 7 A.M. or even earlier. Also, carpools or other forms of transportation needed to be arranged. In September of that year, six pilot classes were inaugurated. Their success led to the addition of seven more that same school year.

Despite the difficulties of time and distance, 461 students flocked to these classes and registered an average attendance of 88 percent during that first year. Three years later, there were fifty-nine classes achieving an average attendance of 92 percent—a tribute to the devotion of students and parents willing to get up as early as 5:30 A.M. in order to attend or help children attend.[20]

Another Church program benefitted from President Hunter's leadership. Soon after becoming stake president, he "was anxious to see a family home evening program developed which would be on the same evening in every home in the stake." It was decided to set Monday evening aside. No other events would be held which would conflict with that "sacred evening."[21] Fifteen years later, in 1965, a Churchwide "Family Home Evening" program was implemented, and in 1971 Monday night was set aside for this purpose. For many years, bumper stickers saying "Happiness is Family Home Evening" could be spotted on California automobiles.

The Church's welfare plan also received attention during the postwar years. President George Albert Smith did not want to build up a huge, centralized system of storage and transportation, so urban stakes were encouraged to secure farm land on which they could raise locally the region's necessary supplies

---

[19] Knowles, 131–32.

[20] William E. Berrett, "A General History of Week-day Religious Education: The Seminaries and Institutes of Religion"; Church Educational System Archives.

[21] Knowles, 125.

of staples such as milk, meat, poultry, eggs, grain, fruits, and vegetables.

Less than four months after he became stake president, Howard W. Hunter received a telegram to meet with Henry D. Moyle of the First Presidency at a special Saturday meeting in Los Angeles. "We wondered what could cause such an emergency," he recalled. It was the purchase of the 503-acre ranch from motion picture producer Louis B. Mayer, in Perris, about fifteen miles southeast of Riverside. The Church intended it to be used as a welfare project, producing farm crops, eggs, and poultry for the Los Angeles Region. President Moyle suggested that ten stake presidents formulate a plan whereby they could raise one hundred thousand dollars as a down payment and then set up a schedule to pay off the remaining $350,000 within five years.

The stake presidents conferred and proposed that they would work over the following six months to raise the necessary down payment. To their astonishment, President Moyle rejected the idea. "In his opinion, if we could not raise it in a month, it was a lost cause," President Hunter remembered. "We talked it over again and decided to show him we could do it." Each of the stake presidents immediately contributed his share and contacted his counselors and high council about the project. In turn, local bishops notified ward leaders and each added his contribution. By mid-afternoon Sunday, the money was collected and wired to Salt Lake City, where it arrived ahead of Elder Moyle.[22]

The ranch was formally dedicated by J. Reuben Clark, Second Counselor in the First Presidency, on 8 June 1951. The following day, the Church also dedicated an eighty-thousand-square-foot industrial building on Soto Street in east Los Angeles which had been purchased the previous year for $175,000. This facility became the Southern California regional welfare center and served as the home base of the area's Deseret

---

[22] Ibid., 125–26.

Regional welfare center in Los Angeles

Industries operation. A few years later it also housed the largest cannery owned by the Church. It processed orange juice, turkey, stews, chili, beans, tomatoes, and many other commodities grown on Southern California welfare farms.[23] The various Church welfare projects scattered throughout the area were coordinated by the Southern California welfare region, over which President Howard W. Hunter presided from 1952 to 1956.

Activities for Young People

During the postwar years the Church provided various activities for its youth. The first all-Church softball tournament played its finals in Salt Lake City in the summer of 1949. Participating in the tournament were more than four hundred teams from all regions of the Church. The winner was the North Hollywood Ward from the San Fernando Valley. The following year another Southern California team, the Linda Vista Ward of the San Diego Stake, won the all-Church championship.[24]

The Church also involved the youth in cultural activities. For example, in the summer of 1954 the Young Men's and Young Women's Mutual Improvement Associations (MIA)

---

[23] Ibid., 133.

[24] *Church News*, 25 September 1949, 10-C; 30 August 1950, 8–9.

held a conference in Southern California, patterned after the successful conferences held at Church headquarters each June. This was the first time such an event was ever held outside of Salt Lake City. "As chairman of the regional council of stake presidents," Howard W. Hunter was the priesthood leader for this event.[25] In conjunction with this conference, some five thousand persons packed the East Los Angeles Junior College auditorium one Thursday night for two performances of a drama festival. Twenty thousand people were present as an orchestra and a chorus of fifteen hundred LDS youth filled the Hollywood Bowl for a Friday-evening concert and a Sunday-afternoon special conference session. Another twenty thousand attended the Saturday-evening dance festival, which filled the playing field of the East Los Angeles Junior College football stadium with over four thousand brightly costumed youth intricately performing folk and modern dances.

A reporter for one of Los Angeles's large daily newspapers remarked, "We have never seen anything like this before. You should tell the world about it." Similar conferences and cultural festivals were held each of the following two years.[26]

A Memorable Era

The years following the close of World War II were memorable to specific groups of Latter-day Saints for various reasons. In 1945 the temple endowment was presented in Spanish at the Mesa Temple—the first time the endowment was available in a language other than English. About two hundred Spanish-speaking Saints gathered from California and other southwestern states. Most made sacrifices, traveling long distances to receive temple ordinances in their native tongue. Some came from as far away as Mexico City. Others lost jobs in order to attend. But, like earlier Latter-day Saint Pioneers, these

---

[25] Knowles, 133.

[26] *Church News*, 14 August 1954, 7; 2 July 1955, 1; 27 July 1956, 2.

endowed members were a substantial and committed base of Saints upon whom future growth was built. During succeeding years, the "Lamanite Conferences" and Spanish temple sessions at Mesa became eagerly anticipated annual events among these California Saints.[27]

For years, the president of the Spanish-American Mission, headquartered at El Paso, had supervised Spanish-speaking members and missionary work from California on the west to Louisiana on the east and from Denver on the north to the Mexican border on the south. In 1950, however, the territory of the mission was reduced to cover only Texas and New Mexico. With this change, California Spanish-speaking branches were placed under the jurisdiction of local stakes, thus ending the long isolation that had existed between the Spanish-speaking branches and overlapping English-speaking stakes and wards.

A major boost to the California Saints' spiritual lives came when the 4 October 1953 session of the Church's general conference in Salt Lake City was carried live on television to Los Angeles. Now members, in their own homes, could both see and hear their chosen prophets, seers, and revelators even as they spoke. This was a remarkable step forward that further unified Saints far removed from Church headquarters. Since that historic day, Saints throughout the Golden State have eagerly anticipated local television broadcasts of general conference and other Church programs. (Interestingly, television had been developed by a Latter-day Saint, Philo Farnsworth. In 1927 he built his first set in a San Francisco building on the corner of Green and Sansome Streets. He refined his invention while living in Southern California just prior to World War II.)

As the Saints were celebrating significant anniversaries and past achievements, they were also looking toward the future. The death of President George Albert Smith on 4 April 1951 touched the Saints with nostalgic sadness and in a sense marked the end of the memorable postwar era. At the same

---

[27] "Lamanite" refers to descendants of the people of ancient America described in the Book of Mormon.

time, however, the California Saints crossed the threshold into a remarkable era of building and sacrifice which lifted the Church in the Golden State to a new plateau.

Buildings and Blessings: 1950–64

19

Even before the excitement of postwar celebrations had faded, a spirit of sacrifice and hard work was beginning to take hold among California Latter-day Saints. As the Saints turned their energies to building the kingdom of God in California, their efforts were met with success. As they worked and sacrificed, they were being blessed. California prospered, giving them the necessary means to build the kingdom. These were years of serious, purposeful work and the rewards that came with it.

Not only was the state graced with beautiful temples and permanent meetinghouses in the 1950s and 1960s, but these years were also productive in other ways. This was yet another period of remarkable growth. California missions, after decades of few convert baptisms, were now numbered among the most successful in the Church. At the same time, thousands of Latter-day Saints from other areas continued to move into the Golden State. Church membership nearly tripled, from just over one hundred thousand in 1950 to almost three hundred thousand in 1965. The number of stakes more than tripled, from eighteen to fifty-nine. Attendance of men at priesthood meetings in the Los Angeles Stake was ninth best in the Church in 1952, and other statistics showed similar patterns.[1] Significantly, a California stake president, Howard W. Hunter, was called to Churchwide service as a member of the Quorum of the Twelve Apostles.

Presiding over this dynamic period of growth was David O. McKay, who was seventy-seven years of age when he succeeded George Albert Smith as president of the Church in 1951. With his noble bearing, flowing white hair, and quiet sense of humor, journalists remarked that he looked and acted like a prophet.

The Building Program Accelerates

Construction of many of the buildings needed for the growing Church had been postponed during the Depression and subsequent war. There now was a need to make up for lost time, and construction on local meetinghouses and other Church buildings was begun at more than a hundred locations in the Golden State. And plans for the two California temples were reactivated.

Over the years, the California Saints contributed nearly half of the money needed for buildings, although the ratio of local to general Church funds for a given project depended on the size, activity, and economic strength of individual congregations. Carrying on such an extensive building program required sacrifice, and the Saints responded.

The Beverley Hills Ward tried for many years to collect enough money for a ward chapel. After many dinners, carnivals, etc., they had little to show for all their efforts. At length they decided to host an evening of entertainment to raise funds. The husband of a member donated a night at his theater. The ward, however, could not find a headliner.

---

[1] Chad M. Orton, *More Faith Than Fear: The Los Angeles Stake Story* (Salt Lake City: Bookcraft), 198–99.

The ward bishop, C. Dean Olson, a successful business-man, used his position as mayor of Beverley Hills to contact the world-famous entertainer Danny Thomas—not a Latter-day Saint but a resident of the community. In the gracious and generous spirit for which he was known, Thomas agreed to help, and over twenty thousand dollars was raised for the ward building fund.[2]

Typical postwar meetinghouse, at Fresno

Experience in designing and erecting hundreds of chapels throughout the Church enabled the General Building Commit-tee to develop a series of standardized plans incorporating the most desirable features and minimizing costs. Generally a simple, pleasant, and functional design was used. Costs were further reduced by designing most meetinghouses to serve two or more congregations. Small buildings that could be ex-panded easily one phase at a time were built in places where congregations were not large. An LDS meetinghouse took on a distinctive, easily recognized look.

Another significant thrust of the Church's building program was to provide facilities for education. Because David O. McKay was the first Church president to hold a college degree and had been an educator prior to his call as an apostle, he became a powerful advocate for the Church Educational

---

[2] Ibid., 202.

System. Brigham Young University in Provo, Utah, which had been a small college since 1875, was expanded into a major university. California LDS college students in large numbers began going to BYU to receive a good education within a Church environment. As they returned, BYU alumni in California swelled to over thirty thousand.

In the 1950s the Church also considered developing a system of junior colleges to provide greater numbers of Latter-day Saint students the opportunity to attend a Church school. Land was acquired for construction of junior colleges in San Fernando Valley, Anaheim, LaVerne, and Fremont City.[3] Ultimately the Church abandoned the junior college idea, opting instead to establish or strengthen institutes of religion adjacent to existing universities and colleges.

President Hunter's Challenge

Like other California stake presidents, Howard W. Hunter faced the difficult task of acquiring funds and property for a stake center. A two-and-one-half-acre site, to be shared between the Pasadena Stake and the East Pasadena Ward, was found in a good Sierra Madre neighborhood. After the site was purchased, the stake members needed to raise $400,000 as their contribution toward the construction of the building.

Under President Hunter's leadership, the stake planned an impressive stake center. The twenty-five-thousand-square-foot building included a 375-seat chapel for worship, and a cultural hall larger than a basketball court for socials, dances, dramatics, sports, and other activities. Like other LDS chapels, this building included numerous classrooms for the Sunday School and other organizations, as well as specialized rooms for Primary, seminary, Boy Scouts, and Relief Society. The

---

[3] Ernest L. Wilkinson and Leonard J. Arrington, ed., *Brigham Young University: The First One Hundred Years* (Provo, Utah: Brigham Young University Press, 1976), 3:148–56.

Stake president Howard W. Hunter at Pasadena groundbreaking

building committee realized that it needed to seize this opportunity to accommodate the large and growing stake and at the same time create an architectural statement reflecting their sense of the stake's excellence.

Although numerous fundraising events followed, the project ran out of funds in the summer of 1953. Stake members were carrying a heavy burden: they had three other chapels and a camp facility under construction. They were also operating multiple welfare projects and were actively raising funds for the Los Angeles Temple. In addition to these contributions they paid tithing (which went to Salt Lake City) and made generous contributions to local missionary funds and ward and stake budgets. They often donated 15 percent or more of their incomes and most of their spare time working on buildings and welfare projects.

One evening at 11:30 P.M. in the summer of 1953, President Hunter announced to the stake's bishops that "they were closing down the project for lack of funds." One of the bishops responded that he thought this would be a mistake: "Why not invite the priesthood of the stake to come and see what they are investing in?"[4]

"The idea caught fire," and a special priesthood conference was set for Sunday, 16 August 1953—the first meeting of any kind in the partially complete stake center. President

---

[4] Susan Kamei Leung, *How Firm a Foundation: The Story of the Pasadena Stake* (Pasadena, Calif.: Pasadena California Stake, 1994), 37.

Hunter and other stake leaders told the group of the predicament and outlined what was needed to finish the building. Then "we sat down and waited for their response," President Hunter recalled. "A long period of silence ensued before, one by one, individuals stood up and pledged their support." The building committee was prepared with blank souvenir checks printed with a picture of the building, pledge forms, and receipts. More than twenty-three thousand dollars was raised on this occasion.[5]

An example of the sacrifices made during the period was related by a bishop: "Among my souvenirs is a small glass piggy bank which recalls happy memories of a successful fund-raising drive. . . . The bank belonged to a young man, Steven Terry, who had been working and saving for a trip to Europe with the All-American Boys' Band. Steven gave up his dream trip to Europe, and brought his piggy bank and entire savings and donated it."[6]

Pasadena stake center under construction

Such sacrifices brought stake members closer together and developed a powerful feeling of unity among them. President Hunter's dream was realized when the stake center was dedicated on 6 June 1954. Not quite two years later, the stake was divided again, and many who contributed became members of the new Covina Stake and started over.

---

[5] Eleanor Knowles, *Howard W. Hunter* (Salt Lake City: Deseret Book, 1994), 129; Leung, 37–38.

[6] As quoted in Leung, 42.

The Los Angeles Temple

During the late 1930s, plans had been prepared for a temple in Los Angeles which would accommodate two hundred persons per session, but further preparations were suspended because of World War II. On 17 January 1949 President George Albert Smith announced at a meeting of Southern California Church leaders that the time had arrived to build the temple. Conferring with city officials, he expressed his desire that the temple be a "contribution to the architecture and culture of the community."[7]

California Saints believed that President Heber J. Grant had been blessed with inspiration a decade earlier when he chose the Santa Monica Boulevard site, as it was "the highest point in elevation between Los Angeles and the ocean." Furthermore, the freeway network, planned years after the site was purchased, would provide excellent access.[8]

President Smith appointed Edward O. Anderson, a member of the prewar board of temple architects, to design the temple. Rapid growth in California prompted President Smith to enlarge the design to accommodate three hundred persons per session, the same as in the Salt Lake City Temple, and to add a large assembly room on the upper floor—the first of only two such facilities to be built in the twentieth century.[9]

Anderson prayed for the same inspiration that had guided earlier temple architects, so that his design "might express in appearance" and facilitate "the spiritual work to be carried on" in the temple. A staff of twenty-eight specialists assisted in preparing the sixty-three large sheets of plans. Anderson and his associates worked closely with the First Presidency, from whom they received inspiration and direction. He later grate-

---

[7] Journal History, 17 January 1949; LDS Church Archives.

[8] Orton, 180.

[9] George Albert Smith Diary, 8 November 1949; Western Americana Collection, University of Utah; Edward O. Anderson, "The Los Angeles Temple," *Improvement Era* 56 (April 1953): 225–26; 58 (November 1955): 804.

fully acknowledged that whenever a problem arose "the answers or individuals we needed were forthcoming."[10]

Plans called for a six-story building, 364 feet long and 241 feet wide, containing about four and one-half acres of floor space, surmounted by a tower more than 257 feet high.[11] Only one other building in Los Angeles was taller: the Los Angeles City Hall. When completed, the temple was visible to ships twenty-five miles out to sea.

President McKay, succeeding President Smith, recognized the influence Church buildings, particularly temples, had in areas such as California where there was often turmoil, and where the Latter-day Saints were a small, sometimes unknown, minority.

Los Angeles attorney and Church member Preston D. Richards donated his services by contacting various government bureaus and explaining the purposes of the temple to them. "When these men realized the importance of the temple and reviewed the record of Latter-day Saints living in California," they were pleased to help "in every way to obtain the necessary permits."[12] Final approval was received from the Los Angeles City Council early in 1951. Ground was broken on 22 September of that same year. LeGrand Richards, Presiding Bishop of the Church and former president of the Hollywood Stake, remarked that the groundbreaking would be "one of the most important events in the history of the world."[13]

Two weeks later, during the October general conference, stake presidents in the temple district met with President Stephen L Richards, first counselor to President McKay, to receive their assignments for fund-raising. They were told that of the building's estimated four-million-dollar cost, one million would be their "fair share." President Noble Waite of the South

---

[10] Anderson, *Improvement Era* 58 (November 1955): 803; *Church News*, 5 December 1953, 9.

[11] *Church News*, 13 December 1950, 2.

[12] Anderson, *Improvement Era* 56 (April 1953): 226.

[13] Orton, 181.

Presidents David O. McKay (left) and Stephen L Richards (second from right) at Los Angeles Temple groundbreaking

Los Angeles Stake and chairman of the fund-raising committee later commented that President Richards did not know how he nearly "knocked out fourteen stake presidents with that statement," as this would average more than seventy thousand dollars per stake. "We kept our chins up," President Waite continued, "and it was only afterwards when we got out, and we confided in each other that really we were staggered. But we had received the commission, and so our instructions before we left were to make a plan, organize, and submit the plan, and get the approval of the First Presidency and then we would be given the green light to go forward."[14]

A pledge card was created, and each individual was invited to "determine for himself and according to his own circumstances the size of his Temple contribution."[15] President McKay came to Los Angeles on 3 February 1952 and officially launched the fund-raising campaign. He told twelve hundred leaders of stakes and wards that the Church was about to begin construction on the "largest temple ever built in this dispensation." He also counseled them to let the "young people, even the children in the 'cradle roll' [nursery], contribute to the

---

[14] In *Conference Report*, October 1952, 75.

[15] Orton, 182–83.

temple fund, for this is their temple, where they will be led by pure love to take their marriage vows."[16]

When one twelve-year-old deacon pledged $150, his bishop thought the boy had inadvertently put the decimal in the wrong place. However, the youth assured him it was no mistake. It took two years, but the young man paid the full amount from his paper-route and lawn-cutting earnings.[17] Throughout Southern California the Saints responded generously, raising over $1,648,000—well over the amount originally requested. During this same period other Church donations did not suffer but actually increased. Tithe paying, for example, rose 45–50 percent.[18]

In August 1952 construction on the temple began. Many workers found it a spiritual experience. Workdays uniformly began with prayer, and construction was completed without serious accident. Though 80 percent of the construction workers were Church members, at least four others asked for baptism for themselves and their families.

The temple was constructed of reinforced concrete, specifically engineered to withstand California earthquakes. It was faced with perfectly matched crushed-stone panels, which were etched with acid in such a way that the stone crystals sparkled in the light. The Buehner brothers of Salt Lake City received the contract to provide the stone, which they regarded as a fulfillment of their father's prophetic patriarchal blessing decades before, which stated that his family would "help erect temples of this Church."[19] One of the brothers reported that when the unique material was chosen for the temple's exterior, "there was just enough to make the stone for this

---

[16] Quoted in Richard O. Cowan, *Temples to Dot the Earth* (Salt Lake City: Bookcraft, 1989), 153.

[17] *California Intermountain News*, 27 September 1955, 46.

[18] *Church News*, 28 March 1981, 3.

[19] Quoted in Cowan, 143.

Los Angeles Temple under construction

building and the Bureau of Information [visitors center]—no more, no less."[20]

The Los Angeles Temple's cornerstone was laid on 11 December 1953. A party of sixty-seven, including more than twenty General Authorities, arrived from Salt Lake City by train. They were met at the downtown depot by local Saints in sixteen cars and were taken directly to the temple site about twelve miles away, escorted by two motorcycle policemen, one of them Albert J. Aardema, bishop of the nearby Elysian Park Ward.[21]

Some ten thousand members—the largest gathering of Latter-day Saints in California to that date—witnessed the placing of the commemorative copper box, containing

---

[20] Carl W. Buehner, *Do Unto Others* (Salt Lake City: Bookcraft, 1957), 153; see also *Church News*, 8 May 1954, 1, 8.

[21] *California Intermountain News*, 27 September 1955, 3, 45.

David O. McKay speaking at Los Angeles Temple cornerstone laying; to his left are his second counselor, J. Reuben Clark Jr., and Joseph Fielding Smith, president of the Twelve

historical memorabilia, into the cornerstone. Countless others listened by radio as the ceremony was broadcast in Los Angeles and Salt Lake City. The Los Angeles County Board of Supervisors honored the Saints by presenting a formal resolution congratulating the Church.[22]

A fifteen-and-one-half-foot statue of Moroni was sculpted by Millard F. Malin and cast in aluminum in New York. In October 1954, the one-ton figure, coated with twenty-three-carat gold, was hoisted to the roof and placed on the tower. At first the angel faced southeast toward the front of the temple. But soon afterwards, at the request of President McKay, it was turned to face east as a symbol of watching for Christ's Second Coming.

The story was told of a neighbor who lived east of the temple and who was asked if she had visited the temple grounds. She replied, "No, I'm waiting until the angel turns around and faces me." She later said, "Imagine my surprise

---

[22] *Church News*, 19 December 1953, 6–12.

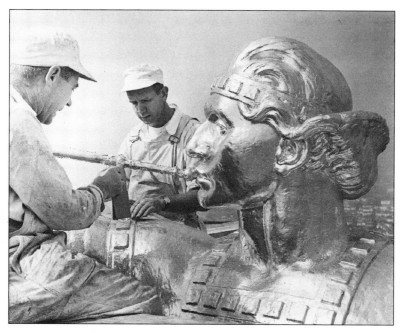

*Workmen put finishing touches on Los Angeles Temple
statue of angel Moroni*

when I woke up one morning and discovered that the angel was looking right down my street."[23]

During construction, so many visitors stopped at the site that a temple mission was created with LDS volunteers to answer questions and conduct guided tours of the grounds so that the work could progress uninterrupted. While full-time laborers did the actual building, Church members—some highly paid professionals—performed clean-up work around the site. They also prepared the thirteen-acre grounds for landscaping.

Olive, palm, pine, and Chinese ginkgo trees, as well as other trees and plants, came from all over the world. Teenage

---

[23] Orton, 187; Cowan, 155–56.

Latter-day Saint girls from the area contributed roses for a beautiful garden.[24]

During a fifty-one-day open house, nearly seven hundred thousand persons—an average of twelve thousand per day—visited the temple, often waiting in line for many hours. A local television station carried an hour-long program featuring the new landmark.

The temple was dedicated in eight sessions, from 11 to 14 March 1956, by President David O. McKay. The services were open to all qualified Church members, and over fifty thousand—nearly sixty-seven hundred per session—attended, seated not only in the assembly hall, but also in many other places inside, where they viewed proceedings over closed-circuit television.

With their new temple, the Southern California Saints no longer felt that they lived in "some sort of 'outpost' either spiritual or temporal."[25] Yet even with the opening of the Los Angeles Temple, some California Saints still had to travel long distances. Two years after the temple's dedication, "the temple advisory committee recommended that the Church construct housing specifically for temple workers on Church-owned property near the temple." These "Temple Patrons' Apartments" were opened in 1966.[26]

The Oakland Interstake Center and Temple

Over the years, Oakland's Temple Hill changed considerably. New freeways were announced, and a neighborhood was developed nearby. The Oakland Stake concluded that Temple Hill would be ideal for its stake center, and the First Presidency approved. In Berkeley, meanwhile, a site had also been acquired and was being developed for another stake center.

---

[24] Albert L. Zobell Jr., "Los Angeles," *Improvement Era* 66, no. 11 (November 1963): 953.

[25] Leung, 44.

[26] Orton, 244.

It was at this time that Stephen L Richards of the First Presidency called a joint meeting of the two stake presidencies. He spoke of the rapid growth of the Church, its demanding building program, and the wisdom of avoiding duplication. He suggested a joint building for the two stakes which eventually could be used by many stakes, an attractive place where members could gather close to a temple.

Berkeley Stake leaders recognized that the two stakes working together could afford a more adequate facility than either one alone. The decision to work together was fortuitous because before construction even began, the Oakland and Berkeley Stakes were realigned to form three stakes: Walnut Creek, Oakland-Berkeley, and Hayward.

On 20 July 1957 ground was broken for "the East Bay Interstake Center." It was dedicated by President McKay and opened on 16 October 1959. The center was originally a large red-brick structure on the northeast corner of the hill. Later, when the white temple was completed, the Interstake Center was painted white to match. It occupies more than seventy-seven thousand square feet—approximately an acre and a half—just five thousand feet less than the adjacent temple. It contains an auditorium seating 2,180 persons, and a recreation hall large enough for two simultaneous basketball games. The recreation hall can seat one thousand persons for banquets and twice that number for meetings. Between the auditorium and the recreation hall is a large stage with curtains front and rear, permitting its use with either room.

Among other things, the facility has been used as a home for Oakland civic light opera, a training center for the city's disaster preparedness team, a practice gym for the Golden State Warriors professional basketball team, a site for Martin Luther King Day commemorations, a hall seating over four thousand to hear football star Steve Young speak, and a theater for a temple pageant.

President David O. McKay at dedication of Oakland Interstake Center

On the way to the airport following the dedication, Oakland-Berkeley Stake president O. Leslie Stone reminded President McKay that there were 120,000 Church members still anxiously awaiting a temple in Northern California. Just over a year later, on 23 January 1961, President McKay summoned the stake presidents in the area to a special meeting and showed them sketches of a proposed temple. He appointed two stake presidents, O. Leslie Stone and David B. Haight (of the Palo Alto Stake), to head the temple committee.

The design President McKay presented features a modern oriental motif, reflecting the San Francisco Bay Area's unique heritage. A rooftop garden graces the top of the first level, and a fountain and artificial brook cascade down through the center of the temple's north gardens. The central tower rises 170 feet, and four tapering pinnacles, one on each corner, rise ninety-six feet. A sculptured panel facing the temple's north court portrays the Savior commissioning his apostles in the Old World, and a similar panel facing south features Christ's appearance in ancient America as described in the Book of Mormon.[27]

As in Los Angeles, the Saints in the north were given a target amount of money, four hundred thousand dollars, to raise. However, the temple committee felt that the people would contribute more and therefore raised the goal to five hundred thousand dollars. As in Los Angeles, one and one-half times the targeted amount was raised.

The San Jose Stake raised their allotment in a single day. As was done in Los Angeles, a day was set aside to visit every household. However, rather than pledge-cards, checks were received. At the end of the day, the stake's entire allotment was deposited. Stake president Horace Ritchie remarked that "it was the finest single achievement accomplished since the organization of the Stake."[28] As had been the case in Southern California, the general level of Church activity accelerated as the temple was built.

On Saturday, 26 May 1962, ground was broken. Work on the temple then continued uninterrupted, and the cornerstone was laid on 25 May 1963 with President McKay officiating.

Prior to its dedication, this temple was also opened to the public, and some 350,000 people toured the $2.5-million building. The temple has 265 rooms and a total floor area of 82,417 square feet—less than half the size of the Los Angeles Temple but still among the largest in the Church. The reinforced concrete structure is faced with Sierra white granite from Raymond, California, which gives it a gleaming exterior. The 18.3-acre site sits on a hill with spectacular views of Oakland, Berkeley, San Francisco, and the Bay's five bridges.

Elder George Albert Smith's 1924 vision of a gleaming white temple on the Oakland hills that could be seen by ships entering San Francisco Bay was literally fulfilled. One Friday

---

[27] Harold W. Burton and W. Aird Macdonald, "The Oakland Temple," *Improvement Era* 67, no. 5 (May 1964): 383, 386.

[28] Delbert F. Wright, "Building the Oakland Temple," 15; Oakland Stake Collection.

afternoon during the public viewing, a chauffeured government car parked at the entrance, and a navy officer stepped out and introduced himself as the commander of a ship which had sailed in through the Golden Gate early that morning. He had observed on the foothills of east Oakland a new landmark. He docked his ship and arranged to come and see for himself what it was.[29] California Latter-day Saints knew that the construction of the Los Angeles and Oakland temples was the fulfillment of Brigham Young's 1847 declaration that "in process of time the shores of the Pacific may be overlooked from the temple of the Lord."[30] It took just over one hundred years, but instead of one, there were now two temples prominently overlooking the Pacific. A third would follow before the end of the twentieth century.

Oakland Temple and Interstake Center

On 17 November 1964 the Oakland Temple was dedicated by President McKay. Now ninety-one years of age, he had recently suffered a stroke that left him virtually speechless and unable to walk or stand. When he came to the dedication, General Authorities and his own family despaired that he

---

[29] Ibid., 70.

[30] Journal History, 7 August 1847; see chapter 6.

would not be able to take any meaningful part and were certain that he would not rise or speak. However, President McKay was brought to the speaker's podium in a wheelchair and assisted as he stood and grasped the pulpit. He began to speak as clearly as he had before his stroke. His son recorded: "[My wife], with tears running down her cheeks, . . . whispered, 'Lawrence, we're witnessing a miracle.' I nodded in agreement. Members of the Council of the Twelve were crying. Father finished his talk and, still standing, dedicated the building."[31]

After the services, Lawrence McKay sought out Dr. J. Louis Schricker, President McKay's physician, and asked if the prophet would be able to deliver the dedicatory prayer again in the afternoon session. Dr. Schricker answered, "Lawrence, this is out of our hands. If I hadn't been here to see it, I wouldn't have believed it." President McKay not only delivered the prayer that afternoon but also in the morning and afternoon sessions of the following day.[32]

The Oakland Temple employed a new method of presenting instructions associated with the endowment. Rather than making the presentation in a series of four rooms with muraled walls, modern audio-visual equipment was used to make the entire presentation in a single lecture room. Two such rooms, each seating two hundred persons, were provided, making it possible for two groups to receive the endowment simultaneously. The temple was also one of the first to take advantage of the Church's new computer system. Traditionally, temples had performed vicarious baptisms, endowments, and other ordinances for individuals whose names had been submitted to them by individual researchers. When the Los Angeles Temple opened, however, the number of ordinances performed in the Church's temples began to exceed the number of names being submitted. Employees at Church headquarters were therefore authorized to identify names from vital records which had

---

[31] David Lawrence McKay, "Remembering Father and Mother," *Ensign*, August 1984, 40.

[32] Ibid.

been microfilmed by the genealogical department and submit them to the temples.

Having these genealogical records on microfilm meant that copies could be reproduced inexpensively. This enabled the Church to develop a vast system of branch genealogical libraries. One of the first, located in the basement of the Los Angeles Temple visitors center, was dedicated on 20 June 1963. It soon became one of the largest in the Church.[33]

A Musical Classic Is Born

While the Church was building beautiful chapels and temples in California, the Golden State made a significant contribution to Latter-day Saints worldwide in a rather different way. Out of this period of struggle and sacrifice emerged a Latter-day Saint musical classic. Mildred Tanner Pettit, of the Pasadena Stake, composed the music for "I Am a Child of God" for a Primary meeting at the April 1957 general conference in Salt Lake City.

After receiving the assignment, she "woke up one night with the music running through her mind and immediately wrote it down." The song's coauthor, Naomi Randall, said the words had come to her "in a similar way."[34] Since then, the song has been a favorite throughout the world. Although a simple children's song, it is powerful enough to move adults. It is now included in the Church's hymnbook.

An Apostle from California

Some of the California leaders who played key roles in planning and constructing the two temples would go on to provide significant Churchwide service. In October 1959 the Pasadena Stake president, Howard W. Hunter, became an apostle. He later described how he received his call. Following

---

[33] Orton, 238.

[34] William W. Tanner oral history, quoted in Orton, 311; Leung, 42.

the opening session of general conference he received word to go to President David O. McKay's office as soon as possible.

> President McKay greeted me with a pleasant smile and a warm handshake and then said to me, "Sit down, President Hunter, I want to talk with you. The Lord has spoken. You are called to be one of his special witnesses, and tomorrow you will be sustained as a member of the Council of the Twelve."
>
> I cannot attempt to explain the feeling that came over me. Tears came to my eyes and I could not speak. I have never felt so completely humbled as when I sat in the presence of this great, sweet, kindly man—the prophet of the Lord. He told me what a great joy this would bring into my life, the wonderful association with the brethren, and that hereafter my life and time would be devoted as a servant of the Lord and that I would hereafter belong to the Church and the whole world. He said other things to me but I was so overcome I can't remember the details, but I do remember he put his arms around me and assured me that the Lord would love me and I would have the sustaining confidence of the First Presidency and the Council of the Twelve.
>
> The interview lasted only a few minutes, and as I left I told him I loved the Church, that I sustained him and the other members of the First Presidency and the Council of the Twelve, and I would gladly give my time, my life, and all that I possessed to this service. He told me I could call Sister Hunter and tell her. . . . I went back to the Hotel Utah and called Claire in Provo, but when she answered the phone I could hardly talk.[35]

The following morning, Church leaders were presented for a sustaining vote to the eight-thousand-member congregation seated in the Salt Lake Tabernacle. "My heart commenced to pound as I wondered what the reaction would be when my name was read," Elder Hunter remembered. "I have never had such a feeling of panic. One by one the names of the Council of the Twelve were read and my name was the twelfth." After the vote he was invited to take his place among the apostles on the stand. "I felt the eyes of everyone fastened upon me as well as the weight of the world on my shoulders. As the conference proceeded I was most uncomfortable and wondered if I could

---

[35] Knowles, 144–45.

ever feel that this was my proper place."[36] Howard W. Hunter would himself become the prophet and president of the Church in 1994.

Howard W. Hunter plays piano at farewell gathering

Upon his return home he "found a large stack of mail, phone messages, and telegrams from well-wishers. His call to the Twelve had been reported in the major Los Angeles newspapers, some with front-page stories. One longtime client who called to congratulate him commented that 'the Church must have made a very attractive offer' to entice him to leave his successful law practice."[37]

Elder Hunter wrote in his journal: "Most people do not understand why persons of our religious faith respond to calls made to serve or the commitment we make to give our all. I have thoroughly enjoyed the practice of law, but this call that has come to me will far overshadow the pursuit of the profession or monetary gain."[38]

The two stake presidents who served as cochairmen of the Oakland Temple Committee also became General Authorities. David B. Haight, mayor of Palo Alto and governor of the San Francisco Bay Area Council of Mayors, gave up these positions to serve as president of the Scotland Mission. He was then called as an Assistant to the Twelve in April 1970 and became a member of the Quorum of the Twelve Apostles six years later. O. Leslie Stone, former vice-president of the Safeway grocery chain, became an Assistant to the Twelve in October 1972.

---

[36] Ibid., 145–46.

[37] Ibid., 151; Leung, 44.

[38] Knowles, 151.

Thus ended a decade and a half which was a high-water mark for the Latter-day Saints in California, climaxing in President McKay's miraculous dedication of the Oakland Temple and the call of a California Saint to be a member of the Quorum of the Twelve. Sacrifice and hard work had brought substantial progress and a feeling of peace and permanence only dreamed of by previous generations. The dedication and spirit of Church members in California were never stronger. But this peace would not last, and strength would be needed to meet the tumultuous challenges ahead.

Challenge and Change: 1964–85

The years covered in this chapter can be described as a time of challenge, change, and yet steadfastness. These were decades of protest as various groups felt that they had been left on the outside looking in and therefore sought to correct what they regarded as society's ills. While the Church responded to these challenges, it also implemented long-planned innovations in its programs and activities to more adequately meet the needs of the Saints.

Still, Church members sought to hold steadfastly to the principles, values, and ideals which they had regarded over the years as central to their religion. Elder Bruce R. McConkie of the Quorum of the Twelve captured this feeling of steadfastness when he declared:

> The Church is like a great caravan—organized, prepared, following an appointed course, with its captains of tens and captains of hundreds all in place. What does it matter if a few barking dogs snap at the heels of the wary travelers? Or that predators claim those few who fall by the way? The caravan moves on.[1]

---

[1] *Ensign*, November 1984, 85.

African Americans and the Church

As California's African American population continued to grow, Blacks joined with others in demonstrating against laws and customs regarded as discriminatory. In the mid-1960s, peaceful marches expressed the concerns of Blacks about their status in society. Some demonstrations, however, grew militant, erupting into violent riots on an unprecedented scale. The Watts section of south Los Angeles endured more than six days of urban warfare after particularly hot weather in August 1965. The carnage left forty million dollars in property damage, 34 killed, 1,032 wounded, and 3,952 arrested.

Because LDS practice long held that Blacks could not hold the priesthood, some militants began targeting the Church and its members. Even though the First Presidency issued a proclamation in 1964 that the Church supported all citizens in their quest for civil rights, many were still not satisfied. Several universities, including Stanford in California, refused to participate in athletic events with Brigham Young University, whose teams were sometimes threatened with violence. Bert Scoll, a member of the Los Angeles Stake high council, watched the destruction of his medical clinic on television even as it happened. A curfew imposed by the police canceled all Wilshire Ward meetings. Even after the curfew was lifted, members felt unsafe in the area at night, so all meetings were held during daylight.

Some time after these demonstrations of protest had subsided, concerned Church leaders continued giving the question of Blacks holding the priesthood deep consideration. Over a period of months in 1977 and 1978, the General Authorities discussed this matter in their regular temple meetings. In addition, Church president Spencer W. Kimball frequently went to the Salt Lake Temple, especially on Saturdays and Sundays when he could be there alone, to plead with the Lord for guidance.

Then, on 1 June 1978, the First Presidency and the Twelve gathered, fasting, for their regular monthly meeting in the temple. After a two-hour session during which each had expressed at length his feelings, there seemed to be a remarkable unity. President Kimball asked them to unite with him in prayer. One of the apostles, Elder Bruce R. McConkie, recalled:

> It was during this prayer that the revelation came. The Spirit of the Lord rested mightily upon us all; we felt something akin to what happened on the day of Pentecost and at the dedication of the Kirtland Temple. From the midst of eternity, the voice of God, conveyed by the power of the Spirit, spoke to his prophet. . . . And we all . . . became personal witnesses that the word received was the mind and will and voice of the Lord.[2]

Others present concurred that none of them "had ever experienced anything of such spiritual magnitude and power as was poured out upon the Presidency and the Twelve that day in the upper room in the house of the Lord."[3] The Church's official announcement affirmed that priesthood blessings would henceforth be given to all "regardless of race or color" (Doctrine and Covenants, Official Declaration 2).

When the revelation was publicly announced, members everywhere rejoiced, particularly Black members: "It's the greatest thing that has happened to the Black man since we have been in this life," declared Paul Devine, a high school physical education teacher from San Pedro. He added that the first thing he wanted to do after receiving the priesthood was baptize his children. Robert and Delores Lang, already carrying leadership responsibilities in the Inglewood Ward, were thrilled with the announcement. "When I came in, my wife was crying," Robert reported. "She had heard the news and was so happy. . . . Delores and I will now get our endowments and

---

[2] Bruce R. McConkie, "The New Revelation on Priesthood," in *Priesthood* (Salt Lake City: Deseret Book, 1981), 126–28.

[3] Ibid., 128.

will be sealed and do temple work for the dead. I know that they have been waiting for this moment, too."[4]

Youth and the "Counterculture"

African Americans were not the only ones working for changes in society. California college campuses also became focal points for protest. Although most students of the "baby boomer" generation had been raised in relative prosperity, many were unhappy and disliked what they regarded as California's prevailing materialism. The well-scrubbed look of the 1950s gave way to an unkempt "counterculture" identified with tattered clothes, sandals, beads, and long hair. Many of these young people indulged in mind-altering drugs and viewed traditional religion as irrelevant. They also espoused their own set of morals, as the birth control pill seemed to replace abstinence, and casual sex became widely accepted. Many, raised under a constant threat of nuclear holocaust, opposed America's involvement in the Vietnam War. Many California youth rebelled and refused to serve in the U.S. military.

The Vietnam War became a deeply emotional and political issue; and as with the rest of the nation, the Saints were divided. While some opposed the war, Latter-day Saint George F. Putnam, a leading Southern California television commentator, reflected the feelings of many other Church members as he vigorously spoke out against those who were burning draft cards and desecrating the U.S. flag.[5] A quota in each LDS ward stipulated that only two draft-eligible young men could be called on missions each year. This placed a burden on the shoulders of stake and ward leaders who had to decide who could go and who could not.

---

[4] *Church News*, 17 June 1978, 3–4.

[5] Ibid., 4 July 1970, 14.

Some LDS youth left home without telling their parents where they were going and went to California to gather with other "hippies." Urban stake leaders sometimes received ten to fifteen contacts a month from concerned parents asking for help in locating lost children. Bishops of wards where these youth gathered spent many extra hours, often in hostile environments, trying to locate young adults and teens.

While some Latter-day Saints felt it was best to try to understand these youth, others were shocked and felt that anyone who showed any sympathy was spiritually disloyal. However, most leaders recognized that simply choosing to dress differently or to listen to popular music was not contrary to God's commandments, and that those involved were souls to whom they needed to minister. Still, the Church's established standards had to be maintained, and when it came to more important issues, such as drug use or premarital sex— behaviors clearly contrary to the commandments of God— leaders stood steadfast.

Challenges to Traditional Family Roles

The traditional family with a father, mother, and several children became increasingly less common. As smaller families became the norm of society, larger LDS families sometimes became the objects of disapproving whispers at supermarkets and shopping malls. Single-parent households—usually mothers with children—became more common as the divorce rate grew. Perhaps the most direct threat to the family came from the growing practice of couples living together outside of marriage. Many, including influential celebrities, openly questioned the benefits of marriage for themselves and their children.

During these years, feminists challenged the traditional roles of women. Strident voices insisted that those roles were demeaning and intended only to keep women subservient to men. Sonia Johnson, an English professor who had left her family and the Church and received much notoriety, insisted in a speech at San Jose State University that "there is no word in our language strong enough to describe the utter horror of most women's lives with men." She boasted that the day she was excommunicated from the LDS Church was "the greatest day in her life."[6]

The Church acted to meet the changing needs of women. As more and more women became employed during the day-time, evening Relief Society sessions were added. The General Authorities encouraged local leaders to invite women to speak and pray more often in Church meetings and to involve them more fully in planning programs and activities. Members of the general Relief Society, Young Women, and Primary presiden-cies were regularly invited to speak in general conferences. To help strengthen the family, the Church instituted a yearly women's meeting that coincided with the October general conference and was broadcast from the Salt Lake Tabernacle via satellite to local stake centers in California and around the world.

Despite these developments, the major objectives of radi-cal feminists still were not met. The policy concerning women holding the priesthood was not modified. Someone confronted Sally B. Nielson, who served twenty-three years in the Pasadena Stake Relief Society presidency: "Well I don't under-stand how you can belong to that church and be belittled as a woman because you can't hold the priesthood." Her response was: "Who needs the priesthood? Being honored as a woman by the priesthood is the most wonderful thing a woman could ask for. In all the years I have served, I have never felt that one priesthood holder set himself up as my superior."[7]

Further, the Church took a stand against the proposed "Equal Rights Amendment" to the United States Constitution, which would have banned gender-based legal distinctions.

---

[6] Notes taken by William E. Homer.

[7] Susan K. Leung, *How Firm a Foundation: The Story of the Pasadena Stake* (Pasadena, Calif.: Pasadena California Stake, 1994), 51.

Church leaders feared that it would abolish laws giving special protection to women and thereby undermine traditional family structures and roles.

At the first of the annual women's conferences in 1978, President Spencer W. Kimball affirmed: "Much is said about the drudgery and confinement of the woman's role in the home. In the perspective of the gospel it is not so. There is divinity in each new life. There is challenge in creating the environment in which a child can grow and develop. There is partnership between the man and woman in building a family which can last throughout the eternities."[8]

Many LDS women in California echoed those sentiments. Helen Andelin of Santa Barbara appeared several times on nationwide television programs to defend the traditional role of women in the family. Similarly, Colleen Pulley of Concord mobilized a group of other Latter-day Saint women to urge the state textbook commission to retain the image of women being happy in their "prime role" as "wives and mothers and teachers of the next generation."[9]

Another threat to the traditional family came from an increasingly vocal homosexual movement. Animosity toward the Church grew among some who viewed its policy on morality as archaic and discriminatory. As early as February 1973, Church president Harold B. Lee branded homosexual conduct as a "grievous sin" in the same degree as adultery and fornication.[10]

As homosexual activists continued protesting, Church members sometimes became involved in defending the stance of the Church. In San Jose, for instance, activists placed before the local voters an initiative granting a city-sponsored "Gay Pride Week." Some of the Church's earliest formal interfaith efforts in that city came as Latter-day Saints joined with other

---

[8] *Ensign*, November 1978, 105–6.

[9] *Church News*, 18 December 1971, 6; 4 January 1975, 13.

[10] *Ensign*, January 1973, 106.

religious groups to oppose the initiative, which was subsequently defeated by the voters.

Adjustments in Meeting Patterns and Programs

In response to the challenges of modern times, the Church
took several far-reaching steps. "We are in a program of defense," declared Elder Harold B. Lee of the Quorum of the
Twelve in 1961. "The Church of Jesus Christ was set upon this
earth in this day '. . . for a defense, and for a refuge from the
storm, and from wrath when it should be poured out without
mixture upon the whole earth' (D&C 115:6)."[11] To this end, and
under Elder Lee's direction, Church authorities examined
carefully the interplay among, and perhaps unnecessary duplication of, various programs to be sure these activities were
helping the Saints meet their challenges. Long and prayerful
planning resulted in what became known as the Church's
priesthood correlation program.

Prior to 1964, several different Church organizations were
involved in visiting families in their homes. All these contacts
were now consolidated under home teachers, who were assigned to visit each family monthly and minister to its needs.
To further strengthen the Saints, the Church published its first
family home evening manual in 1965. It provided lessons for
parents to teach and included suggestions for a variety of
family-centered activities. Five years later, Monday nights
were freed from all other Church activities so families could
have this time together.

Further steps were taken to facilitate the coordination of
Church activities. Priesthood executive committees and correlation councils were established at the ward and stake levels.
Youth age groupings were adjusted to be the same from one
organization to another. In the process, such long-established
names as *M Men* and *Gleaners* gave way to the more descriptive

---

[11] In *Conference Report,* October 1961, 81.

designation, *Young Adults*. Calendars were synchronized to have all organizations begin their curriculum years at the same time. Rather than having each organization publish its own magazine, in 1971 the *Ensign* replaced the *Improvement Era* and other publications as the Church's periodical for adults.

The energy shortage of the 1970s provided the setting for carrying out yet another long-anticipated move. For decades, the priesthood and Sunday School met Sunday mornings, sacrament meetings convened Sunday afternoons or evenings, and Primary activities and Relief Society meetings were conducted during the week. However, in the early 1970s several local units, including Los Angeles's Spanish Branch, adopted a consolidated schedule with all meetings except youth activities on Sunday. Meetings were scheduled back-to-back to better serve these Saints, some of whom came great distances.

A similar three-hour block of meetings began Churchwide in March of 1980. Not only did this cut energy costs for transportation, heating, and air conditioning, but it also gave Church members more time for families, service, and community involvement. The benefits of this consolidation were especially great in California, where Latter-day Saints typically traveled some distance to attend church meetings.[12]

Helping Groups with Special Needs

During these years the Church also devised programs to serve members with special needs. California played a leading role in these developments.

Many deaf people had come to Southern California during World War II because they could work comfortably in noisy defense industries. As early as 1941, a special Sunday School class for the deaf was organized in the Vermont Ward of the South Los Angeles Stake. A deaf branch was formed eleven years later in the more centrally located Los Angeles Stake.

---

[12] *Church News*, 9 February 1980, 3; 8 March 1980, 3.

Oakland-Berkeley Stake deaf softball player and coach

Over the years, Church units in other areas sponsored programs for deaf members. The Oakland-Berkeley Stake, for example, organized a softball team of deaf players.[13]

In 1968, the first deaf missionaries in the Church were called to serve in Los Angeles. Within a year, eighteen conversions were made, including two brothers who were deaf, blind, and could not speak. Through a "slow, laborious process," the missionaries taught these brothers by drawing out in the palms of their hands the letters of the alphabet. After their baptisms "the two, with tears streaming down their faces, embraced each other and then the missionaries who had so lovingly and painstakingly taught them the gospel." Soon "they were given the priesthood and, with the assistance of a member of the branch who could see, began to pass the sacrament." With the assistance of such missionary work, the deaf branch grew in membership to almost three hundred.[14]

Southern California played a key role in Churchwide work with the deaf. During the summer of 1972, the Church's Social Service Department conducted a twelve-day seminar at California State College in Northridge for deaf Latter-day Saints and their interpreters. Together, they planned a dictionary of signs for unique LDS terms. A film on how to perform sacred ordinances when one cannot speak attracted special interest.[15]

Another group with special needs, particularly in urban areas, was the large number of single members. People were marrying later and divorcing more; men were also dying sooner than women, leaving more and more singles, young

---

[13] Ibid., 23 September 1972, 6.

[14] Chad M. Orton, *More Faith Than Fear: The Los Angeles Stake Story* (Salt Lake City: Bookcraft, 1987), 248.

[15] *Church News*, 19 August 1972, 7, 12.

and old. Even suburban and rural wards often had more than most members realized. The mobility of some members created challenges for leaders. In the Pasadena Ward, for example, there were 429 personnel changes in ward administration in one year.[16]

Singles and seniors needed special consideration. With priesthood correlation's emphasis that all Church programs should focus on and strengthen families, some single adults wondered where they fit in. The Los Angeles Stake led the way in developing a program for them. The problem was addressed as early as 1946, when Bishop Jay Grant began "Get Acquainted" firesides and socials for singles in his Wilshire Ward.

A quarter of a century later the stake leadership gave new emphasis to this activity, providing the basis for a Churchwide single adult program. In March 1969 stake leaders discussed with General Authorities the possibility of establishing a singles ward. President Harold B. Lee, who had a special affinity for single members, explained, "We have been neglecting some of our adult members—those over eighteen who have not yet found their companions, or who are perhaps widowed or divorced. They have been saying to us, 'But you have no program for us. . . . ' We have said to them 'We want to find out what you need.'"[17]

Finally, on 27 January 1974, at a special meeting of the UCLA Ward, "the first singles unit outside Salt Lake City" was organized. Branch leaders "found that almost half were attending Church for the first time in their adult lives. . . . Between 1979 and 1984 seventy-eight marriages took place between branch members."[18] Soon singles wards were organized in many other California stakes.

Another challenge facing widely scattered California Latter-day Saints was how to make seminary instruction avail-

---

[16] Leung, 53.

[17] Harold B. Lee, *Ye Are the Light of the World* (Salt Lake City: Deseret Book, 1974), 349.

[18] Orton, 272–74.

able where there were not enough students, where distances were great, or where there were no Church buildings. The answer came in 1966. The young people studied seminary lessons at home during the week and then met as part of their regular Sunday meetings to go over this material with a volunteer teacher. In 1972 the program was expanded to include college-level institute study as well.

Sharing the Gospel

During the difficulties of the 1960s and the 1970s, Latter-day Saints felt more than ever that the gospel had the answers society needed, and they were eager to share it with their neighbors. However, communicating with California's diverse population posed a significant challenge, but modern technology could help. President Spencer W. Kimball remarked, "When we have used the satellite and related discoveries to their greatest potential and all of the media—the papers, magazines, television, radio—all in their greatest power . . . then, and not until then, shall we approach the insistence of our Lord and Master to go into all the world and preach the gospel to every creature."[19]

These words reinforced an effort that had already been underway for some years. In 1968 the Church had purchased Southern California's radio station KBIG-AM and -FM.[20] The Church also acquired station KOIT-AM and -FM in San Francisco.

Following the creation of the Church's Public Communications Department in 1972, a full-time public affairs office was opened in Los Angeles. Keith Atkinson, a media professional, was hired to head this office. During the next two decades he built a public relations network that culminated in a public affairs council in nearly every stake. Through these efforts,

---

[19] Regional Representatives Seminar, 4 April 1974.

[20] *Church News*, 20 April 1968, 2.

Edward Fraughton's statue of Battalion soldier in Presidio Park, San Diego

local members were able to raise public awareness of the Church, answer questions, and build bridges of understanding.

As Latter-day Saints recalled past achievements, they discovered new opportunities to share their message. On 22 November 1969, Hugh B. Brown of the First Presidency dedicated a nine-foot bronze statue of a Mormon Battalion soldier by LDS sculptor Edward J. Fraughton. This monument stood atop a wooded hill in San Diego's Presidio Park, not far from where the Battalion had completed its historic march nearly a century and a quarter earlier. It was paid for through a variety of projects conducted by California chapters of the Sons of Utah Pioneers (SUP).[21] Three years later, on 3 November 1972, Church president Harold B. Lee dedicated the

Mormon Battalion visitors center at Old Town in San Diego

Mormon Battalion Memorial visitors center. This one-story building of traditional Spanish American architecture was built in San Diego's "Old Town," just a few hundred yards

---

[21] Ibid., 27 April 1968, 3; 29 November 1969, 8–9, 14.

Reconstructed courthouse at Old Town in San Diego

from Presidio Park. Its displays reminded visitors that the Battalion soldiers were the first to introduce the restored gospel to Southern California and that the Latter-day Saints were a patriotic people loyal to their country.[22]

Another opportunity to focus on the Mormon Battalion's contributions came with the restoration of nine buildings in the San Diego historic district. While six of the structures were rebuilt with public tax funds, the restoration of the old courthouse was paid for by private groups. These groups included local legal associations and the Utah-based Mormon Battalion, Inc., which raised one hundred thousand dollars. Originally erected by Battalion men, this building was destroyed by fire in 1872. The restoration was aided when nearby excavations unearthed old bricks the soldiers had made for the original structure.[23]

Also in Northern California, attention was directed to early Latter-day Saint history. In 1971 the "Mormon Boys' Cabin" was moved from high in the mountains to become a permanent part of the historic park at the gold-discovery site (see picture in chapter 22). The restoration was a joint venture of the U.S. Forest Service, the California State Department of Parks and Recreation, and the SUP.[24] The wagon road first carved out over Carson Pass in 1848 by homeward-bound Mormon Battalion veterans was designated as a historic trail in August 1992. In October of the following year, a nearby mountain was officially named "Coray Peak" by the U.S. Board of Geographical Names, honoring Melissa Coray, who traveled with the Battalion road builders. On 30 July 1994 the SUP

---

[22] Ibid., 22 April 1972, 6; 11 November 1972, 3, 10.

[23] Ibid., 23 May 1981, 7; 28 November 1992, 7.

[24] Ibid., 12 June 1971, 6.

unveiled a plaque in the pass commemorating the accomplishments of the 1848 group.[25]

The Church explored yet other means of reaching the public. Beginning in the 1970s, thousands of beautiful Christmas lights were installed on the grounds at both the Los Angeles and Oakland temples to commemorate the light that was brought into the world with the birth of Jesus Christ. Mayors of both cities began visiting the temple grounds each year in order to turn on the lights and deliver a Christmas message to their respective communities.

Pageants also became an important means of sharing the Church's message. The Mormon Battalion's exploits were recalled in *My San Diego*, a musical production written by R. Don Oscarson. This pageant was presented each night for a week during October 1977 in Balboa Park's Starlight Bowl.[26]

The Oakland Temple pageant, *And It Came to Pass*, was another attempt to reach out to those outside the Church. Originally performed on Temple Hill in the 1960s, the pageant portrayed the apostasy from the New Testament Church, the latter-day Restoration, and the Pioneer trek to Utah. It was first presented annually in the Center, then in Oakland and San Jose on alternate years, then every three years. Initially written to tell the Church's story to non-LDS audiences, the pageant became immensely popular as a testimony builder for Church youth.

Meanwhile, Pasadena's famed New Year's Day Rose Parade became another opportunity for the Church to share its message. The Pasadena Stake was represented over the years by many Eagle Scout honorguards, and in 1970 Pam Tedesco reigned as parade queen, the only Latter-day Saint to do so. Then in 1976 a local Los Angeles LDS public communications council entered a family-oriented float in the famed parade. Individual contributors donated thirty-five thousand dollars

---

[25] Ibid., 13 August 1994, 3–4.

[26] Ibid., 22 October 1977, 13.

to pay for the float, and five hundred volunteers worked many hours gluing thousands of rose petals, orchids, camellias, and chrysanthemums to its surface. The float's message, "The Family Is Eternal," was received not only by the million who lined the parade route but also by other millions of television viewers worldwide.[27] Another float the following year, entitled "Family Home Evening," featured the popular Osmond family, professional Latter-day Saint entertainers.[28] A third float in 1978 carried seven children representing different ethnic cultures to illustrate the theme "I Am a Child of God,"[29] taking the words of Pasadena Saint Mildred Pettit's song to the world. These were the first floats from any church accepted by parade officials since 1926.

In keeping with the family theme, in 1977 the Church produced and aired a national television program entitled "The Family and Other Living Things," again featuring the Osmonds and other popular entertainers. Viewers were invited to write or call for a free brochure (a condensed version of the Church's family home evening manual) to help them with family relations. This was the Church's first attempt at inviting viewer response from a national television program, and it was followed by others to various targeted audiences over the ensuing years. About a decade later when the Church produced another television special, "Together Forever," hundreds of Southern California LDS volunteers, by means of personal visits, phone calls, or announcements left on doorknobs, invited nearly a half million people to watch the program. These efforts not only resulted in hundreds of missionary referrals but also brought a greater feeling of unity between missionaries and local Saints.[30]

Another media success was the Brigham Young University football team, which won widespread prominence,

---

[27] Ibid., 20 September 1975, 3; 10 January 1976, 5.

[28] Ibid., 20 November 1976, 4; 8 January 1977, 8–9, 12.

[29] Ibid., 7 January 1978, 3.

[30] Ibid., 12 August 1989, 5.

including a national championship in 1984. The team's partici-pation in internationally televised post-season bowl games became an annual event. BYU's first appearance at San Diego's Holiday Bowl in December 1978 attracted President Spencer W. Kimball, who addressed approximately seventeen thou-sand people at a pregame devotional on the subject of "putting Christ back into Christmas."[31]

Keeping in Touch with the Saints

While the Church was attempting to communicate with a non-LDS public, its own members were not forgotten. In 1981, the Church installed satellite receiving stations in each of its stake centers, including those in California. In addition to general conference broadcasts, which up to this point had been carried live by only a few local television operators, these receiving stations made it possible for the Saints to attend Churchwide firesides and instructional programs and to watch live broadcasts of BYU sports events at local stake centers. Now, for the first time, California Church members could experience the spirituality of a General Authority's talk, the beauty of Temple Square in Salt Lake City, or the excitement of a BYU team's or athlete's victory.

To deliver their messages to ever-growing and more di-verse Church audiences, Church leaders began conducting meetings for larger groups of Latter-day Saints. In May 1980 an area conference was held at the Rose Bowl in Pasadena. Two apostles originally called from California, Howard W. Hunter and David B. Haight, accompanied President Kimball and other general Church leaders to the conference, which resulted in the largest gathering of Latter-day Saints in history as nearly eighty thousand attended the Sunday conference, which was translated into seven languages. Since regular attendance at the multiplying number of local stake conferences was now a

---

[31] Ibid., 30 December 1978, 4–5.

physical impossibility for the First Presidency and Quorum of the Twelve Apostles, many members felt that this might be the only chance in their lifetimes to see and hear their prophets and apostles in person.

In his keynote address, President Kimball stressed the need for reaching out with the gospel message to every individual, family, neighborhood, and cultural and ethnic group.[32] "It is not left to our discretion or to our pleasure or to our convenience. Every man and woman should return home from this conference with the determination that they will take the Gospel to their relatives and their friends."[33]

This was followed by a series of smaller area and regional conferences throughout California, including one of the first two multi-stake conferences in the United States, which was held at San Diego on 8 January 1984. This conference was conducted by Elders Howard W. Hunter and James E. Faust of the Quorum of the Twelve and Robert L. Backman of the Seventy, who would be appointed just a few months later as Area President of California.[34]

The attendance record set at the 1980 Rose Bowl conference was surpassed by attendance at an LDS dance festival held five years later at the same location. More than one hundred thousand people attended, setting a new record for Latter-day Saints at a single event. U.S. president Ronald Reagan sent a telegram to the performers, commending them and their leaders for a "commitment to excellence."[35]

Holding Steadfast

Out of the turbulent 1960s and 1970s came a hope for a brighter future as the Saints lived and shared the gospel of Jesus Christ. The Church's progress in California was reflected

---

[32] Ibid., 24 May 1980, 4–5.

[33] Remarks at Rose Bowl Area Conference, May 1980.

[34] *Church News*, 15 January 1984, 4.

[35] Ibid., 28 July 1985, 12.

in the organization of new stakes. Because these units, headed by local leaders, are net givers rather than receivers of Church resources, their creation indicates real Church progress better than does a mere increase in membership. Quietly, and almost unnoticed, the formation of the Palm Springs Stake in 1967 meant that Isaiah's figurative tent was stretched and staked over the entire state of California. No matter where in the Golden State they lived, Latter-day Saints now were "gathered into stakes" (D&C 115:5–6) and had the benefit of more complete involvement in the Church's programs and activities.

Although the latter part of the twentieth century brought many challenges, the Saints steadfastly held to their basic principles and continued to move forward. While responding to the needs of ethnic minorities and other groups, the Church would seek additional opportunities to reach out to an even broader audience.

Building Bridges: 1984–96

21

The continued multiplication of stakes and missions created a significant Churchwide challenge. The long-standing structure of stake and mission presidents reporting directly to the apostles was stretching the Twelve beyond reasonable limits. Other levels of administration had to be put into place. The 1976 organization of the first Quorum of the Seventy and the subsequent formation of a Second Quorum gave the Church an administrative structure well suited for growth and expansion far into the future.

In 1984 the Church was divided into thirteen (later expanded to over twenty) large areas, and three men from among the Seventies quorums were called to preside over each as presidencies. California and Hawaii became the North America West Area, with Robert L. Backman as president, and native Californians Paul H. Dunn and John K. Carmack as counselors. This was a most significant milestone, because for the first time since 1923, when the Los Angeles Stake had been separated from the California Mission, all of the Golden State was included within a single ecclesiastical subdivision under one presidency.

One major challenge faced by the new area presidency—indeed by the Church as a whole—was that of building bridges to more people, including the growing numbers who spoke little or no English.

Changing Demographics

Internal U.S. migration to California finally slowed during the early 1970s, with 300,000 entering and 350,000 leaving in 1972.[1] However, this slow-down in growth was short-lived. The century-old vision of California as the promised land was just reaching such far-off places as the Middle East, India, China, and the Pacific Islands. Unprecedented numbers from those regions began joining the long-term flood into the state. Neighborhoods began looking like a miniature United Nations as Anglos, Blacks, Hispanics, and various Asian families lived together in close proximity.

Not only were the numbers large, but California was more culturally diverse than ever. The Anglo majority that had prevailed for nearly 150 years became a minority in some urban areas. Los Angeles's 1990 population was 40 percent Hispanic compared to only 36 percent Anglo; 14 percent was African American, and 10 percent Asian.

The shift in San Jose was particularly dramatic. Between 1980 and 1990 the Hispanic population increased from 23 percent to 27 percent, while the Asian population expanded from 8 percent to 20 percent. *Reader's Digest* remarked that "America [particularly California] is experiencing the biggest influx of immigrants since the great wave that ended in the 1920s. . . . It's becoming a new America. . . . Let's call it the 'Sunday stew'—rich, various and roiling, and all of it held together by a good strong broth." These immigrants "paid us the profoundest compliment by leaving the land of their birth to come and spend their lives with us."[2]

---

[1] T. H. Watkins, *California: An Illustrated History* (Palo Alto, Calif.: American West, 1973), 516.

[2] *Reader's Digest*, July 1991, 39–40.

Typically these newly arrived groups brought a strong sense of ethnic identity and pride. While this provided newcomers with a sense of security, it sometimes stood in the way of their assimilation into the larger society. The Church faced the challenge of helping these peoples maintain their cultural traditions while melding into a new community. Urban LDS congregations became dotted with many cultures. On one Sunday in the late 1980s, for example, San Jose's Almaden Second Ward had four young priests prepare and administer the sacrament: one White, one Black, one Hispanic, and one Chinese. All later served missions.

During these same years many families moved to the suburbs. Some central urban stakes were left with only a dozen or so Aaronic Priesthood youth, a thousand or more widows, and thousands of other singles and retirees. What had been homogeneous wards of close-knit, white, middle-class families originally from Utah became heterogeneous wards of less-affluent ethnic peoples, mobile singles, and senior citizens. In 1974, of the 3,571 members in the Los Angeles Stake, for example, "almost one thousand belonged to the student wards, the singles branch, the Deaf Ward, or the Spanish Branch," showing how diverse this stake had become. And "60 percent of the families had no Melchizedek Priesthood holder in the home, a statistic that reflected not only the growing number of widows but also the consequence of so many marriages outside the faith."[3]

In November 1958, Church officials had given approval to disband the downtown Adams Ward in Los Angeles and dispose of its chapel. The historic mother ward of Los Angeles, which traced its roots back to the first Los Angeles Branch in 1895, and its building, the first urban LDS chapel in California, were no longer needed. The building's beautiful stained-glass window was eventually acquired by the Church Museum of History and Art in Salt Lake City (see photo on page 2).

---

[3] Chad M. Orton, *More Faith Than Fear: The Los Angeles Stake Story* (Salt Lake City: Bookcraft, 1987), 275, 220.

Twenty years later, the same debate arose over the fate of the landmark Wilshire Ward chapel. This time stake leaders saw "the future of the chapel as sound and exciting. . . . It was being used more than ever before, and by a wider variety of people." While Anglos were moving out of the ward, "other groups such as Blacks, Koreans, Filipinos, and Latins were filling the void. . . . It was clear that the chapel's best days could still be ahead." Instead of tearing the building down, a sum of one hundred thousand dollars was spent renovating it.

Stake president John Carmack received "a powerful spiritual confirmation of the decision. . . . A vision came to him in which he saw that while the building then served as a home for only one Spanish-speaking branch, it would one day serve many Spanish wards and be a center of Spanish activity."[4]

In some ways, these two buildings epitomized the early twentieth-century Church, deeply intertwined with a Utah heritage, and mostly White. The demise of one building and renovation of the other underscored the fact that Mormonism was no longer a religion of Utahns or Anglo Americans but a church for "all nations, kindreds, tongues and peoples" that would find new ways to minister effectively to them.

Diverse Ethnic Congregations

Ethnic branches were not new, dating back to pioneer times in Utah. Yet Church leaders pondered whether it was better to have separate, non-English-language branches or to expect ethnic groups to blend into the established English-speaking units. Within the Church, some Anglo members found it difficult to adjust to the changes that immigrants were bringing. By the 1970s, Church leaders became convinced that it was important to make the gospel available to groups of new

---

[4] Ibid., 267–70.

arrivals in their own language and to help them develop their own leaders.[5]

In the San Jose Stake, an independent Spanish-speaking branch had sacrificed over the years to build, from meager means, their own building, only to have the branch disbanded, its members assigned to English-speaking wards, and the building taken over by the stake for a genealogical library. However, when attendance at English-speaking meetings plummeted, a Spanish-speaking bishop was called, a Spanish-speaking ward organized, and their building partially restored to them. Church activity among this language group again blossomed.

Meanwhile other ethnic groups also proliferated in California. As the Vietnam War came to a close during the mid-1970s, many Southeast Asian refugees poured into the state. Local LDS congregations in several areas launched efforts to reach out to these newcomers. As a result of efforts by Latter-day Saints in Stockton, some 143 refugees from Laos and Cambodia attended Church services one Sunday early in 1981.[6]

Similarly, in Long Beach a Cambodian family and several friends responded to a missionary's invitation to attend church even though they could not speak English. The Saints' warm welcome encouraged more to attend, and after six weeks the number of Cambodian visitors passed the hundred mark.

Surprisingly, an inactive member who knew Cambodian was discovered right in the neighborhood. As he was enlisted into service, his faith revived, and soon he was sustained as a counselor in the newly formed branch presidency. Although most of the children could not speak English, they learned to sing some songs in that language.[7]

By 30 October 1966, an independent Spanish-speaking branch had been formed in the Los Angeles Stake. As this and other branches gained leadership strength, the time came to

---

[5] *Church News*, 17 June 1989, 8–9.

[6] Ibid., 21 February 1981, 13.

[7] Ibid., 17 January 1981, 7.

consider forming an entire ethnic stake. Since Spanish-speaking members constituted the largest ethnic minority, it was fitting that they should be the first to achieve that milestone.

"As early as 1972, a recommendation was made that a Spanish-speaking stake should be created in Los Angeles."[8] Finally on 3 June 1984, Spanish Saints from the Huntington Park, Inglewood, Los Angeles, and Santa Monica Stakes crowded in the Huntington Park stake center for the momentous occasion. Presiding was Elder Howard W. Hunter of the Council of the Twelve.

The new Huntington Park West Stake, with seven wards, had a membership in excess of twenty-two hundred. The stake president was Rafael Seminario, former bishop of the Los Angeles Third Ward. He thanked the Anglo members who had helped his Spanish brethren learn Church leadership and expressed confidence that the new stake's members would be equal to the challenges they would face.

And challenges there were. Many Hispanic families had barely enough resources to survive. They worked hard and long hours at low-paying jobs. Yet they found the faith and strength to fill Los Angeles Temple sessions on Saturdays at 6 A.M.—often their only day off.

Even though many members had to rely on public transit, often involving several transfers, Spanish-speaking units averaged over 60 percent attendance at sacrament meeting before the stake was created and over 65 percent afterward. These figures stood in stark contrast to the surrounding English-speaking wards and stakes, where the average was around 40 percent. The Spanish-speaking stake accounted for over half the region's baptisms—enough to create one ward per year. The Spanish-speaking Saints proved they were more than ready to shoulder stake responsibilities, because within a decade the original stake had become four.

---

8 Orton, 303.

The next ethnic group to be organized into a stake was the Tongans, who began settling in the Bay Area in the late 1950s. During the next third of a century their numbers grew to the point that in July 1991, Princess Salote Mafile'O Pilolevu Tuita came to San Francisco to help these Latter-day Saints celebrate the Church's centennial in their homeland. She honored them by appointing Hengehenga (Joe) Tonga a *matāpule* ("Talking Chief"). In attendance was Elder John H. Groberg, the General Authority who presided over Church affairs in California. He had been a champion of the Tongan people and a close personal friend of Princess Pilolevu since serving as a missionary and mission president in Tonga.

The new San Francisco East Stake was formed on 10 May 1992 from existing Tongan wards in Foster City, Millbrae, and Oakland. Like the Spanish-speaking members, the Tongans had higher-than-average temple activity and sacrament meeting attendance and were faithful tithe payers. They were also known for their great musical talent, as Tongan choirs often provided music for the Oakland Temple Christmas lighting ceremony and other special Church events.

The number of ethnic Latter-day Saints continued to grow even faster than Church membership as a whole. By the mid-1990s, there were over two hundred of these congregations in California, approximately one-sixth of the total wards and branches in the state.

Responding in Times of Disaster

As the Church continued maturing in California, the state was struck by a series of natural disasters that included earthquakes, floods, fires, and drought in a seemingly endless succession. However, the Saints were prepared to build bridges by taking love and support to everyone affected, including those who knew little of Christianity and even less about the Church.

On 2 May 1983, at least eleven Latter-day Saint families lost homes in an early-evening earthquake that shook the town of Coalinga. The Saints were well prepared for this calamity because just the day before, the ward bulletin had outlined what should be done in case of an earthquake. Following these instructions, home teachers, visiting teachers, and priesthood leaders accounted for the safety of all Church members in the affected area within two hours.[9]

Then came the fires. In July 1985 at least two LDS families lost homes in a blaze near San Diego. A month later, a massive inferno swept through the Santa Cruz mountains in the north, destroying or damaging a half dozen homes among members of the Alma Branch. However, the branch united with the congregations of three other faiths to work side by side, coordinating cleanup and relief efforts among themselves and their neighbors.

This same mountain area was one which experienced heavy flooding the following winter. However, once again, Church units were well prepared to meet the needs of their members.

These disasters were just a prelude. On 17 October 1989 a powerful earthquake rocked the region just prior to the second game of the first-ever Bay Area baseball World Series. The seven billion dollars in property losses made it the costliest natural disaster in U.S. history.

Few escaped unaffected. Priceless heirlooms and glass tumbled from shelves and shattered on the floor. Chimneys were cracked and broken. Entire buildings were destroyed. Dozens of Latter-day Saint homes were leveled, including the Alma Branch president's mountain home—a home that had earlier escaped the fires and floods. Approximately ten of the seventy-five LDS buildings in the quake zone suffered damage. However, the Oakland Temple, built on solid rock, escaped with only a few minor cracks.

---

[9] *Church News*, 8 May 1983, 13.

In San Francisco's hard-hit Marina Ward, several members were involved in dramatic rescues. "There was a real spirit of community among the ward," commented San Francisco Stake president Quentin L. Cook. Bishop J. Stanford Watkins added, "We usually do home teaching by assignment, but when something like this happens, we do it just by natural Christian instinct."[10]

Three Church members were among the seventy who lost their lives. Two members were killed in an Oakland freeway collapse. Another died in Santa Cruz when an old brick storefront collapsed.

When wildfires swept the hills surrounding Santa Barbara in late June 1990, fourteen Latter-day Saint families, including stake president Gerald Haws, lost their homes.[11] Then, in October of the following year, a massive fire swept through the hills in Oakland, destroying hundreds of homes and leaving the city—which had not yet recovered from the earthquake—stunned. However, no members' homes were lost and there was no damage to the temple.[12]

Looming in the background through all these problems was a ten-year drought that caused severe water rationing and widespread anxiety. The drought ended shortly after the Area Presidency called upon members statewide to fast and pray for rain.

A different kind of disaster hit Southern California in late April 1992. Eight Church members lost their businesses when riots swept south-central Los Angeles. Once again, the Los Angeles Stake had just conducted an emergency preparedness drill the Saturday before the riots broke out, so members were able to put the procedures into effect when the crisis occurred. Church members joined people of other faiths to preserve peace and order in their neighborhoods. "I found it inspiring and gratifying," remarked Keith Atkinson, the Church's Direc-

---

[10] Ibid., 28 October 1989, 3, 7–10.

[11] Ibid., 14 July 1990, 8, 10.

[12] Ibid., 26 October 1991, 5; 2 November 1991, 6.

tor of Public Affairs in California, "to see good-hearted people draw together to protect businesses and homes in their community."

In the aftermath, hundreds of Latter-day Saint volunteers with brooms and rakes joined thousands of others in cleaning up the debris. One afternoon the Long Beach Stake was asked to provide meals for the police and National Guard who had been called in to secure the peace. By 4 P.M. spaghetti and other casserole dinners were delivered. The soldiers and police officers were happy to have good home-cooked food.

When Los Angeles Stake president Howard B. Anderson attended testimony meeting in the Korean branch, whose members had been hit particularly hard by the looting, he was amazed to hear them singing "Come, Come, Ye Saints," with its affirmation "All is well, All is well." He had always associated this hymn with the early Pioneers, but he added, "I will never hear that song again and not think of those Korean people and their upbeat attitude."[13]

San Diego members gather relief supplies following Tijuana floods

When floods hit Tijuana, Mexico, in January 1993, Latter-day Saints in the San Diego area offered a helping hand across the border, strengthening contacts between members in the two countries. A new bond developed with the construction of

[13] Ibid., 9 May 1992, 5.

the San Diego Temple, when five stakes in northern Mexico were assigned to its temple district. It was through the temple committee that leaders in the United States first learned of the urgent needs in Tijuana. Within a few days a caravan of thirty-five pickup trucks was on its way with forty to fifty tons of food and clothing to aid the Tijuana Saints and their neighbors.[14]

Continuing Efforts at Building Bridges

The Church also joined with others in promoting measures to improve the moral character of society. Pornography was a particularly offensive problem. Elder John K. Carmack, former Los Angeles Stake president and now a General Authority and a member of the area presidency, spoke before the California state legislature in favor of tighter laws. In 1990 the Los Angeles County Board of Supervisors recognized the Church's role in the passage of stiffer laws against child pornography: "Without the help of The Church of Jesus Christ of Latter-day Saints and similar religious organizations you helped bring together, this bill would not have passed."[15]

In the San Francisco Bay Area, a local effort at working with an interfaith group to broadcast religious programming caught the Church's attention, and in September 1989 the Church joined a national coalition of twenty-eight religious groups in forming a national religious cable network known as VISN or Vision Interfaith Satellite Network (later renamed the Faith and Values Network). Leon Davies, who had been one of the founders of the Bay Area Religious Channel (BARC) was called with his wife on an indefinite mission to New York City to help launch the new national network.

California's challenges also brought opportunities. After the 1989 quake, an interfaith group was organized in San Jose. Church representatives were welcomed, perhaps due to the

---

[14] Ibid., 23 January 1993, 3, 5.

[15] Ibid., 5 December 1987, 5; 17 March 1990, 3, 13.

enormity of the disaster and partly because religious leaders were divided over an anti-Mormon film that had been shown in some Protestant churches. Some ministers of other faiths embraced opportunities for friendship to counterbalance their colleagues' involvement with the film. As earthquake relief efforts were carried out, new friendships were formed and new understandings reached, not only in San Jose but throughout the state, as Church leaders encouraged participation in interfaith groups wherever Latter-day Saints could be welcomed without compromising their principles or doctrine.

The Church has taught its members that their good example is the best way of sharing the gospel. For instance, Steve Young, a descendant of Brigham Young, became a star quarterback for the San Francisco 49ers. He not only became a favorite role model for Latter-day Saint youth, but he also attracted considerable goodwill for the Church.

Steve Young, San Francisco 49ers quarterback

Since its dedication in 1959, the Oakland Interstake Center on Temple Hill had been the focus of many Church and community programs, as well as home for three stakes, several wards, and a dozen or more small ethnic branches. Civic and other local leaders often referred to the Oakland Temple as "our temple." Though few had ever been inside its walls or contributed to its construction or maintenance, the temple was nonetheless part of their community. It was the only Oakland landmark included in each of the convention and visitors bureau's seven major city tours.

The Interstake Center was used for rescue operations after the devastating earthquake and fire. It seemed more than coincidence that during the city's hours of crisis those administering physical and emotional relief wanted Temple Hill as a base of operations.

A new twenty-two-thousand-square-foot visitors center was dedicated on Temple Hill on 12 September 1992—a prototype of others to be built around the Church. Nearby residents were sent special invitations to be guests at an open house prior to its dedication. Like the city's leaders, hundreds of citizens expressed their "ownership" of Temple Hill, citing the uplifting influence it was to them even though they were of other faiths or of no faith at all.

This center focused on the mission of Christ and the strengthening of families—two subjects which research showed were of interest to all people. The visitors center was built with large windows that took advantage of the magnificent view of the Bay Area. It featured a large statue of Christ and the latest interactive electronic displays that allowed visitors to hear answers to their questions about the Church.[16]

In the early 1990s, public affairs leaders began suggesting that the temple was the most visible, recognizable, and accessible symbol of the Latter-day Saint faith to those both inside and outside the Church. They recommended a program to bring more people to Temple Hill—qualified members to enter the temple itself, and others to at least come to the grounds where they could feel its influence. Outsiders had already recognized the Oakland Temple as a special place, as it had long been a popular backdrop for local Asian wedding pictures. Though non-Latter-day Saints could not enter the temple itself, almost every week an Asian wedding party would come and stroll through the grounds and take pictures with the temple in the background. They seemed to recognize

---

[16] Ibid., 19 September 1992, 3–4.

instinctively that there was something special about marriage and the temple, even though most were not Christians.

After the new Oakland Temple visitors center was dedicated, public affairs missionaries—full-time couples having been called the previous year—moved into these facilities. Their efforts, together with the attractive new center, increased the number of visitors to the hill nearly fourfold, from 34,364 in 1991 to 126,313 two years later. In mid-1994, Temple Hill public affairs and cultural arts councils were formed to further promote activities there.

New Houses of Worship

A challenge posed by continued Church growth and increased attendance at meetings was the need for more houses of worship. A 1984 national survey revealed that in an average week, 53 percent of all Latter-day Saints attended worship services—the highest number of any religious group in the study.[17] The Saints' increased faithfulness in paying tithes enabled the Church to more easily meet the need for more buildings. Over the years, local units had paid about 50 percent for the construction and maintenance of buildings. Beginning in April 1982 the Church announced that the local congregations' share was being reduced. In California, members were amazed that during a time of rising prices and taxes, the Church was able to lessen the financial burden of its members.

In November 1989, the Church announced that all building construction and maintenance costs would be paid from general Church funds. This was a real boon to the growing number of poor urban ethnic congregations, as funds for Church buildings and programs were all allocated from Salt Lake City without regard to local financial circumstance. A major criterion for receiving funds was sacrament meeting attendance, something at which many ethnic congregations excelled.

---

[17] Ibid., 10 February 1985, 3.

Throughout the state, older buildings were expanded and refurbished at general Church expense, bringing all buildings to a standard of maintenance and building code compliance never before seen.

Further, the consolidating of meetings under the Church correlation program paved the way for more compact building designs, and local chapels were reduced in size from approximately nineteen thousand to fourteen thousand square feet. On the other end of the scale, large chapels, capable of housing an entire stake, appeared. The LDS pioneer town of Fremont soon boasted two of them—one on the north end of town and one on the south. Another was built on the southeastern edge of San Jose, where it was anticipated that city growth would eventually result in new wards needing a home.

*Center for first
Spanish-speaking
stake in
Los Angeles*

In Oakland, members of several ethnic branches attended services at the Interstake Center on Temple Hill. But as they found it burdensome to travel across town, land was purchased to erect a new building for them in a more centrally located ethnic neighborhood. Likewise, following the riots in south-central Los Angeles, the Church was among the first to announce a new building in this district. It would be a large facility for the Spanish-speaking stake in the area. Such a thing would have been unthinkable just a few years before, and some grumbled at the Church for planning new buildings in what they perceived to be decaying neighborhoods.

However, some members, as well as other religious and civic leaders, expressed pride in a church that offered hope in areas where it was most needed. Many saw the Church's action as a partial fulfillment of its mandate to be with and minister to people where they lived and as a sign that the Church believed in its ability to lift and bless people in every circumstance.

In addition, after the Los Angeles and Oakland temples had been in service for a quarter century, the time came for the facilities in each to be improved and expanded. The Los Angeles Temple was closed for an extended period in 1980–81, as was the Oakland Temple nine years later. In each case, additional rooms were provided for presenting the endowment, enabling a new session to begin every half hour.[18]

The San Diego Temple

The major building project during the twentieth century's concluding decade was the construction of California's third temple. As early as 1977, Donald R. McArthur, a regional Church official in San Diego, was impressed that a temple should be built on vacant property he had observed adjacent to the I-5 freeway just south of La Jolla Village. Plans to construct a temple in San Diego were announced publicly in 1984, and the 6.9-acre site was acquired early the following year. One individual referred to the Church's early practice of building temples on hilltops and declared the visible freeway site to be "the modern urban equivalent of those early temples."[19] As had been the case with the Los Angeles and Oakland temples a quarter of a century earlier, the Saints in the San Diego Temple district raised 50 percent more funds than the assigned amount.

---

[18] Ibid., 14 March 1981, 11; 5 November 1988, 2.

[19] *Los Angeles Times*, 4 January 1993, A22.

Ground was broken for the new temple on 27 February 1988, and actual construction commenced two years later.[20] The building gradually took shape in full view of tens of thousands traveling the I-5 freeway each day. It has two towers, each 190 feet high, and a fourteen-foot-tall gold-leafed statue of the angel Moroni surmounting the eastern spire. Gleaming white marble chips were blown into the temple's exterior plaster to give the building a glistening look. The temple has a to-

San Diego Temple

tal floor space of fifty-nine thousand square feet, including four endowment presentation rooms.

In May 1992, as the temple neared completion, the First Presidency named Floyd L. Packard to be the temple president. At the same time, his brother, H. Von Packard, was named to preside over the Los Angeles Temple. Area president Elder John H. Groberg noted that "this is the first time in the history of the Church that brothers have simultaneously served as temple presidents."[21]

Daily newspapers asserted that the $24.4-million LDS temple was "destined to become a San Diego landmark" and

---

[20] Donald R. McArthur, *From Small Things: San Diego Stake, Its People and Its History* (San Diego Stake, 1990), 287–96.

[21] *The San Diego Seagull*, April 1993, 30.

Presidents Gordon B. Hinckley, Thomas S. Monson, Howard W. Hunter,
Elder Boyd K. Packer, and Susan Elizabeth Cardenas Vargas
at dedication of San Diego Temple

"a highly visible manifestation of the important contributions Mormons have made to San Diego for over a century."[22]

A Jewish rabbi compared the temple to medieval cathedrals which used "architecture to create a space that invokes the celestial heavens that is awesome, that transcends the place and the moment, transporting people from the here and now to thoughts and images of God's presence. . . . We thank [our Mormon friends] for reminding us how holy a place a mere building can be."[23]

The temple was dedicated in twenty-three sessions beginning on 23 April 1993. President Gordon B. Hinckley, counselor to Church president Ezra Taft Benson, opened the dedication by declaring: "The significant things about this temple are the

---

[22] *San Diego Union-Tribune*, 27 February 1993; *San Diego Evening Tribune*, 19 February 1993, B6.

[23] *San Diego Jewish Times*, 25 March 1993.

ordinances of the gospel that will be administered here. . . . There would be no purpose to build temples if there was no immortality."[24]

Three dedicatory sessions were conducted in Spanish for the benefit of Church members from Mexico and Spanish-speaking Saints from Southern California. In two of these sessions President Hinckley "spoke with emotion" about the heritage of these Saints: "You come from two great ancestral lines, from the people of Spain and from the people of Jerusalem, Lehi and his children. Great is your inheritance and marvelous are your blessings. . . . You are a beautiful people . . . with beautiful testimonies, with the light of the gospel of Christ in your lives. You represent a miracle this day in the house of God. [You are] people who love the Lord and are loved by the Lord."[25]

Bringing together not only the living and the dead but also the Anglo and Hispanic communities in its area, the San Diego Temple exemplified the connecting power of the Church. Building on foundations laid in earlier times, the Church in California reached out to build bridges of love and understanding. It sought to bless members of varied ethnic groups, to render assistance in the wake of disasters, and to help improve the moral climate of society and the quality of life for all. With visible and invisible bridges in place, the California Saints increasingly took advantage of opportunities to share their precious gospel treasure.

---

[24] *Church News*, 1 May 1993, 3.

[25] Ibid.

California Saints Today and Tomorrow

A s the Church approached the milestone of a century and a half in California, the time seemed right to take stock of what had been accomplished and to look forward to the Saints' future in the state.

Though the Church and its members had passed through times of trial and challenge, life was now generally good. An eight-year study by the UCLA School of Public Health revealed that "10,000 active Latter-day Saints in California" had "one of the lowest mortality rates ever recorded." The death rate among high priests who lived the Word of Wisdom was only 22 percent of the mortality rate for middle-aged white males as a whole, and the life expectancy of this LDS group was eleven years longer than that of the general population.[1] These conclusions simply confirmed what many already knew: living the restored gospel of Jesus Christ results in a happy, fulfilling, and healthy lifestyle. California Latter-day Saints were eager to reach out and share with their neighbors what they had.

During the closing decades of the twentieth century, the Church in California continued to grow. By 1990 the state had

---

[1] *Journal of the National Cancer Institute*, 6 December 1989, quoted in *Church News*, 9 December 1989, 7, and *Ensign*, February 1990, 80.

grown to be nearly ten times more populous than it was in 1920. But the rate of Latter-day Saint growth was nearly twenty times that of the state as a whole, from about four thousand members in 1920 to 725,000 in 1990. The 34-percent Church growth rate during the 1980s was nearly double the 19-percent increase for the state as a whole and significantly higher than Utah's Church growth rate of 21 percent during the same period.[2] Latter-day Saints had become the next-to-largest faith group in California, second only to the Roman Catholics. Statewide there were twenty-five Latter-day Saints for every one thousand in the population.

By the mid-1990s, California boasted 161 stakes, 15 missions, and over 1,300 local congregations.[3] However, shifting population patterns have caused some urban stakes and wards to be eliminated through consolidation. In more recent years, especially in some urban areas, certain foreign-language congregations once again have become parts of mission districts rather than of stakes.

California's Contributions

During their century and a half in California, the Latter-day Saints have made a variety of contributions to the Golden State. The arrival of Samuel Brannan's colony on the *Brooklyn* tripled the population of the community which would soon grow into the great city of San Francisco. Men from the Mormon Battalion dug the first wells, made bricks, and built the courthouse in San Diego. They also raised the American flag as part of Los Angeles's first Fourth of July celebration. Brannan published the state's first newspaper completely in the English language, and a young LDS girl in his colony taught California's first English-speaking school. Soldiers from the Mormon Battalion played a key role in the discovery of gold,

---

[2] *Church News*, 8 June 1991, 3–4.

[3] *1995–96 Church Almanac* (Salt Lake City: Deseret News, 1994), 114.

and one of their diaries fixed the exact date of that momentous event. John Horner, the first man to use a harrow in the state, was honored as "California's first farmer." The city of San Bernardino had its beginning as a Latter-day Saint colony. In more recent years, a growing LDS presence has provided a stabilizing influence of high morals and family values. Contributions of individual Latter-day Saints to business, politics, education, and cultural life are too numerous to list.

But the Golden State has also made significant contributions to the Church of Jesus Christ of Latter-day Saints. Those contributions have been varied, perhaps beginning when Samuel Brannan taught the Pioneers how to make adobes—a skill that helped the Saints survive during their first winter in the Salt Lake Valley. Mormon Battalion members' observations of irrigation in the Southwest helped the Saints develop similar projects in the mountains. Gold from California helped finance early development in the Great Basin, just as tithes from faithful California Saints helped support worldwide Church programs a century later. Mormon Battalion pay enabled Captain James Brown to purchase Miles Goodyear's cattle ranch at the mouth of Weber Canyon, providing a needed source of meat for Utah Pioneers. The first seed wheat in the Great Basin also came from California. For many years, John Horner sent seedlings, especially of fruit trees, to the Saints in Utah.

During the 1880s, California provided a haven for those fleeing from persecutions because of plural marriage. In a similar manner, during the present century, California became the place where Intermountain Saints could go to find economic opportunity. It allowed the Latter-day Saints to have a broader influence than if they had stayed only in the valleys of the mountains. California gave the Church its first experience with establishing stakes in predominantly non-LDS urban areas. In this setting, programs were launched that became important Churchwide. Southern California's Good Will enterprises set the pattern for the Church's own Deseret Industries.

California became the home for the largest group of Latter-day Saints in any state or nation outside of Utah. Here the Church built what was at the time its largest temple, in Los Angeles.

In early years the Golden State provided significant experience for several who were or became general Church leaders—Parley P. Pratt, Amasa M. Lyman, Charles C. Rich, George Q. Cannon, Joseph F. Smith, and Moses Thatcher to name just a few.

Likewise during the twentieth century a growing number of General Authorities were called from California. These included Hyrum G. Smith, called as Patriarch to the Church in 1912; Robert L. Simpson, called to the Presiding Bishopric in 1961; Paul H. Dunn, named to the First Council of the Seventy in 1964; and David B. Haight, who became an Assistant to the Twelve in 1970 and one of the Twelve Apostles six years later. Other Californians who became members of the Quorums of the Seventy in the later twentieth century included Ronald E. Poelman (1978), John K. Carmack (1984), Cree-L Kofford and Joseph C. Muren (1991), and Lance B. Wickman (1994). In addition to these, L. Tom Perry, who became an assistant to the Twelve in 1972 and a member of the Twelve in 1974, lived in Sacramento from 1953 to 1962 while serving as controller of a department store chain. Also, Henry B. Eyring, who became a counselor in the Presiding Bishopric in 1985 and a member of the Twelve ten years later, lived in the Bay Area for nearly a decade while teaching at Stanford University's Graduate School of Business. Of course, heading the list of California's contributions to Church leadership was Howard W. Hunter, who became an apostle in 1959 and served as president of The Church of Jesus Christ of Latter-day Saints from 1994 to 1995.

One of California's most important contributions is often overlooked. A revelation given through Joseph Smith speaks of the latter-day Zion being the only place of peace and safety in the midst of widespread calamities and disasters. "With one heart and with one mind," the faithful from "every nation under heaven" will gather there for refuge (D&C 45:65–69). Some California Saints have a vision of the Golden State as a laboratory to which representatives of many nations have been "gathered" to learn how to live together in peace.[4] With beautiful temples amid the diversity of three of the world's most oft-visited cities, the California Saints have the potential of becoming a Zion people. Their experience, in turn, can bless the entire world.

A Prophet from California

Upon President Ezra Taft Benson's death, Howard W. Hunter became the Church's fourteenth president on 5 June 1994. For over a third of a century he had pursued his career as a father, Church leader, and corporate attorney in Southern California. Then, for another similar time period, he served in the Quorum of the Twelve.

He had learned to relate peaceably and effectively with people of many backgrounds. He was comfortable meeting with Arabs in Egypt, Arabs and Jews in the Holy Land, or with Polynesians and Asians in Hawaii. He created a record number of fifteen stakes in Mexico City on a single weekend and also organized the first Spanish-speaking stake in Los Angeles. "We look upon no nation or nationality as second-class citizens," affirmed Elder Hunter.[5]

His ministry as an apostle more fully opened the Church to the world and the world to the Church in new ways. His background put him in the forefront of the Church's transformation from a Utah or American institution to a global one. Elder Hunter's apostleship was summed up by President Thomas S. Monson: "His mission was marked by monumental events. . . . Truly he was a pioneer, one who, according to Webster, goes before, showing others the way to follow."[6]

---

[4] *Ensign*, June 1995, 75.

[5] Ibid., June 1979, 74.

[6] Ibid., April 1995, 32.

President Howard W. Hunter

Though he served as Church president for less than a year, President Hunter was able to quickly focus members' attention to their temples and their Lord. He immediately challenged them to make the temple "the great symbol of your membership" and repeated this theme as he traveled throughout the world. As he had done earlier as a leader in California, he also asked the Saints to be more charitable and forgiving in their dealings with one another. He welcomed those "who have transgressed or been offended" back into the fold, and to those who were "hurt or . . . struggling and afraid," he said, "Let us stand with you and dry your tears."[7]

Powerful Prophetic Blessings

After decades of sustained growth, Church membership in California leveled off during the early 1990s. Some Latter-day Saints were among the Californians who left the state to escape from natural disasters, increasing crime, a softening economy, and other changes they regarded as a deterioration in lifestyle. But the future remained bright for the Church in the Golden State. Both Presidents Howard W. Hunter and Gordon B. Hinckley personally journeyed to California where

---

[7] Ibid., November 1994, 8.

they gave encouragement, inspired counsel, and powerful promises to the Saints.

Only two weeks after being sustained as President of the Church, Howard W. Hunter returned to his old stake in Pasadena—"an especially satisfying moment for him."[8] He took this occasion to reflect on the unique opportunities and challenges of the Latter-day Saints in his beloved California and to pronounce a blessing on them:

> What a marvelous opportunity is yours to live where the Church is generally well regarded and where there is a strong base of those who have similar values and opportunities together. . . . Truly the faithful Latter-day Saints represent the leaven in the loaf of the state of California. Your influence, through righteous living, appropriate community involvement, and effective missionary work, will bless the people who reside within . . . the whole state of California. I feel the Church will continue to grow in strength and vitality in this area.
>
> Without doubt there are significant challenges facing the Latter-day Saints, both here and elsewhere in the world. We hope that you will not be overcome with discouragement in your attempts to raise your families in righteousness. . . . If you will diligently work to lead your families in righteousness, encouraging and participating in daily family prayer, scripture reading, family home evening, and love and support for each other in living the teachings of the gospel, you will receive the promised blessings of the Lord in raising a righteous posterity.
>
> In an increasingly wicked world, how essential it is that each of us "stands in holy places" and commits to be true and faithful to the teachings of the gospel of Jesus Christ.
>
> Certainly there continues to be a need in this area to appropriately blend into the gospel and the Church the many diverse nationalities and cultures which have become a part of California. Much positive work has been done in this regard. We hope that you will reach out to your brothers and sisters of every background and circumstance and welcome them in as "fellow citizens with the saints, and of the household of God," as was said in the book of Ephesians (Eph 2:19).
>
> I repeat, I see the future of the Church in California as bright. Those things which will bring us the peace and happiness we so desire are contained within the teachings of the Master. We encourage you young people present today to be diligent and faithful in living the

---

[8] Ibid., April 1995, 26.

standards of the gospel, setting an example before your friends and your associates. We trust that you young men and young women are finding appropriate fellowship within the body of the Saints so that you will not be tempted to involve yourself in destructive activities, such as gangs, drugs, sexual immorality, or other things which are not in harmony with the teachings of the gospel.

My beloved brothers and sisters I feel impressed to leave my blessing with you. I bless you that you may feel the love and confidence of our Heavenly Father and the Lord Jesus Christ in your daily lives. I bless you as parents with the confidence to raise your children in faith that they may receive an added measure of strength to avoid the temptations of Satan. I bless you with an increased desire to live your own lives worthy of the privilege of entering the house of the Lord and enjoying the blessings of the temple both for yourselves and for your kindred dead.

That you may live in such a way to merit the eternal promises of the Lord I humbly pray as I leave my witness with you of the reality of the restored gospel of Jesus Christ.[9]

Following Howard W. Hunter's death in March of 1995, Gordon B. Hinckley succeeded him as President of the Church. Just a few weeks earlier, President Hinckley had spoken to a multi-regional conference at San Jose. He admonished the Saints to take serious thought before moving from California to Utah or other places. He indicated that the Church must continue on in California.

Then, soon after being sustained as the Church's leader, President Hinckley addressed another multi-regional conference, this time in Sacramento. He reminded his listeners of their heritage. "There are Mormon footsteps over this part of the world, over this part of California," he maintained. "This is not the first time Mormons have been here. . . . There was Mormon heroism, there was Mormon sacrifice, there was Mormon faithfulness long before any of us came on the scene."[10]

During his address at Sacramento, President Hinckley also testified: "I have seen miracles in my time, my brothers and

<hr />

[9] Howard W. Hunter remarks at Pasadena Stake conference, 16 October 1994, typescript; see also *Church News*, 22 October 1994, 3–4.

[10] *Church News*, 27 May 1995, 3.

Church president Gordon B. Hinckley and area president Loren C. Dunn
with their wives in front of Mormon Battalion cabin at Coloma

sisters. The greatest miracle of all, I believe, is the transformation that comes into the life of a man or a woman who accepts the restored gospel of Jesus Christ and tries to live it in his or her life." He then challenged the California Saints to enrich their own lives and to bless others through the gospel. "It is indeed a marvelous work and a wonder which has been brought to pass by the power of the Almighty in behalf of His sons and daughters in such a way that we of this season in His work can serve in a work of salvation in behalf of the whole human family." After testifying that "the work is true," President Hinckley concluded: "I leave my blessing upon you that you may find peace and happiness and love in your homes."[11]

With the blessings of these prophets upon their land and in their hearts, and as significant as their legacy is, California Saints may anticipate an even greater future. Though there are still problems, the Saints again march as pioneers seeking that

---

[11] Ibid., 5.

which is more precious than gold. The long-held dream of California as a "promised land" will be realized more than ever before, and the Golden State Saints, like those who laid some of the state's foundations 150 years before, will be an integral part of it.

From the small colony aboard the old sailing ship which entered San Francisco Bay 150 years earlier, the California Saints grew to be nearly three quarters of a million strong. As interesting as their first century and a half was, they turn their faces forward, rather than backward, in anticipation of even greater possibilities the future will yet bring.

APPENDIX A
CALIFORNIA HIGHLIGHTS

Year	Date	Event
1819	2 March	Samuel Brannan born in Saco, Maine
1820	Early spring	Joseph Smith's First Vision
1830	6 April	Church of Jesus Christ of Latter-day Saints founded
1844		*The Prophet* published in New York City
	27 June	Joseph Smith killed in Illinois
1845		Brannan publishes *New-York Messenger* at New York City
	19 Nov	New York conference approves sending group to California by sea
1846	4 Feb	*Brooklyn* sails from New York; Pioneers leave Nauvoo
	16 July	Mormon Battalion enlisted at Council Bluffs, Iowa
	31 July	*Brooklyn* party arrives at Yerba Buena
1847	9 Jan	First issue of Brannan's *California Star*
	10 Jan	Battalion crosses Colorado River into California
	29 Jan	Mormon Battalion arrives at San Diego
	30 June	Brannan meets with President Brigham Young in Wyoming
	16 July	Mormon Battalion discharged at Los Angeles
	2 Dec	Addison Pratt named San Francisco Branch president
	Dec	Jefferson Hunt group arrives in Southern California to buy supplies
1848	24 Jan	Gold discovered at Sutter's Mill

Year	Date	Event
	March	"Mormon Volunteers" take first wagons over southern route
	1 April	*Star* special announces gold discovery
	3 July	Wagon train leaves Northern California for Salt Lake City via "Mormon Emigrant Trail"
1849	25 May	Elder Amasa M. Lyman and Porter Rockwell in California
	14 July	Mormon gold train leaves for Salt Lake City with tithing
	22 Nov	First missionaries to Hawaii leave San Francisco
1850	8 Jan	Elder Lyman and Rockwell confront Brannan
	15 Feb	Elder Charles C. Rich arrives in San Francisco
	April	Last "gold missionaries" sent
	28 June	Apostles receive five hundred dollars from Brannan
	17 Aug	Elder Lyman leaves for Utah with tithes
	9 Sept	California admitted to the Union as a state
	5 Oct	Elder Rich and Rockwell leave for Utah
		John Horner builds school/church near Mission San Jose
1851	23 Feb	Three apostles called to missions in California
	March	Elders Lyman and Rich head large group to San Bernardino
	10 June	Brannan helps revive Vigilance Committee
	11 June	Colonists arrive in Southern California
	6 July	Stake organized at San Bernardino
	11 July	Elder Parley P. Pratt arrives in San Francisco
	1 Sept	Brannan disfellowshipped

Year	Date	Event
	5 Sept	Elder Pratt leaves for mission in Chile
	22 Sept	Purchase of San Bernardino ranch consummated
1852	21 May	Elder Pratt returns from Chile
	29 Aug	LDS practice of plural marriage announced
1854	2 July	Elder Pratt returns to San Francisco as mission president
1855	March	Elder Pratt publishes prospectus for newspaper
	21 April	San Bernardino election intensifies divisions
	June	George Q. Cannon replaces Elder Pratt
1856	23 Feb	Cannon publishes *Western Standard* in San Francisco
	Dec	"Reformation" launched in San Bernardino
1857	24 July	President Young learns of approaching U.S. Army
	3 Dec	Cannon leaves for Utah
1858	Feb	San Bernardino ranch sold
1871		Aaron Garlick becomes president of Sacramento Branch
1876	27 Dec	Job Smith arrives as missionary to California
1877	29 Aug	President Young dies in Salt Lake City
1880	10 Oct	John Taylor becomes president of the Church
1882		Edmonds Law sparks anti-polygamy "raid" in Utah
1884		Eliza Woollacott and family arrive in Los Angeles
1887	15 Sept	Wilford Woodruff seeks help for Utah statehood
1889	7 April	Wilford Woodruff becomes president of the Church
	April	President Woodruff's second trip; first visit by Church president

Year	Date	Event
	May	Brannan dies at San Diego
1890	July	Lindsey family arrives in Oakland
	24 Sept	"Manifesto" announces end of plural marriages
1892	10 Aug	Luther Dalton named California Mission president
	2 Oct	Oakland Branch created
1894	Jan	Karl G. Maeser organizes exhibit and heads Mission
	25 July	Henry S. Tanner becomes mission president
1895	20 Oct	Los Angeles Branch created
1896	4 Jan	Utah statehood
	April	Tabernacle Choir concerts create goodwill
	Nov	Ephraim H. Nye becomes mission president
1898	24 Jan	Jubilee celebration of gold discovery
	2 June	San Diego Branch created
	2 Sept	President Woodruff dies in San Francisco
	13 Sept	Lorenzo Snow becomes president of the Church
1901	10 April	President Cannon dies in Monterey
	June	Joseph E. Robinson becomes mission president
	17 Oct	Joseph F. Smith becomes president of the Church
1906	18 April	Earthquake and fire devastate San Francisco
		Mission headquarters moved to Los Angeles
	22 Nov	LDS settlers from Idaho arrive in Gridley
1908	Autumn	President Smith tours mission
1909	4 July	Liberty Social Hall opened at Gridley
1912	9 May	Hyrum G. Smith called as patriarch to the Church
	Nov	Chapel completed at Gridley

Year	Date	Event
1915	29 July	Elder James E. Talmage speaks at San Francisco fair
1917	Fall	Soldiers from Utah in training near San Diego
1918	23 Nov	Heber J. Grant becomes president of the Church
1919	April	Elder Joseph W. McMurrin becomes mission president
1923	21 Jan	Los Angeles Stake created
1924	Aug	Missionary work opened among Mexicans in Los Angeles
1927	Feb	Daughters of Utah Pioneers chapter organized at Los Angeles
	10 July	San Francisco Stake created
1929	28 April	Wilshire Ward chapel dedicated by President Grant
	29 Oct	Stock market crash foreshadows Great Depression
1931		*Messenger* published in Oakland
		Weekly LDS broadcast on Oakland radio station
	13 Jan	Church's first "Deseret Club" organized at UCLA
1932		Church Employment Office opens in Los Angeles
1934	18 Nov	Los Angeles choir on national "Church of the Air" program
1935		*California Intermountain News* published in Los Angeles
		Church opens own exhibit building at San Diego fair
		Elder John A. Widtsoe teaches at USC School of Religion
1936	April	Churchwide Welfare plan launched

Handwritten annotation: 1922 3 JULY J WEST BORN LONG BEACH CA

Year	Date	Event
	28 June	Spanish American Mission created at meeting in Los Angeles
1937	23 March	Los Angeles Temple site purchased
1938		Deseret Industries created
1939		Church exhibit at Golden Gate International Exposition
1940	Sept	Howard W. Hunter becomes bishop of El Sereno Ward
1941	May	Hugh B. Brown becomes LDS Servicemen's Coordinator
	7 Dec	Attack on Pearl Harbor brings U.S. into World War II
1942	Jan	California Mission divided
1943	16 Aug	Oakland Temple site purchased
1945	21 May	George Albert Smith becomes president of the Church
	14 Aug	World War II ends
	Nov	First Spanish-language temple sessions at Arizona Temple
1949	17 Jan	Plans announced to build Los Angeles Temple
1950		California LDS membership surpasses 100,000
	26 Feb	Howard W. Hunter becomes Pasadena Stake president
	March	Mormon Battalion trek celebrated
	9 Sept	Centennial of California's becoming a state
	Sept	Early morning seminaries begun in Southern California
	Nov	Spanish American branches transfered to stakes
1951	9 April	David O. McKay becomes president of the Church
	9 June	Welfare Center dedicated in Los Angeles

Year	Date	Event
	22 Sept	Ground broken for Los Angeles Temple
	7 Oct	Mormon Choir of Southern California first performs
1953	4 Oct	General conference televised live from Salt Lake City
	5 Oct	Goodwin J. Knight becomes California governor
1954	Aug	MIA conference and festivals in Los Angeles
1956	11 March	Los Angeles Temple dedicated
1958	3 July	Ft. Moore Monument dedicated in Los Angeles
1959	10 Oct	Howard W. Hunter sustained in Quorum of the Twelve Apostles
	16 Oct	Oakland Interstake Center opened
1963	20 June	Branch genealogical library dedicated adjacent to Los Angeles Temple
1964	17 Nov	Oakland Temple dedicated
1969	22 Nov	Mormon Battalion monument dedicated in San Diego
1970	23 Jan	Joseph Fielding Smith becomes president of the Church
	6 April	David B. Haight becomes a General Authority
1972	7 July	Harold B. Lee becomes president of the Church
	3 Nov	Mormon Battalion visitors center opens in San Diego
1973	30 Dec	Spencer W. Kimball becomes president of the Church
1976	1 Jan	First LDS float in Rose Parade
1978	1 June	Revelation extends priesthood to all races
	22 Dec	BYU's first appearance in San Diego's Holiday Bowl
1980	18 May	80,000 at Rose Bowl area conference

(handwritten annotation: "25 MAR J WEST JOINS CHURCH")

Year	Date	Event
		California LDS membership reaches 541,000
1984	8 Jan	Multi-stake conference in San Diego
	April	North America West Area announced
	3 June	First Spanish-speaking stake in U.S.
1985	20 July	100,000 at dance festival in Rose Bowl
	10 Nov	Ezra Taft Benson becomes president of the Church
1989	17 Oct	San Francisco earthquake kills three members
1990		California LDS membership reaches 725,000
1992	12 Sept	New Oakland Temple visitors center opens
1993	25 April	San Diego Temple dedicated
1994	5 June	Californian Howard W. Hunter becomes president of the Church
1995	12 March	Gordon B. Hinckley becomes president of the Church

APPENDIX B
CALIFORNIA GROWTH

Years	California Population	Percent Increase	Calif. LDS Population	Percent Increase	LDS Per Thousand
1850	93,000		600		6.5
1860	380,000	308.6			
1870	560,000	47.4			
1880	865,000	54.5			
1890	1,215,000	40.5			
1900	1,485,000	22.2			
1910	2,380,000	60.3	898		.38
1920	3,427,000	44.0	3,967	342	1.15
1930	5,677,000	65.7	20,700	422	3.65
1940	6,900,000	21.5	44,800	116.4	6.49
1950	10,600,000	53.6	102,000	127.7	9.62
1960	15,900,000	50.0	217,600	113.3	13.69
1970	20,000,000	25.8	368,000	69.1	18.40
1980	23,800,000	19.0	541,000	47.0	22.73
1990	28,300,000	18.9	725,000	34.0	25.62

APPENDIX C
CALIFORNIA MISSIONS

Date	Mission	Total
3 February 1851	Pacific (San Francisco; discontinued 3 December 1857)	1
August 1892	California (San Francisco; moved to Los Angeles 1906)	1
2 January 1942	Northern California (San Francisco; renamed California North 1966; renamed California Sacramento 1974)	2
10 July 1966	California South (renamed California Anaheim 1974)	3
1 July 1969	California Central (renamed California Oakland 1974)	4
7 July 1969	California East (renamed California Arcadia 1974)	5
20 June 1974	**(All mission names changed to include state and headquarters city)**	
1 August 1974	California San Diego	6
1 July 1975	California Fresno	7
1 July 1978	California San Jose	8
1 July 1978	California Ventura	9
1 July 1980	California San Bernardino	10
1 July 1985	California Santa Rosa	11
1 July 1990	California Riverside	12
1 July 1993	California Carlsbad	13
1 July 1993	California Roseville	14
1 July 1994	California San Fernando	15

APPENDIX D
CALIFORNIA STAKES

Date	Stake	Total
6 July 1851	San Bernardino (discontinued 1857)	1
21 January 1923	Los Angeles (renamed South Los Angeles 1939)	1
22 May 1927	Hollywood (renamed Los Angeles 1939)	2
10 July 1927	San Francisco	3
4 November 1934	Gridley	4
4 November 1934	Sacramento	5
2 December 1934	Oakland (discontinued 1956)	6
3 February 1935	San Bernardino [new]	7
19 April 1936	Pasadena	8
3 May 1936	Long Beach	9
1 October 1939	San Fernando (renamed Van Nuys 1974)	10
19 November 1939	South Los Angeles (Los Angeles renamed; discontinued 1984)	
	Los Angeles [new] (Hollywood renamed)	
26 November 1939	Inglewood	11
9 February 1941	San Diego	12
3 June 1946	Palo Alto (renamed Menlo Park 1974)	13
13 October 1946	Berkeley (discontinued 1956)	14
25 April 1948	San Joaquin (renamed Stockton 1974)	15
4 December 1949	Glendale	16
12 February 1950	East Long Beach	17
26 February 1950	East Los Angeles (realigned 1993)	18
7 January 1951	Santa Rosa	19
18 March 1951	Santa Barbara	20
20 May 1951	Fresno	21
27 May 1951	Bakersfield	22
1 July 1951	Santa Monica	23

Date	Stake	Total
26 October 1952	Mt. Rubidoux (renamed Riverside 1974)	24
30 November 1952	San Jose	25
27 June 1954	Orange County (discontinued 1975)	26
12 December 1954	Sacramento North	27
29 May 1955	Redondo (renamed Torrance North 1974)	28
26 February 1956	Covina	29
26 August 1956	Oakland and Berkeley discontinued	
	Oakland-Berkeley (renamed Oakland [new] 1974)	
	Hayward	
	Walnut Creek	30
16 September 1956	Reseda (renamed Chatsworth 1974; discontinued 1992)	31
	Burbank (renamed North Hollywood 1974)	32
15 September 1957	San Mateo (renamed Pacifica 1974; discontinued 1992)	33
22 September 1957	San Luis Obispo	34
8 December 1957	Santa Ana (renamed Orange 1974)	35
2 March 1958	Monterey Bay (renamed Monterey 1974)	36
20 April 1958	San Diego East (renamed El Cajon 1974)	37
26 October 1958	Norwalk (renamed Cerritos 1974)	38
19 April 1959	Huntington Park (renamed Downey 1986)	39
26 April 1959	Whittier	40
3 May 1959	West Covina (renamed La Puente 1974; renamed Walnut 1985)	41
3 May 1959	Torrance	42
16 August 1959	Mojave (renamed Barstow 1974)	43
6 December 1959	American River (renamed Sacramento East 1974)	44
17 April 1960	Napa	45
6 November 1960	Palomar (renamed Carlsbad 1974)	46
13 December 1960	Redding	47

Date	Stake	Total
21 May 1961	San Leandro	48
25 June 1961	Garden Grove	49
8 October 1961	Canoga Park	50
22 October 1961	Redwood (renamed Eureka 1974)	51
21 January 1962	Pomona (renamed LaVerne 1974)	52
21 October 1962	San Diego South (renamed Lemon Grove 1983; renamed Sweetwater 1988)	53
23 June 1963	Concord	54
15 September 1963	Fresno East	55
20 October 1963	Santa Maria	56
10 November 1963	San Jose West (renamed Saratoga 1974)	57
7 June 1964	Modesto	58
14 March 1965	Orange County discontinued	
	Fullerton (renamed Placentia 1974)	
	Anaheim	59
20 March 1966	Rialto	60
5 June 1966	Huntington Beach	61
11 December 1966	Fremont	62
12 February 1967	Fair Oaks	63
23 April 1967	Arlington (renamed Riverside West 1974)	64
27 August 1967	Palm Springs	65
17 September 1967	El Monte (renamed Hacienda Heights 1978)	66
10 December 1967	Simi Valley	67
11 February 1968	San Jose South	68
31 March 1968	Newport Beach	69
12 May 1968	Antelope Valley (renamed Palmdale 1974)	70
23 June 1968	Marin (renamed San Rafael 1974)	71
15 June 1969	Sacramento South (renamed Elk Grove 1993)	72
22 June 1969	San Diego North	73
24 August 1969	Visalia	74

Date	Stake	Total
15 February 1970	Anaheim West (renamed Cypress 1974)	75
17 May 1970	Roseville	76
29 May 1970	**(Stake names adjusted to place directional words second rather than first; e.g., East Los Angeles became Los Angeles East)**	
7 June 1970	La Canada (renamed La Crescentia 1974)	77
16 August 1970	Mt. Whitney (renamed Ridgecrest 1974)	78
30 May 1971	Ventura	79
6 February 1972	Chico	80
13 August 1972	Upland	81
20 August 1972	San Jose North (renamed Santa Clara 1974; discontinued 1992)	82
24 September 1972	Escondido	83
14 January 1974	**(Many stakes renamed to more acurrately reflect their location including adding the name of the state; e.g., Escondido California Stake.)**	
19 May 1974	Santa Clarita	84
18 August 1974	Newbury Park	85
8 September 1974	Cerritos West	86
15 September 1974	Merced	87
8 December 1974	Pleasanton	88
16 February 1975	Fairfield	89
4 May 1975	San Jose East	90
24 August 1975	Los Altos	91
21 September 1975	Fullerton [new]	92
26 October 1975	Modesto North	93
30 November 1975	San Diego East [new]	94
18 January 1976	Palos Verdes	95
14 March 1976	Blythe	96
8 August 1976	Camarillo	97
19 September 1976	Chula Vista	98
14 November 1976	Glendora	99
14 November 1976	Santa Ana	100

Date	Stake	Total
28 November 1976	Lancaster	101
16 January 1977	Huntington Beach North	102
23 January 1977	Concord East (discontinued 1986)	103
13 March 1977	Granada Hills (discontinued 1992)	104
24 April 1977	Stockton East (renamed Lodi 1981)	105
24 April 1977	Santa Cruz	106
8 May 1977	Mission Viejo	107
15 May 1977	Morgan Hill	108
9 October 1977	Arcadia	109
30 October 1977	Ukiah	110
4 June 1978	San Bernardino East (renamed Redlands 1987)	111
18 June 1978	Bakersfield East	112
6 August 1978	Hanford	113
17 September 1978	Hemet	114
8 October 1978	Vista	115
19 November 1978	Corona	116
19 November 1978	El Dorado	117
27 May 1979	Auburn	118
10 June 1979	Anderson	119
26 August 1979	Poway	120
14 October 1979	Chino	121
14 October 1979	Quincy	122
4 November 1979	Yuba City	123
9 December 1979	Ontario	124
17 February 1980	Lawndale (discontinued 1993)	125
16 March 1980	El Centro	126
22 June 1980	Citrus Heights	127
22 June 1980	Davis	128
22 June 1980	Cordova (renamed Rancho Cordova 1985; renamed Sacramento Cordova 1994)	129
22 March 1981	Manteca	130

Date	Stake	Total
3 May 1981	Antioch	131
20 June 1982	Laguna Niguel	132
30 January 1983	Victorville	133
12 February 1984	Fresno North	134
	Fresno West	135
3 June 1984	Huntington Park West [Spanish]	136
	Los Angeles South discontinued	
25 November 1984	Carmichael	136
24 February 1985	Anaheim East	137
24 February 1985	San Francisco West	138
8 December 1985	Santee	139
12 January 1986	Fremont South	140
16 February 1986	Concord East discontinued	
	Walnut Creek East (renamed Danville 1989)	140
23 March 1986	Turlock	141
22 June 1986	Fontana	142
21 September 1986	Penasquitos	143
14 December 1986	Bakersfield South	144
11 January 1987	Thousand Oaks	145
22 February 1987	Hesperia	146
12 April 1987	Irvine	147
28 June 1987	Rancho Cucamonga	148
23 August 1987	Lompoc	149
13 September 1987	Livermore	150
27 September 1987	Moreno Valley	151
31 January 1988	Long Beach North (dicontinued 1993)	152
6 March 1988	Sacramento Antelope	153
20 March 1988	Murrieta	154
7 January 1990	Del Mar	155
9 December 1990	Jurupa	156
19 May 1991	Lancaster East	157

Date	Stake	Total
26 May 1991	Vacaville	158
5 January 1992	Santa Ana South [Spanish]	159
2 February 1992	Valencia	160
9 February 1992	Escondido South	161
21 February 1992	Pacifica discontinued	
19 April 1992	Rocklin	161
10 May 1992	Santa Clara discontinued	
10 May 1992	San Francisco East [Tongan]	161
6 December 1992	Chatsworth and Granada Hills discontinued	
	San Fernando [new; became Spanish]	160
17 January 1993	Santa Margarita	161
21 February 1993	Lawndale discontinued	
14 March 1993	Highland	161
27 June 1993	East Los Angeles [Spanish (Los Angeles East realigned)]	
7 November 1993	Long Beach North discontinued	
9 January 1994	Yucca Valley	161
6 November 1994	Covina [Spanish (Covina and surrounding stakes realigned)]	
15 October 1995	Menifee	162

APPENDIX E
CALIFORNIA HISTORIC SITES

Following are a few of the sites important to LDS history in California. Numbers in braces refer to pages in the text where more information can be found.

American River. Its North, Middle, and South Forks were the sites for some of the richest gold mining locations. Such key LDS sites as **Mormon Island** and **Salmon Falls** have been covered by the waters backed up by the Folsom Dam but are still reflected in place names surrounding the lake {106–17}. See also **Coloma.**

Calistoga. Located in the Napa Valley north of San Francisco, it was founded and developed by Samuel Brannan as a health and leisure resort. One of the original cottages Brannan rented to wealthy vacationing San Franciscans is preserved as part of the Sharpsteen Museum at 1311 Washington Street, a block north of Lincoln {220–22}.

Carson Pass, "Mormon Emigrant Trail." Although the pass had been traversed earlier at least by Kit Carson and John C. Fremont, the first wagon road was developed by Mormon Battalion men and *Brooklyn* Saints headed for the Great Basin in 1848. From Placerville take state highway 49 south to Pleasant Valley Road. Proceed east through **Pleasant Valley**, where the 1848 group met before traveling the mountain pass. Continue on E16 through Sly Park to Jenkinson Lake, where the designation **"Mormon Emigrant Trail"** officially begins. A marker at **Tragedy Spring** recalls the ambush of three Battalion scouts. A portion of the tree with the carved inscription describing the massacre is now at the Marshall Gold Discovery State Park in Coloma {119–22}.

Coloma. The Marshall Gold Discovery State Park includes a full-sized replica of **Sutter's sawmill**, a **log cabin** recalling where the Battalion men lived, and a portion of the actual tailrace where gold was discovered in 1848. The **Tragedy**

Springs inscription is found inside the entrance of the visitors center {106–10, 374, 409}.

Comet **Marker.** A monument located in the Mossdale Crossing County Park between Tracy and Manteca near the junction of the I-5 and 120 freeways commemorates the first sailing ship to ascend the San Joaquin River {53, 321}. This is also the site of the final bridge which extended the transcontinental railroad to the San Francisco Bay Area in 1869.

Fremont. "California's first farmer" is honored in the name of the John Horner Middle School. Although Horner's original schoolhouse/chapel no longer exists, it is celebrated by a plaque in front of the Centerville Ward LDS meetinghouse, 38134 Temple Way at the corner of Peralta Boulevard {144–47, 215–16}. The Mowry Avenue freeway exit off I-880 is named for the Mowry family, *Brooklyn* passengers.

Gridley. This Sacramento Valley farming community became an LDS enclave with the arrival of a large group of settlers from Idaho in 1906. Here the Church erected its first California buildings. Although the **1909 Social Hall** is no longer standing, it is recalled by the name Social Hall Road south of town on which an LDS chapel is now located. The **1912 chapel** at the corner of Sycamore and Vermont is now used by members of another faith {253, 256}.

Los Angeles. The Mormon Battalion helped construct **Fort Moore** and participated in the city's first Fourth of July celebration here {90–92}; a huge memorial on Hill Street immediately north of the Hollywood freeway (US 101) can be reached from the civic center exits {323–24}. The magnificent **Wilshire Ward chapel**, dedicated in 1929, is at 1209 South Manhattan Place, one block west of Western and one block north of Pico (I-10) {276–78, 384}. The **Los Angeles Temple**, largest in the Church when dedicated in 1956, can be reached by driving north on Overland from the Santa Monica freeway (I-10), or east on Santa Monica Boulevard from the San Diego freeway (I-405) {343–50, 396}. The beautiful stake center of the Church's first ethnic stake in the U.S. is located at the corner of

Jefferson and Vermont near the University of Southern California campus {395–96}.

Mormon Battalion Trail. I-8 roughly follows the route of the Battalion's march across the Imperial Desert between Yuma and Ocotillo. Their route then turned northwest (paralleled by highway S2) through **Box Canyon**, where the soldiers had to chisel their way through the narrow rocky passage to **Warner's Ranch** near the crest of the Coast Range (nearly one mile east of the junction of highways S2 and 79). State highway 79 then follows the Battalion route through the beautiful Temecula Valley. I-15, state highway 76, and I-5 approximate the route to its destination in San Diego {75–79}. (See also **San Luis Rey Mission.**)[1]

New Hope. This 1847 LDS agricultural colony was located near the junction of the San Joaquin and Stanislaus Rivers {51–53, 86–87}. It is recalled by a marker in nearby Ripon's city park at Fourth and Locust Streets {321}. The actual site is near the Caswell Memorial State Park.

Oakland became the first branch when missionary work was resumed during the 1890s {235}. The **East Bay Interstake Center** and **Oakland Temple** and **Visitors Center** are on Lincoln Avenue, immediately west of the Warren freeway (13) {350–56, 392–94}.

Sacramento. Sutter's Fort, at L and Twenty-seventh Streets, was a base of supply for those living in or traveling through the area during the later 1840s and early 1850s. **"Old Sacramento"** on the river front includes restored buildings in the area where Samuel Brannan was a major developer {82–123}. One of California's earliest branches was also located at Sacramento {218, 235}.

San Bernardino was a major LDS colony from 1851 to 1857. Key sites dating from this period were concentrated in the area downtown now bounded by Second and Ninth Streets on the north and south and by F Street and Waterman Avenue

---

[1] For more details, see Stanley B. Kimball, *Historic Sites and Markers Along the Mormon and Other Great Western Trails* (Urbana, Ill.: University of Illinois Press, 1988), 227–32.

on the east and west. What was originally the "temple block" was bounded by E, F, Fifth, and Sixth Streets. The original Lag ranch house and the pioneer stockade were located at the present site of the **County Courthouse** (between Third and Fourth, and Arrowhead and Mountain View); a large marker was placed near the southwest corner in 1932. About twelve miles northwest, at the Glen Helen Recreational Park, just west of I-215, is a monument identifying the site of the **sycamore grove** where the Latter-day Saints camped for several weeks before purchasing the San Bernardino Rancho. About seven miles farther to the northwest, near the mouth of **Cajon Pass** on a service road just southeast of the intersection of I-15 and highway 138, is a marker commemorating the Latter-day Saints and other pioneers who traversed this route to and from the Great Basin. A marker on highway 18 to Lake Arrowhead recalls the old **Mormon Mountain Road** {167–84, 211–15, 280}.

San Diego. Buildings in historic Old Town include a restoration of the **courthouse** erected by members of the Mormon Battalion. Edward Fraughton's **statue of a Battalion soldier** is on the crest of the hill in Presidio Park. Nearby is the **Mormon Battalion Visitors Center** at the corner of Juan and Harney Streets {73, 78–79, 89–90, 373–74}. **Samuel Brannan's grave** is located in Mount Hope Cemetery, entered from Imperial Boulevard just east of the I-15 freeway; the cemetery office, open until mid-afternoon, can provide directions {223–24}. The **San Diego Temple** is situated along the east side of the I-5 freeway in La Jolla {396–99}.

San Francisco. Originally named *Yerba Buena*, this was essentially a "Mormon town" from the arrival of the *Brooklyn* on 31 July 1846 at what is now the corner of Broadway and Battery Streets until the beginnings of the gold rush two years later. The original plaza is now **Portsmouth Square**; a monument at the southwest corner commemorates San Francisco's first schoolhouse, which Brannan helped to finance. The surrounding area where most Latter-day Saints settled is now part of Chinatown. While in or near Chinatown, look for Mormon street names: Union, Glover, Stark, Fisher, Hyde, Joice, Brooklyn, Pratt, St. George, Aldrich, Jasper, Reed, etc. **Brannan Street** parallels Market, about five blocks to the southeast {38–51, 54–56, 81–82, 100–4, 147–49, 185–99, 219}. The Victorian **Trumbo Mansion**, on the southeast corner of Sutter and Octavia Streets, is where Wilford Woodruff died {244–45}. **Ina Coolbrith Park**, which commemorates Joseph Smith's niece, California's Poet Laureate, is at the corner of Taylor and Vallejo Streets and affords an excellent view of the Bay {217–18, 252–53, 259}. The **Fairmont Hotel**, from which in 1924 Elder George Albert Smith envisioned a temple across the Bay, is on Powell at California Street {268–69}.

San Luis Rey Mission. Near where the Battalion had its first view of the Pacific, the mission was repaired when most of the soldiers were subsequently quartered here for a month and a half {77–78}; it is located near Oceanside on highway 76, five miles east of the I-5 freeway.

Photo Acknowledgments

We express appreciation to the following agencies or individuals who provided key photographs:

The pictures on pages 7, 69, 130, 133, 138, 174, 177, 186, 197, 212, 219, 230, 242, 243, 244, 248, 256 (right), 257 (right), 265, 273, 276, 285, 304, 341, and 406 were provided by the Historical Department of The Church of Jesus Christ of Latter-day Saints, Salt Lake City, Utah, and are published with their permission.

The illustrations on pages 46, 106, 145, 325, 345, 352, and 354 originally appeared in the Church's *Improvement Era*. The photographs on pages 52, 146, 239, 249, 256 (left), 257 (left), 266, 268, 279, 293, 297, 298, 299, 312, 322, 326, and 332 originally appeared in Leo J. Muir's *A Century of Mormon Activities in California*, published by Deseret News Press. These illustrations are included here with the permission of the Church. The Forever Young Foundation provided the photo on page 392.

The *Church News* section of the *Deseret News* has given permission for us to reproduce the pictures appearing on pages 370, 390, and 398. Pictures appearing on pages 2 and 5 are used courtesy of The Museum of Church History and Art, Salt Lake City. The latter photograph is used also with the permission of Buddy Youngreen.

Mrs. Jean Cowan Simpson photographed several sites especially for this book. Her pictures appear on pages 53, 73, 75, 77, 88, 103, 107, 115, 121, 221, 224, 277, 323, 373, 374, and 395. The picture on page 339 is courtesy of Richard W. Jackson. S. George Ellsworth supplied the photo on page 101. The picture on page 137 is used courtesy of Leonard J. Arrington. Josephine DeWitt Rhodehamel provided the picture on page 217. The pictures on pages 250 and 251 were supplied by Jeni Broberg Holzapfel. Susan Kamei Leung provided the photos on pages 342 and 358. The photograph on page 397 was taken by Robert Marriott.

The photographs on pages 347, 348, and 349 were taken by Paul Garn. The picture on page 409 was taken by Lowell C. Hardy, secretary to President Gordon B. Hinckley. The Bancroft Library, University of California at Berkeley, provided the photographs on pages 148, 188, and 220. The Sharpsteen Museum of Calistoga, California, supplied the photo on page 13. The painting on page 35 originally appeared in two books by Conway Sonne.

Index

A

Aardema, Albert J., 347
Adams Ward, 257, 271-73, 276, 278-80, 302, 383
Adams, George J., 14-15
Alameda Conference, 235
Alameda County, 144, 218, 321
Alhambra, 270, 272
Allen, Ezra, 121
Allen, James, 62, 65, 68
Alma Branch, 388
Almaden Second Ward, 383
Alta California, 123
Alturas Branch, 285
American River, 83, 95, 105, 109-10, 112, 154, 200, 431
Anaheim, 214-15, 340
And It Came to Pass, 375
Andelin, Helen, 367
Anderson, Edward O., 343
Anderson, Howard B., 390
Anderson, Willard J., 288
Antioch, 50, 144
Arcadia Ward, 325
Arizona, 72, 74, 266-67, 274, 309
Army of the West, 63, 87
Asia, refugees from, 385
Atherton, William, 226
Atkinson, Keith, 372

B

Backman, Robert L., 378, 381
Badlam, Alexander, 11
Badlam, Alexander, Jr., 230-31
Badlam, Mary Ann, 11
Bakersfield, 266, 276, 285
Baldwin Park Ward, 288
Ball, Isaac B., 293
Ballantyne, Joseph, 258
Ballard, Melvin J., 286, 294
Bancroft Library, 299
Bancroft, Hubert H., 43, 190

Bank of America, 254, 271
Barger, William W., 108
Barnson, Stephen, 257
Barstow, 275
Bartlett, Washington A., 55, 85, 100
Battalion, Mormon
    See Mormon Battalion
Bay Area Religious Channel (BARC), 391
"Bear Flag Revolt," 42-43
Bear River, 83, 93
Beckworth Pass, 259
Belvedere, 270, 272, 279
Benecia, 151
Benson, A. G., 27, 60
Benson, Ezra T., 210
Benson, Ezra Taft (counselor in Adams Ward), 272
Benson, President Ezra Taft, 315, 398, 405
Benson, Jerome, 181
Bergen, Edgar, 324
Berkeley, 350, 353
Berkeley Institute of Religion, 298
Berkeley Ward, 274, 311
Berry, John W., 162
Beverley Hills Ward, 338
Bidamon, Emma, 156
Bidamon, Louis C., 156
Biddy, 178
Bigler, Henry W.
    Battalion member, 93
    gold discoverer, 108, 113, 137-41, 243
    journal of, 106
    missionary, 162, 193
Blackburn, Abner, 98, 154
Bliss, Robert, 65
Blood, Henry H., 299
Boggs, Lilburn W., 4, 56, 134-35
Bohemian Club, 244

Boley, Samuel, 63
Bowen, Albert E., 303
Bowron, Fletcher, 322
Box Canyon, 75, 433
Boyle Heights, 270, 272
Boyle, Henry G., 90, 94, 180, 201-3, 211
Brannan, Eliza, 220, 222
Brannan, Harriet, 219
Brannan, Samuel
   early life, 11-14
   described by contemporaries, 18
   service with Eastern Saints, 13-22
   leads *Brooklyn* voyage, 19-39
   San Francisco
      early years, 41-57, 81-87, 100-4, 135, 149, 208
      street named for, 115, 435
      firm of S. Brannan & Co., 54-55, 102, 123
      and gold, 109-25
      meets Brigham Young on Plains, 86, 95-100
      relations with Church, 130-31, 151-53, 171, 187-90
      later life and death, 219-24, 434
Brannan, Thomas, 12
Brannan-Fowler Hotel, 152
Brawley Branch, 285
Brentwood, 325
Brewster, William, 19
Brier, J. W., 141
Brigham Young University, 325, 340, 362, 376
Broadway Street, 45, 186, 320
Broberg family, 251
Brooklyn Saints, 46, 57
Brooklyn ship, 23-39, 46, 49
Brooklyn, route of, 32
Brooklyn Street, 115
Browett, Daniel, 121
Brown, Almira, 219
Brown, Daniel, 219
Brown, Hugh B., 303-4, 323, 373

Brown, James (Battalion captain), 97-100
Brown, James S. (gold discoverer), 106, 108, 137, 152, 243, 324
Brown, Jesse, 100
Brown, John H., 48-49, 51
Brown, Mary A., 219
Buchanan, James, 208-9
Buckeye Branch, 202
Buckeye County, 202
Buehner brothers, 346
Buildings, Church, 256-57, 275-78, 338
   See Temples
Burdette, Stephen C., 24
Burnett, Peter, 163, 165
Burr, John Atlantic, 33

C

Cajon Pass, 118-19, 168, 170, 238, 434
California Intermountain News, 292
California Irrigated Land Company, 253
California Mission, 266, 285, 290-92, 309
California Society of Pioneers, 219, 223
California Star, 56, 81-82, 100, 102-3, 110, 113, 122, 125, 235
California Trail, 86, 92, 98, 132, 154
California Utah Women, 320
California Volunteers, 51, 90-92
Californian, 44, 82, 110, 122-23
Calistoga, 200, 220-21, 431
Cambodia, refugees from, 385
Campbell, Eugene E., 324
Cannon, Abraham H., 241
Cannon, Elizabeth, 197
Cannon, George Q.
   missionary, 13-38, 140, 162, 193
   in San Francisco, 196-99, 201-4, 210, 220
   in First Presidency, 227-28, 230, 234, 242, 244

death, 245
Cannon, James H., 254
Cape Horn, 17, 19, 22, 27, 32-34, 39, 125, 196
Carmack, John K., 381, 384, 391, 404
Carpenter, George C., 251
Carson Pass, 120, 374, 431
Carson Valley, 154, 156, 160, 197, 230
Centennial Celebrations, 319-24
Chamberlain, Solomon, 154, 156
Chile, 33, 176, 191
Chinatown, 115
Christian Advocate, 193
Clark's Point, 45
Clark, Hiram, 155-56, 159, 163
Clark, J. Reuben, Jr., 294, 331, 348
Clawson, Hiram B., 244
Clawson, Rudger, 268, 274
Clayton, Peter A., 302
Clayton, William, 95-96
Clinton, 218
Cluff, William W., 193
Coalinga, 388
Cole, George, 253
Coloma, 83, 95, 109, 117, 122-23, 125, 200, 321, 409, 431
Combs, Abraham, 26
Comet, 53, 321
Comet monument, 52, 432
Congress, U.S.S., 36-37
Consumnes River, 56, 83, 109, 200
Cook, Quentin L., 389
Cooke, Philip St. George, 68-75, 78, 90-91, 214
Coolbrith, Ina, 217, 252, 259
  Mount, 259
  Park, 435
Cooper, Gary, 324
Cooper, William, 240
Coray Peak, 374
Coray, Melissa, 120, 374
Coray, William, 120
Cornwall, J. Spencer, 324
Coronado Hotel, 240
Corwin Street, 115
Corwin, Eliza Ann, 14

Corwin, Fanny, 14, 159
Cosgrave, Luke, 235
Covina Stake, 342
Cowdery, Oliver, 215
Cowley, Matthias, 250
Cox, Henderson, 121
Creek, Lytle, 175
Crosby, Caroline Barnes, 155-56, 158, 196
Crosby, Jonathan, 196
Crosby, William J., 173
Crow, Robert, 128, 131
Cucamonga, 172
Culver City, 267
Culver, Harry, 267-68
Cummings, James B., 235
Curle, Archibald, 236
Customs House, 54, 187
Cutler, Bishop, 233

D

Dalton, Luther, 234-236
Daly City Ward, 274
Daughters of Utah Pioneers (DUP), 280, 294, 320-21, 323
Davies, Leon, 391
Davis, H. Frederick, 326
Day, Lorraine, 324
Deaf, programs for, 370
Death Valley, 141
DeMille, Cecil B., 324
Dempsey, Jack, 325
Depression, Great, 283-99
Deseret, 164-66
Deseret Club, 297
Deseret Industries, 288-89, 314-15, 331-32
Deseret News, 222-23, 251
Devore, 171
Dewsnup, J. F., 253
Dimond Park, 274, 293-94
Dixon, John, 162
Dolores Mission, 49, 159
Done, G. Byron, 298
Doniphan, Alexander W., 68
Donner Lake, 83, 98
Donner Party, 82-85, 93
Donner Pass, 56, 83

Donner, Mary, 85
Drummond, W. W., 208-9
Dry Creek, 56, 203
Dunford, Grover C., 321
Dunn, Loren C., 409
Dunn, Paul H., 381, 404

E

Eager, Thomas, 218
East Pasadena Ward, 340
Eastern States Mission, 13, 60, 270
Edmunds Act, 227
Edmunds-Tucker Act, 228, 230
Educational System, Church, 298, 330, 339-40
El Monte, 288
El Paso, 235, 291-92, 334
El Sereno Ward, 303, 309, 328
Elmhurst Ward, 274
Elysian Park Ward, 347
Emigrant Gap
    See Donner Pass
Employment Office, Church, 286
Endowment House, 231
Ensign, 369
Equal Rights Amendment, 366
Escondido, 75, 285
Eureka Branch, 285
Evans, Richard L., 320
Evans, Thomas St. Clair, 297
Evans, William, 134
Eyring, Henry B., 404

F

Fairbanks, Avard, 258, 322
Fairmont Hotel, 268, 435
Fairs, 258-59
Faith and Values Network, 391
Farnsworth, Philo, 334
Farrer, William, 162
Faust, James E., 129, 378
Feather River, 253
First Dragoons, 91-92
First Vision, 2
Fisherman's Wharf, 186-87
Flake, James, 138

Florence Ward, 272
Fort Moore, 92, 94, 238, 323, 432
Foster City Ward, 387
Fowler, Jerusha, 135
Fowler, John, 135, 163
Fraughton, Edward, J., 373, 434
Freestone, John W., 255
Fremont, 172, 340, 395, 432
Fremont, John C., 7-8, 51, 53, 81, 87-88, 90-92, 120
Fresno, 83, 242, 285, 339
Friend, Honolulu, 37
Frost, Lafayette, 72
Fruitland, 234
Fruitvale, 234

G

Gadsden Purchase, 74
Garlick, Aaron and Mary, 218, 225, 234-36
Garra, Chief Antonio, 173, 175
Garvanza, 270, 272
Gates, Harvey H., 254
George, Henry, 217
Germany, 302, 314-5
Gilroy Branch, 285
Glendale, 270, 272, 284, 288, 297, 303
Glover Street, 115
Glover, William, 34, 47, 49-51, 85, 101-2, 117, 133, 169
Gold
    discovery, 105-8, 243
    impact on California, 112-17, 127, 143
    impact on Great Basin Saints, 123-25, 127-29
    missionaries, 124, 160
    aftermath, 143-44
    reconstructed mill site, 107
"Gold Discovery Jubilee"
    gold discovery site, 321
    reconstructed mill site, 107
Golden Gate Exposition, 299
Gonzales, Juan M., 291
Goodwill Industries, 288
Goodwin, Laura, 34

Goodyear, Miles, 403
Graham, A. B., 313
Grant, Heber J.
  early visits to California,
    240-41, 267
  political views, 287, 299
  as president of Church, 264-65,
    268, 270-73, 276-77, 284, 294,
    315, 343
Grant, Jay S., 278-79, 371
Great Salt Lake Trading Co., 162
Green, Talbot, 188
Greenwood, 152
Gridley, 83, 253, 256, 432
Gridley Hotel, 253
Gridley Stake, 285, 288
Griffin, John S., 89
Groberg, John H., 387, 397
Grouard, Benjamin, 180, 191-92
Guadalupe-Hidalgo, Treaty, 117
Guaymas, 222

H

Haight, David B., 352, 358, 377,
  404
Hall, Thomas, 235
Hammond, Francis, 121
Hancock, Levi, 89, 92-95, 99
Hanford Branch, 285
Hangtown
  See Placerville
Hanks, Ebenezer, 182, 210
Hanks, Ephraim, 155
Hannah, 178
Harding, George F., 271
Harris, Silas, 111
Harris, William, 55
Harte, Bret, 217
Haskell, Ashbell, 116
Hawaii, 25, 33, 35-38, 55, 161-63,
  192-93, 196, 211, 215-16, 405
Hawk, Nathan, 111
Hawk, William, 111
Hawkins, James, 162
Hayes, Benjamin, 179
Hayward Stake, 351
Hemet Branch, 285
Hilton, Eugene, 293, 296, 306, 313

Hinckley, Alonzo A., 290
Hinckley, Gordon B., 294, 321,
  399, 406, 408
  at Mormon Battalion cabin, 409
  at dedication of San Diego
    Temple, 398
Hoag, Charles, 240
Holiday Bowl, 377
Hollywood, 254, 263, 270, 272
Hollywood Bowl, 326, 333
Hollywood Stake, 273, 276, 284,
  288, 293, 344
Holmes, Jonathan H., 120
Home Gardens, 270, 295
Hopkins, Richard, 173, 176,
  180-81
Horner, Elizabeth, 144
Horner, John M.
  sails on *Brooklyn*, 26-27
  agricultural endeavors, 50-54,
    86-87, 144-47
  schoolhouse of, 146
  middle school named for, 432
Howard, W. D. M., 188
Howell, Elizabeth Bird, 320
Howells, Adele Cannon, 298
Howells, David, 273
Hudson, Wilford, 109, 116
Huffaker wagon train, 152
Hunt, Jefferson, 65-66, 88-89,
  93-95, 99, 118-19, 137-39, 141,
  150, 167, 169, 177, 212
Hunt, John, 213
Hunter, Claire, 357
Hunter, Howard W.
  early life, 264, 302-3
  comes to California, 264
  as bishop, 302, 309-10
  as stake president and
    regional leader, 329-33, 338,
    340-42
  as apostle, 356-58, 377-78, 386,
    398
  as president, 404-8
Huntington Park, 270, 272, 276,
  386
Huntington Park West Stake, 386
Huntington, William D., 155

Hutchins, Colleen, 325
Hutchins, Mel, 325
Hyde, John, 199
Hyde, Orson, 197

I

"I am a Child of God," 356, 376
Ide, William Brown, 42
Imlay, Elizabeth, 26
Improvement Era, 242, 369
Indio Branch, 285
Inglewood, 260, 270, 272, 324, 363, 386
Institutes of Religion, 298
Ivins, Anthony W., 268, 291
Ivy Street, 288

J

Jackson (town), 187, 200
Jackson Street, 45
Jackson, Alden M., 187, 216
Jackson, Carolyn Joyce, 45
Jacobs, Sanford, 111
Jacobson, Hans C., 240
Jenkins, John, 189
Jensen, Harold R., 251
Jewell, Amelia, 240
Johnson's Ranch, 82-84
Johnson, J. Edward, 274
Johnson, Sonia, 365
Johnston, William J., 108, 243
Joice Street, 115
Jorgensen, James Peter, 234-35
Joyce, Carolyn, 38-39, 49, 134, 187
Juan Fernandez Island, 32, 34, 36

K

Kane, Thomas L., 60, 213
Kawai, Hideo, 312
KBIG, 372
Kearny, Camp, 259
Kearny, Gen. Stephen W., 29, 60-61, 63, 68-69, 75-76, 87-88, 90, 92, 209
Keeler, James, 162
Keller, Alva, 235

Kemble, Edward, 18, 28, 35-36, 82, 122
Kendall, Amos, 27, 60
Kerr, Basil T., 272
Kimball, Heber C., 128
Kimball, J. Golden, 290
Kimball, Spencer W., 362-63, 367, 372, 377-78
King, Sophia Patterson Clark, 236
Kirkham, Oscar A., 321
Kittleman, Sarah, 49
Knight, Goodwin J., 255, 328
Knight, Jesse, 255, 328
Knudsen, Vern O., 298
Koening, Irmgard Kreipl, 280
Kofford, Cree-L, 404

L

Ladd, Samuel, 38
Lamanite Conferences, 334
Lancaster Branch, 285
Lane, Martella, 254
Lang, Robert and Delores, 363
Lankershim Branch, 270
Laos, refugees from, 385
Larkin, Thomas O., 41-42, 188
Larsen, Charles, 253
Latham, Rachel, 280
Latrobe, 242
LaVerne, 340
Leach, G. T., 13-14
Leavenworth, T. M., 136
Lee, Ettie, 255
Lee, Harold B., 303, 308, 322, 367-68, 371, 373
Lee, J. Bracken, 322
Lee, John D., 225
Leese, Jacob P., 188
Leuba, Philip, 225
Lewis, Eugene B., 254
Lewis, John, 159
Liahona Club, 327
Liberty Social Hall, 256
Light, James, 50
Lillywhite, Daniel, 254
Lincoln, Seth, 113, 152
Linda Vista Ward, 332

Lindsay, Clyde W., 274
Lindsey, Mark, 233-34
Little, Jesse C., 59-60, 62, 101
Livermore, 53
Lloyd, Harold, 296
Lompoc Branch, 285
London, Jack, 217
Long Beach, 270, 272, 276, 385, 390
Long Wharf, 188
Los Angeles
    Mormon Battalion in, 76, 87-92, 94
    early activity in, 118, 186, 219, 221
    Church activity revives, 236, 238, 242, 255, 257
    stakes organized and buildings constructed, 271, 278, 284
    ethnic groups in, 362-64, 382-87, 389-90, 385
    varied activities in, 279-80, 286, 290-92, 294, 297, 302, 309, 319-24, 329-31, 334, 370-72, 377
Los Angeles Stake, 271-93
Los Angeles Stake Journal, 279, 292
Los Angeles Temple
    site and early planning, 267, 296, 313, 343, 346
    construction and dedication, 347-50
    remodled, 396,
    See Temples
Lost Spring, 67
Lovett, Angeline, 49
Ludington, Lt., 66
Lugo brothers and Rancho, 171-72, 179
Lund, Anthon H., 257
Lund, Wallace E., 279
Lyman, Amasa M.
    at Pueblo, 96
    assignment to California, 125-33, 149-65
    in San Bernardino, 168-86, 197, 280
Lyman, Francis M., 173

M

M Investment Company, 279
Macdonald, W. Aird, 268-69, 274, 290
Maeser, Karl G., 235-37
Malin, Millard F., 348
Manifesto, 231-33
Marin Peninsula, 50, 200
Marina Ward, 389
Mariposa, 151
Marsh's Landing, 50-51, 53, 83
Marsh, John, 50-51
Marshall, James, 56, 105, 107-8, 110-11
Martinez Branch, 274-75
Marysville, 82-83, 149, 154, 200
Mason, Richard, 93, 95, 100, 110, 117, 121, 125, 135
Matthews Ward, 272, 279
Maw, Herbert, 320
Maycock, George H., 235, 240
McArthur, Donald R., 396
McBride, William, 192, 195
McConkie, Bruce R., 361, 363
McCune, George W., 270-73, 266, 277
McDonald, Howard S., 293
McKay, David Lawrence, 355
McKay, David O.
    groundbreaking at Los Angeles Temple, 345
    cornerstone laying at Los Angeles Temple, 348
    at dedication of Oakland Inter-stake Center, 352
McLean, Eleanor, 195
McMurrin, Joseph W., 227, 266-72, 274-75, 280-81, 290
Mendocino County, 203
Merritt, Ezekiel, 52
Merriweather, Frederick, 236
Messenger, 82, 292, 328
Mexican Mission, 291-92
Mexican War, 87, 209
Mexico
    war with, 20, 27, 36, 39, 59-60, 71, 84, 88, 125

Church activities in, 292,
  390-91
Brannan's dealings with,
  222-23
immigrants from, 291
Millbrae Ward, 387
Millennial Star, 81, 194
Miller, Joaquin, 217
Miller, Nephi E., 254
Mission Ward, 274
Missionary work
  in San Francisco, 185-87
  in 1850s, 199-204
  slowed/suspended during
    late 19th century, 210
  slowed by Great Depression
    and war, 290-92, 310
  post-war years, "sharing gospel,"
    369, 372-77, 391-94
Missions, early Franciscan
  See Dolores, San Diego, San
  Gabriel, San Jose, San Luis Rey
Missourians, 66, 91, 209
Modesto, 83, 200, 275
Mojave Desert, 213, 255
Mojave River, 141
Monson, Thomas S., 398, 405
Monterey, 37, 41, 43-44, 82-83, 92,
  95, 100, 200, 203, 245
Montez, Lola, 208
Montgomery, John B., 43, 45-47,
  50, 55
Moore, Benjamin D., 76, 92
Morey, Sister, 159
Mormon Bar, 113
Mormon Battalion
  call of, 61-62
  march, 63-79
  service in California, 87-95
  reenlistment/discharge, 94
  and gold, 106, 109
  memorials, 73, 322, 373-74
  Southern California, 326-27
Mormon Battalion, Inc., 374
Mormon Choir of Southern
  California, 326-27
Mormon Corridor, 169, 176
Mormon Emigrant Trail, 431

Mormon Gulch, 113
Mormon Herald, 196
Mormon Island, 109, 111, 113-14,
  117, 123, 154, 163, 431
Mormon Mountain Road, 434
Mormon Station, 230
Mormon Tabernacle Choir, 241,
  294, 320
Mormon Volunteers, 119
Moroni
  statues of on temples, 348,
    397
Morris, Thomas, 162
Moss Landing, 321
Mountain Meadows Massacre,
  209, 225
Mountain View, 203
Mowry, Barton and family, 186,
  190, 432
Moyle, Henry D., 331
Muir, Leo J., 271, 273, 319, 324
Mulford, Prentiss, 217
Muren, Joseph C., 404
Murphy, Lavinia, 56, 84
Murphy, Mary, 56
My San Diego, 375

N

Napa, 200, 202
Narrimore, Mercy, 49
Natress, Joseph, 235
Nethercott family, 233-34, 237
Nevada, 171, 266, 309
New Helvetia, 110
New Hope, 51-53, 83, 85-87, 102,
  321, 433
New York City, 1, 13-19, 23,
  26-28, 30, 36-37, 82, 127, 129,
  186, 190, 196, 270, 348, 391
New York Herald, 28, 125
New-York Messenger, 15-16, 24
New York Volunteers, 91
Nibley, Charles W., 268, 271
Nielsen, Hans Benjamin, 272
Nielson, Sally B., 366
Nogales, 223
North Hollywood Ward, 332
Northern California Mission, 309

Nuttall, L. John, 244
Nutting, Lucy, 49
Nye, Ephraim H., 242

O

Oakes, George, 189
Oakland, 83, 218, 226, 232-35,
    237, 241, 293, 313, 353, 375,
    389, 395, 433
Oakland Branch, 233, 235-36
Oakland earthquake, 388
Oakland, Interstake Center,
    350-54, 375, 392-93, 395, 433
Oakland Lyceum, 194
Oakland Region, 287
Oakland Seventh Ward, 218
Oakland Stake, 286, 290, 313-14,
    327, 350-51
Oakland Temple
    George Albert Smith prophecy,
        268-69
    site acquired, 296, 313-14,
        352-53
    committee, 358
    construction and dedication,
        353-55
    remodeled, 396
    See Temples
Oakland Visitors Center, 433
Oakland Ward, 274, 387
Oakland-Berkeley Stake, 351-52,
    370
    deaf softball team, 370
Oakley, Howard, 85
Ocean Heights, 267
Ocean Park, 270-72, 276, 279
Ogden Tabernacle Choir, 258-59
Old Spanish Trail, 69, 86, 118, 138
Olson, C. Dean, 339
Olson, Culbert L., 298-99
Orr, Thomas, 154-55
Osborn, Alice H., 286
Oscarson, R. Don, 375
Osmond family, 376

P

Pacific Mission, 185-87

Packard, Floyd L., 397
Packard, H. Von, 397
Packer, Boyd K., 398
Pajaro, 195, 200, 203-4
Palm Springs Stake, 379
Palo Alto, 352, 358
Panama Canal, 314
Panama-California Exposition,
    258
Panama-Pacific International
    Exposition, 258
Pardoe, T. Earl, 255
Parry, Morris R., 295
Pasadena
    activities in, 270, 288, 308, 366,
        371, 375
    Howard W. Hunter, 309, 329,
        340, 342, 356, 407
Patton, Anna and Stanley, 311-12
Pell, E. Ward, 29, 152, 163, 236
Penrose, Charles W., 271
Perpetual Emigrating Fund, 149,
    161
Perris, Fred T., 238
Perry, Horace T., 254
Perry, L. Tom, 404
Pettigrew, David, 71, 89, 95
Pettit, Mildred, 356, 376
Phelps, Harold E., 326
Phillips, Norman, 233-35, 237
Pickett, Agnes, 216-17
Pickett, John, 233-34
Pickford, Mary, 254
Pico, Pio, 42
Pike, Harriet, 84
Pike, Naomi, 84
Pinto, 248
Placerville, 109, 120, 154, 285
Pleasant Valley, 120, 154, 431
Plural marriage
    announced publicly, 192
    Saints flee persecution, 227-28
    abandoned, 231-33
Poelman, Ronald E., 404
Polk, James K., 20, 27, 60-61,
    126-27
Polynesia, 101, 137, 152, 155,
    158-59, 175, 191

Pomona, 91, 168
Porter, John C., 280
Porterville Branch, 285
Portsmouth, 39, 43, 45-46
Portsmouth House hotel, 49, 51
Portsmouth Square, 49, 103, 115,
    149, 189, 434
Pratt Street, 115
Pratt, Addison
    in San Francisco and gold fields,
        101-5, 110, 112-16, 150-52,
        191-92
    missionary to South Pacific, 8,
        137-39, 155, 158, 180
    in Southern California, 213-14
Pratt, Elizabeth, 186, 191
Pratt, Ellen, 213
Pratt, Louisa Barnes, 155, 158-59,
    192, 214
Pratt, Orson, 16-17, 21-22, 97,
129,
    210
Pratt, Parley P.
    and Eastern Saints, 14-16
    and plans for California settle-
        ment, 8
    leader in California, 169,
        171-76, 185-97, 204
    prophecy on Samuel Brannan,
        222-23
    death, 195-96, 209
Pratt, Phoebe, 186, 191
Pratt, Rey L., 291
Presidio, 38
Prophet, 13, 15-16, 82
Pueblo, Colorado, 67, 69-70, 96
Pulley, Colleen, 367
Putah Creek, 202
Putnam, George F., 364

R

Radio, Publicity, and Literature
    Committee, 294
Randall, Naomi, 356
Raymond, 353
Reagan, Ronald, 378
Redding Branch, 285
Redondo Branch, 270

Reed, Rachel, 121
Reese, John, 230
Reid, Rose Marie, 324
Relief Society, 226, 278, 286, 289,
    340, 366
Religious Conference Building,
    297
Reorganized Church of Jesus
    Christ of Latter Day Saints, 215,
    218, 226, 233
Reugg, Theodore, 321
Rhoads, Daniel, 56, 84
Rhoads, John, 56, 83-84
Rhoads, Thomas, 56, 133
Rich, Charles C.
    assignment to California, 130,
        137-42, 149-63
    in San Bernardino, 167-86, 197
Rich, Emeline, 174
Richards, LeGrand, 266, 284-85,
    344
Richards, Preston D., 298, 344
Richards, Stephen L, 273, 329,
    344-45, 351
Richardson, Abel W., 24, 27-28,
    31, 34, 36, 38, 49
Richardson, Edward, 24
Richmond, 274, 306
Ripon, 321
Ritchie, Horace, 353
Robbins, Ann, 26
Robbins, Georgiana Pacific, 33
Robbins, Isaac, 26, 29, 134
Robbins, John, 33, 134
Robinson, Joseph E., 248-60, 290
Rockwell, Orrin Porter, 118-19,
    125, 130, 132-34, 152, 155, 158,
    162-63, 216
Rose Bowl, 377-78
Rose Parade, 375
Rosencrans, Lt.,74
Rowen, Lizzy, 178
Russon, John M., 326

S

Sacramento, 83, 109, 200
    Samuel Brannan develops,
        110, 122-23, 134-35

early branch, 218, 225, 234-35, 240-41
important stopover and political center, 133-35, 149, 151-52, 154, 163
Church growth in, 275, 285
President Hinckley speaks at, 408-9
See Garlick, Aaron and Mary
See Sutter's Fort
Salinas, 51, 83, 200, 203, 285
Salmon Falls, 109, 154, 431
San Antonio Redwoods, 218
San Bernadino
Colony, 167-84, 187, 191, 193, 195, 201, 204
abandoned, 210, 212
Saints return, 215-16
later activity in, 236, 238, 240, 242, 280, 285, 291, 320-21, 326, 403, 433
San Diego
Mormon Battalion in, 76-79, 88-90, 93-94, 99, 119
Samuel Brannan in, 223-24
later Church activity in, 236, 240, 257-59, 276, 279, 291, 304, 321, 332, 378, 390-91
Battalion statue and visitors center, 73, 373-74, 434
San Diego Temple, 396-99
See Temples
San Fernando Valley, 288, 332, 340
San Francisco
early developments in Yerba Buena, 38-39, 41-51, 54-56, 81-87, 93-94, 99-104
impact of Gold Rush, 105-17, 122, 124-25, 134-37, 143-48
Elders Lyman and Rich in, 132-34, 149-53
in 1850s, 147-49, 159, 163, 166, 171-72, 185-206, 219
Brannan returns to, 223
California Mission reorganized, 233-37, 239-41
later Church activity in, 217, 241, 244, 258-59, 268, 274, 309, 320-21, 334, 372
disasters, 136, 149, 249-53, 388-89
San Gabriel Mission, 118, 168
San Joaquin River and Valley, 51-53, 57, 83, 95, 200, 321
San Jose (city), 83, 150, 165, 195, 200, 241, 266, 285, 366-67, 375, 385, 391-92, 395, 408
San Jose Mission, 83, 144-47, 191, 200, 203
John Horner near, 144-47, 204-6
San Juan, 203
San Luis Obispo, 303
San Luis Rey Mission, 76, 88, 90, 435
San Marcos Pass, 296
San Mateo County, 203
San Pasqual, 76
San Pedro, 151, 172, 186, 270, 272
San Rafael Branch, 285
Sanderson, George B., 63, 66
Sandwich Islands, 32, 161
Santa Anna, 168, 275
Santa Barbara, 92, 285, 389
Santa Clara, 53, 192, 195, 203
Santa Cruz, 50, 195, 200, 203, 242, 285, 388-89
Santa Fe, 60-61, 65-70, 78
Santa Fe Railroad, 238
Santa Fe Trail, 65
Santa Monica, 257, 265, 279, 386
Santa Rosa Branch, 83, 200, 285
Sausalito, 50
Schenck, George, 189
Schricker, J. Louis, 355
Scoll, Bert, 362
Seely, David, 173, 215
Seminario, Rafael, 386
Seminary, 330, 340
Sherman, William Tecumseh, 117, 199-200, 204
Sherwood, Henry G., 179-80
Shupe, Orville, 288
Sierra Madre, 340

Sierra Nevada, 50, 82-83, 93, 95, 110, 121-22, 132, 154, 164-65
Simpson, Robert L., 404
Sims, Emily Brinton, 297
Sinclair, Upton, 287, 298
Sirrine, George, 152
Slapjack Bar, 109, 162
Slater, Richard, 111
Sloat, John D., 43
Smith, Albert, 99
Smith, Andrew Jackson, 66-67, 165
Smith, Azariah, 67, 70, 99, 108, 116, 119, 243
Smith, Charles, 87, 99, 110, 123
Smith, Don Carlos, 216
Smith, George A., 21
Smith, George Albert
    visits California, 257, 271, 274, 320
    vision of Oakland Temple, 268-69, 296, 353
    president of Church, 317-18, 322, 330, 343-44
    death, 334
Smith, Henry, 321
Smith, Hyrum G., 255, 404
Smith, Job Taylor, 225, 227
Smith, John Henry, 267
Smith, Joseph, Jr., 3, 5-6, 12, 42, 118, 163, 215, 259, 404
    in Nauvoo Legion uniform, 5
    prophesies of Saints in Rocky Mountains, 6
Smith, Joseph F.
    in California as young man, 192-93, 211-12
    in First Presidency, 227, 230, 241, 247-64
Smith, Joseph Fielding, 291, 322, 348
Smith, Josephine Donna, 217
Smith, Nicholas G., 290
Smith, O. K., 138-41
Smith, Robert, 178
Smith, William, 14
Smoot, Reed, 292

Snow, Lorenzo, 241, 247-48
Society Islands, 101, 158, 175
Sonoma, 83, 135, 200, 202
Sons of Utah Pioneers (SUP), 320-23, 373-75
South Los Angeles Stake, 273, 344-45
Southern Pacific Railroad, 238-39, 245
Spanish-American Mission, 334
Sparks, Quartus, 53, 180
Spencer, William, 73
St. George, Utah, 295-96
Standage, Henry, 65, 74
Stanford University, 328, 362, 404
Stanford, Leland, 231
Stanislaus River, 53, 83, 200
Star
    See *California Star*
Stephen, Alexander, 108
Stephens, Evan, 241
Steptoe, Edward, 216
Stewart, Boyd, 162
Stockton, 83, 200, 242, 385
Stockton, Robert F., 37, 135
Stoddard, Charles Warren, 217
Stone, O. Leslie, 352, 358
Stout, Thomas, 52
Stout, William, 85-86, 123, 150, 180
Stuart, David M., 200-1
Summerhays, Alma B., 279
Sunset Ward, 274
Sutter's Fort, 50, 83-84, 87, 94-95, 99, 109-11, 114, 117, 123, 132, 433
Sutter's Mill, 105, 109, 111, 125, 243, 431
Sutter, Capt. John A., 95, 120, 122-23, 224
    and gold, 105, 108-10, 114-15
    on Samuel Brannan and tithing, 152-53
Sycamore Grove monument, 280, 434

T

Tabernacle Choir, 241, 294, 320
Talmage, James E., 258, 293
Tanner, Henry, 237, 242
Taylor, John, 8, 227-30, 248
Taylor, Zachary, 164, 166
Tedesco, Pam, 375
Temples
  Brigham Young prophecy, 98
  excursions, 295-97
  Los Angeles
    site and early planning, 267,
      296, 313, 343, 346
    construction and dedication,
      347-50
    remodeled, 396,
    See Los Angeles Temple
  Oakland
    George Albert Smith prophecy,
      268-69
    site acquired, 296, 313-14,
      352-53
    construction and dedication,
      353-55
    remodeled, 396
    See Oakland Temple
  San Diego, 396-99
    See San Diego Temple
Terry, Steven, 342
Thatcher, Hezekiah, 202
Thatcher, Moses, 202-3, 404
Thomas, Albert Henry, 255
Thomas, Danny, 339
Thomas, Louis, 278
Thurber, Albert, 160, 169
Tijuana, 390-91
Tonga, Hengehenga (Joe), 387
Tongans, 387
Tragedy Springs, 109, 121, 431
Treasure Island, 294, 312
Truckee Canyon, 98
Trumbo house, 244, 435
Trumbo, Isaac, 230-31, 245
Twain, Mark, 217
Twelve, Quorum of
  and New York affairs, 14-17,
    22

  and California affairs, 97, 103,
    127-42, 149-53, 157-63
  directs San Bernardino Colony,
    167-84
  presides over mission, 185-204
  members visit California,
    240-41, 257-58, 268, 271, 285-86,
    291-92, 298, 303, 324, 378,
    381, 386
  Californians become
    members of, 357-59, 404
Tyler, Daniel, 71-72, 75, 77, 99

U

UCLA Ward, 371
Ukiah Branch, 285
Union City, 147, 195
University of California
  at Berkeley, 259, 299
  at Los Angeles (UCLA),
    296-98, 401
University of Southern
  California, 255, 298, 324
Utah
  and California statehood,
    163-66
Utah War, 207-15
Utah Women's Club, 320
Utley, Roy, 326

V

Valparaiso, 34
Van Denbergh, John Peter Philip,
  235, 237
Vargas, Susan Elizabeth
  Cardenas, 398
Vermont Ward, 369
Vietnam War, 364
Vigilance Committee, 188-89, 219
Virgin, George, 188-89
Vision Interfaith Satellite
  Network (VISN), 391
Visitors Centers
  at Los Angeles Temple, 350,
    356
  at Oakland Temple, 393-94
  at San Diego, 373-74

W

Waite, Noble, 344-45
Walker's Pass, 138
Wall's Diggings, 201
Wallace, W. Ed, 254
Walnut Creek Stake, 351
Wandell, Charles W., 203
Warner Ranch, 75-76, 433
Warner, John, 76
Warren, Earl, 321-22, 328
Watkins, J. Stanford, 389
Watsonville, 200, 219, 285
Watts, 362
Weaver, Franklin, 121
Welfare
    during Great Depression,
        385-89
    post-war activities, 314-15, 341
    assistance during disasters,
        387-91
West Bay, 147
West Union, 203
Western Standard, 197-99, 210,
    220, 244
Wheeler, Benjamin Ide, 259
Whitlock, Harvey, 204
Whittier, 275, 326
Whittle, Thomas, 162
Wickman, Lance B., 404
Widtsoe, John A., 298
Williams Ranch, 91, 118-19, 142,
    150, 168-72
Williams, Henry B., 235, 240
Williams, Orlando C., 292
Willis, Ira and Sidney, 109, 111-12,
    116
Wilshire Ward, 260, 273, 325-26,
    362, 371, 432
    Chapel, 276-77, 384
Wilson, John, 164-65
Wimmer, Elizabeth Jane and
    Peter, 57, 105, 108
Winner, George K. and Hannah,
    57, 186, 190
Wood, Philo B., 186
Woodruff, Emma, 244-45
Woodruff, Wilford

on conditions in New York,
    14-15
as president of Church,
    229-33, 242, 244, 248
Woollacott, Eliza, 239, 255
Workman, Andrew, 116
World War I, 259, 263, 302-3
World War II, 296, 301, 317, 319,
    323, 333-34, 343, 369
Wright, Parley T., 240

Y

Yerba Buena
    See San Francisco
Yolo County, 202
Young, Brigham
    becomes president of Church
    and plans westward
        migration, 6-9, 16-22, 62, 81
    and Mormon Battalion, 62-63,
        66
    and Samuel Brannan, 16, 20-22,
        95-96, 102-4, 112, 130-31,
        151-53, 224
    and California gold, 112-31
    motion picture about, 294
Young, John R., 215-16
Young, Steve, 351, 392
Young, Waldamer, 254
Yuba City, 149